On the Road to Baghdad
or
Traveling Biculturalism

On the Road to Baghdad or Traveling Biculturalism

Theorizing a Bicultural Approach to Contemporary World Fiction

Edited by Gönül Pultar

With an Introduction
by William Boelhower

New Academia Publishing, LLC
Washington, DC

Copyright © 2005 by Gönül Pultar

New Academia Publishing, 2005

All rights reserved. No part of this book may be reproduced or transmitted in any form or by any means, electronic or mechanical, including photocopying, recording, or by any information storage and retrieval system.

Printed in the United States of America

Library of Congress Control Number: 2005931209
ISBN 0-9767042-1-8 paperback (alk. paper)

New Academia Publishing, LLC
P.O. Box 27420, Washington, DC 20038-7420
www.newacademia.com - info@newacademia.com

Contents

Foreword   1
Gönül Pultar

Introduction   7
William Boelhower

Part I Biculturality

1. Bi- or Mono-Culturalism?: Contemporary Literary Representations of Greek-American Identity
   Theodora Tsimpouki   15

2. "Meaningful Wor(l)ds": Patricia Grace's Bicultural Fiction
   Paloma Fresno Calleja   27

3. Güneli Gün's *On the Road to Baghdad* or Traveling Biculturalism
   Gönül Pultar   47

4. The Intricacy of Spices: A Bicultural Reading of Salman Rushdie's *Midnight's Children* and Banerjee Divakaruni's *The Mistress of Spices*
   Mita Banerjee   65

Part II Transculturation and Cultural Translation

5. Transculturation and Biculturalism: Latina Writers of the United States at/as a Crossroads
   Esther Alvarez Lopez   89

6. José Maria Arguedas and Vikram Chandra: Bridging Cultures, Living Translation
   Dora Sales Salvador   109

7   From Hybrid Original to Shona Translation:
    How *A Grain of Wheat* Becomes *Tsanga Yembeu*
    Katrina Daly Thompson   141

Part III Hybridity and Interculturality

8   Hybridity and the Artist in *Out of Africa*
    Rachel Trousdale   169

9   Magical Realism and Myth in Salman Rushdie's *Haroun
    and the Sea of Stories* and Maxine Hong Kingston's
    Tripmaster Monkey
    Kuldip Kaur Kuwahara   191

10 "Cracking India": Tradition versus Modernity in Attia Hosain's *Sunlight on a Broken Column* and Manju Kapur's *Difficult Daughters*
    Nadia Ahmad   199

11 Rabindranath Tagore, Cultural Difference and the
    Indian Woman's "Burden"
    Sriparna Basu   219

Part IV Transnationalism and Postmodernism

12 The Cultural Mirroring in-between Two Symbolics:
    A Lacanian Reading of John Okada's *No-No Boy*
    Fu-jen Chen   249

13 Postmodern Blackness and Unbelonging in the Works
    of Caryl Phillips
    Paul Smethurst   273

14 Locating Global Links: Arundhati Roy's *The God of
    Small Things*
    Lalitha Ramamurthi   289

Works Cited   299
Notes on Contributors   322
Index   326

Foreword

Gönül Pultar

As we move forward into the twenty-first century, the master-word of globalization increasingly looms as an all-consuming process capable of reshaping the world we live in. Attendant and parallel developments, such as the perspective horizon of transnationalism, and the convincing emergence of first-class diasporic authors have helped to collapse the conventional boundaries of national literatures. More and more authors are now writing from "outside the nation," as Azade Seyhan puts it (*Writing Outside the Nation*, 2001). A new sort of world literature that is very different from the one conceptualized by Goethe has now taken center stage. A product mainly of migration and relocation as well as of the aftermath of the colonial experience, this new literary community is created for the most part by authors writing in a language different from the one they were born into and has given rise to the neologism *literatures in English*.

It is evident that this new literature originates from various non-English linguistic, literary and cultural heritages, with authors consciously and deliberately rejecting linguistic and cultural tenets which the Polish-born Joseph Conrad or the Russian-born Ayn Rand, to name but two "transplants" on both sides of the Atlantic, had felt bound to when composing in English. Such literature summarily turns away from the traditional study of English literature descending from and involving *Beowulf* and *The Canterbury Tales*—in other words, from Old English and Middle English texts. It also founders the very basis upon which English literature was established, just as it burns all bridges with the recently dominant Arnoldian and Leavisite traditions. What is more, it embodies the *Weltschmerz* of the age, with its representation of a culturally complex world alerting us to power struggles in world cities and postcolonial sites where individuals fight entrenched value systems and undergo experiences of deracination and migrancy. This new body of literary works requires new formulations and a remapping within current cultural and literary studies.

As the special issue on "Globalizing Literary Studies" of the Modern Language Association's *PMLA* in 2001 illustrated, this is a question that has begun to preoccupy scholars and critics in search of ideas capable of radically revising the by now conventional paradigms of multiculturalism and post-colonialism—the latter having emanated from deconstructionism and postmodernism which themselves have become passé. Multiculturalism and post-colonialism tend to overlook, when not incriminating, the Western grand narrative that has remained, in spite of postmodernism, very much in evidence and has even been given new life with U.S. president George W. Bush's post-9/11 discourse. Multiculturalism and post-colonialism also acquiesce to the basically imperialist-conditioned position of "subalternity" of those groups in whose name they articulate grievances, thereby reinforcing the "inferior" standing of these.

It is the exhaustion of prevalent approaches that has led Gayatri Chakravorty Spivak to write in 2003, "in loving memory" so to speak, of the "death" of the discipline of comparative literature (*Death of a Discipline*), whose concern should have been the emergent fiction, but whose present conceptualization remains far behind and below the reach of this fiction. It is again frustration with current theory that claims to compartmentalize and explain away—within the post-Leavisite, "Birmingham-style" cultural studies context—the new developments in fiction, that has led Terry Eagleton in his *After Theory* of the same year to take for granted this announced death and undertake a post-mortem assessment which offers a rather harsh indictment of the state of the art. The present volume, devoted to theorizing a bicultural approach to contemporary world fiction, is one endeavor to go beyond tribute and condemnation alike, and offer in turn, in all modesty, an approach capable of addressing the demand for new insights. The deaths in 2003 and 2004 of Edward Said and Jacques Derrida, respectively, herald the end of an epoch and render such search imperative.

One major aspect of the emerging world fiction is the fact that it has increasingly come to require the cognizance and analysis of a culture other than the one in the language it is written. The product of a cross-cultural fertilization and mutual transculturation, this fiction constitutes a meeting ground of cultures and makes possible a juxtaposition that is at the core of the complex relationship(s) between East and West. In addition, such fiction, rather than being "post-colonial," "ethnic" or "multicultural"—all labels under which it has been categorized so far (and that suggest the existence of a putatively hegemonic culture, calling at once for its denigration)—is in reality "bicultural." For, when examined closely this fiction is seen to reflect a biculturalism that is the amalgam of two cultures both of which are hegemonic in their own ways. This volume adopts a "bicultural approach" to study the work of authors who have produced this fiction. Such an approach, while providing insight into the works discussed by uncovering and retrieving elements of the seemingly "other," non-European culture, elevates both cultures to the same level of consideration and confers an equal status on them.

The present collection has its genesis in the very many conferences which I have attended since the mid-nineties, and the many conversations at these venues I had with colleagues who, like myself, were Western-educated but originated from the "rest" of the "West," and who had been following (as best we could) the latest literature in critical and cultural theory. We felt that the well-polished words we were hearing in the sessions somehow did not encompass the whole picture of the works treated in the conference presentations. Edward Said in his seminal *Orientalism* (1978) neglected to underscore the fact that the "orientalized" was also a subject/agent who had articulated over the centuries a more than substantial discourse of his/her own. And although Homi Bhabha rightly criticizes British colonialism in India for having imposed his/her "book" (*The Location of Culture*), he, too, failed to record that the medium which the colonial officers were tinkering with was no *tabula rasa*: whether as Persian and Arabic poetry, that in Sanskrit and other local languages, or popular literature dating back to *The Thousand and One Nights*, literature in India had a very ancient tradition and an impeccable pedigree.

The "Mughal" Turks erected splendors of architecture in India that the British only knew how to loot and very poorly emulate. Yet none of this was ever pointed out. And we, from the rest of the West, were all too busy going over the twenty-minute presentation we were soon to make, and too happy to have been s/elected by Western colleagues to committees in US- or Europe-based associations, too thankful to them, too much imbued with Eastern *sensibilité*, to protest, and/or oppose prevailing views. Recognition in present-day Ganges or the Bosphorus rests, much more than on the authorship of any dissertation or monograph of whatever merit, on acceptance on the shores of the Thames or Charles rivers—as we have all had occasion to learn, to our detriment. Thus we remained silent, and were even impressed to see our cultures being portrayed by our peers with fashionable buzzwords such as *subaltern* and *hybrid*. We knew, however, that no discussion on Salman Rushdie's *Midnight's Children* (1980) could ever be complete or even satisfactory without a consideration in its own right of Eastern oral story-telling in general, and of Indian story-telling and epics, myths and legends in particular. Even the most Western aspect of the novel, its nation-building, "community-imagining" characteristic (that appears to derive from the tradition established by Walter Scott's novels), needs to be examined *also*, and perhaps before anything else, within the tradition that has produced the Persian-language *Shahnama* (Book of Kings, ca 1000) of Firdawsi (see B.W. Robinson for a recent rendering in English).

In 1998 I organized at the "Crossroads" conference in Tampere, Finland, a panel entitled "World Fiction as Meeting Ground of Cultures: A Bicultural Approach." The idea for the present volume takes its origin from it and includes some of the essays—subsequently reworked—from the panel and additional ones added later. (My own essay, for example, is based on a presentation I made at the 2000 MELUS-India conference in Hyderabad, India.) I would like to thank the contributors for their important and often incisive essays as well as for the patience and enthusiasm they have shown all along. Two of the contributors have already published their essays elsewhere, but I am including them here as initially planned, to capture the critical moment of the book project as originally conceived. Thus, of the two articles published earlier, one is "Postmodern Blackness and Unbelonging in the Works of Caryl Phillips" by Paul Smethurst, which has appeared in *The Journal of Commonwealth Literature*. It is reprinted in this volume by permission of Sage Publications (copyright Sage Publications, 2002). The other is "*Cracking India*: Cultural and Religious Representation in Indo-Anglian Literature (1947 to Present)" by Nadia Ahmad (who retains the copyright), in the 2001 thematic issue on "Power and Recolonization" of *Queen: A Journal of Rhetoric and Power*, and is an earlier version of Ahmad's chapter in this volume.

The collection includes fourteen chapters written by scholars coming from different cultures, literary traditions and disciplines, who examine authors writing in English, Spanish and Bengali, reflecting a cornucopia of other languages, literary traditions and cultures. So much so that William Boelhower notes in the Introduction "the almost borderless inventory of authors studied here—as if the scholars themselves had met by chance in an airport waiting lounge." In fact, the contributors were "recruited" through the Internet, in response to two calls for papers, one for the Tampere panel and the other for additional essays for this volume. Indeed, the scholars could very well have met at some airport waiting lounge, ready to depart for a destination in some out-of-the-way site, an "exotic" postcolonial metropolis somewhere between Rushdie's real-life Mumbai and a Marienbad imagined by Kazuo Ishiguro, to attend a conference at which they would be presenting their latest work.

What the Tampere panelists, the later contributors, and I have tried to underscore here is that there exists a growing body of fiction that possesses a significant dimension other than the one quite manifest for the linguistic culture—the so-called home audience—in which it is published. As one reads the chapters in this volume, one will find discussions about an immensely rich and effervescent world, a universe teeming with a variety of individuals and their passions, an almost boundless space inflected with innumerable hues, sounds and smells. In fact, although only fictional works are examined (mostly novels, but also an occasional play or poem), what emerges is larger than fiction, whether mimetic or postmodern. For example, one can catch a glimpse of the late Andreas Papandreou, who will go down in history as prime minister of Greece, while yet married to a WASP American woman, chairing the department of economics at Berkeley University, with "his Adlai Stevenson liberalism and rhetoric from the Berkeley free-speech movement," espied by his son in the seclusion of their home dancing the *zebekiko*. One will also encounter the wife of Tagore's elder brother, closer in age to Tagore than her own husband and therefore bonded in friendship (and perhaps more) to Tagore rather than her husband, later committing suicide when Tagore in turn gets married. In short, as the reader will bear me out, a whole teeming humanity is here, feeling, suffering, and revealing for the reader sentiments and scenes ranging from tragedy to the joys and pathos of everyday bicultural life.

I hope that the scholarship in *On the Road to Baghdad or Traveling Biculturalism: Theorizing a Bicultural Approach to Contemporary World Fiction* will provoke new connections and insights in the study of world literatures in a renewed and truly comparative context. I trust that the material in the volume will prove useful to the widest possible range of readers, be they scholars or students of literary studies, comparative literature, ethnic studies, cultural studies and any other related or emerging fields, or merely literature aficionados seeking to gain a new perspective.

I would like to thank William Boelhower not only for his competent introduction but also for his editorial help in going over the whole manuscript. My thanks also go to Nilüfer Eren Pultar, whose meticulous proofreading went well beyond mere proofreading; to Gökçe Sert who helped me organize the "works cited"; to Duncan Chesney for additional proofreading; to Şule Tarakçıoğlu for all the administrative assistance she provided; and as always, foremost to my husband, Mustafa Pultar, not only for the patience and understanding he has shown all along but for the assistance he has given in all matters technical.

Introduction

William Boelhower

Today, many of the writers who have contributed to the burgeoning canon of international literatures in English—such as Bharati Mukherjee, Salman Rushdie, Wilson Harris, Derek Walcott, Marjorie Agosin, Iva Pekarkova, Eva Hoffman, Manthia Diawara, Yvonne Vera, and a host of others—have become, in the critic Tim Brennan's phrase, "Third World cosmopolitan celebrities." In confirmation of this, where we once focused our critical attention almost exclusively on immigrants, the processes of assimilation and acculturation, and the ideological division of nations into two blocks, we now talk of migrants, flexible citizenship, and the global civil society. And where once ethnic authors were studied solely in literature departments, writers like those mentioned above are now discussed in cultural, postcolonial, critical theory, and gender studies courses. Criticism of literature also has developed radically new premises; figures like Franz Fanon, C.L.R. James, Gayatri Spivak, Judith Butler, Edward Said, Homi Bhabha, Mary Louise Pratt, Elleke Boehmer, and Dipesh Chakrabarty, to name only a few, have revolutionized the way we talk about texts, their worldliness, and our own ethical standpoint as gendered readers. It is on the foundations of this vast overhauling of literary studies that the present volume of essays, edited by the well-traveled cosmopolitan scholar Gönül Pultar, builds.

The essays Pultar has brought together here concentrate their attention on elaborating a bicultural approach to a wide-ranging, international pantheon of authors including the Greek American Nikos Papandreou, the New Zealand Maori writer Patricia Grace, the Turkish American Güneli Gün, universally recognized cosmopolitan stars like Salman Rushdie, Arundati Roy, and Vikram Chandra, the Chinese American Maxine Hong Kingston, the Kenyan Ngugi wa Thiong'o, the Peruvian writer José Maria

Arguedas, the Danish writer Isak Dinesen, the Indian writers Chitra Banerjee Divakaruni, Attia Hosain, Manju Kapur, Rabindranath Tagore, the black British writer Caryl Phillips, and the Japanese American John Okada. Perhaps only a decade ago, such an ambitious, world-spanning project would have seemed absurd outside a congress of anthropologists or bankers. Today, it represents a state-of-the-art sensibility reflecting the efforts of an equally various geocultural assembly of scholars. The implications for a community of readers not only interested in but competently sensitive to such far-flung narrative geographies is equally stunning.

And yet, if we look at recent attempts in the social and political sciences to theorize postnational (and transnational) exchanges in our now rather visible global village and compare them with this volume's table of contents, it is immediately evident that there is a rather strong homology between the study of "world literature" in English and the space of flows we take for granted when talking about financial markets, the Internet, or even the more arduous flow of migrants following the global job market. How, for that matter, could it be otherwise, when it is in the very nature of literature to construct a detailed and synthetic *mundus* out of the existential, social, political, and economic forces at work in the structures of our infraordinary lives. As the world goes, so goes its literature; and students of the latter, conscious as never before of their place in the world, are patently caught in between. Evidently, it is with this self-reflective burden in mind that Gönül Pultar has provided four topical groupings for the essays here: 1) biculturality; 2) transculturation and cultural translation; 3) hybridity and interculturality; 4) transnationalism and postmodernism. How these categories are employed by the individual contributors and how successful they are in labelling an as yet largely inchoate global reality marks the challenge and the achievement of these essays.

Having started by noting the almost borderless inventory of authors studied here—as if the scholars themselves had met by chance in an airport waiting lounge—I should immediately add that the above topical ordering already provides us with what is arguably the most nuanced vocabulary that an equally cosmopolitan criticism has so far cobbled together. And it is to the credit of many of the contributors that they have used these categories not only to explore their chosen set of texts but also, in doing so, to test the usefulness and limits of the heuristic tools themselves. In effect, both the new conditions brought about by globalization and social science theories with a cosmopolitical reach start from the same scripts describing what happens when individuals, coming from different cultures and speaking different languages, encounter each other as they travel and work their way around the globe.

The converging linguistic particles "bi-," "trans," and "inter" in the section titles of this volume apparently anticipate what these scripts counsel when it comes to learning how to live positively in a plural society with cosmopolitan, rights-based underpinnings. And for the most part the essays confirm that they do, especially when it comes to rethinking what kind of subject is best fitted to live in a fluid and increasingly rootless world as a protagonist. Here theoretical meditation on the nature of the bicultural subject is mandatory, and many of the essays (Mita Banerjee's, Esther Alvarez Lopez's, and Theodora Tsimpouki's, for example) are interesting precisely for their sustained discussion of a certain performative lightness of being typical of a postmodern, high-riding subject. While fluidity, hybridity (the condition as well as the art of "in-betweenness"), and empathy are important traits of the bicultural subject, there is also a less buoyant, more conflictual, side that has been expressed in terms of identity politics, the politics of recognition, or in more extreme instances, cultural survival.

In her essay on the Maori writer Patricia Grace, for example, Paloma Fresno Calleja discusses a major issue in postcolonial politics and literatures, namely the fight to take back what was lost—not only land but also a people's cultural heritage. In such struggles, the central subject is usually a community or at least a transindividual collectivity and herein lies the very strength that is needed to carry on a lengthy, sustained battle on several fronts. In these large battles, the individual subject is often the spokesperson for a set of values handed down from a timeless past. And the issues are national and often revolutionary. For the individual to aspire to universal values or to want to rise above the ethnic limitations of a narrowly observed parochial tradition may lead to tragedy, as it does in Arundati Roy's linguistically exuberant novel *The God of Small Things* (see Lalitha Ramamurthi's essay). For Roy, history seems cyclical, and caste, class, and religion weigh in heavily when it comes to an individual's freedom of choice.

In Sriparna Basu's discussion of the work of Rabindranath Tagore, we are presented with a cultural trajectory that begins in universal humanism (his first novel *Gora*) and ends in a tragic split between East and West (his novella *Char Adhyay*). At first Tagore believed in the value of empathy and the possibility of constructing a transnational hybrid subject in India, but as time passed cultural nationalism and the agenda of revolutionary struggle gained the upper hand. Basu also explores what this means at the symbolic level for the feminine subject, used by Tagore to filter and distinguish between cultural and political nationalism. The regimenting effects of anticolonial struggle on theories of free-forming subjectivities can also be looked at in other ways, such as the face-off between tradition and modernity (see Nadia Ahmad) or the restraining role such categories as gender and race often have on women and people of color.

In effect, the category of culture looms as large as any of those used to head the various sections of this volume, and all the contributors find themselves having to deal with it either directly or indirectly. In some instances, for example Rachel Trousdale's essay on Dinesen's *Out of Africa*, it seems that a hybrid culture can be invented without too much sacrifice by taking into account the talents and knowledge of all those living together in a given place and according to a shared economy. This symbiotic achievement is a hard-won victory of sorts and even then one on a very small scale. But when it comes to such large Orientalist divisions as East versus West, colony versus mother country or, much more generally, the traumas suffered by first generation immigrants in any of the big industrialized nations (see Paul Smethurst's essay on the oeuvre of Caryl Phillips and Fu-jen Chen's fresh reading of John Okada's powerful novel *No-No Boy*), then we are dealing with an altogether steeper challenge.

If we consider culture as somehow equivalent to Manuel Castells' space of flows, Arjun Appadurai's global ethnoscapes, or James Clifford's poetics of travel and then reposition these in terms of, say, the category of diaspora, quite a different set of questions regarding culture emerges: questions that summon up tragic histories, particularly those of the Jews and then the Africans in the centuries-long build-up of the slave trade. There are, of course, numerous other "lesser" diasporic experiences that could be cited here. In truth, there is enough hard evidence in many of the essays in this volume to stir us to be vigilant as we entertain new interpretative paradigms engendered by globalization, cosmopolitics, and other effects resulting from our now living in a global village.

Diaspora evokes broken histories, the obligation both to remember and to forget in order to move forward in time, and the moral call to serve as a witness and to shoulder the burdens inherent in belonging to a community. All of these diasporic-related commitments tend to discourage any attempt to create an exclusively formal theory of biculturality. In addition, the ethical responsibilities of diaspora remind us how thoroughly embedded *all* of Gönül Pultar's topical categories—not only biculturality but also transculturation, hybridity, interculturality, transnationalism, and postmodernism—are. What is more, both Edward Said's example of critical worldliness and the very nature of literature as a webbed *mundus* of countless details call for this same embeddedness. Nowhere is this shared ontology more evident than in the painstaking deliberations of translation, as Katrina Daly Thompson's important essay on how Ngugi wa Thiong'o's *A Grain of Wheat* became *Tsanga Yembeu* demonstrates.

Translation, Thompson notes, is a productive struggle sanctioned by the patronage of the African trickster Legba. This lexical "warfare" is further explored by Dora Sales Salvador in her informative discussion of the notion of "living translation." She focuses on the recently revalued Peruvian writer José María Arguedas and the Indian writer Vikram Chandra, both of whom belong to two language-cultures and create a unique literary poetics by translating their knowledge of oral and folk traditions from one language into another. As the etymon of the word *translation* suggests, the translator is saddled with the burden of carrying something, whether that be from one language to another or from one culture to another. In her engaged scrutiny of Latina writers in the United States, Esther Alvarez Lopez weaves psychic and geographical space into one discursive strategy and uses the concept of "mestizaje" as an ideal interstitial site for defining the role of both writers and readers. As Lopez (and earlier, Mita Banerjee) argues, identity itself requires constant negotiation and translation as we move from place to place. Here, then, is the connecting link between the work of textual translation and that of cultural translation, both of which had an important role in creating an influential school of border studies.

Almost all of the essays included in this volume make it quite clear that a superficial understanding of biculturality will end up drowning in its own shallows. A full reading of them reveals how again and again the authors insist on linking cultural strategies and subject performances to location, standpoint, community, region, nation, and beyond. The notion of "world literature" is as much a critical construct on trial as it is a global reality in the making. In probing it with their worldly, self-conscious questioning, the volume's contributors have no intention of taking this phenomenon as something merely given. For that matter, the writers they study certainly require new readerly skills and multidisciplinary competencies. As Gönül Pultar points out in her smart reading of Güneli Gün's entertaining novel *On the Road to Baghdad*, the ideal reader must truly be bicultural in order to catch the uniquely Turkish American playfulness and postmodern sleights of hand at work in it.

Pultar shares with Kuldip Kaur Kuwahara, who offers us an instructive reading of Salman Rushdie's *Haroun and the Sea of Stories* and Maxine Hong Kingston's *Tripmaster Monkey*, what is perhaps the central aim of this volume, namely that in moving from the national to the cosmopolitan scale of attention, the reader should simultaneously seek to deconstruct any ethnocentric *forma mentis* harboring a set of cultural values the provenance of which remains unexamined. If, as Kuwahara suggests, it is the vocation of art to transcend reality through stories, then it must also be said that it does so through synthesis, syncretism, disjunctive ploys, and radical criticism. Indeed, the kind of bicultural pragmatics that emerges from these essays is one that is meant to construct a reader capable of coping with being at home in the world at large, beyond the increasingly ineffective horizon of the nation-state. The bicultural subject, as Gönül Pultar and her contributors seem to construe it, is both a minimal and a maximal sign, a relational conduit for making visible the tensions and transactions of an ontologically social self, a self that is both a singularity but also an *esse cum* (a being-with). It is this theoretical understanding that allows them to escape the ill effects of any form of substantialism or essentialism and to embrace, instead, the intrinsically dynamic and performative aspect of the minimally conceived bicultural self.

PART I

BICULTURALITY

1
Bi- or Mono-culturalism?
Contemporary Literary Representations of Greek-American Identity

Theodora Tsimpouki

> "We are ethnics committed to a politics of transliteration."
> Olga Broumas, *Beginning with O*

The Politics of Subjectivization

The advent of post-structuralism and deconstruction has led to a profound transformation of the debate surrounding the category of the "subject." No longer is it assumed to be a stable category. Rather, as "transcendental signified," to use Jacques Derrida's terms, the subject is "under erasure"; it has become the site of ontological and epistemological contestation ("Structure, Sign and Play in the Discourse of the Human Sciences" 249). The political and rhetorical impact this reality has had on ethnic American writing and critical discourse is undeniable, but not always welcome. Just as ethnic groups have begun, since the 1960s civil rights movement, to define and construct their subjectivity, the category of the "subject" has suddenly become an issue of critical inquiry. "Somehow it seems highly suspicious," writes Nancy Hartsock,

> that it is at this moment in history, when so many groups are engaged in "nationalisms" which involve redefinitions of the marginalized Others, that doubt arises in the academy about the nature of the "subject," about the possibilities for a general theory which can describe the world, about historical "progress." Why is it, exactly at the moment when so many of us who have been silenced begin to demand the right to name ourselves, to act as subjects rather than objects of history, that just then the concept of subjecthood becomes "problematic"? (26)

Mimicking poststructuralist terminology for increased parodic effect, Elizabeth Fox-Genovese in turn points out that "[T]he death of the subject and of the author may accurately reflect the perceived crisis of Western culture and the bottomless anxieties of its most privileged subjects, white male authors who have presumed to define it" (67).

In reclaiming an integrated self, ethnic authors often seek their discursive legitimization by either falling back on essentialist modes of representation, or by securing the sovereignty of one part of their bicultural identity at the expense of the other. Such a deconstruction of binary divisions changes the cultural or subjective contents of identity but the subject continues to be constituted within the same essentialist form. In her stimulating reading of colonial discourse, Meyda Yeğenoğlu foregrounds a different view of the subject according to which "the 'other' is not what the subject distinguishes itself apart from, but the necessary possibility that makes the subject possible, *again and again, each time anew*" (emphasis added). Only such an approach, Yeğenoğlu argues, "can develop a notion of agency as an active and transformative principle" (9).

Taking the lead from Yeğenoğlu's insightful reading of Orientalism, I propose a reading of contemporary Greek-American texts as sites of contestation, where both cultural identities, the American and the pre-American (the identity of descent) are complementary and mutually implicated in each other, and neither part exists in a fully constituted entity. Following the ethnic paradigm, contemporary Greek-American authors also engage in the process of recovering their individual subjectivities, which may often include the contradictory aspects of their gender, ethnicity and class. Their texts attempt to come to terms with the notion of identity as a cultural construct, which emphasizes the dynamic and changing character of the self, encourages the fluid movement of differences and resists homogenization. To foreground the constituted character of the subject, however, is not to suggest that it is determined. The subject, Judith Butler reminds us, is "never fully constituted, but is subjected and produced time and again through," what she terms, a "forcible reiteration of norm"; it is because "bodies never quite comply with the norms by which their materialization is compelled" that "instabilities" and "possibilities for rematerialization" are opened up which call into question the hegemonic force of the regulatory laws (*Bodies that Matter* 2). Drawing on a postcolonial theorizing of hybridity, this chapter focuses on questions of bicultural identity raised in the texts, and aims to reveal how the illusive desire for a fixed or self-contained self is precluded by the notion of difference.

Parental Models Displaced

In his extensive work on Greek-American literature, Yiorgos Kalogeras has repeatedly pointed out the difficulties of the contemporary Greek scholar who attempts to define a Greek-American canon that would not only have to establish the "genealogy" of his subject but also the legitimacy of the subject's status (see e.g. his "Greek American Literature: Who Needs It? Some Canonical Issues Concerning the Fate of An Ethnic Literature"; and "Greek-American Literature"). While most contemporary Greek-American novels are written in English, their authors have either already formed their aesthetic sensibilities by the time of their arrival in the United States or they contextualize Greece in ways that lack identifiable ethnic situations and themes within the American literary framework. This "radical alterity," as Kalogeras put it, has resulted in the systematic exclusion of Greek-American authors from the ethnic paradigms which American critics "have extrapolated from a limited number of texts or literatures such as that of the Jewish or the Italian-American" ("Greek-American Literature" 259), supplemented in recent years by Latino/a and Asian-American texts, besides those of the Native Americans and the African-Americans.

Taking these problematics of canonization into consideration, I will examine here two semi-autobiographical novels by authors of Greek-American descent. Born in the United States and removed, by at least one generation, from their respective immigrant parent, Nicholas (Nikos) Papandreou and Catherine Temma Davidson return to their ancestral parentland in order to explore their ethnic roots and come to terms with a part of their identity silenced by American upbringings. Both works reflect in their beginnings the ambiguities of speaking through an orientalizing discourse that constructs Greece as a place of sensuality, irrationality, mystical religiosity, backwardness, and attendant expressions of exoticism. Later, both texts depart from the representation of an immanently exotic culture and introduce an awareness of the influences their ethnic heritage has asserted in their quotidian—influences that express doubly informed identities. These books demonstrate graphically, and viscerally, the process that moves from an initial desire by the authors to assume full control of the ancestral land to a voluntary surrender to the complexities of their ethnic Greek culture. In order to achieve this ability of surrender, both authors displace the inherited parental/authoritative narratives of Greece in order to centrally position themselves in their narratives of their ancestral land. The initial neo-colonial scaffolding that dominates their discourse is dismantled to gain access to a sense of achieved difference—a difference metonymically associated with their Greekness. Thus, both narratives signify a turning point in the writers' fictional biographies as they record experiences of becoming relocated within Greek culture. Through first-hand encounters with the subjectivity of the native Greeks and the varying forms of resistance to stereotypical cultural representations, these contemporary Greek-American authors come to question their prefabricated understanding of Greece. The titles of both novels are indicative of appropriated cultural clichés, which, in the texts, are undermined in a narrative process that revises them. Papandreou's *Father Dancing* (the title of the British Penguin edition, 1997; all page references are to this edition) vividly recalls a "Zorba-the-Greek" national type that has long contributed to an Epicurean image of Greek culture in the Western mind. On the other hand, Davidson's *The Priest Fainted* (1998, all page references are to this edition) is the literal English translation of *imam baildi*,[1] a popular eggplant dish whose genealogy reaches back to the Ottoman period of Greece.

Once back in their ancestral land, both of these Greek-American authors are confronted with the realization of their polymorphous, complex cultural heritage. Drawing on Kalogeras's formulation of the ways Greek-American travelers experience their ancestral parentland, I contend, with him, that contemporary Greek-American authors also perceive Greece "as a space" rather than "a topos," as "relations among sites"; that is, their experience of Greece becomes "a series of relations that represent, contest, and invert real sites within a civilization or culture" ("The 'Other Space' of Greek America" 704). Their physical if temporary appropriation of the ancestral land and their encounters with historical specificity allow them to contest the hegemony of the American vision of their Greek identity: both writers come to voluntarily re-inscribe themselves in the Greek cultural context. Different as they may be in their narratological as well as ideological concerns, *Father Dancing* and *The Priest Fainted* demonstrate the empowering effect of a Greek ethnic heritage in the formation of their authors' identities.

"A Crowded Heart"[2]

Papandreou's book is immersed in Greek modern history. Using a first-person narrative point of view, the young narrator gives us a vivid fictional account of his family's history from 1965 to 1974, a period before and after the Junta Occupation in Greece.[3] What makes the young boy's narration especially interesting is that his family story follows the history of a family responsible for much of contemporary Greek history. The boy's grandfather was the "old man of democracy," George Papandreou, Greece's prime minister at the time the dictators seized power. His father,

Andreas Papandreou, was the liberal academic who chaired the economics department at Berkeley, entered politics by his father's side to help organize Greek resistance abroad to the seven-year dictatorship and, later, governed the country for almost fifteen years until his death in 1996.

Born in the United States by an American mother, the eight-year-old boy is "forced to inhabit two worlds" (3) that initially seem incompatible with each other. Between the *baklava* and the apple pie, the "evil eye" of superstition and its rational negation, the Greek *Little Hero* and *Batman*, the narrator is exposed from an early age to both cultural worlds. Yet, in several narrative instances he identifies himself as American in appearance, style and habits: "I had blond hair, blue-green eyes and a freckled face" (9); he struggles embarrassingly over the complexities of the Greek language: "Greek Grammar. What a humiliation if I used the feminine article for a masculine noun" (12). And, perhaps most importantly, he resents the public role he is forced to play as son and grandson of his famous progenitors: "I hated them for being so strange, so Greek" (45). He rebels against the people whom he does not understand until he becomes "autistic to all things Greek" (20). Elsewhere, when his father is jailed by the dictators, he imagines himself protected, hiding behind Californian license plates (96). Or he invests in a neo-colonial belief that casts America, the so-called bastion of democratic principles in the modern world, in the role of Greece's savior from dictatorship (102): he yearns for its intervention to ensure his father's release from prison. This last, culturally divided attitude is shaped by the narrator's father, whose intellectual formation—"his Adlai Stevenson liberalism and rhetoric from the Berkeley free-speech movement" (5), marriage to an American woman, and double citizenship are in no apparent conflict with his all-empowering political role as the defender of Greece's sovereign rights and independence. Moreover, because the narrator is aware that his privileged position among the native Greeks stems from his paternal origins rather than from his own understanding of, or active participation in, Greek cultural life, he accepts, initially at least, his father's view of Greek culture as the authentic one.

Paradoxically, in order for the narrator to dismantle his (inherited) neo-colonial rhetoric and form his own textualization of Greece, he has to challenge and ultimately disempower the very forces that sustain him in his privileged role as son and grandson to two historically powerful Greek men. In other words, every time the narrator discovers some sense of his own Greekness, it is eclipsed, and his agency negated by the greater historical shadow of a parental model. The narrator confronts this perversity by displacing the image of the father, by substituting the father's "originary," "authentic" discourse of Greece with his own discursive version. The father's voice (which mesmerizes crowds, tames them, ignites their wrath and their laughter in public speeches) is the same voice that whispers in the boy's soul the "correct" and "Greek" way of everything. The paternal exercise of power and control is shown to be dependent on his knowledge, scientific as well as ethnic. Thus, the father becomes not only the possessor of ethnic knowledge but also the creator of a discourse that constructs the very reality he is in the process of describing (Said, *Orientalism* 94). The more the father demonstrates his ethnic male exceptionalism, the more urgent it becomes for the son to discover a different Greece that will displace the paternal one. Adolescent revolt against paternal authority translates as resistance to the influences of Greek culture as long as Greece remains homologous to the father and his notions of order, control and maleness. The following incident describes a father-son confrontation as the father performs the ritualistic *zebekiko* dance. In exile, "hyphenated Greeks" who believed in the cause of liberation gathered in the father's house of exile in Canada. One night the boy awakens to the "strangled bouzouki notes" and walks down the stairs to see the following:

> head down, one hand tucked behind his back, the other holding worry beads, my father moved slowly with heavy responsible steps. He swayed like someone drunk. He careened from one side to the other, as if about to fall, lifted himself from a bent position and spun, then crouched and slapped the parquet with both hands, back and forth as if he were sweeping the floor. (165)

"Faced with all this Greekness," the narrator rebels against the music with its "absurd beat" and its "other-worldly words," but also against the exhibitionist masculinity and absolute authority of the father: "This was family stuff, and in this family father ruled and son obeyed, especially such a father, their leader, and such a son, this half-clothed apparition with long hair" (167). Confronted with such a father, one who rarely acknowledges the son's presence or makes an effort to include him in his activities, the son, subdued and conquered, feels "like a *hanger-on*, like an observer of a *foreign* organization" (171, emphasis added). A sense of distance and alterity characterizes the boy's feelings. Not accidentally, his rebellion against his father becomes a simultaneous search for another Greece, one not colonized by the father. "The real Greece, the country of my childhood, certainly existed, I just hadn't found it yet" (173). The "real" Greece no longer coincides with his father's picture of it but with his own lived experiences and reminiscences of his ancestral homeland. He is able to substitute the father's "essentialist" discourse of Greece with another one, which both subverts and supplements the first one. The son opts for a full ethnic return and never considers the possibility of following his father's career as a politician; instead, through his agonizing search for *his* Greece, he discovers his vocation as a writer. In writing, he displaces paternal models in yet another way: his written text displaces his father's public speeches, his writerly loneliness marginalizes the father's performative charisma in front of Greek crowds. As for the *zebekiko* dance, a quintessentially male dance, it becomes a metaphor and a sign for his understanding of a Greekness constituted by diverse and heterogeneous cultural practices: "Over the years I have discovered my own dancing style," the narrator admits, in this way revising a paradigmatic ritual dance as one of the assets of his own Greek identity. Despite parental attempts to maintain control over the son and keep his identity framed in pre-established categories, the son emerges as capable of belonging to both cultures in an apparently unproblematic manner.

"There Is Only One Way to Tell This Story"[4]

The majority of reviews of Davidson's novel *The Priest Fainted* describe it as a "female *Odyssey*" that masterfully combines "the mythic and the mundane" (Shea F1) by locating these two elements in a postmodern, ethnic paradigm; and also as an artful pastiche of myths, recipes, and fragments of memories and family stories. However, interest in *The Priest Fainted* lies with questions of narrative construction and hybridity that arise from a postcolonial reading of the novel. Though the heroine (who remains unnamed throughout the novel) most frequently identifies herself as American rather than Greek, she longs to recover her lost Greek identity, repressed or silenced by her Jewish-American upbringing. In order to do this, she takes a return trip to Greece, the same way her Greek-American mother did some thirty years before. The unraveling of the circumstances of her mother's sojourn in her motherland as well as the reasons of her voluntary return to America serve as the heroine's pretext to visit Greece (233).

After a one-year stay in Greece that leads her to replace her mother's story of hybridity with her own, the heroine-narrator believes she has resolved the conflicting aspects of her bicultural identity. Her efforts to rediscover her Greek roots by displacing the maternal model empower her as a bicultural individual able to choose from various cultural traditions. However, the uneasiness that characterizes the heroine's allegiance to her American identity, the blatant uses of binary oppositions of insider/outsider, difference/sameness, Western reason/Oriental sensuality, and the representation of the Greek Other as a stereotype or as the heroine's own "dark reflection" (Bhabha, *The Location of Culture* 44) point toward a more complicated notion of bicultural identity, one that is already discursively construed through its relation to the Other, and already informed by the ambivalence of its own constructions of difference.

The problem with the heroine's adherence to her American past is not only that it undermines her critique of American cultural domination and superiority (47, 155), but also that it is predicated on an essentialist discourse invested in homogeneous and cohesive views of Greek national identity. The primacy awarded to traditional Greek peasant culture; the representation of native Greek women as subordinate, yet nevertheless occupying an inner, sacred and inviolable locus of the culture (108); and finally, the ambivalent relation of the heroine to her sense of Greek Otherness all suggest her investment in given stereotypes.

The heroine's perception of Greek national identity demonstrates her own discursively constructed identity through her early exposure to the non-assimilated Greek community of America. Greeks are the descendents of a glorious classical past toward which they show deep-felt pride. They are depicted as ethnocentric, always passionately defending the purity and uniqueness of their cultural achievements in poetry (135), music (46), and history (155). The statement that "Greeks are a people addicted to risk, to extremes of emotion" (253) is an example of the way in which the heroine formulates her vision of an authentic, coherent national identity. Elsewhere, she identifies with the Zorba stereotype while fully endorsing the literary representations of Greece by Lawrence Durrell (see his *Bitter Lemons*; and *The Greek Islands*) and Henry Miller ("his [Miller's] book [*The Colossus of Maroussi*] has become my constitution" [49], she maintains).

This idealized depiction of Greece is best illustrated by the village communities, which are, according to the author, the heart of the authentic folk culture. Distanced from the metropolitan center geographically, temporally, and culturally, the little villages of the plains and the mountains (the grandmother's birthplace) represent the virtues of an original and untarnished folk culture that is untouched by modernity or contact with foreign cultures: "The villages had been there during hundreds of years of occupation, protective and strong, their social codes passed down from mother to daughter in a feat of Darwinian survival, an entire language and religion saved from a conquering power that did its best to wipe them out" (51). If a Greek national identity is to be found in a peasant culture and its defining proximity to nature, it is no wonder that everywhere they went, the Greeks of the "great diaspora . . . re-formed into villages, fragmented but still clear in outline" (52). In dramatic contrast to this delineation of cultural coherence, the heroine's itinerary through Athens exposes her to a variety of dangers and traps that contest the notion of a cultural homogeneity. The city directly tests the heroine's ability to anchor her identity within the metropolitan community. Athens emerges in the novel as a space of "relations among sites," a place of difference and transformation.

Interestingly, individual transformation is presented as a possibility available only to foreigners or cultural hybrids. This sense of exclusion is especially true for women since Greek cultural and social practices cast them in secondary and subordinate roles. While the heroine grants women a special kind of power in spite of their domestic seclusion ("Feminine power is hidden under the Greek culture" [237]), she nevertheless excludes them from personal or public agency. Instead, it is only the women with double or foreign origins, people like herself, who are considered privileged subjects. In fact, both mother and daughter experience Athens as the site of a variety of subversive actions. Specifically, their anonymity and distance from the parental gaze allow them both sexual and social freedom. In Greece, they experience an unprecedented liberty denied to them in the oppressive Greek community of the New World. While their conduct implies the author's assumption that Western/American women enjoy greater freedom than Oriental/Greek women, curiously enough they come to exercise this (American) freedom in an ancestral land. It is as if they wish to protest against the social and sexual structures that reduce Greek women to a condition of dependence and subjection. Or, they seem to wish to contest Greek phallocentric hegemony by assuming sexual liberties traditionally attributed to men. In a sense, they take up the masculine position within Greek society, which confers on men the role of hunting and sexual agency. Evidently, this freedom is granted to the mother only periodically, when she pledges allegiance to her American identity. In this way she shares the privilege of participating in Western women's sexually emancipated status. Such agency is never bestowed on the grandmother or even on contemporary Greek women who are always depicted as living in a state of subordination. The mother, therefore, makes the "right" choice by dropping all marriage proposals and flying back to America. The metonymic association between Greece's cultural traditions and its despotic men makes it all the more necessary for the mother to advise her daughter never to marry a Greek man. As a result, the daughter does not seriously consider such a possibility, especially since she already enjoys more sexual freedom than the mother, given the chronological and cultural distance between the two women.

Pointing to the intimate connection between femininity, nature and the Orient, Yeğenoğlu, following Luce Irigaray (see her *The Speculum of the Other Woman* and *This Sex Which is Not One*), provides (in her *Colonial*

Fantasies: Toward a Feminist Reading of Orientalism) an approach that affords a psychoanalytic reading of the heroine's representation of Greek society. The heroine-narrator herself reflects that even after its political and economic unification with Europe, Greece is still considered "the edge of Europe, the back alley, faintly seedy and litter-strewn" (26). Moreover, Greece is associated, literally as well as figuratively, with the maternal: as the origin, the womb of the world, with Delphi as "the belly button of the universe" (28). It is the land that has engendered the heroine's grandmother who upon her arrival in the New World gives birth to generations of women. However, it is also the place that has given birth to one of the foundational cultures of the Western world. I suggest that the women's return to Greece does not constitute so much a "break with the [American] past" (182), as a desire to go back into the womb; to establish "continuity" (81) and retrieve the grandmother's broken story, which was "in even smaller, more jagged shards" (106). In this way, these two generations of women enact the possibility of reestablishing a sense of community with their origin, and, thus, re-inscribing their identity within a *bi-* rather than a *mono-* cultural framework. Given the stark contrast in sexual mores between the New and the Old Worlds, America and Greece, the women have to take up the masculine position to (literally!) penetrate Greek cultural traditions and move skillfully within them. In a way, they accept the cultural challenge to search for a feminist discourse that will unify both components of their bicultural identity.

Despite the ambivalent authorial stance toward female identity and the social status of women in Greece, the site where the heroine's Americanness and Greekness converge is gender. It is feminist universalism (another essentialist trope that runs through the novel) that binds Western/American and Greek cultures together. The need to unveil the female power, hidden or subdued, and to release the voice, strangled or silenced, becomes the heroine's primary goal. "Women," she affirms, "are not taught that their bodies can be a source of power to themselves, other than through the power to attract and manipulate desire. A woman's journey can take her far or as long as she wants, but she must learn to travel in her own body" (160). Elsewhere she states that: "In [men's] stories, we women live by love, waiting passively on the sidelines, for the reward or the temptation. Underneath that version lies another, where the goddesses do more than chase around the gods; they also shape the world" (15). If women are to achieve a liberated status, the novel seems to imply, they have to contest traditional structures and displace maternal narratives. "Abandoning the tracks in the earth laid out for her" (193) is what the heroine's mother does; and, in doing so, she "has made a choice, kept what she has wanted from her [own] mother's past and discarded what tasted sour or cost too much"

(219). Similarly, the heroine regards her ethnic identity as a performance, an *act* or a choice. "I have entered a role and participated in a drama; whenever I want to, I can drop my mask and go" (189), she asserts.

The antagonistic, almost condescending rhetoric that characterizes the heroine's allegiance to her ethnic identity should not surprise the cautious reader. The deep-seated ambivalence that permeates the heroine's relation to her Greek identity is described by Homi Bhabha as the colonial subject's positionality toward its colonized other: the colonial subject both fears and desires the familiar unfamiliarity that the stereotype produces (*The Location of Culture* 77-81 *passim*). Hence all the references to dark, dangerous and primitive elements of Greek culture: the "dark line in the [heroine's] blood" (68); the "old rusty trap" of marriage she has to avoid (192); the "darkness" that only "Greeks know how to savor" (198); and the "black waters" of the cultural current she plunges into (233). On the other hand, the text is permeated with images of Greece as providing a sense of belonging, and as a site of safety and protection. Despite such apparent ambivalences, by the end of the novel the heroine seems to have reached the naïve conclusion that she has resolved the tensions and conflicts of her bicultural identity by containing and regulating the articulation of her difference.

Toward a Bicultural Identity

Toward the end of Papaendrou's *Father Dancing*, the narrator seems to have achieved a balance in relation to both facets of his identity. The son's "crowded heart"—peopled by his uncontested allegiance to American culture, his father's imposed discourse on authentic Greekness, and his own first responses to his ancestral land—is progressively transformed into a "reconciled" space, where the crowds no longer conflict but move in dialogic opposition. This seemingly unproblematic point of view is informed by the narrator's particular perception as an adolescent male. Complexities that might develop as a result of adult experiences of gender or historical and cultural specifications are absent in the narrative.

On the other hand, the unnamed heroine of Davidson's *The Priest Fainted* launches on an adventurous trip to "reshape" and "re-create" ancestral narratives while insisting on the variety, and at times conflicting versions, of her past. Instead of privileging any single mode of narration, as one of her chapter headings ironically suggests, she attempts to face the complexities of her female adulthood and sexuality. Her gendered identity becomes, within the context of Greek patriarchal traditions, the site of fragmented and contradictory experiences of self-affirmation.

Nevertheless, the heroine's confident, but problematic, belief that ethnicity can be invoked at will is founded on socio-historical formulations long since discredited. Although sociologists such as Richard D. Alba and Mary C. Waters have, in conjunction with Herbert Gans's suggestion of "symbolic ethnicity" (193), demonstrated the freedom American whites enjoy in affiliating and disaffiliating themselves at will, this view of ethnicity is considered insufficient as it dissimulates or conceals "the contingent, temporally, and socially situated character of our beliefs and values, of our institutions and practices" (Hollinger 60). The subject's historicity and ethnic affiliation becomes performative only in its normative force, when, in Butler's words, "its power to establish what qualifies as 'being'" is assumed. As Butler explains, in regard to the crafting and signification of the sexed body, "performativity is neither free play nor theatrical self-presentation" (*Bodies that Matter* 188, 96), and the power of the subject is not the function of an originating will; it is derived by the *citationary* nature of its acts, by originating experiences that create themselves *as* they locate themselves. Thus, the heroine's notion that she is free to exercise an "ethnic option," to go back and forth between the roles of visitor and native, outsider and insider, is misleading. She barely understands that the performative nature of ethnicity works precisely through the reiteration of ethnic norms, as much as through their exclusion. Viewed in this way, the two identities, American and pre-American, are complementary and mutually implicated; the difference between the two cultures is maintained while hierarchy is denied. Only such an understanding of the subject's bicultural heritage could uncover the density and depth of his/her identity and attribute equal, dialogic emphasis to both of one's ancestral origins.

Notes

[1] The appellation comes from the Turkish *imam bayıldı*. İmam is a religious leader in Islam, functioning in practice as the equivalent of priest, and *bayıldı* is the past tense of the verb *bayılmak* which means both to adore and to faint. Legend has it that the imam fainted because the dish, consisting basically of eggplant and onion cooked in olive oil and eaten cold, was too succulent. Editor's note.

[2] The book's title as it appears in the American publication (1998).

[3] In April 1967, a group of colonels seized power and held to it until 1974. The Greek junta was known around the world for its suspension of civil liberties, torture of political prisoners and brutal repression of a student revolt in November 1973.

[4] Reference to one of the chapter titles of *The Priest Fainted*.

2
"Meaningful Wor(l)ds"
Patricia Grace's Bicultural Fiction.

Paloma Fresno Calleja

Biculturalism in New Zealand

In 1952 *Te Ao Hou* magazine, the official publication of the Maori Affairs Department in New Zealand, came out announcing in its "Editorial" that "a true Maori world [was] slowly shaping itself to stand beside the Pakeha[1] world" (1). The editor's words not only revealed optimism with respect to the literary materialization of Maori culture, but also responded to a generalized concern with the promotion and recovery of traditional art forms, occurring in the country since the beginning of the twentieth century, that had not been reflected in literature as much as in other artistic manifestations. *Te Ao Hou* became a platform for most of today's best-known Maori writers, inaugurating a bicultural trend in New Zealand's literary history by means of which the nation began to be, following Benedict Anderson, "imagined" in Maori as well as Pakeha terms. The contents of the magazine, therefore, should be mainly valued in a political sense, since they contributed to illuminate the unknown aspects of *Maoritanga* (Maori culture), allowing them to serve a purpose at a national level.

In the following years a few scattered examples, such as Hone Tuwhare's collection of poems *No Ordinary Sun* (1964), and the short story collections *Pounamu, Pounamu*[2] (1972) by Witi Ihimaera and *Waiariki* (1975) by Patricia Grace, reinforced the sense that there was in New Zealand another world, that had remained hidden but was progressively coming out "into the world of light."[3] These early works established in the last five decades the basis of a literature which has undergone a process of emergence, consolidation, and diversification, and which is, at the beginning of the twenty-first century, still facing some of the old challenges that inspired those works.

As Grace pointed out in an interview, "[New Zealand] literature isn't defining us properly and the overall picture we get is a false one. That's why Maori literature has such an important place" (qtd. in Kedgley 63). Thus, one of the remaining challenges is to increase Maori literary output, and Grace herself occupies an outstanding position amidst the variety of voices trying to fill this as yet existing bicultural emptiness. Grace's work has in fact helped to fill not one but many gaps: that of Maori writing in Aotearoa/New Zealand, that of Maori women's writing, and that of New Zealand literature in a more international context. Her commitment to the inscription of a Maori cultural identity has taken her to re/create traditional notions that do away with static definitions of her ethnicity, and with official models of biculturalism unable to account for the way in which she has experienced the interaction between both cultures at a personal as well as an artistic level.

The discourse of biculturalism and the political measures associated with it have had a relatively short history in New Zealand, although, strictly speaking, a factual biculturalism has been operating in the country since the very first moment of contact in the colonial period, and has become a reality for the majority of Maori people since then. This bicultural *modus vivendi* seems to be as old as the colonial process itself, despite early efforts to assimilate the native population to European standards, and constitutes the inevitable result of their belonging to a culture that has managed to preserve some of its constituents while necessarily being forced to embrace European forms.

Maori people had become bicultural even before biculturalism took the form of an official policy, despite monocultural trends imposed from 1840, the starting point of British colonization. In that year, representatives of the Crown and several Maori chiefs signed the Treaty of Waitangi, a document that inaugurated an ethic of "partnership" between the two peoples inhabiting the Isles who, following Captain William Hobson's[4] oft-quoted words, should from then on become "one people." For the British, the treaty was apparently meant to avoid conflicts that had occurred in other colonies, and aimed at the establishment of a *single* nation of British subjects, an ideal that could only be forged through assimilation of the Maori tribes towards European culture. In contrast, the native inhabitants saw the treaty as a formal agreement that would allow them to maintain their sovereign status as *tangata whenua* (people of the land), while agreeing to cede the administration of the territory to the Crown. The details surrounding the signing of the document and its different versions still remain a rich source of controversy, but underlying these opposed interpretations are, on the one hand, the belief of the Maori tribes that they could maintain their cultural specificity while becoming part of a nation, and on the other, the settlers' idea that the existence of two separate peoples would hinder the process of settlement and subsequent national consolidation as they (and later their descendants) would wish it. The British settlers believed assimilation to be the only option for a people they considered to be the last of a "dying race," despite the fact that these had managed to survive in the changing world, thanks to their capacity of adaptation and the practice of an unacknowledged type of biculturalism.

The agreement established with the Treaty of Waitangi is also the origin of the dual pattern that, in the absence of an official policy of multiculturalism, dominates the New Zealand political scene today. The treaty is considered to be a binding document between the native inhabitants and any other people (as an entity) living in Aotearoa; therefore, the term *multiculturalism*, which intends to be inclusive and indicative of other minorities (i.e., other than the whites), mainly from Asia and the Pacific Islands, has been rejected by those who place their claims to the land in a secondary position with regards to those of the Maori community. Although demographically and culturally New Zealand is obviously multicultural today, at an official level biculturalism has not given way to multicultural procedures.

The mismatch between the social reality and the political measures is also reflected, albeit in another manner, in literature: the number of Maori (and other minority) writers is still considerably inferior to that of Pakeha writers. This reveals that, at least at the level of representation, biculturalism is still to be achieved and should therefore constitute the primary focus of attention before further measures are taken. As Grace has explained:

> We have a treaty . . . signed by representatives of the Crown and representatives and leaders of the Maori people. At that time and just after that we had a bicultural society—two cultures living alongside each other. . . . Biculturalism means Maori people on the one hand and all the other people on the other. . . . We must not confuse the rights of many different cultures with the rights of indigenous people, because they are two separate issues entirely. (qtd. in Sarti 44)

The adoption of an official policy of "biculturalism" was preceded by other alternative models, namely the policy of colonial assimilation (envisioning monoculturalism) mentioned above, and, in the postcolonial period, measures based on "integration"—a term used in this context by Jack Kent Hunn in his *Report of the Department of Maori Affairs* (1961). The term aimed at defining the contours of what apparently constituted a new attitude regarding intercultural relations, but proved in fact that some of the old trends were still operative. Hunn assumed that since much of the "essence" of Maori culture had already disappeared, the only possible alternative would be to safeguard whatever remained, while ensuring that Maori people were urbanized, educated and lived according to a Western lifestyle. He saw integration as a combination, never a fusion, "of the Maori and Pakeha elements to form one nation wherein Maori culture remains distinct" (8). The need to keep the two cultures apart had, however, nothing to do with positive discrimination; rather, it was the result of the whites' pervasive view of Maori culture as a way of life about to vanish. In Hunn's eyes this way of life could safely be preserved through a set of what was for him stereotyped practices—"the chief relics" being "[l]anguage, arts and crafts, and the institution of the marae"[5] (9)—which were not to transcend their purely symbolic value in the otherwise "homogeneous" New Zealand culture.

New Zealand's bicultural discourse was initiated in 1968, when Erik Schwimmer edited *The Maori People in the Nineteen-Sixties,* a work in which, in an article entitled "The Aspirations of the Contemporary Maori," he defined bicultural individuals—rather than biculturalism—as those who accept "as legitimate the values of a second culture, [are] to some extent familiar with these values, and can turn to them, if necessary, for subsidiary relationships" (13). His definition was intended to be a guiding principle against and away from previous policies, and shaped substantially what otherwise—either in its presence or absence—had been a tangible reality since the European settlement. It recognized for the first time the existence of cross-cultural interaction between the two communities, while emphasizing the importance of mutual recognition.

In its most basic definition, biculturalism stressed, not only the need for awareness, acceptance, and tolerance of the other community; but also interaction between the two groups—what Schwimmer called making "creative use of each other" (13). It seemed obvious, however, that cultural interaction was neither a novelty nor a question of choice for a group of people (the Maoris) who had been brought up learning to bridge the differences between two cultural heritages, whereas it certainly appeared to be so for the Pakeha majority. The latter, kindly invited to learn about traditional Maori protocol, a few token greetings, words or symbols, had not felt the need up until then to make the elements of the other culture part of their everyday life.

What follows, thus, is that most Maori people today enjoy a *de facto* biculturalism: one which is the product of intermarriage and dual upbringing, that can neither be rejected nor embraced as a set of laws. It results from the (inevitable) fact that cultures are never compact wholes opposed to one another but come into contact with each other and are in constant transformation. The case for most Maori in the past was one of *having* to be bicultural in order to survive, a necessity that has, nowadays, turned, at a personal and quotidian level into a question of *being* bicultural. As Grace herself suggests, "Maori people, being in a minority position, *become*, of necessity, bicultural, and *are* often bicultural by parentage and upbringing as well" (qtd. in McRae, "Interview with Patricia Grace" 290).

Thus, at the point when Grace began writing, biculturalism was not only the unavoidable result of two coexistent cultures, but also testimony to a culture of survival capable of adopting new ways of life, while adapting ancestral traditions to a contemporary context in order to accord them permanence. This distinction between a personal and a more political type of biculturalism, that can be traced in the writings of many Maori authors, has been drawn by Andrew Sharp with the term "bicultural selfhood," which he uses to distinguish the more personal way of experiencing a dual cultural belonging from a more social and external meaning. In the second case, he talks of biculturalism applied to the *personae*, "to our selves as bearers of rights and duties, as actors on a public stage," which, in turn, differs from a more political usage, deriving from the public procedures intended to guide these *personae* in the political arena (121, 120, 126). Sharp's division is relevant for my purposes here because it is from the assumption of her bicultural selfhood and her mixed heritage that Grace works to build up a strong literary universe. This is a universe in which bicultural *personae* interact, through an enormously complex and often problematic process of intercultural communication based on dialogue, which Sharp places as the common goal, needed in order to achieve mutual understanding and recognition.

My analysis in this chapter focuses precisely in the way in which these two sides of the coin interact in Grace's works: the personal and the political, the individual and the communal, the unavoidable cultural interaction and the strategic separation of these two worlds by means of which she emphasizes their differences but also points out their similarities, in the hope that New Zealand culture can be equally enriched by both. Grace's allegiances have always been with the Maori, but it is precisely her privileged position as a communicator between the two worlds that has allowed her to tell the story of her community in dialogue with itself and with the Pakeha world. I examine below five works of fiction by the author, published during a period extending over two decades (1975-1998), to engage in the issues of intercultural communication and dialogue she problematizes.

Patricia Grace's Literary Output

Examining the importance of recognition in the articulation of individual and communal identity, as well as the philosophical precedents shaping the quest for authenticity experienced by many indigenous cultures today, Charles Taylor proposes the concept of a social and dialogical search, by means of which identity would be derived from external contact and understanding between cultures—as opposed to Herder's view that one's original identity can only be found inwardly. As Taylor puts it:

> [The] crucial feature of human life is its fundamental *dialogical* character. We become full human agents, capable of understanding ourselves, and hence of defining our identity, through the acquisition of rich human languages of expression. . . . But we learn these modes of expression through exchanges with others. People do not acquire the languages needed for self-definition on their own. Rather, we are introduced to them through the *interaction* with others . . . (32, emphases added)

Taylor explicitly links his political theory with a Bakhtinian conception of language, understood as the variety of modes of expression that interact in an interplay of forces ruled simultaneously by centripetal and centrifugal impulses, and that represent the ideological conceptions of different groups and individuals (Bakhtin 272). Taylor's definition of identity is eminently dialogical; he assumes the convenience and inevitability of dialogue both as a means of self-definition and eventually as a key to solve cultural conflicts. This is in agreement with Sharp's proposal and with many other theoretical and political approaches to bi/multiculturalism in different countries today and finds an evident correlation in the way in which Grace constructs her polyphonic communities. Although individual Pakehas cannot be forced to become bicultural in the sense that most Maori people are today, as Sharp points out, intercultural communication, as a process of recognition, understanding and tolerance, should be "a precondition of a public life inclusive of all who wish to join in" (122, 123). A mere set of political measures and relocation of resources is not enough, the struggles for self-definition at a personal and a social level must be negotiated through a dialogue between the two groups. I believe that throughout her literary production, Grace, understanding the importance of articulating meaningful words in order to find the true significance of the Maori and the Pakeha worlds, has managed to establish the conditions that can meet this intercultural exchange.

Grace's work is an extremely careful construction of complex linguistic worlds determined by two simultaneous impulses: on the one hand, a process of dialogic cooperation, which sets her characters in search of an identity that can only be obtained and gain sense through a process of communal interaction; on the other hand, a process of dialogical confrontation, in which opposing points of view are set against each other, although they cannot be analyzed in mere confrontational terms (see Fresno for more on this). The individual and communal identity of her characters is shaped not only in opposition to others, but thanks to an interaction with them; this has made Grace's literature a rich source of cultural polyphony whose variations have been superb reflections of the evolving social conditions of the last four decades of New Zealand history.

Her first works constitute firm, although not strictly political, claims towards intercultural understanding and the need of Pakeha recognition in particular. As Raj Vasil indicates, in the 1970s (when Grace started writing), the search for a distinctive identity undertaken by Maori people "was seen mostly in cultural-linguistic terms rather than in political and economic terms" (28). This explains to a great extent the kind of works published at the time, including Grace's, in which the focus was placed on the evocation of typically Maori scenes in rural landscapes and the close imitation of Maori idiom, intended basically to inscribe the lost voice of the culture. The protagonists of these works became the inhabitants of nostalgic vignettes, of "lyrical evocations of a world that once was" (Ihimaera, "Maori Life and Literature: a Sensory Perception" 50), with writers expressing more or less unconsciously their interest in reconstructing their "emotional landscape" (Grace and Ihimaera, "The Maori in Literature" 82). As a result, most reviewers took these writers to task for approaching the process of cultural recovery in a sentimental or overtly didactic fashion. These first works seemed to reveal mainly the individual's struggle with his/her bicultural self, the hardships of having to grow up in a dual environment, and the conflicts resulting from deficient social interaction.

In an article co-written with Ihimaera in 1978, Grace affirms: "I am a person of mixed racial origins, being Maori and Pakeha both by birth and upbringing. So, although I have always identified myself to myself as Maori, my Maori experience has been limited" ("The Maori in Literature" 80). This need to give advocacy to the hidden part of that bicultural self constitutes the main effort of her early works.

Waiariki

In *Waiariki* (1975), the first collection of short stories published by a Maori woman, Grace managed to sow the seed of intercultural dialogue in a series of stories that evolve around conflicting discourses of individual and communal identity, informed respectively by the urban environment to which most Maori people belong since the mid-twentieth century and the rural settings where the old generations were striving to keep the notion of community alive.

In "A Way of Talking," the opening story, Rose returns to her village from university, after having been in contact with that other world and having managed to acquire a new way of talking and, consequently, a new way of understanding the relationship between the two worlds connected inside her. In the story, Rose, who is now able to perceive the nuances between what are still different ways of talking and of understanding the world, confronts a Pakeha woman for referring to "the Maori" with a generic label. Grace concentrates the essence of the dissonance that has so far failed to assure a fruitful understanding in a very short but powerful exchange:

> Jane said, "That's Alan. He's been down the road getting the Maoris for scrub cutting." . . .
> "Don't they have names?"
> "What. Who?" Jane was surprised and her face was getting pink.
> "The people from down the road whom your husband is employing to cut scrub." Rose the stink thing, she was talking all Pakehafied.
> "I don't know any of their names." . . .
> "Do they know yours?"
> "Mine?"
> "Your name."
> "Well. . . . yes."
> "Yet you have never bothered to find out their names or to wonder whether or not they have any." (Grace, *Waiariki* 3)

In these early stories Grace rejects the empty agenda of a false biculturalism which still seems to hide a tendency towards assimilation and where acceptance of Maori culture is literally limited to a set of stereotyped practices, very much in the line of Hunn's ideas. Through the portrayal of young, urban, educated protagonists Grace shows the capacity of her community to react against injustices, which in the surface are of a linguistic or symbolic type, but deep inside hide more complex implications. The anonymity of Maori culture can only be overcome at this point by characters like Rose or like the protagonist of "Parade," another student who goes back home for the annual carnival and witnesses how her people are placed on a platform and made to perform in a "moving" museum:

> [D]uring my time away from here my vision and understanding had expanded. I was able to see myself and other members of my race as others see us. . . . 'Is that what we are to them?' Museum pieces, curious, antiques, shells under glass. A travelling circus, a floating zoo. People clapping and cheering to show that they know about such things. (Grace, *Waiariki* 84)

Mutuwhenua[6]

In her first novel, *Mutuwhenua* (1978), Grace tackles some of the same issues while expanding the profile of a bicultural character. Linda/Ripeka—the double name revealing her double background—struggles to become a Pakeha girl, wishing to escape the constraining embrace of the family traditions, despite her grandmother Ripeka's attempt to resurrect "the old ways" in her. Linda's struggle is one of choice between the new glittering life in the city, after marrying a Pakeha man, and the life (at times asphyxiating) in her small community. The novel is constructed around the metaphor of a tree with deeply embedded roots, symbol of a culture that has remained linked to the land it has sprung from, but also with long leaping branches, which demonstrate its adaptability. The image is also related to the Maori myth of Rona, the woman dragged to the moon's surface as a punishment for her swearing to it for not enlightening her way. As Rona is drawn to the sky with the tree she has clung to in order to remain on earth, she becomes an in-between figure, a commuter between both worlds, a cultural amphibian capable of combining her two heritages. The fact that the tree is uprooted from the soil clearly refers to Linda's displacement, but its capacity to grow in an unknown surface symbolises the permanence and adaptability of Maori culture.

However, it is thanks to its branches, which still serve to shelter Rona, that one sees the connection between Linda's life in the city and her tribe in the ancestral land. Linda's final decision to take her new-born son to her family to be educated by her grandparents according to traditional Maori mores and her husband's easy acceptance contrast with the lack of understanding between the two which Grace narrates throughout the novel. Linda's inability to open the doors of her culture to her husband—"I was afraid of what I might come to know about him and me, of what there could be between us" (Grace, *Mutuwhenua* 3)—reflects the limits of intercultural communication, but also the possibility of change, if responsibility is undertaken equally by both parts. At this point dialogue may not yet be possible; however, Grace does not resort to the easy solution of blaming it all on the Pakeha side.

Potiki

As opposed to the early reflections on the more personal and familial aspects of biculturalism seen in *Waiariki* and *Mutuwhenua*, and while such considerations still constitute an important part of her subsequent production, Grace's work in the 1980s is characterized by a strong political emphasis.

From the mid-1970s onwards, the political climate in the country had been defined by a more radical approach towards Maori sovereignty and the adoption of new political measures, with the Treaty of Waitangi as its basis. These contributed to spread a bicultural conscience among all New Zealanders, who in turn became more aware of their own ethnicity in a country which still remained inevitably linked to "Britain" but was also beginning to be defined in Pacific terms. These were controversial years in which it became obvious that the mere recognition of a mixed heritage would not be sufficient to ensure an actual equality between the two peoples. At this point, the echoes of Schwimmer's bicultural theories turned into sound protests, centred mainly on the recovery of Maori land, the recognition of Maori cultural specificity, and the emphasis on the "dual partnership," that came to be understood not as a describing feature but as a weapon for a new generation of Maori people aware of their position within New Zealand society. Political radicalism crystallized in more challenging literary works such as Keri Hulme's *the bone people* (1983), which, in the experimental character it projected, brought about a new way of conceiving Maori literature, and was acclaimed internationally as the postcolonial paragon of New Zealand literature; or Ihimaera's *The Matriarch* (1986), in which territorial issues were tackled from a historical perspective showing that the struggle of the Maori community had in fact existed uninterrupted since colonial times.

This was the year also in which Grace's second novel came out. *Potiki* (1986) is the story of a Maori rural community struggling to remain on their ancestral land that is being threatened by Pakeha developers. Its plot is loosely based on the incident of the Raglan Golf Course, a *cause célèbre* at the time concerning an area borrowed as an aviation field during the Second World War which had not been returned to the tribes, and was about to be turned into a golf course. Once again, the central issues of the novel evolve around conflicting discourses of individuality and community, power and powerlessness, and two radically different types of allegiance to the land—the material and the spiritual. Yet this time the confrontation is developed more explicitly, as the novel sets out to condemn Pakeha domination in economic, cultural, and political terms. The opposition between the coastal community and the developers causes the destruction of the community's *marae*, the flooding of the village, and the death of Toko, the youngest child or *potiki*, in what seems as an evident victory over the community. However, Grace's characters are never presented as victims, but rather as powerful individuals who stand up and raise their voices in efficient narrations and dynamic linguistic exchanges.

The novel implies a step ahead in the process of intercultural communication, as Grace manages to represent both groups in very clever dialogues which, although still distilling an enormous amount of bitterness, demonstrate to what extent her Maori characters have embraced a bicultural language and are equipped to fight social injustices from within. All characters undertake the dialogic confrontation, but Tangimoana, the young educated protagonist, is placed in charge of the protests. She constitutes a good example of linguistic and cultural maturity, paradoxically because she has left her village and entered "Pakeha territory." She embraces biculturalism in a way that is very different from Linda's "Pakehafied" ways in *Mutuwhenua*. It is not mannerism, but a powerful weapon to confront the developers with their own weapons. When the developers come to the village Tangimoana is the one entitled to confront them:

> "Is there anyone in particular you would like to see?" Tangimoana asked.
> "The chief," he said.
> "Perhaps I can help you?"
> "Well who's in charge?"
> "Of what?" Her replies were becoming shorter.
> "Of . . . Of. Well I haven't got much time. And if I could go straight to the top?"
> "What of? A tree?"
> "Look, I just want to know who is in charge here so I can get permission. I want some photos and I need some people . . ."
> "This is where we live. We are all in charge." (Grace, *Potiki* 118)

Affirming that in Grace's work "[c]ommunication between these two peoples [Maori and Pakeha] often lacks reciprocity and a sense of completeness," Jane McRae writes about the author's concern for "complete communication," not so much as a terminated process but as an aim to be achieved to ensure the harmonious relationship between the two communities ("Patricia Grace and Complete Communication" 68). Despite the fact that the reader only witnesses painful monologues or violent confrontations where there is no hint of understanding, instances such as the above-quoted encounter certainly reveal that a basis for further exchanges is already being established by these young characters' gaining linguistic agency. Although at this point one still perceives a cultural mismatch and the impossibility of dialogue as a way of solving conflicts, as reader, one is capable of overcoming the impression that the novel is based on "vociferous exchanges, most often bitter, but no dialogue," words which Ihimaera used to refer to earlier literary pieces ("Maori Life and Literature: A Sensory Perception" 53). The characters have acquired the linguistic weapons necessary to initiate an exchange, even if at this point the Pakeha flank is still dubious of Maori linguistic capacities. As Otto Heim rightly remarks, the novel is the result of presenting the characters' bilingual abilities through a combination of the "dialogic dissonance by which the text dramatizes the confrontation" between the two groups, and the linguistic unity and "the sense of cooperation that pervades community life in its economic, cultural and spiritual dimensions" (132, 136).

The gallery of characters through which Grace manages to convey this double process, the confrontational and the cooperative, is especially relevant: Mary and Toko, mentally and physically handicapped, are the weak victims of the external conflicts, but develop powerful ways of communicating and serve Grace to subvert the notion of Maori as children in need of education. Tangimoana has been chosen to study law and to mediate with legal weapons in what constitutes a modern alternative to the warrior spirit of traditional Maori society. James becomes the carver entitled to carry out the history of his community in wood, and therefore functions as a modern artist who manages to recover an old artistic language making it fit into a contemporary context. Last but not least, the parents Hemi and Roimata are rewritings of Rangi, the Sky Father, and Papa, the Earth Mother, the gods of the Maori creation, yet appear to be subverting Western gender hierarchies, since Hemi, the father, is presented as the earth keeper and Roimata, the mother, is described as the sky dweller, escaping thus the constraining association between the land and the female body. With them, Grace is offering, not at all a gallery of cardboard characters, but quite the opposite: a series of very distinct discursive positions that fit into the polyphony that the novel presents. The different voices become contrapuntal ways of looking at what might otherwise seem a mere dual confrontation; the versions of the events are retold once and again, and fit into one another, because, as the reader is reminded throughout the novel, "although the stories all had different voices, and came from different times and places and understandings . . . each one was like a puzzle piece which tongued or grooved neatly to one another" (Grace, *Potiki* 41). Through her storytelling, that involves this communal process, Grace presents her community as a living entity, whose cultural contents are borrowed from a multiplicity of sources all of which contribute to create a complete picture of their identity. While the community recovers from the physical destruction of their lands, they initiate the verbal reconstruction of their heritage in cooperation, not only of different voices but also of materials borrowed from both worlds:

> The stories I had to share were childhood stories . . . I had other stories too, known from before life and death and remembering . . . When James and Tangimoana came home from school they brought their stories with them. School had a place from them. . . . James's school stories were about the earth and the universe. . . . Tangimoana had stories of people. Some of these were book stories of queens and kings . . . In the evenings Hemi would come home with his work stories, . . . Mary would tell us her stories too, which were not always exactly the same if you listened carefully . . . There were the stories that Granny Tamihana had to tell which were weavings of sorrow and joy . . . Then there were the stories from newspapers and television that we read and viewed each day. And there were the stories we found in library books which we went to exchange every few weeks. (Grace, *Potiki* 39-41)

In this sense, the novel presents the process of cultural recovery as an example of what Marie Louise Pratt has called "transculturation" (4), the bi-directional influence between colonizers and colonized when they come into contact, a process of a conscious choice with respect to the elements that are appropriated from the dominant culture and, hence of a more active participation than the accounts on colonial domination normally bargain for (7). Moreover, the novel constitutes a magnificent example of Grace's bicultural artistic legacies. To describe most characters, Grace makes use of mythical associations coming from both cultures, especially in the case of the child Toko, who is a contemporary rewriting of Maui, the Maori trickster, and also that of Jesus. To shape the story, she turns traditional novelistic conventions into a polyphonic narrative resembling the format of a *whaikorero*, a traditional oration. To reflect on the act of writing itself, she draws parallels with the art of the carver, whose wooden figures speak up from the "womb that is a tree" (Grace, *Potiki* 7), as the characters' voices mature progressively throughout the story and emerge in a contrapuntal sequence. And to inform the narrative organization, she weaves a Western linear temporality and a Maori spiral one in simultaneous fashion.

A work of fiction in which she established for the first time the basic guidelines of her own bicultural politics, *Potiki* is to this date Grace's most representative novel.

Cousins

In 1992 Grace published *Cousins,* a novel which reinforces her faith in dialogue as a means of solving conflicts. It represents a multiplicity of linguistic struggles both inside and outside the Maori community through the development of three very different female characters: Mata, Missy and Makareta, whose lives are determined by opposite ways of conceiving familial relationships and tribal allegiances. By placing the action of the events in the 1950s Grace looks back to some of the problems that still exist today. In contrast, the sense of community that she presupposes in her previous novels is not taken for granted here but described and contested from its origin; so, the linguistic relations acquire new and unexplored nuances.

Mata grows up without a family and her life is determined by the lack of *turangawaewae*, of a standing position from which to define her self in a meaningful way. The opening scene of the novel, in which she is described as an aimless walker on an empty road, already announces her lack of direction. She has been cut off from her roots in her childhood, and is searching for her own linguistic and familial identity, unable as she is to share the words of the people who surround her: "Everybody knew each other, knew how to finish each other's sentences, knew what to do and say, belonged to each other. There was a secret to it that she knew nothing of" (Grace, *Cousins* 90). Missy grows up in the country, and is made to marry a man chosen by her family to ensure that their lands are joined. Through Missy's character, Grace questions for the first time some of the practices of a family who remains anchored in the past and places communal interest over individual needs and wishes. Missy's expectations evolve around a romantic conception of love inspired by Hollywood films, but she ends up quietly agreeing to marry Hamu and accepting others' words as a way to define herself: "I managed to be who they all wanted me to be . . . I was carried along on words—called words, words spoken, words sung"

(Grace, *Cousins* 230). Despite the differences in their upbringing, these two characters represent two similar discursive positions: neither one is able to articulate her needs, and to contribute to the supposedly dialogic quality within the community. Makareta occupies, however, the opposite position. She becomes one of Grace's cultural amphibians, rejecting a prearranged marriage and going to the city where she becomes an activist of Maori cultural claims. Throughout the novel the reader regrets Mata's lack of power and Missy's resignation, but shares Makareta's determination to escape familial rules and, despite obvious difficulties, bridge the gaps between the two cultures.

In *Cousins*, Grace takes the notion of dialogue not only as a weapon to confront injustices, but also as a way of healing one's own scars. The voices chosen to orchestrate the narrative are meaningful only when they come into contact with others. The first part of the novel is formed by three sections: Mata's life is told from an omniscient point of view, Missy's has hers narrated by her brother (an unborn narrator addressing her in the second person), and Makareta's mother completes the account of her daughter's childhood. In the second part of the novel, the three protagonists recover their linguistic agency and complete it with an autobiographical narrative through a consummated process of dialogical cooperation. Intra-cultural dialogue between the members of the family is thus established, as a precondition to more complex intercultural linguistic exchanges.

Baby No-eyes

The combination of individual needs and communal impositions, linguistic agency and muteness, cooperation and confrontation, and biculturalism understood as an enriching dialogue and as a system still dominated by polarized identities can be observed in Grace's fourth novel, *Baby No-eyes* (1998). The novel progresses in polyphonic fashion, as one hears different voices, belonging to several members of a family, who undertake the process of narration from several different perspectives, that serve to provide accounts of injustices exerted against them at personal, tribal or social levels. Grace leads the different narrators through separate but intertwined discursive paths: political issues are presented, as in *Potiki*, in the form of territorial conflicts, this time through the eyes and voice of Mahaki, a Maori lawyer helping his community to recover lands illegally appropriated by the government. A parallel account of historic injustices deriving from the colonial past is provided, in short vignettes interspersed throughout the novel, by the grandmother, Kura, who goes back to key events in the history of race relations, such as the signing of the Treaty or the Land Wars. The mother Te Paania is entitled to reconstruct her life for the sake of her children, offering descriptions of a youth spent in a monocultural and restrictive environment.

Maori concerns are taken in this novel to a new frontier through the theme of genetic engineering and the destruction of indigenous intellectual property. The death of Baby, Te Paania's first child, whose eyes are removed from her body to be used in some unspecified experiment, is the event that binds all the issues together. The incident, based on a real event which took place in a New Zealand hospital, culminates with Baby's eyeless body being returned to the land but remaining with her family as a spiritual presence. The loss of Baby's eyes has a metaphorical implication, as it enlarges her mere physical disability into a cultural blindness. At a cultural level, the treatment that the body receives at the hospital implies not only a lack of awareness of Maori death and burial traditions but also a deprivation of the baby's physical entity that in Maori terms implies a communal deprivation. When Kura undertakes the task of recovering the child's body to return it to her tribal land to be buried, she experiences cultural disagreements similar to those experienced by the community confronted with the developers in *Potiki*:

> [T]here were these words that I didn't like . . . these people have their words and we have ours. They are doctors, professionals, high-up people. Their words are different . . . You think that people know, think that they are high-up people, then you discover that all they are is different. To you they are empty, and you know it. (Grace, *Baby No-eyes* 60-64)

The issues of confrontation engaged in the novel do not seem to have changed, when one looks back at Grace's previous works. The author is still concerned with the unsolved matters on the agenda, aggravated by new conflicts such as the one surrounding Baby's death. And yet she continues to propose the same solution in confronting the new challenges, solution which she seems to delineate with precision and efficiency in this novel.

The faith in communal cooperation as the means of survival can be found in the relationship between Baby and her younger brother Tawera, in charge of guiding her in the dark and unknown world, a task which he carries out thanks to a very precise verbal reconstruction of the shapes, colours and materials which Baby cannot perceive. As soon as Tawera is born, he has to get accustomed to living with a sister whom *he* can see but who remains an invisible presence for other people. The relationship established between the two children is one of complementation, similar to that of Toko and Manu in *Potiki*, or Missy and her twin in *Cousins*. In order for Baby to become integrated into the genealogy of ancestors, her presence has to be acknowledged by other members of the family and, implicitly, by the reader who is made to share this search for agency as a metonym for the more complex search of the Maori community at a national level. To express this wider search, Baby's quest is not presented as an isolated journey and is eventually completed with a communal process in which all the characters take part. Tawera becomes Baby's basic reference in an unseen world as he finds information about his own past asking his mother:

> "All right Mum," I said, "tell us about yourself and about this sister of mine who has no eyes. Stolen? How come?"
> "She died in an accident," Mum said, "If we are going to tell about the accident we'll have to tell everything."
> "We?"
> "Gran Kura and me, and all of us in our different ways. You too, you'll have to do your part. It could take years." (Grace, *Baby No-eyes* 19)

The telling does take years, and in fact becomes a journey into their remote past, in which the reader is made to witness a continuous series of injustices of which the hospital incident is the last stage. Because Baby cannot see the world around her, Tawera has to leave the visual material behind and tell his part of the story relying exclusively on words. In that way, the whole family is implicated in a blind journey, an inner search that will only be accomplished through the communal retelling of their stories.

This novel is, once again, the result of putting together voices and stories coming from very different perspectives and understandings, enriched with bicultural sources. But while, internally, communication seems to flow, external confrontations still remain very much irreconcilable.

Conclusion

Although the general tone of Grace's works is far from pessimistic, her view of race relations in New Zealand is never based on obsolete conflicts, but enlarged to new problems, insisting that in order to achieve biculturalism, a fair representation of distinctive discursive positions is a basic precondition for dialogue and respectful communication. The words pronounced by Makareta in *Cousins* constitute a precise declaration of Grace's intentions:

> [C]ulture is deep. It is deep. Even the remnants or the memories of it are deep. It is not something that can be explained to those of another culture, but neither should it need to be explained, I think. It only needs, at the least, to be allowed, to be let be, to be trusted. (209)

The question is, therefore, not merely attempting to increase the amount of Maori material or to explain the complex meaning of each other's cultures. Grace intends to recover the contents of Maori culture and to reinforce the links between both worlds to form a comprehensive picture of New Zealand culture as truly bicultural.

With a few notable exceptions, to this day, it is mainly Maori writers such as Patricia Grace who are concerned with the articulation of bicultural politics into an aesthetic frame. Until a more general concern about biculturalism trespasses the mere political agenda and adopts a literary form through the works of non-Maori authors, biculturalism in New Zealand will certainly remain blind to the multiplicity of social and personal nuances that Grace has managed to reflect in her works.

Notes

[1] *Pakeha* is the term used in New Zealand to refer to people of European descent, who are, as Paul Spoonley defines them, "New Zealanders of a European background, whose cultural values and behaviour have been primarily formed from the experiences of being a member of the dominant group of New Zealand." However, "[t]he label excludes," remarks Spoonley, "those European groups which retain a strong affiliation to a homeland elsewhere and which reproduce this ethnicity in New Zealand" (57).

[2] *Pounamu* is the Maori word for greenstone or jade, the sacred stone used by Maori people in their carvings and ornaments, which plays an emblematic role in Ihimaera's collection.

[3] A translation of the Maori expression *Te Ao Marama*, a name given to the last stage of cosmological creation in which the previous stages of darkness gave way to light and life. The expression was used in 1982 to name the very first anthology of Maori writing, *Into the World of Light*, co-edited by D. S. Long and Witi Ihimaera; and has also been used to name the latter's subsequent five-volume compilation, with others, of Maori literature, *Te Ao Marama* (1992).

[4] William Hobson (1792-1842) was born in Ireland and joined the Royal Navy early in life. He arrived in New Zealand in 1840, and after helping to draft the Treaty of Waitangi and gathering some of the Maori chiefs' signatures, he became

the first governor of the country.

⁵ The *marae* is the public space that constitutes the centre of Maori community life. It is formed by several buildings, of which the *wharenui* or meetinghouse occupies an outstanding position as the centre of traditional ceremonies and celebrations.

⁶ The word *mutuwhenua* refers to the phase of the moon at which it is invisible. The "darkness" associated with this state can be interpreted as a metaphor for the intercultural misunderstandings which occur in the novel.

3
Güneli Gün's *On the Road to Baghdad* or Traveling Biculturalism

Gönül Pultar

Introduction

Umberto Eco, scholar and creative writer, distinguishes between the novel as genre and what he terms *"le besoin narratif"*[1] — the need to tell and be told stories — which he indicates is nowadays taken over by the cinema and television. For Eco, the novel remains in existence nevertheless because it retains a key function: since Marcel Proust, James Joyce, Thomas Mann and Franz Kafka, it is through the novel that all the great myths and ideas have been conveyed (Anquetil 73-74).[2] V.S. Naipaul in turn suggests that, "perhaps it is, of all forms, the novel that has come nearest to managing the mixture of realities, myths and cultural possibilities through which we try to find our own writerly way into the future of history and experience." Citing Naipaul, Malcolm Bradbury writes that in the present-day "multicultural, international world where there are so many forms of human imagination to include, so many tales to tell, this multi-angled aspect of fiction is of ever greater value" (12). As we move on in the twenty-first century, and while newer means of communication such as the Internet compete with film in devising ways of fulfilling the need for narratives, myths (whether timeless or newly developed) as well as ideas continue to be conveyed through the novel, which is more than ever the vital mixture Naipaul refers to. This chapter introduces a novel that has "so many tales" to tell, Turkish-American woman author Güneli Gün's *On the Road to Baghdad*, published in 1991. It is a novel that attempts, through the amalgam of the representations of two cultures, from which emanate its tales, to offer, in a "writerly way," an alley of comprehension to the current history and experience, that have become, not only multicultural and international, but also transnational and globalized.

Subtitled "A Picaresque Novel of Magical Adventures, Begged,

Borrowed, and Stolen from the Thousand and One Nights," the novel duly delivers what it promises: the greater part of its text consists of rewritings of the tales of the classic Eastern work. As such—that is, as a work of fiction that is authored by a hyphenated American writer and that includes non-Western elements—one would readily assume that it falls, basically, into the same category as the texts of such authors as Maxine Hong Kingston and Amy Tan, to name but two American "multicultural"/ "ethnic" writers. In fact, it would not be wrong to surmise that it is the success of the works of authors such as these two that made possible the emergence of a novel like Gün's. By the early 1990s, multicultural/ethnic fiction had fully developed as a sub-genre in the U.S., and moreover acquired its *titre de noblesse* within the mainstream with its commercial success and the widespread popularity it enjoyed among the reading public (a public that went well beyond the "ethnics" concerned). On the other side of the Atlantic, postcolonial fiction, taking the mantle from Commonwealth literature, had also acquired, with the likes of Salman Rushdie and Kazuo Ishiguro, a prestigious position within the republic of letters by invigorating the British novel and freeing it from the post-World War II neo-realistic mode of the "angry young men" discourse it had imprisoned itself in.

However, although reprinted as a pocket book (1994, all page references are to this edition), *On the Road to Baghdad* never attained the fame or stature of works like those of the two Chinese-American authors mentioned above. One reason may be that the existing Turkish-American community is smaller than the Chinese-American one (or any other equivalent hyphenated group), and naturally even much smaller than the larger Asian-American one, for whom the works of Kingston and Tan struck a chord, touched a nerve, bringing about recognition and popularity—and sales. Another, even more important, reason is that *The Woman Warrior* (1976) and *The Joy Luck Club* (1989), the first texts of Kingston and Tan that propelled them to fame, are the renderings on paper of American experiences, with the non-American element they both contain consisting of the engagement of *American*[3] authors with their parents' non-American culture. *On the Road to Baghdad*, on the other hand, presents a totally different image. It appears to narrate the life and times, so to speak, of one Hürü, a woman protagonist who lives in the sixteenth century, in Istanbul (or, as Westerners would call it at the time, Constantinople), the capital of the Ottoman Empire, and whose picaresque adventures, in this postmodernist/magical realist novel, take her further back in time to the eighth century, to Baghdad, during the reign of the Abbasid Caliph Haroun-er Rachid. As such, the content seems far from embodying the predicament of, and therefore awakening much interest in, the present-day small Turkish-American community, let alone the general American reading public.[4]

On the other hand, when the novel was translated into Turkish (1993), widely publicized in Turkey as the work of a Turkish author who "made it" (i.e., succeeded in getting published) in the U.S. (the sole superpower by then), it did not at all receive attention proportionate to the publicity that was deployed to launch it. As coming from the U.S., Turkish readers would have expected and valued a Turkish-American (Mary Antin's) *The Promised Land* (1912) or (Abraham Cahan's) *The Rise of David Levinsky* (1917), to name but two by now classic immigrant success stories. A fictionalized account of the American Dream achieved would have made them proud. The subject matter of *On the Road to Baghdad* left them cold when it did not repel. Geared towards the "Western" type of fiction and its cultural semantics, Turkish readers did not have much taste for the Eastern "matter," preponderant in the novel, which they tended to identify with the paradigm they had formally left behind, first with the Edict of Tanzimat of 1839[5], then even more vigorously with the establishment of the republic in 1923. Nor did they have much appreciation for the elements of magical realism found in the novel, such as supernatural happenings that allow characters to travel between centuries, which they associated not so much with the fiction of Gabriel Marcia Marquez or with that of those ethnic writers in the U.S. who emulated him, as with a lack of rationality that denotes downright ignorance and primitivism. Postmodernist features such as an eighth-century Arab woman in Baghdad wishing to order take-out Chinese food (178) were too foreign to be savored—both in the sense of the practice being unfamiliar, at least at the time; and of the anachronistic use of uncommon fictional material.

I wish to argue in this chapter that in order to arrive at a just appraisal of *On the Road to Baghdad*, we need to regard it as a *bicultural* novel: neither purely as a work of American (ethnic or multiculturalist) fiction, as would be natural for a novel written in English and published in the U.S. by someone who "lives in Ohio" and "has taught creative writing and Women's Studies at Oberlin College" as stated in the front-matter of the novel (i);[6] nor purely as a work of Turkish fiction, as Turkish scholar Rezzan Kocaöner Silkü does, when she sees Gün as a Turkish woman author of the diaspora, whose position enables her to pose a detached eye on developments within her (Turkish) culture, which she metaphorically represents in *On the Road to Baghdad*. It is not that either view is unfounded. But each one misses something. *On the Road to Baghdad* is arguably a bicultural novel par excellence: two cultures are combined, intertwined; and an understanding of the two cultures involved is necessary for a satisfactory appreciation of the work. Following Werner Sollors who entitled his book on interracial literature *Neither Black Nor White Yet Both* (1997; this edition 1999, all page references are to this edition), I wish to examine *On the Road to Baghdad* as a bicultural work of fiction that is neither Turkish nor American yet both; and to illustrate how the biculturalism is achieved in it.

In this, I wish to go beyond the concept of *hybridity*—a model I do not reject but which I believe should be transcended. As defined by Bill Ashcroft, Gareth Griffiths, and Helen Tiffin, hybridity is "the creation of new transcultural forms within the contact zone produced by colonization" (*Key Concepts in Post-colonial Studies* 118; see also their *The Empire Writes Back* 33-37; for a discussion of hybridity, see also Young). As conceptualized by Homi Bhabha, the critic who most championed it in his book *The Location of Culture*, the term presupposes the ascendance of a culture that is hegemonic over another one that is subaltern. Believing it generates ambivalence, Bhabha is inclined to view hybridity as deconstruction, as a critique of the dominant text/language/culture, and a counter-narrative in itself. However, insofar as hybridity connotes a crossbreeding that subverts, perverts, sullies and/or mars the purity of a text/language/culture, it simultaneously recalls by this very act an original, immaculate wholesomeness, to which is posited (in opposition to what that wholesomeness stands for) a "Third World" text that can perhaps only be a palimpsest. This text is inevitably produced within the experience of colonialism and imperialism and, by its very existence, is testimony to power imbalance and servitude (see Fanon and Ngugi wa Thiong'o's *Decolonising the Mind*). It is a repositioning—either as "white," by the use of the white's language, with Fanon's *peau noire* (black skin) nevertheless visible in the background; or as national allegory (see Jameson, "Third World Literature in the Era of Multinational Capitalism."), aiming to fight back against colonialism; when it is not mimicry plain and simple (see Naipaul, *The Mimic Men*; and also Bhabha, such chapters as "Of Mimicry and Man" in *The Location of Culture*)—with (each time) the point of reference/fulcrum being the dominant white/colonizer/imperialist identity/culture.

Traveling Biculturalism

I intend to frame my engagement with the bicultural aspects of *On the Road to Baghdad*[7] with James Clifford's theory of "traveling cultures." Calling attention in his essay "Traveling Cultures"(1992)[8] to the fact that nowadays those (non-Western) informants of (Western) anthropologists are themselves aware of being travelers, Clifford conceptualizes culture "*as travel*" (emphasis in the original), and "cultures" as "sites traversed" (103).

For him,

> Anthropological "culture" is not what it used to be. And once the representational challenge is seen to be the portrayal and understanding of local/global historical encounters, co-productions, dominations and resistances, then one needs to focus on hybrid, cosmopolitan experiences as much as rooted, native ones. . . . the goal is not to replace the cultural figure "native" with the intercultural figure "traveler." Rather, the task is to focus on concrete mediations of the two, in specific cases of historical tension and relationship. In varying degrees, both are constitutive of what will count as cultural experience. . . . If we rethink culture . . . in terms of travel, then the organic, naturalizing bias of the term culture . . . is questioned. Constructed and disputed *historicities*, sites of displacement, interference, and interaction, come more sharply into view. ("Traveling Cultures" 101)

Following Clifford, I suggest situating both cultures represented in *On the Road to Baghdad* as "sites of displacement, interference, and interaction"—where the "other," within the novel, is both Turkish territory (including its former possessions) and culture/the East *and* U.S. territory and culture/the West, depending on the eye of the beholder or the positionality/perspective of the narrative stance. This creates a narrative tension, following the "historical tension" Clifford alludes to, that produces a unique cultural experience. Throughout the novel, the two cultures simultaneously and mutually "other" each other even as they complement each other. Transformed into both object and subject interchangeably, the two cultures are so imbricated that it is almost impossible to distinguish components of one from those of the other. I suggest calling this positionality *traveling biculturalism*.

Putting on stage various historical characters such as Harun er-Rashid, as well as the Ottoman Sultan Selim I (known as Yavuz [the Brave] Sultan Selim), *On the Road to Baghdad* at first gives the impression of being a work of historical fiction. However, one realizes soon enough that along with historical personalities and fictionalized characters such as Hürü and members of her family, the novel also features such traditional characters of Turkish folk literature as Keloğlan (Bald Boy),[9] and characters from *The Thousand and One Nights* whose adventures are recounted as happening to personae Hürü meets during her travels. These treks in turn establish the novel as a road novel in its most conventional sense in American culture.

The novel's discourse is purely twentieth-century mainstream American parlance, comprising slang, an aspect that the reader at first finds staggering, and at times sacrilegious towards illustrious historical personalities or classical characters of the Eastern narrative heritage, when not in poor taste—as when Shahriyar describes Shahrazad[10] as "a great broad" (268). Yet both the anachronism and the linguistic relocation constitute features the reader has no difficulty adjusting to. One realizes that this novel is, as Georg Lukács aptly noted in writing about the "so-called historical novels of the seventeenth century," "historical only as regards the purely external choice of theme and costume. Not only the psychology of the characters, but the manners depicted are entirely those of the writer's own day" (15). This means that while some of the characters, descriptions, and episodes could withstand verification, *On the Road to Baghdad* is not to be evaluated as a historical novel—or as a realist one, for that matter.

The fantastic tone quickly sets in when, in what is yet the beginning of the novel, the mere adolescent girl Hürü is deserted in the woods by her elder half-brother Mahmut Jan who was supposed to take her to their parents. She is helped by the tree to which he had tied her, a tree which very conveniently turns into a Green Knight-like figure, out of the "Sir Gawain and the Green Knight" romance of the Arthurian legend: "a venerable gentleman with intense green eyes, swathed in green robes, a huge green turban on his head. Even his beard and skin seemed tinged with green" (37). He turns out to be "Hidir," the "Green Old Man" or "the special guardian or teacher of wandering Sufi mystics," as the author explains (369). The fabulation that ensues belies once and for all any pretense at historical veracity.

At the same time, while on the one hand the Green Knight[11]-like figure points towards a quest novel within purely Western parameters that subsume the road novel, it concurrently indicates a Sufi quest. In Turkish, *Hıdır* or *Hızır* (a term of Islamic origin) is a "legendary person who attained immortality by drinking from the water of Life." The word is used in the expression *Hızır gibi yetişmek*, meaning "to come as a godsend; to come to the rescue at the right moment"; and in the Ottoman Turkish expression *Hızr-ı râh* (today archaic), meaning "road-guide who suddenly turns up when one is puzzled" (*New Redhouse Turkish-English Dictionary*, 12. ed.). As can be seen, elements of the two cultures are so enmeshed as to be inseparable. This novel is no *The Joy Luck Club* where Chinese/Eastern/non-American vignettes can be easily plucked out.

While still in the woods, Hürü comes across a shepherd with whom she exchanges clothes, which allows her from then on to "pass" as a young man. *Passing* is an important feature in this novel: Hürü lives transformed thus during at least half of the novel and in that state finds herself married off to a woman with whom conjugal life inevitably turns into a lesbian relationship. Lady Safiye (whose tale is based on "The Story of Zumrut" in *The Thousand and One Nights*) and Shahrazad are two other women characters in *On the Road to Baghdad* who will pass for men, the first to rule a princedom, the second to attend a seminary(!); and another character, Barsoom, a Christian, will pass for Moslem—until he is caught. Yet, "passing," however universal an impulse it may be, is first and foremost an American feature—the term itself is "an Americanism not listed in the first edition of the *Oxford English Dictionary*" (247), Sollors specifies. As the title of Nella Larsen's *Passing* (1929),[12] one of the best known American works of fiction on the theme, indicates, the term is used within the American context for a black person passing for white. The predominant gender switching in *On the Road to Baghdad* evidently makes a different, metaphorical statement, whether within the American/Western or the Turkish/Eastern societies, both being essentially patriarchal ones to date.

When putting on the shepherd's clothes, Hürü also dons on her head a sheep's bladder, which the shepherd again very conveniently happens to be in possession of. The bladder on Hürü's head makes her appear to be bald, i.e. turns her into the traditional Turkish folk character Keloğlan – Bald Boy.[13] As the author herself explains, "As a folk hero, Keloglan goes back to tales told by the Turkoman, a term that denotes all the Turkic tribes that spread out of their original home in Central Asia" (362). The "Historical Note" at the end of the novel specifies that the story of Hürü is based on "a folk tale localized to Kalejik, a province of Ankara [capital of present-day Republic of Turkey, successor of the Ottoman Empire]" (362). Stressing further that Hürü's tale is "localized even more specifically to the household of the Aga of Kalejik, grandfather of the author" (362), the said author, Gün, points out: "I come from a country where the oral tradition is still not dead" (355). She explains that what attracted her in the "Kalejik"[14] tale was the fact that "the heroine solves her traveling problem by turning herself into an orphan boy, Keloglan," a strategy she describes as "an old but sophisticated storytelling device through which one fictional character impersonates another" (362).

"Re-recounting" the Tales of *The Thousand and One Nights*

Fictional characters impersonating others is a device Gün uses even more frequently in her "re-recounting" of the tales of *The Thousand and One Nights*. *Alf layla wa layla* (the title in Arabic), or *The Arabian Nights*,[15] as it is also known, is a collection of stories blending popular themes, and heroic and romantic tales with the teaching of wisdom, and knowledge of good and evil.[16] It is known to have originated from three distinct cultures and storytelling traditions: that of India,[17] Persia, and Arabia. Literary history records that it first appeared in its (written) Arabic form around the middle of the ninth century. Drawing attention to the fact that names such as Shahrazad and Dunyazad are Persian, chroniclers have also maintained that the tales were derived from a Persian book of folk tales entitled *Hazarafsaneh* (A Thousand Stories). "Like many folk tales, The Arabian Nights may have originated from true stories which were embellished over time for entertainment value," Hanan Ramadan believes.

Reminding the reader that "the tales found their final shape as The Thousand and One Nights in the early sixteenth century when the Ottoman Turks conquered the territories that belonged to the Arabs," Gün conjectures that

> it must have been the Turkish annexation that stimulated the Arab culture to define and formalize its fictional heritage. Shahrazad . . . seen, in this light . . . takes on the job of ennobling Arabs, who now feel impotent before their Turkish conquerors, by telling them the tales of their golden past, especially the reign of Harun-er-Rashid." (363)

Daniel Beaumont draws attention to another Turkish aspect of the tales when he maintains that these stories, although purportedly taking place in the eighth century, "may reflect popular notions about how a Turkish sultan lived in the fifteenth century rather more than they reflect such images of the way Harun lived six hundred years earlier." He explains:

> Not that ornate palaces, gardens, wine drinking, cup bearers and slave consorts were not features of the Abbasid court, but as found here these features often seem like those of the Ottomans. An obvious example comes in the frame story, in the scene in which King Shahriyar's wife commits adultery in the garden with a black slave; the lover and the enclosed garden are stock elements in any Ottoman Turkish *gazel*[18] or love poem.

The "frame story" of *The Thousand and One Nights*, probably one of the best-known stories in the world, acts as a catalyst for the others that are thus stories within stories. When the mythical ruler Shahriyar discovers his wife is unfaithful to him, he has her executed and from then on marries only virgins, whom he invariably has put to death the morning after he consummates the marriage, before they have had the time or opportunity to dally with other men. As a result, families with marriageable daughters all flee town, and there is no maiden left for Shahriyar to wed. When he asks his vizier (chamberlain) for help, the vizier's daughter Shahrazad volunteers to become Shahriyar's bride. On the wedding night, Shahrazad requests that her sister Dunyazad be allowed to join her, and her wish is granted. Dunyazad asks Shahrazad to tell Shahriyar and herself a story. Shahrazad obliges and starts to recount a tale that turns out to be so captivating that Shahriyar wants to hear more the next day. "Her story, or stories, since many tales are interwoven and imbedded into the first, lasts for two years and 271 days, if we are to take the 1001 nights literally," Ramadan calculates. Shahrazad's life is thus spared. Her fantastic stories also captivated the French diplomat Antoine Galland (1646-1715) who discovered the text while posted in Istanbul in the eighteenth century, translated and introduced it to the West. Galland began publishing his French translation—that would become the twelve-volume *Les Mille et Une Nuits, Contes Arabes Traduits en Français*—in 1704.[19] *The Thousand and One Nights* has had a tremendous career since, with over the centuries numerous translations into other languages, including English. And, needless to say, many poets, fiction writers and dramatists, as well as composers, both in the West and the East, have not tired to this day of repeating, recreating, and being inspired by the stories.

There is in Gün's *On the Road to Baghdad* a nod to American postmodernist novelist John Barth,[20] who published *Chimera* (1972), a novel consisting of three intertwined novellas or tales, one of which recounts the thousand and *second* night from the perspective of Dunyazad. Almost twenty years later, Barth published *The Last Voyage of Somebody The Sailor* (1991), another rewriting of *The Thousand and One Nights*. Recalling that Barth's *The Last Voyage of Somebody The Sailor* is basically a parody of the latter work and that it contains "a whole section written in the style of [Sir Richard Francis] Burton," its principal translator into English, Jonathan Raban writes that it is "an extended copulation between the two narrative worlds . . . giving birth to a style of high irrealism." The same may be said of Gün's novel, that it is "an extended copulation between two narrative worlds."

To give a sense of what *On the Road to Baghdad* is about and how the "copulation" and the high "irrealism" that accompanies it are achieved, I wish to discuss how Gün's reader meets John Barth, called Jann Baath in the novel. It is in fact not Hürü but Shahrazad who encounters Barth-Baath. In chapter 16, entitled "Face to Face: Hürü Wakes Up in the Courtyard of Shahrazad" (the first chapter of Part III, itself entitled "Return: Hürü is Snatched Back into Real Time and a Life Waiting to be Lived"), Hürü has been whisked back from the eighth century (the period of Harun er-Rashid) and has reincorporated her own, namely, the sixteenth century. She meets and befriends "plain old Shahrazad of Baghdad," as the latter calls herself, who, the narrator informs us, sits "cross-legged" at her "low writing table . . . scribbling like a common scribe, day in, day out" (227). In the next chapter, entitled, "The False Caliph"—which is itself the title of one of the tales of *The Thousand and One Nights*—Shahrazad explains that she met Shahriyar "at the Seminary" which she attended by "passing" as a "young man," and where he (Shahriyar) "was doing post-graduate work." They slept together, and she proposed! This is the kind of discourse I indicate as being twentieth-century American speech. They got married and had children, but have been estranged since. As Shahrazad relates to Hürü, one day she was sitting at home wondering what to do with her life, as a middle-aged mother separated from her husband. Thinking she needs a genie to help her, and even appealing out loud to Jann Bath (meaning *the resurrected genie* in Arabic, or "the Spirit Reawakened" as Shahrazad herself explains[21]) to come and help her, Shahrazad suddenly finds in front of her a "creature" who turns into a man and asks her: "You called?" He continues:

> "Can I really believe my eyes? You are Shahrazad, aren't you? I was on my boat talking to a friend. I had just said, 'even Shahrazad has run out of tales . . .' when you called me by my name. And here I am, at your service." (241)

And Shahrazad to Hürü: "We fell to exchanging stories. He said he too was a writer of fictions, like me. Pray tell, what fictions did I write? [I asked him.]"

"'Your *The Thousand and One Nights*,' he said. 'Your work . . . has never been off my desk.'"

To which Shahrazad asks incredulously what "the thousand and one nights" are. From Barth-Baath's response, "I finally understood," Shahrazad informs Hürü, "I was meant to write an opus that would survive for all time. . . . I already knew all the stories I was to pen. The material existed in the popular domain. I was shocked. How vulgar!"

Shahrazad then goes on denigrating the "tales that evolved among illiterate peasants from the land of the Maghrabis all the way to China." Next she tells her friend, "Turns out, however, that the structure of the tales was what intrigued this genie. 'Oriental,' he said . . . 'Patterns within patterns.'"

Shahrazad did not understand the significance of the term "Oriental." "Oriental as opposed to what?" she wanted to know (242). And Barth-Baath went on explaining (*avant la lettre*, what the twenty-first century reader construes as Derrida and Said, *différance* and logocentrism, culture and imperialism) and encouraging her, convincing her finally to become a writer.

And he succeeds: Shahrazad conveys her worries to Hürü: "Do you realize how much it will cost to reproduce a book this size? I can't even afford publication" (244). If Shahrazad gives the impression in this episode of being a coarse and dim-witted middle-class matron, she herself explains why, when she makes fun of Barth-Baath who "was only perceiving the Shahrazad in his own mind's eye" (242).[22]

"Othering" the U.S.

In Gün's novel, the fictional Shahrazad is only a character—a mature, feisty woman who sees no scruples sleeping with her good friend Hürü's husband the Sultan Selim. The stories that Shahrazad tells in *The Thousand and One Nights* are in *On the Road to Baghdad* stories that happen to others or, as tales within tales, stories told by other characters. To illustrate, in the chapter entitled "Lady Zubaida's Tale," which is another reworking of a tale of *The Thousand and One Nights*, Lady Zubaida, Harun er-Rashid's contemporary and a successful business woman,[23] narrates how she went on a sea voyage where she encountered a "strange harbor," describing for the reader a Pompeii-like scene more awesome than that of New York in the movie *Planet of the Apes* (dir. Franklin J. Schaffner, 1968):

> Even as we glided into the harbor, we knew something strange was up.... we'd never heard about or dreamed of structures so tall; man-made towers that ascended hundreds of stories into the sky. We sailed by a small islet on which stood the figure of a giantess holding up a torch in one hand and a stone tablet in the other, wearing a serene expression and a diadem shaped like a star.... We docked without seeing a soul. (133)

Lady Zubaida's experiences include eating "hot meat patties inside small sesame-seed rolls, and drinking "a dark, sweet and bubbly refreshment," provided from "metal boxes that lined the hall," who were, "instead of people," the "shopkeepers" in this land. As to the population, "we found all the inhabitants converted into black stones" (133), "petrified" (135). "Never was there a city so laden with material goods and so destitute of a public that might enjoy the riches," Lady Zubaida comments (134). "The captain thought the inhabitants must've been fire worshippers," she adds. "He'd seen a wondrous little box which showed pictures that moved, and through the moving picture was recorded the wrath of their god," who must have been, he believed, a sort of fire "that burned from within," the reason why the inhabitants had turned into coal (139). Lady Zubaida concludes:

> I felt sorrow for these people who'd been so intelligent, so inventive, so developed in their comforts and work-saving devices; they seemed to have ... unlocked the mysteries of the universe. Yet, they hadn't foreseen the catastrophe that awaited in the form of a fire that burns only the living. Or perhaps ... their inventions, like some demons, had gone out of hand. (140)

"You penetrated into the future," will be the comment of a *jinniye*[24] to Lady Zubaida.

This passage illustrates perfectly what I mean by the "othering" of the U.S. There is obviously a critique here; a statement about the U.S. that is Gün's "writerly way" of offering a version of current American history and experience. Lady Zubaida's tale is part of the American "matter"; it is an American tale, not a Turkish/Eastern narrative, although it appears to be. A careless reader would easily fail to perceive this and consequently fail to grasp the gist of the novel.

Whether Hürü's travels are related in her "real" time, the sixteenth century; or in the eighth century; or in the time of the other characters, one thing is certain: everyone is on the move and *On the Road to Baghdad* is a road novel. In so far as American literature has its antecedents in English literature, it stems from the tradition of "life as journey" narratives for which John Bunyan's seventeenth-century *The Pilgrim's Progress* (1678) serves as prototype. Perhaps an earlier work, Sir John Mandeville's *Travels* (1356), should also be mentioned. More specifically, within the framework of American literature, the novel is very much in the vein of Jack Kerouac's *On the Road* (1957) and many others that have followed suit. Patterned on the great journey in American fiction, *On the Road to Baghdad* both reenacts and parodies it, in a postmodernist mode that is both its feat and its undoing—so many personae are involved and so much is happening, all of which ever more discordant, that it becomes almost impossible to keep track of any unity or line of thought.

In Kerouac's *On the Road*, the West has a symbolical significance. It stands for freedom and is a "route for escape," as Orm Øverland terms it, explaining, "The West that Kerouac's hero and narrator, Sal Paradise, is drawn to has no specific geographic location ... the place is of the mind, a construct of the imagination fed by images of the West accumulated from the beginnings of American history.... [In] *On the Road* the West is a land of dream and legend" (452). The same can be said of Hürü's Baghdad. Her first trip to Baghdad seems predestined and inevitable, as she is to join her parents who have left her behind to go on the pilgrimage to Mecca but who have second thoughts when they hear worrisome news about her. The second one, after she has been reunited, years later, with her parents in Istanbul, is a trip in reverse: it is as a parent herself that she takes to the road, a bereaved mother who wishes to pay a visit to the site where her baby died. "Married" to Yavuz Sultan Selim who did not wait long to desert her, she gave birth to a son who drowned during her trip back to Istanbul. This time, her destination is the lagoon near Konya, in central Anatolia, where he lost his life. Yet, both trips are admittedly also voyages that are made in search of identity and freedom, and indirectly salvation. This last, Gün seems to intimate, can only come through adherence to Sufism, a point indicated by both Silkü and Kader Konuk.

The many guises under which the reader encounters Hürü and the many characters she impersonates ultimately turn into a farce, preempting any serious consideration of issues of identity. I suggest that the search for freedom in *On the Road to Baghdad* has to be interpreted within a twentieth-century American context. Statements such as "I am not yet free to stay" (326-327), as words coming from a sixteenth-century Ottoman daughter, however avowedly not dutiful, are just too anachronistic, too adverse to the Ottoman *Weltanschauung* (whether in the historical past or prevailing in fiction/fabulation) to make any sense. I suggest that the author's own assertion that "[o]ur Hürü was a truly liberated soul" (xiv) needs to be received as the concern of an intentional fallacy. As an American woman's search for freedom, Hürü's travels and travails seem one long exercise in futility, as they do not reach any destination proper and the novel ends, with Hürü vanished, the reader knows not where. Thus, I hesitate to categorize *On the Road to Baghdad* as "female fabulation," as Lidia Curti employs for the expression in fictional terms of feminist criticism. There is at the end some hint, divested of gravitas because of the fantastic framework within which it is encased, to look for salvation in Sufism. Yet, emptied today of any significance (a mere tourist attraction) by obliging whirling dervishes, Sufism itself remains a mere anachronism and part of the absurdist paraphernalia of the novel, and so the suggestion cannot be taken seriously. The road to Baghdad leads nowhere. Even the protagonist of Voltaire's *Candide* (1759) has fared better, reaching Constantinople and cultivating a garden there.

Conclusion

On the Road to Baghdad, published in the U.S. in the last decade of the twentieth century, seems at first look one more product of American multicultural literature. Seen from an American viewpoint, the text, written originally in English, is that of a first-generation immigrant. It is an ethnic text reflecting a cultural baggage that is totally alien, as in "resident alien." Its distinctiveness and "otherness" labeled and proclaimed, its presence is accepted among "Americans," as being part of their universe. To illustrate, the magical realism in *On the Road to Baghdad*, which is conveyed through an alien-looking Eastern framework, makes it American in multicultural America—not American as in "American as apple pie," but American as in *The Woman Warrior*.

Yet at the same time, both the title and the subtitle indicate a totally different narrative heritage: a Turkish/Eastern one. The protagonist is Turkish, and the stories within stories that make up most of the material of the novel, the "re-recountings" of the tales of the *Thousand and One Nights*, are very much part of Turkish narrative lore and *appear* to have nothing to do with any other tradition except perhaps the larger Eastern one. In effect, notwithstanding the fact that this novel is written in English and published in the U.S., the first impression is that this is a *Turkish* work of fiction. The informed reader knows that there is already an antecedent: Turkish author Halide Edip Adıvar wrote and published her novel *The Clown's Daughter* (1935) in English, while she was in exile. On her return, she translated the novel into Turkish as *Sinekli Bakkal* (The Flea-ridden Grocer, 1942), and *that* version is part of the Turkish literary canon today.

I argue that both views, without being incorrect, fall short of appraising Gün's novel. It needs to be construed as a bicultural novel, and both of the cultures that are represented in it have to be taken into consideration. I further argue that in the novel both cultures mutually "other" each other and interchangeably act as subject and object. While, with the iconoclasm manifested by the desacralization of eminent Eastern historical figures, deconstruction is extended to Eastern lands; "subjects" that never existed, in Western eyes, convert those very "Western subjects" into objects. This bicultural aspect I label "traveling biculturalism," following Clifford, in order to call attention, firstly to the shifting, unstable nature of the cultures imbricated in the novel, neither one of which is more hegemonic than the other; and secondly, again following Clifford who indicates that the non-Western cultures can now be studied in the West, to the fact that, within the context of literary studies, the non-Western culture(s) can now be located—and should be studied—along with the Western one(s). The non-Western culture(s) need to be given importance equal to the latter in contemporary world literature written and published in the major Western languages.

On the Road to Baghdad is not an easy novel. Perhaps it tries to do too much: it is as if Lewis Carroll's *Alice in Wonderland* (1865) and Daniel Defoe's *Moll Flanders* (1772) were fused into one, supplemented by Washington

Irving's "Rip van Winkle" (1819) and *The Thousand and One Nights*, and more . . . *ad absurdum*. Thus, although with its many stories within stories it satisfies the universal urge for narratives Eco calls attention to, it must perforce remain a novelist's novel—which may explain its neglect by critics[25] and lack of success with the general reader. It reflects, however, a new trend in contemporary world fiction, written in a *post*-colonial, globalized world. If stories are indispensable, so are myths, as they are the best metaphors ever; and myths, whether ancient or generated anew and however universal, are now being more and more transmitted through a bicultural fictional medium.

Notes

[1] In French in the original, in an interview he gave to the French periodical *Le Nouvel Observateur* in 1990.

[2] I have discussed Eco's proposition elsewhere, in my *Technique and Tradition in Beckett's Trilogy of Novels* (1996).

[3] That appears to be the reason why these works of fiction obtained the interest of mainstream/Eurocentric readers, who chose to interpret the content in their own way, as stories of initiation and Americanization, or novels of "redemption" as Fu-Chen defines them in chapter twelve in this volume. This is especially evident, for example, in the cinematic version of *The Joy Luck Club* (dir. Oliver Stone, 1994): everything to do with China is oppressive, retrograde; everything to do with the U.S. is polished, glossy, pleasant—which is not all what the novel conveys.

[4] A third reason is probably the one that Theodora Tsimpouki mentions in the first chapter of this volume a propos of Greek-American literature: quoting Yiorgos Kalogeras, Tsimpouki alludes "to the systematic exclusion of Greek-American authors from the ethnic paradigms which American critics 'have extrapolated from a limited number of texts or literatures such as that of the Jewish or the Italian-American.'" That a Turkish-American author would be faced with a similar and even greater exclusion is only to be expected.

[5] The word *tanzimat* means "ordering" or "organizing" in Turkish, and would also signify "reordering" or "reorganizing. The Edict of *Tanzimat* decreed political, legal and cultural reforms that were aimed at Westernization. The first such formal move in Ottoman history, it was a turning point for Ottoman Turkish culture.

[6] Gün has also published *A Book of Trances* (1979). She is moreover the translator, from Turkish into English, of *Night: A Novel* by Bilgé Karasu (1994); *The Black Book* by Orhan Pamuk (1994); and *The New Life* by Pamuk (1997).

[7] It is a very complex novel that employs many different poetic codes—as a postmodern novel, as a novel of magical realism, as a novelist's novel pondering issues of literary creation and reality, fiction and meta-fiction, etc.—to do justice to which a mere chapter would not suffice, but not all of which yield positive results. To illustrate, it is an extremely sophisticated rewriting of *The Thousand and One Nights* and requires a serious comparative study; yet it is also ensconced within a

self-exoticizing, self-orientalizing mode that is almost revolting.

⁸ See also his "The Transit Lounge of Culture" (1991) and *Routes Travel and Translation in the Late Twentieth Century* (1997).

⁹ See Paksoy for a rendering in English of the Keloğlan tales; and Alangu for a rendering in Turkish.

¹⁰ I adopt in this chapter the spelling in Gün's novel.

¹¹ The Green Knight of the Arthurian legend is demoniacal, whereas the venerable apparition in *On the Road to Baghdad* is on the contrary supportive; but I do not believe that this prevents the reader from construing the work, in Western terms, as a typical or traditional quest novel.

¹² See Sollors 247-284 for many other fictional works treating the same theme.

¹³ Paksoy explains that the "bald-head of Keloglan is generally simulated by others by simply molding a sheep's or calf's stomach, turned inside out, over the hair. . . . Many a maiden has transformed her outer appearance into a *Keloglan* to suit the needs of her circumstances and troubles" (24).

¹⁴ Spelled as *Kalecik* in Turkish (and pronounced Kaledjik), the area is known today for its vines producing the *Kalecik karası* (the black of Kalecik) grape from which the much-prized wine of the same name is made.

¹⁵ That is how one of the most recent translations into English, by Husain Haddawy (1990), is entitled.

¹⁶ According to Hanan Ramadan, the tales "bear three main elements or notions which are typical of all the stories in the collection: 1) If there is a problem, there is a solution; 2) Endurance can enable a crisis to reach a resolution; and 3) Fantastic elements help the protagonists to maintain their endurance."

¹⁷ That is (one reason) why Salman Rushdie will so readily reappropriate the tradition as one of the narrative components of his *Midnight's Children* (1980). His *Haroun and the Sea of Stories* (1990) also includes elements of the *The Thousand and One Nights*, starting with the name of Haroun in the title.

¹⁸ A "gazel" is a "lyric poem of a certain pattern (comprising 4-15 couplets, with the first couplet rhyming, and all the second hemistichs rhyming with the hemistichs of the first couplet)" (*New Redhouse Turkish-English Dictionary*, 12. ed.).

¹⁹ To commemorate its tercentenary, a three-volume edition of Galland's translation, entitled *Les Mille et Une Nuits Contes Arabes*, was published in 2004, with an introduction by Jean Paul Sermain and Aboubakr Chraïbi.

²⁰ For sceptics, the "List of Characters" at the end of the novel makes it clear that Jann Baath is "John Barth, American writer" (370).

²¹ While *jinn* is Arabic for genie, *jann*, which author Gün takes to be synonymous with or "another form of" *jinn* (370), is a word of Persian origin meaning *spirit*. Moreover, the Turkish *can*, to be pronounced as *jann* would be, means *soul* or *life*. Edward Lane, one of the principal translators of *The Nights* into English, explains that:

> The species of Jinn is said to have been created some thousands of years before Adam. According to a tradition from the Prophet [Mohammed], this species consists of five orders or classes; namely, Jánn (who are the least powerful of all), Jinn, Sheytáns (or Devils), 'Efreets, and Márids. The . . . Jánn are transformed Jinn; like as certain apes and swine were

transformed men (Qurán 5:65). It must however, be remarked here, that the terms Jinn and Jánn are generally used indiscriminately, as names of the whole species (including the other orders above mentioned) whether good or bad; and that the former term is the more common. (qtd. in Crocker)

[22] Much can be made of this episode, as it can be conducive to the discussion of the art of writing in general as well as to the nuances between fiction and reality.

[23] A proposition that is much less surprising and anachronistic than most other statements in Gün's novel after all, as the Prophet's first wife had also been a successful businesswoman.

[24] Female *jinn* (371).

[25] So far, the only scholars having written on the novel seem to be Konuk and Silkü.

4
The Intricacy of Spices
A Bicultural Reading of Salman Rushdie's *Midnight's Children* and Banerjee Divakaruni's *The Mistress of Spices*

Mita Banerjee

Perhaps biculturality, as the interaction of two distinct cultures, has become unreadable in the contemporary climate of multiculturalism that revolves around biculturality as hybridity. For hybridity, as it is deployed in postmodernist and postcolonial discourse, is often inseparable from the decentering of the West by an East that is constituted as cultural *difference* only in the act of this decentering. As an antidote to this reading of the "East" only in terms of its "use value" for the West, I propose in this chapter an alternative reading of biculturality through the concept of spices as it emerges in both Salman Rushdie's *Midnight's Children* (1980; this edition 1981, all page references are to this edition) and Chitra Banerjee Divakaruni's *The Mistress of Spices* (1997). For far from merely "spicing up" the West, spices are themselves part of an intricate culture, a culture in which they hold a meaning completely other than the mere coloring of Western blandness. As *The Mistress of Spices* illustrates, within Indian culture itself, spices are anything but unreadable; instead, they possess a healing power known only to the (culturally) initiated. Similarly, the concept of the "nation" emerges in *Midnight's Children* with an ironic twist: for it is the Indian nation itself that is chutneyfied in all its multicultural diversity. Complexity, then, does not originate in the West; as the spices tell us, it is an intrinsic part of the Other culture that ceases to be "other" in the very reading of biculturality as a fusion of equally intricate cultures.

Can a spice be other than what it does? This is not as much of a rhetorical question as it may seem. For what I would like to explore in this chapter is the assumption that spices can be read as cultural signs, circulating between the "East" and the "West" as cultural currency as part of a system of power that may be unequal. Spices, from this perspective, are both trivial and culturally significant.

Moreover, this very exchange of spices as cultural currency is not as clear-cut as it may appear. Because of the pitfalls of Orientalist projection, I wish to argue, the space of cultural difference has in fact become unreadable today, or so postcolonial theory seems to suggest. It is perhaps all the more tragic that this unreadability ensues directly from a highly salutary and culturally progressive project: the deconstruction, by postcolonial theory as well as literature, of the cultural misrepresentation of Orientalism. Given the ossification of the Other culture, the structuralist writing up of what the Orient means,[1] I believe that even to speak of the Orient today makes us cringe. More crucially, this cringing hardly abates even if "Orient" is substituted by another marker of cultural difference: the "East," of course, is a poor candidate here. To speak of cultural difference, then, becomes impossible in a setting in which this Otherness is read by the mainstream as always already intelligible, and intelligible only as exoticism. This intelligibility as cultural ossification, in turn, seems to be resistible only through its opposite: the contention that cultural difference simply is not, is nothing at all.

This dilemma is inextricably interwoven with the fusion of cultures in the contemporary Western metropolis. For given a (white) normative mainstream that refuses to negotiate the sameness *and* difference of the Other, it is hard not to resort to the claim that the difference of the Other is *only* a projection: in Berlin, the "Turkish" (now in quotation marks) person next door is not as Other or "Oriental" as the mainstream would have it: s/he is as Other only as the man from Frankfurt who just moved in across the street; as German as *Apfelstrudel* (which, incidentally, is Austrian). To speak of Turkish-German, then, is at once to privilege sameness over the projection of difference. Given the trajectory of this chapter, however, I would like to ask whether the "Turkish" in "Turkish-German" remains readable at all.

Similarly, in the contemporary anti-essentialist readings of cultural difference, there is no "real" cultural difference in the Western metropolis precisely because the projection of Orientalism must be resisted: the Other is never as Other as s/he may seem. Thus, Anthony Appiah has recently argued for a de-essentialization of ethnic identity: "[r]acial identity can be the basis of resistance to racism; but even as we struggle against racism . . . let us not let our racial identities subject us to new tyrannies" ("Race, Culture, Identity: Misunderstood Connections" 104). Culture is thus seen as the ossification of a collective identity that infringes on the free play of individuality. To be uniquely individual, then, is to be post-ethnic. This individuality of ethnic identity, in turn, intersects with the anti-Orientalist claim of the margin's sameness. What emerges, I would suggest, is a double entendre of this very claim of the not-so-Other: while this claim is fundamentally subversive in an anti-racist, anti-Orientalist context since it forces the mainstream to engage with its own definition of what exactly difference *is*, the same reasoning seems precarious in the context of an overall engagement with the extent to which cultural difference persists despite this misrepresentation. Is difference only what it is *not* for the mainstream Orientalist?[2]

Moreover, given the unreadability of the space of cultural difference due to its entanglement with the misrepresentation it resists only by ruling out difference as such, there can be no true interculturality. For interculturality is the interaction of two distinct, and culturally intelligible, elements; even as each element transforms the other beyond recognition in the course of this interaction, the prior distinctness of each of the elements fused is indispensable to intercultural negotiation. Again, I am immediately trapped in misrepresentations of interculturality even as I make this claim. In a dilemma strikingly similar to the anti-essentialist view of cultural difference in the (Western) metropolis, Maxine Hong Kingston's character Wittman Ah Sing, in her novel *Tripmaster Monkey* (1989; this edition 1990, all page references are to this edition) is caught up in anti-essentializing the reception of his own play. Desperately seeking to counter "intercultural" (and interculturally racist) reviews of his play as a mixture of apple pie and chop suey (which can only be inedible), he counters the projection of difference by a proclamation of sameness: in this sense, ironically enough, it is salutary that chop suey happens to be a *Western* invention of Chineseness:

> "You can't like these reviews. . . . Look. Look. 'East meets West.' 'Exotic.' . . . 'Snaps, crackles and pops like singing rice.' 'Sweet and sour.' . . . I'm having to give instruction. There is no East here. West is meeting West. This was all West. This is The Journey *In* the West. I am so fucking offended." (307-308)

I would like to argue, however, that salutary as Wittman's indictment of the projections of Orientalism is, the other side of this indictment is the unreadability of cultural difference. Given this unreadability of "Chinese" in "Chinese-American," the politics of hyphenation has clearly lost its critical edge.

Given this unreadability of the "inter-" in "intercultural," as in Wittman's fusion of the same and the same, ethnicity is thus unintelligible except in terms of what ethnicity *does*—and, I would add, what it does for the *West*. As Rajagopalan Radhakrishnan has asked,

> [if] ethnic identity is a strategic response to a shifting sense of time

and place, how is it possible to have a theory of ethnic identity posited on the principle of a natural and native self? Is ethnicity nothing but, to use the familiar formula, what ethnicity does? (205)

Precariously enough, Orientalism seems to meet its critique in its functionalizing of cultural difference. For Orientalism, cultural difference is misconstrued as exoticism; in the *critique* of Orientalist conceptions of the Other, the same cultural difference is geared only towards the decentering of Western claims to cultural homogeneity. In both instances, cultural difference exists only for Orientalism or its critique; the norm remains the sole point of reference. Ethnicity as cultural difference remains unreadable, then, outside of this deconstructive project even for those who are its most ardent champions—and of course, the culturally hyphenated themselves. Given the fact that most postcolonial critics do what they are, so to speak, this downplaying of cultural difference in the face of Orientalist appropriations of it also equals a politics of self-italicization: the professing by the Other that s/he is not. Ironically enough, we have thus perhaps come full circle, returning to a different kind of assimilationism: the mainstream call for the culturally different to divest themselves of their Otherness, a call which was first opposed by the insistence on one's difference, is now "countered" by the margin's own critique of essentialism: "we" are really the same. How much continuity is there between assimilationism and the anti-essentialist critique of cultural difference?

It seems to me, then, that the denial of cultural difference outside of deconstruction, the insistence on the Other's sameness, ensues directly from the recognition of what diplomacy Étienne Balibar has called a "differentialist racism" (21). According to Balibar,

> It is a racism whose dominant theme is not biological heredity but the insurmountability of cultural differences, a racism which, at first sight, does not postulate the superiority of certain groups or peoples in relation to others but "only" the harmfulness of abolishing frontiers, the incompatibility of life-styles and traditions ... (21)

Balibar thus anticipates Samuel Huntington's *Clash of Civilizations* (1996)—the idea of the clashing of the same and the different that hence becomes visible as the "neo-racism" it is. It is this very juncture that is crucial: for predicated as this new racism is on the very incommensurability of the same and the culturally Other, there seems to be no other defense than the denial of difference as such.

The unreadability of cultural difference is thus the other side of culturalist racism, the racism of cultural incompatibility—an incompatibility, what is more, that is at once pathologized: Balibar speaks of a "neo-racism whose preferred target is not the 'Arab' or the 'Black,' but the 'Arab (as) junky' or 'delinquent' or 'rapist' and so on, or equally, rapists and delinquents as 'Arabs' and 'Blacks'" (49). The mainstream myth of the black rapist is countered, on the part of postcolonial theory, by the deconstruction of ethnic meaning as such. The question which I would like to explore in this chapter, then, is whether or not cultural meaning can be inscribed without closure—an absence of closure in which meaning itself would be wrested from the anthropological quest for cultural characteristics. This simultaneity of inscription and disruption defies neo-culturalism without the (self)destruction of culture. There is thus a double entendre of the answer to the equation of ethnicity and delinquency: that ethnicity holds meaning. Understood deconstructively, of course, there should just be no end to this reiteration. I am wondering, however, whether the second meaning of this absence of ethnic meaning is not the unreadability of (the Other) culture as such.

Similarly, looking at Homi Bhabha's concept of *the unhomely* my doubts about the unreadability of culture outside of its decentering of the "West" clash with the subversiveness of Bhabha's project. For in the context of the Western metropolis, there is never indeed anything more salutary than the disruption of the mainstream conception of "home" by those who, the mainstream alleges, do not belong; the disruption, through the simple act of including the unhomely, of homeliness as such. Turning its very interculturality, the absence of any single home in particular, into an asset, the unhomely celebrates itself as the new norm; those who can only conceive of belonging in monolithic or narrowly national terms have themselves become obsolete. For, as Bhabha emphasizes, "[t]o be unhomed is not to be homeless" (*Location of Culture* 9). In my quest for interculturality, I would like to disturb Bhabha's own deconstructive use of the intercultural as unhomely without in any way disagreeing with the urgency of this project. While his understanding of the intercultural seems to imply the richness of those who inhabit two cultures simultaneously, I believe that we lose sight of the other side of the equation: for outside of the unhomely disturbing the dichotomies of the West, is there a space to which the unhomely belongs, a home defined differently? I would suggest that the very concept of the unhomely, in its negation of home and Western normativity, is unable to exist in its own right. Culture remains cultural difference.

However, I want to propose that the threat of the cultural closure imposed by the mainstream, the mainstream's certain answer to what ethnicity *is*, can be opposed by something other than its opposite, the claim that it is nothing at all. Instead, this very argument of the absence of cultural difference could be redefined into an absence of closure: while there is cultural difference, it can never be contained in the definition of (the Other) culture; it can only be discursively negotiated.[3]

Midnight's Children

It is this reality of a cultural difference without closure that I would like to trace to Rushdie's novel *Midnight's Children*. Since, as I have attempted to outline above, this space is virtually absent from contemporary theory, I turn to fiction for an exploration of an interculturality in which both elements interact on the same level, without either culture being relegated to the sphere of mere reaction or deconstruction.

In my search for the intelligible space of difference, it is significant that the story Rushdie's novel tells should be set in India, not in the "West." For it is India that is the multicultural nation, as if in an uncanny transposing of the multicultural metropolis onto a different context: the negotiation of the same and the other is by no means a property (or predicament) of the West. The sides are reversed by the dramatization, in *Midnight's Children*, of the knowledge that in India, to be *Indian* does not mean a thing. By essentializing the interaction between, say, the Indian and the normative whiteness of Britain, the mainstream in fact contemplates an absence.[4] For this Indianness is meaningful only when contrasted with the whiteness of the norm: *Midnight's Children* restores the other side of the equation by unraveling this absence or projection of difference into the multiplicity it conceals. It is precisely by restoring the other side of the equation, moreover, that cultural difference (re)gains meaning outside the West. Complexity, then, hardly originates in the West; India is a nation that, like Saleem's narration, tumbles over itself in the intricacy of cultural negotiation.

The metropolis which is always on the verge of disintegrating, on this side of the equation, is not in the West—just as rice is not being "exported" to London: "But still, in the city, we are great rice eaters. Patna rice, Basmati, Kashmiri rice travels to the metropolis daily, so the original, ur-rice has left its mark upon us all . . ." (93). I believe that the very unreadability of the Other in postcolonial theory makes for a certain ambiguity of this passage; the equation of the metropolis "sampling" fragments of other cultures—Patna, Basmati, or Kashmiri rice—with its Western location in fact renders this sentence unintelligible. Indian rice, of course, is nothing at all. Rather, India is itself an ongoing negotiation of its diverse cultures, not only from Kashmir and Patna.

Similarly, Bombay is a multicultural city regardless of British presence: it is always already multicultural outside of the stock scenario of "East meets West." Saleem exclaims,

> Our Bombay, Padma! It was different then, there were no nightclubs or pickle factories or Oberoi-Sheraton Hotels or movie studios; but the city grew at breakneck speed, acquiring a cathedral and an equestrian statue of the Mahratta warrior-king Sivaji which (we used to think) came to life at night and galloped awesomely through the city streets. (93)

Hybridity, what is more, was not "invented" only when the Western norm and its Others fused. Bombay emerges in *Midnight's Children* as a fundamentally hybrid metropolis, a vibrant real that is negotiated only in the dialogue (or cacophony) of the many cultures it harbors.

In *Midnight's Children*, there is thus an alternative ethnicity which is outside of what it does: a sense of Indianness which even as it seems happily unencumbered by Orientalist misapprehension of it as well as the "foreign" presence itself, never slides into the essentialism of cultural closure. The narrative does not counter corruption with purity, nor does the cacophony of the Western metropolis with *Indian* cultural homogeneity. India *is* even as it is discursively produced and constantly re-negotiated. If in Methwold's estate, the exhortation to the new "native" tenants to preserve what is given to them "lock, stock, and barrel" (95) parallels the claim that the interaction with the West has transformed the Other beyond repair, this claim is disproved by an Indian cultural vitality—not essentialism—which can indigenize Englishness: "'Even if we're sitting in the middle of all this English garbage,' my mother was beginning to think, 'this is still India, and people like Ramram Seth know what they know'" (100). *Midnight's Children* provides an alternative to postcolonial skepticism in the very injunction that India *is*, that there is indeed a space in which the soothsayer Ramram Seth is himself, not a part of the Orientalist nightmare of *voodoo*. Moreover, if "India" is seen as discursively produced, the other side of Orientalism does not have to be nativism, the way it is in the appropriation of the voodoo Other, seen as the vibrancy of a culture which "others" itself. It is here, I believe, that the contemporary critique of essentialism finds itself unable to choose between Orientalism and nativism, and opts out of defining cultural difference as such: in this critique, Ramram Seth must remain an absence. Thus, the sense of culture being itself is foreclosed because this naturalness of culture has become inseparable from the organic selfhood proclaimed by nativism. There seems to be nothing outside the strategic, where culture is performed and never preexists the performative. Radhakrishnan wonders,

> Among these mutable, changing traditions and natures, who are we to ourselves? Is the identity question so hopelessly politicized that it cannot step beyond the history of strategies and counterstrategies? Do I know in some abstract, ontological, transhistorical way what "being Indian" is all about and on that basis devise strategies to hold on to that ideal identity, or do I—when faced by the circumstances of history—strategically practice Indian identity to maintain my uniqueness and resist anonymity through homogenization? (210)

I am probing for a space of culture, then, where culture can at the same time be and be performed, an inscription of culture without closure. It is in this quest that I turn, finally, to the spices, which are at once intelligible (cumin is cumin, so to speak) and open-ended: the taste is in the balance of all spices taken together.

Spices and the "Indian" dishes they are integral to, then, are the epitome of a cultural reality that is nevertheless discursively produced. For even as each dish is still intelligible as what it is (say, fish *tikka masala*), it is nevertheless a performative negotiation of culture: no two dishes are ever exactly the same; culture is open to negotiation. The cultural script, furthermore, is thus constantly redefined by the particular subject position of its creator: the reality of India emerges only as the sum total of all the culinary performances of "Indianness" in which the idiosyncratic must always be weighed against the culturally determined:

> Mary Pereira took the time to prepare, for the benefit of their visitors, some of the finest and most delicate mango pickles, lime chutneys and cucumber kasaundices in the world. And now, . . . Amina began to feel the emotions of other people's food seeping into her—because Reverend Mother doled out the curries and meatballs of intransigence, dishes imbued with the personality of their creator; Amina ate the fish salans of stubbornness and the birianis of determination. (139)

Returning to the issue of indigenizing Englishness as well as the danger of nativism, of countering foreign corruption with internal purity, I would like to turn to the Indian historical debate. In the context of Indian historical specificity, the balance between cultural inscription and an absence of closure is all the more indispensable because the other side of this lack of closure may be Hindu chauvinism and religious communalism. It is in the crucial sense of maintaining this balance that Sudipta Kaviraj's historical account of Indian modernity, a space of "Indianness" curiously undisturbed by colonialism, and the mutability of this space coincide. For without this latter mutability, we risk the ossification of "Indianness" into the timelessness of Hindu tradition—the claim of Hindutva that dismisses Muslim and Christian Indian communities as both "modern" and "Western." The exuberance of Kaviraj's account of modern India, of the appropriation by Indian intellectuals such as Swami Vivekanada, Mahatma Gandhi and Rabindranath Tagore of the Western concept of nationalism (146), thus parallels the survival, in *Midnight's Children*, of Indian cultural vitality: beneath all this English garbage, this is still India. It is significant, then, that historically Indian religions both persisted in the face of colonialism and evolved in response to colonialist pressures. Kaviraj emphasizes,

> [i]n India, remarkably, despite very energetic Christian missionaries, the two major religions stood their ground. Hinduism and Islam remained largely undestroyed by colonialism, partly because English colonial rule was vastly different from the brutal excesses of Spanish conquests in Latin America. The presence of Christianity, however, caused enormous transformations within Indian religious life. . . . [B]y drawing Hindu intellectuals into religious and doctrinal debates on rationalist terms with Protestant missionaries, it forced Hindu doctrinal justifications to change their character. (146)

This inscription of Indianness (literally, of Indian nationalism) and a simultaneous acknowledgment of its mutability is thus a negotiation rather than a collapsing of sameness and difference. While Indianness remains distinct from Britishness and defies colonial rule, this difference is not that of Orientalist closure—a closure that recurs in contemporary Hindu communalism. Finally, it is in the debate on communalism that history and contemporary politics in India parallel the fictional dramatization in *Midnight's Children* of India as a multicultural nation. For the negotiation between cultural specificity or difference and mainstream sameness recurs in the very debate in Indian politics about what is and what is not normative, and what is or is not Indian.

The Mistress of Spices

Similarly to Rushdie's narrative, Divakaruni's *The Mistress of Spices* revolves around the readability of spices in terms of a certain amount of cultural depth—a depth, however, that is not necessarily synonymous with cultural closure. For, as I am trying to suggest in this chapter, given the contemporary climate of anti-essentialism and postmodernism, to speak of cultural depth has itself become impossible without being misconstrued as nativist. Instead, in a Western multiculturalist haven in which henna and yogi chai[5] circulate freely as exotic fragments of a one-world culture, this depth is itself contested. For the circulation is made possible precisely through the unmooring of the sign from a particular cultural context. Culture is readable, once again, only as cultural *difference*, a difference that is always already predicated on the Other culture's being alternative to the West—an alternative which is inextricable from the projection of essentialism, primitivism, cultural closure or the myth of a one-world culture.

Disturbingly enough, however, given the mainstream's craving for the exoticism of an Other culture, to speak of cultural depth could at the same time be understood as a self-Orientalizing catering to mainstream fantasies. The act of openly inhabiting an Other culture is unreadable except in the failure of being a sell-out; to wear a chong-sam[6] for an Asian-American woman in the West today would be unreadable except as complicity with Orientalist projections, never their critique.[7] It is in this sense that the concept of spices may become more precarious in *The Mistress of Spices* precisely because the novel is set in Oakland, California, not in Bombay. While *Midnight's Children* contextualizes the spices of chutneyfication in a sphere they literally originate in, I believe that the intricacy of spices becomes yet more unreadable in Oakland. Is Divakaruni's novel a project of self-Orientalizing or proof of the cultural depth of a culture that exists *not* as an alternative, not as a disruptive presence for the decentering of the West? For in *The Mistress of Spices*, cultural depth comes home with a vengeance as Tilo, the mistress of spices who heals the culturally wounded in Oakland, revels in her own knowledge of culture:

> I know their origins, and what their colours signify, and their smells. I can call each by the true-name it was given at first, when earth split like skin and offered it up to the sky. Their heat runs in my blood. From amchur[8] to zafran, they bow to my command. At a whisper they yield up to me their hidden properties, their magic powers. (3)

Even as I have called for a (re)mooring of the sign not in cultural difference but in the meaningfulness of culture, then, I am profoundly disturbed by what I can only read as self-Orientalizing. I cringe as this Indian-American text meets the mainstream projection of the hot-blooded Oriental woman (both passionate and submissive) through its own internalizing of the organic knowledge of culture. Above all, I search for an absence of closure, the awareness that this cultural "running in the blood" is itself discursively negotiated, created only in the contestation of the constant reinvention of culture. My need for the postmodernist indeterminacy of (cultural) meaning clashes with the fact that the meaning of spices, in Divakaruni's novel, must not be polysemic. For a spice to heal, its meaning must be distinct; cough drops are never the same as aspirin.

Moreover, taking pleasure in the depth of one's culture is blurred by the Orientalist need for the *colors* of difference, or the reduction of difference to colorfulness. This blurring creates an ambiguity, I fear, in which the mistress of spices invents her culture in mainstream simulations[9] of the absolute visual difference of the Other. Or does she? "But the spices of the true power are from my birthland, land of ardent poetry, aquamarine feathers. Sunset skies as brilliant as blood . . ." (3).

Even so, there is a sense in which this same cultural depth does seem subversive after all: the mistress's knowledge of cultural depth exposes the senselessness of henna fetishists. It confronts those who have unmoored the spices from a cultural context, rendering them depthless in order to better consume and circulate them, with the meaning of culture: "Yes, they all hold magic, even the everyday American spices you toss unthinking into your cooking pot" (3). Yet I believe that the effectiveness of this subversion once again hinges on the concept of magic. My critique of Divakaruni's cultural politics is thus refusal to engage with the obvious: that hers is a mythical tale, a dream of culture, against which my charge of cultural essentialism seems unfounded because a fairy tale never aspires to telling the truth.

Ironically, it is here that I find myself yearning for a critique of essentialism that I have so far faulted for foreclosing the exploration of a culture that is no longer "other." I am disturbed by the novel's use of magic and time immemorial. For I believe that in the context of Divakaruni's novel, the claim that, as *Midnight's Children* so eloquently dramatizes, India is a civilization as ancient as it is complex, at once collapses into the distancing of the Other culture into an essentialized, mythical past. While in Rushdie the mythical and the contemporary coexist in a space in which culture is constantly contested, this contestation of mythical Indianness seems absent in *The Mistress of Spices*: "If you stand in the centre of this room and turn slowly around, you will be looking at every Indian spice that ever was—even the lost ones—gathered here upon the shelves of my store" (3).

Perhaps, however, this negotiation of the ancient and the modern emerges only in these "magic" spices being put to contemporary use. For the intricacy of spices and the knowledge of this intricacy is what makes life bearable for the South Asian migrant in Oakland. In this sense, then, Tilo *does* reinvent the ancient for the contemporary in a performance in which culture is redefined:

> I did not want to hear more. I sensed his past already in the lines rising ridged and dark as thunder from his palms. From under the counter I took a box of chandan,[10] power of the sandalwood tree that relieves the pain of remembering. I sprinkled its silk fragrance onto Haroun's hands, careful not to touch. Over the lines of his life. (27)

The question is, then, whether the magic of the spices in Divakaruni's novel is a mere instance of self-Orientalization or, much more subversively, of what Gerald Vizenor calls the reinvention of (Native) culture in the cities: a reinvention of the cultural that is at once dynamic and open-ended; the reinvention of India in an Oakland spice shop. Vizenor speaks of a "postmodern potlatch in the city," and of "new trickster stories in the suburbs" (*Fugitive Poses* 53). Is Tilo, then, a self-Orientalizing sell-out or an Indian trickster in a grocery shop disguise?

The Mistress of Spices is intriguing also in its reinvention of the mainstream projection of the Oriental grocery shop. Outside of the Orientalist's projection, the grocery shop comes to life, endowed with the meaning of those who know what they are buying: while outside there is the simulation of cultural difference, inside there is the intricacy of culture. Divakaruni's novel creates a tension between what the mainstream can and cannot see: the sign or façade of the Asian grocery store, and what is behind it:

> Looped letters that say SPICE BAZAAR faded into a dried-mud brown. Inside, walls veined with cobwebs where hang discoloured pictures of the gods, their sad shadow eye. Metal bins with the shine long gone from them, heaped with *atta* and Basmati rice and *masoor dal*. Row upon row of videomovies, all the way back to the time of black-and-white. Bolts of fabric dyed in age-old colours, New York yellow, harvest green, bride's luck red. (4)

The Mistress of Spices does inscribe Indian culture outside this simulation, not as an alternative space but as a space in itself. At the same time, this alternative space remains a negation of mainstream simulations of Asian grocery stores. Thus, in this very reading of the Oriental grocery shop in Divakaruni's novel, I too seem caught up in the claim that to speak of culture is impossible except deconstructively, in the decentering of Western projections of Otherness.

Moreover, it could also be argued, quite on the contrary, that the spice bazaar is far from subversive and is instead a gesture of self-Orientalizing. The mainstream may find in Divakaruni's novel only what they were looking for: an inside view of the Other, a guided tour of the Oriental bazaar. It is at this juncture that I would like to consider Sau-ling Wong's exploration of the cultural politics in Maxine Hong Kingston's work. As Wong has argued with regard to the controversy over Kingston's *The Woman Warrior* (1976) the problem is precisely the danger of a mainstream public reading ethnic fiction as sociological fact. A fictional text is thus seen as conveying the meaning of an Other culture. Significantly, Wong emphasizes that these issues are not limited to either Kingston herself or Chinese-American literature in general; they are at the heart of the reception of ethnic literature as a whole. According to Wong,

> the critical issues raised in this debate are not merely of passing interest. Rather, they lie at the heart of any theoretical discussion of ethnic American autobiography in particular and ethnic American literature as a whole. (248)

My suspicion about the possibility of *The Mistress of Spices* catering to mainstream simulations of exotic Indianness thus parallels the charge, on the part of Kingston's critics, that *The Woman Warrior* takes those anxious for the ineffably Chinese on a "guided tour" of Chinatown; an acquiescing by the ethnic author herself to the mainstream belief in ethnic representativeness: the meaning of culture. As Wong goes on to affirm, "such a conviction may easily degenerate into the accommodating mentality of a friendly guide to an exotic culture" (261). The "magic" of the spices in Divakaruni's novel—a magic that is, what is more, timeless in scope—could thus be taken by mainstream readers as a confirmation of their projections of Indianness: an Indianness in which unique unspeakability intersects with a lack of historicity; a lack that parallels, as Wong puts it, "the distressing tendency of white readers to confuse Chinese-Americans with [the] Chinese in China and to attribute a kind of ahistorical, almost genetic, Chinese essence [to them]" (261-262).

Significantly, however, Wong puts in relief the fact that the narrative itself can provide crucial safeguards against its own catering to mainstream expectations of exoticism. In this sense, *The Woman Warrior*, according to Wong, is itself an attempt to piece together a tentative understanding of what it means to be Chinese-American; a cultural self-reflexivity and piecemeal reassembling that, I would suggest, implies an absence of closure. It is in this absence of closure, Wong emphasizes, that Kingston's narrative defies both Western exoticism and Chinese-American critics on their quest for cultural purity. Significantly enough, this twofold defiance mirrors the suspension of cultural closure in an Indian context: the search for the solace of closure by both the Western mainstream (ironically, the closure of an unspeakably different culture) and the cultural purists of Hindutva. This is Wong's endorsement, contra white anthropologist readers and Chinese-American cultural nationalists, of the piecemeal reinvention of Chinese-Americanness:

> It is the protagonist's American-born generation who must "make it up as they go along." The emigrant parents' expectation of a "continuous culture" is, if entirely human, ahistorical and therefore doomed. (So, one might add, is the critics' similar demand for cultural authenticity. Purity is best preserved by death; history adulterates.) (268)

Returning to the spices, then, the question is whether or not, as Divakaruni's narrative progresses, magic is replaced by a cultural reinscription that is more tentative.

As the novel unfolds, there does seem to be an awareness of the project of self-Orientalizing, which may complicate my charge of the exoticism of Divakaruni's novel. Buying gifts for the mainstream, the culturally different deliberately and strategically give the mainstream what it wants, proof of the fantasy that its simulation of the Other is indeed correct. This gift giving, in turn, is emphasized, by the narrative itself, to be a deliberate gesture of self-Orientalizing. In this vein, self-Orientalizing becomes readable as strategy. Tilo describes "the glass case heaped with gaudy handicrafts that Indians buy only when they need to give gifts to the Americans" (20). For if one takes the threat of self-Orientalizing that is not a strategy to the limit, it would be impossible for a South Asian author to write a book about spices, just as it is impossible for an (East) Asian-American woman to wear a chong-sam in Oakland.

The rupture of self-reflexivity that Wong has traced in *The Woman Warrior* emerges in *The Mistress of Spices* in its explicit critique of racism. For what does it signify, then, this powerlessness of the spices of ancient India in the face of those who do not care to read them? Tilo is suspended in-between the knowledge of culture and the *meaning*, in the West, of cultural difference: "'Sonofabitch Indian, shoulda stayed in your own goddamn country'" (170). The cultural mooring of spices is of no avail here as the signs of Indianness are unmoored in a spree of violence in which their foreignness is enough:

> But the pain's not as bad as he feared, not so bad that he can't pick up the stone and pitch it at the young man who's kicking at the cart until it comes crashing down and the kababs and *samosas* that Veena so carefully rolled and stuffed scatter everywhere in the dirt. (170)

What is the relevance of myth here, the narrative seems to ask, if *this* is the context in which culture is negotiated? It is perhaps in the unmooring of racism that the space of culture can only be imagined *mythically*, as a land of ardent poetry and bloodred sunsets, a space that is essentialized in the superior beauty the racists disavow. It is perhaps the contrast between the mythic and the contemporary that makes the novel's indictment of racism all the more scathing: "Months later in his apartment when he hears of the acquittal he will scream, a high, moaning, on-and-on animal sound, will bring down the crutches, hard and shattering, on whatever he can reach" (171). After the onslaught by the ignorance of a mainstream that cares little about what culture means, cultural signification has itself collapsed as culture and the difference it signifies in the West are forever inextricable: spices will never again have meaning. The spices proved powerless to prevent what happened to Mohan; we can split *kalo jire*[11] all we want, drown the assailants in turmeric, and the silence will still prevail. And so will the consequences of what is misconstrued as the meaning of difference:

> He stops screaming then. Doesn't speak another word. Not then, not in the coming weeks, not in the Air India plane when the neighbours finally pool together the ticket money to send him and Veena back home, for what else is left for them in this country. (172)

Perhaps, then, survival will depend on the invention of new stories of ethnicity. Spices were never meant to heal a nation run amok. Divakaruni's novel seems to move beyond the space of culture—even in its reinvention through the spices that are not about cultural *difference*—towards an alliance of the different: (almost) everybody who is shown entering Tilo's store is non-white. The suffering the spices must help cure is thus raced; the meaning of spices transcends what is transmitted *in the blood*, in an opening up of cultural meaning that is constantly renegotiated: "I will split again tonight *kalo jire* seeds for all who have suffered from America. For all of them and especially Haroun, who is hurting inside me, whose name each time I say it pulls my chest in two" (173).

Ethnicity, at the end of *The Mistress of Spices*, must thus become what Vizenor captures in his "new stories" in the cities—an urban reinvention of culture in the very city in which, surprisingly enough, Vizenor's Native tricksters and Divakaruni's India converge: Oakland, California. True interculturality can emerge only as the space between what is culture and what is cultural *difference* is constantly renegotiated. Significantly, this renegotiation is itself made possible only by a provisionalizing of the *reality* of Indian culture. Fracturing the very dichotomy of the cultural knowledge the store holds and the depthless, mainstream reinvention of henna, Tilo provisionalizes the wisdom of spices: which is the real culture? Provisionalizing knowledge, the reimagining of culture as open-ended begins with a swallowing of the anger at ignorance:

> I look up and they are there, three bourgainvillaea girls, the prettiest and youngest yet, all fizzy laughter and flutter lashes. . . . They look like they've never cooked a meal—certainly not an Indian meal—in their lives. . . . I put aside my annoyance to think. It's a challenge, to find a party dish simple enough so they couldn't ruin it in fixing. (254-255)

Interestingly enough, Divakaruni's "bourgainvillaea girls" recur in Sunaina Maira's investigation of the real-life politics of henna and hip hop (see her "Henna and Hip Hop"), precisely in Maira's wavering between her skepticism towards mainstream ignorance and her refusal to indict mainstream appropriations of Indianness once and for all on the grounds of cultural authenticity. Maira's juxtaposition of the mainstream appropriation of henna and the South Asian appropriation of (Black) rap makes her wary of the dichotomy between appropriation and cultural knowledge. Yet, her very language betrays the difficulty with which anger is suppressed: as Orientalism, this latest "mainstreaming" of India is nothing new. Maira observes,

> [t]his turn-of-the-millennium fascination has produced a new Orientalization of India that recreates the countercultural appropriations of Indian styles from thirty years ago, through the consumption of imported goods that signify exotic cool. (329)

In this scenario, it is Madonna herself who becomes a bourgainvillaea girl.

As Maira points out,

> it was super-chameleon Madonna whose MTV performance in 1998 emblematized the ultimate cross-over spectacle for Indo-chic. In the video for the single, "Frozen," from her album *Ray of Light*, Madonna performed pseudo-Indian dance moves with henna-painted hands. (342)

In a world that is proclaimed by the metropolitan mainstream to be of one culture, culture is stripped of its cumbersome depth: it is here that Vizenor's new stories in the cities meets Madonna's pseudo-Indian dance. For can there be a monopoly on who is to invent these new stories of culture? An army blanket worn "Indian style" in Native American painting; or a henna painting on the hands of a white superstar who swears that her life has been changed by yoga: who is to say which is more legitimate? I would like to reintroduce a difference between Vizenor and Madonna, however, by insisting on Vizenor's concept of the absence of closure. Cultural depth can be reintroduced, contra Madonna, even as it need not be ossified into the closure of cultural meaning negatively understood: the mythic Indian. However, my own argument here seems to recreate the mainstream blurring of ethnicities in collapsing (South Asian) Indian into (American) Indian. While I am aware that this collapsing always needs to be negotiated against historical specificity, I do believe that both cultures overlap in mainstream simulations of the Other: the noble savage recurs in the deceitful (South Asian) Indian even as both meet Balibar's black rapist and Arab junky.

This mooring of the cultural sign in some kind of depth, however open-ended, is crucial for the mainstream "reinvention," in the colorblindness of a one-world culture, to have some kind of closure. For this is the other side of the deconstructionist allegation that ethnic culture does not hold meaning: a henna painting can be anything at all. Maira goes on to describe how

> [t]he anxieties of appropriation . . . are rationalized by the "one world" credo among tribal ravers or New Age worshippers, who are deeply invested in the recasting of mehndi [henna] as a mythical practice or spiritual ritual, but one that is available to all. Henna seems to have been *reinvented* to fit within the parameters of popular American traditions, whether as New Age ritual, feminist beauty practice, bridal shower, or sex toy. (344-345; emphasis added)

Conclusion

How, then, do Kingston, Indian historians, new stories in the cities, Madonna and henna fetishists come together in this chapter, a motley crew of cultural difference and its appropriations? I would like to insert my reading of the interculturality of the spices in Rushdie's and Divakaruni's narratives into a larger, historical as well as cultural context of the circulation and containment of difference. Taking my cue from Wong's essay, I thus investigate the texts as cultural signs in their own right, a semiotics of culture that levels the distinction between the fictional and the actual.[12]

In *The Mistress of Spices*, then, cultural ignorance is countered by something other than its opposite: not authenticity, but the absence of closure even as culture is negotiated in its reality. Tilo does not abandon, but only reinvestigates her own knowledge of the meaning of spices. Similarly, as long as the specter of authenticity or nativism remains, Tilo's relationship to her Native American lover, Raven, can never be an intercultural one. In this sense, the non-whiteness of the alliance the spice shop symbolizes does not mean a thing: non-whiteness is not a safeguard against the assumptions of cultural authenticity. Those who themselves inhabit simulations of Indianness (as the projections of what Native Americans are) are by no means immune from projecting closure onto an Other culture:

> "You're authentic in a way they'll never be," he adds.
> *Authentic.* A curious word to use. "What do you mean, authentic?" I ask.
> "You know, real. Real Indian."
> I know he means it as a compliment. Still, it bothers me. Raven, despite their fizzy laughter, their lipstick and lace, the bourgainvillaea girls are in their way as Indian as I. And who is to say which of us is more real. (255-256)

Interculturality can be negotiated, then, only if the reality of culture has no closure. In this sense, spices are provisionalized even as they are culturally negotiated. The meaning of spices becomes an open negotiation in which everyone with a certain amount of cultural sensitivity can engage; the "bourgainvillaea girls" are redeemed from their ignorance, in that sense, by the simple act of entering Tilo's spice shop. Yet, I would suggest that the deconstructive argument of the presence of henna in the mainstream—the racing of the mainstream through henna, so to speak— is hardly subversive here; presence is not enough. We have to wonder, instead, at the terms for this inclusion; and the framework of a one-world culture is hardly salutary here. Thus, the narrative does make a distinction between Tilo herself and the bourgainvillaea girls even in their openness to Other spices. There does seem to be a privileged readability of the spices on Tilo's part; even as cultural knowledge is provisionalized, the cultural remains.

Interculturality becomes possible, then, only if the space of culture is not that of projection, of the simulation of cultural difference; and provided that this provisionality applies to both insiders and outsiders of a given culture. For Tilo is no less liable to essentialize the space of Indian culture than Raven is. It is here that the narrative resists the Orientalizing of spices by explicitly subverting the message of magic it begins with. As the novel progresses, this magic is itself dissolved through an investigation of what cultural depth *means*, as well as what it does not mean. In order for intercultural negotiation to become possible, Tilo has to deconstruct her own image as the mistress of spices:

> American, it is good you remind me, I Tilo who was at the point of losing myself in you. You have loved me for the colour of my skin, the accent of my speaking, the quaintness of my customs which promised you the magic you no longer found in the women of your own land. In your yearning you have made me into that which I am not. (290)[13]

At the end of the novel, interculturality is emphatically not the paradigm of fixed, distinct cultural meaning that Raven has been looking for: interculturality cannot exist outside of the cumbersome reality of lived cultural interaction as it unfolds the world over. If interculturality is to divest itself of the fantasy of cultural closure, there must be a constant negotiation of what it is to be Indian and what it is to be (Native) American, even before the actual interaction of these two elements neither of which can be defined in terms of "what it does" for the other: "Our love would never have lasted, for it was based upon fantasy, yours and mine, of what it is to be Indian. To be American" (292).

It is thus in the convergence of an inscription of culture outside of cultural difference and a simultaneous absence of closure that Rushdie and Divakaruni can be said to converge after all; a convergence that testifies to the fact that, contrary to my initial skepticism, (inter)cultural identities can be forged in Oakland as well as in Bombay. Spices, in India as much as in the rest of the world, remain a presence that is never transparent, a presence that testifies to what must be an ongoing negotiation of the meaning of culture.

What is significant about Rushdie's politics of spices is that the spice metaphor resists even as it seems to invite a facile, exoticizing definition of what it means to be "Indian": *Midnight's Children* is thus an important counterpart to *The Mistress of Spices* because it reminds us that "interculturality" must not be limited to East/West encounters. Rather, it can also pertain to the Indian nation-space as such. Rushdie's novel achieves a remarkable transvaluation, as it were, of the concept of spices: far from mere agents of self-exoticization, spices in *Midnight's Children* denote the absence of closure. As markers of multiplicity, they define an alternative space of Indianness *outside* the West. *The Mistress of Spices* could thus well be read as a continuation of *Midnight's Children*. For Divakaruni's novel "takes up" the spice once it has been imported into the West. As the other side to the US-American exoticism portrayed by Divakaruni, *Midnight's Children* reminds us that spices may be an indication of an alternative multiculturalism, an Indian one. Through the open-ended sign of an "exotic" spice, Salman Rushdie's *Midnight's Children* and Chitra Banerjee Divakaruni's *The Mistress of Spices* announce that even seeming tokens of exoticism are in fact markers of complex bicultural encounters. By juxtaposing the "special" politics of Rushdie's and Divakaruni's texts, the aim of this chapter has thus been to point to a transnational investigation of bicultural encounters. A spice is never what it seems.

Notes

[1] Critiquing the structuralist search for the "characteristics" of the Other culture, a search which must reduce the multiplicity of cultural performances to the anthropologically intelligible, Gerald Vizenor maintains: "The theories of structuralism, the myths of universal and unexpected harmonies, and objective dissociations of natural tribal reason are dubious tropes to power in the literature of dominance" (*Manifest Manners: Postindian Warriors of Survivance* 9).

[2] I am deliberately conflating the academic discipline of "Orientalism" with everyday projections, by the mainstream, of what the Other *is*; both converge, I would suggest, in the essentialist closure of the Other's cultural difference.

[3] My plea for an absence of cultural closure in the definition of difference is based on the work of Gerald Vizenor, especially his *Fugitive Poses: Native American Indian Scenes of Absence and Presence* (1998) and *Manifest Manners* (1994).

[4] This contrasting of absence and presence, once again, is based on the work of Vizenor, especially his *Fugitive Poses: Native American Indian Scenes of Absence and Presence*.

[5] A blend of ginger, cardamom, cinnamon and cloves. Editor's note.

[6] A traditional, formal outfit worn by Chinese women, the *chong-sam* (or *cheongsam*) is a fitted dress typified by a high collar, long length, and button or frog closures near the shoulder, that is often made in shimmering silk or embroidered

satin. Editor's note.

⁷ I am indebted to Thy Phu and Jodi Kim for this point.

⁸ Ground mango powder. Editor's note.

⁹ This term, once again, is Vizenor's (passim in both *Manifest Manners* and *Fugitive Poses*.

¹⁰ Sandalwood. Editor's note.

¹¹ Black cumin seed. Editor's note.

¹² This view of a semiotics of culture in Sau-ling Wong's more recent writing is based on a lecture entitled "'Race,' Writing and Deference? Asian Canadian and Asian American Literary Studies in Comparative Perspective" Guy Beauregard gave on 9 November 2000 as the John A. Sproul Lecture in Canadian Studies at the University of California, Berkeley.

¹³ The conflation of Native American with (quintessential) Americanness does seem problematic here. Even as the narrative seems aware of the dangers of cultural conflation in other instances, as in its exploration of the proximity of the two "Indian" cultures (South Asian and American Indian) as mainstream *simulations*, Divakaruni's equation of Native culture with quintessential Americanness appears debatable.

PART II

TRANSCULTURATION AND CULTURAL TRANSLATION

5
Transculturation and Biculturalism
Latina Writers of the United States at/as a Crossroads

Esther Alvarez Lopez

In 1987 Chicana[1] theorist, poet, and fiction writer Gloria Anzaldúa published her seminal *Borderlands/La Frontera: The New Mestiza*, a path-breaking work in contemporary American criticism and fiction. Anzaldúa's physical, psychological, sexual and spiritual borderlands soon became a fashionable metaphor, and border studies/theory a new field to explore. Although Anzaldúa situated her borderlands on the Texas-American border, this initial point of departure was expanded "to include nearly every psychic or geographic space about which one can thematize problems of boundary or limit" (Michaelsen and Johnson 1-2). On the other hand, feminism found in the border a (discursive) strategy to deconstruct ossified structures such as patriarchy, and also problematize questions of identity and representation. The border became "the trope of difference and potential conflict, between races, between cultures and between sexual preferences" (Humm 6), a site of erosion, resistance and contestation, where ideologies are traversed and hegemony loses the privileged center.

Latina writers of the United States have widely used the metaphor of the border to reflect on their bicultural identity. They are, in JanMohammed's words, "border intellectuals" ("Worldliness-Without-World, Homelessness-As-Home: Toward a Definition of the Specular Border Intellectual" 97),[2] an expression that designates "an authorial subject position that occupies the interstitial space of the crossroads as a site of potential transgression—interrogation and production—in a contested living and working domain" (Henderson 2). In alter/native narratives that spring from this social space where cultures meet—a space that Mary Louise Pratt calls "contact zone" (4),[3] and José David Saldívar *"transfrontera* contact zone" (13-14)—the bo(a)rders re-imagine their culture/s, their nation/s, and themselves. In this new cartography of wor(l)ds, the border dwellers create a literature that questions hegemonic cultural assumptions and transgresses gender and genre boundaries, thus destabilizing both cultural and literary hierarchies. I discuss below *Borderlands/La Frontera* and three other works by Latina writers, Cuban American playwright Dolores Prida's *Coser y Cantar* (first performed at Duo Theater in New York City in 1981, published in 1990), Chicana writer Sandra Cisneros' *The House on Mango Street* (1984; this edition 1991, all page references are to this edition), and the poem "Child of the Americas" (in *Getting Home Alive*, 1986) co-authored by Puerto Rican-American Aurora Levins Morales and her Puerto Rican mother Rosario Morales. I argue that through writing, they aim to articulate a sense of their (plural) subjectivities, by interweaving the polarizations that make up their personal and social milieu. In their hybrid works (in some cases a mixture of fiction, poetry, memoir and essay) Latina writers deal with the problems derived from their transculturation, from the juxtaposition of languages, cultures, worldviews, and languages.

Transculturation and *mestizaje*

In 1940 Fernando Ortiz coined the term *transculturation* to refer to the sum of the different phases that are involved in the transitive process of one culture to another (this edition 1963, all page references are to this edition). He asserts that such a process does not only imply acquiring a different culture (*acculturation*), but it also necessarily entails the loss or uprooting of the old culture (*deculturation*) and the consequent creation of new cultural phenomena (*neoculturation*) (134-135). Though painful, this process is nevertheless enriching. [4]

The new border culture, born as the result of the contact of two cultures, is characterized by hybridity and *mestizaje*—that has traditionally been considered synonymous with damnation, with treachery:[5] it is a reminder of the humiliation of the Conquest, of the destruction of a highly developed culture, and of the annihilation of a people's signs of identity. In most present-day criticism and fiction, however, *mestizaje* is an example of, and a metaphor for, "both impurity and resistance," adopted "as a central name for impure resistance to interlocked, intermeshed oppressions" (Lugones 459). In "Elogio del mestizaje" ("Tribute to *mestizaje*") Mexican writer Carlos Fuentes celebrates *mestizaje*, defined by its openness to change and by its capacity to move, as a positive asset in the formation of identity. Fuentes maintains that a fixed identity is also a dead one, and that a real identity is formed only in contact with others and with other cultures. Identity must thus be flexible, and in perpetual evolution (9). In fact, according to general opinion, *mestizaje/hibridismo*'s most salient characteristic is mobility, "the reluctance ... to firmly inhabit one place" (Egerer 23); mobility demands constant negotiation between the different elements that form part of the *mestizo*'s subjectivity. For Chicano theorist Alfred Arteaga, *mestizaje* is an opportunity for negotiating difference. The hybrid subjectivity of the *mestizo* is played out in *difrasismo*, which he defines as the means of representing something in the coupling of two elements: "Not only does it yoke together different elements, it keeps present the separate elements *and the new concept it creates*. It is not quite dialectic or metaphor[ic], nor does it efface the originals in the new. It is a sign of hybridizing, of leaving bare the work of coming to be" (18, emphasis added). Like Anzaldúa's "third country" (25), Arteaga acknowledges the existence of a third state, the result of the coexistence of the other two, a product of the articulation of that "apparently impossible simultaneity" (Young 26), that is the bringing together of the various components that are part of the two halves merging into a single whole. For Gustavo Pérez Firmat, however, it is not clear that the non-conflictive cohabitation of dissimilar cultures "necessarily engenders a synthetic third term" ("Transcending Exile: Cuban-American Literature Today" 5), an idea that I believe Homi Bhabha likewise sustains, since he does not consider hybridity as a third term that resolves the tensions between two cultures (*The Location of Culture* 114).

The *mestizo*/bicultural hybrid lives in the interstices/cracks of two worlds, juggling them. S/he is a "cultural chameleon," to use Judith Ortiz Cofer's expression (17), with a complex identity that is the result of the combination of multiple and even contradictory defining forces, and whose ambiguous position is both that of insider and outsider, "neither/nor, but kind of both, not quite either ... in the middle of either/or" (Lugones 459). Insofar as *mestizos*/hybrids live in-between cultures, with a foot on each side and straddling both, they have been engaged in the task of rethinking what lies behind the signifier "culture" and the nature of "the cultural." Renato Rosaldo did so in terms of "borderlands":

> The fiction of the uniformly shared culture increasingly seems more tenuous than useful. Although most metropolitan typifications continue to suppress border zones, human cultures are neither necessarily coherent nor always homogeneous. More often than we usually care to think, our everyday lives are crisscrossed by border zones, pockets and eruptions of all kinds. Social borders frequently become salient around such lines as sexual orientation, gender, class, race, ethnicity, nationality, age, politics, dress, food,

or taste. Along with "our" supposedly transparent cultural selves, such borderlands should be regarded not as analytically empty transitional zones but as sites of creative cultural production that require investigation. (qtd. in Lugo 207-208)

The cultural hybrid acknowledges heterogeneity[6] rather than homogeneity as the social and cultural norm. By positioning him/herself on the border(s), s/he "seeks to traverse rather than occupy a great variety of 'middle grounds'" (Krupat 25), trying to always think the *between*, that is, "thinking with, against, and across categories" (Egerer 25), a process that Mae G. Henderson calls "worrying the lines," or how to critically engage with living on the border, probing binary oppositions and negotiating difference. Following Bhabha, Claudia Egerer believes that the border is not a space of beginnings or endings, but a moment of transit, understood "as positioned *between* conceptual categories" (42), a place that can erode the hegemony of the privileged center and challenge the dominant cultural norms. (Border) Culture is thus rethought as fragmentation and contestation rather than as coherence and uniformity; it is a site of social differences and struggles, of resistance rather than consensus. The locality that best reflects this poetics of (in)-betweenness is the hyphen, which is taken to be not only a "marked (or unmarked) space that both binds and divides," but also "a crucial location for working at the ambivalences in hybridity" (Wah 60). For Sonia Saldívar-Hull the hyphen is a new space, a bridge where people with double affiliations can negotiate "an empowering racial, gendered, working-class, political terrain we also call mestizaje" (*Feminism on the Border* 44-45). The hyphen is thus conceived as an instrument of resistance, disturbance and dislocation.

Borderlands/La Frontera

Anzaldúa is one of the first theorists to remark on the position of the disjunctive liminality of the cultural hybrid and the possibilities that occupying this middle ground engendered. She develops in her *Borderlands/La Frontera* a whole theoretical and revolutionary border politics/poetics where she weaves in her conception of what she calls "fronterista," the border feminist, or "frontera dwellers with feminist leanings" in Saldívar-Hull's words (*Feminism on the Border* 11). Anzaldúa's *fronterista* is embodied in her work in the figure of the "new mestiza," a multi-faceted Chicana who negotiates conceptual borders and reconciles warring ideologies and traditions. The mark of the *mestiza* is her tolerance for contradictions, for ambiguity:

She learns to be an Indian in Mexican culture, to be Mexican from an Anglo point of view. She learns to juggle cultures. She has a plural personality, she operates in a pluralistic mode—nothing is thrust out, the good, the bad and the ugly, nothing rejected, nothing abandoned. Not only does she sustain contradictions, she turns the ambivalence into something else. (101)

The *new mestiza* shows her discomfort with a fixed positionality, an experience that is characteristic of those inhabiting the locus of hybridity. *Nepantilism*, an Aztec word meaning torn between ways, describes this mental state. Befitting her in-between position as a "boarder" or dweller of borders, the *mestiza*'s subjectivity is characterized by "a state of perpetual transition" (Anzaldúa 100) from one cultural system to another in an endless dialogical interaction. She is a traveler, an image that, in Edward Said's words, "depends not on power, but on motion, on a willingness to go into different worlds, use different idioms, understand a variety of disguises, masks, rhetorics... [T]he traveler *crosses* over, traverses territory, abandons fixed positions, all the time" ("Identity, Authority and Freedom: The Potentate and the Traveler" 81). Alfred Arteaga holds a very similar view: he contends that *mestizaje* is itself a process; and that consequently the *mestizo* is an unfinalized subject. This unfinalizability stems from the length of time the process of *mestizaje* takes, its meaning never fully attained as it is forever in a state of becoming. The *mestizo* is therefore a subject in process, a pluralized identity never fixed or finished, a fact that leads Arteaga to conclude that one cannot really ever *be* a *mestizo* (95).

Anzaldúa's *mestiza* is also engaged in this dynamic process that presupposes as a first step to dismantle received assumptions, monolithic epistemologies, and monologic constructions of self. She moves away from received cultural assumptions and uncontested dogmas toward a more whole, personal perspective, based on inclusion rather than exclusion. From her dialectical, decentered perspective the *mestiza* seeks to balance possibilities and conflicting points of view, resolving contradictions, and uniting what is separate. The outcome of this process is, however, not merely an assembly of disparate elements or a balancing of opposing powers but "in attempting to work out a synthesis, the self has added a third element which is greater than the sum of its severed parts" (101-102). That comprehensive, empowering third element is what she calls "mestiza consciousness," whose energy "comes from continual creative motion that keeps breaking down the unitary aspect of each new paradigm" (102). Like Said or Arteaga, Anzaldúa conceives her *mestiza* subjectivity in terms of movement and transformation.[7] Under the bilingual heading entitled

"La Encrucijada/The Crossroads," Anzaldúa elaborates on the *mestiza*'s multiple subjectivity. Conscious of the traditional definition of women as the (absolute) Other, as a category depending on negation, a not-self, not-man, not-the-phallus (Frye 994), she constructs her own self-definition by opposing to that negative subjecthood a positive self-supporting one, constituted along the axes (race, gender, sexual and political—feminist—orientation) that make her the Other, both in/by Anglo-American and Chicano cultural systems:

> As a *mestiza* I have no country, my homeland cast me out; yet all countries are mine because I am every woman's sister or potential lover. (As a lesbian I have no race, my own people disclaim me; but I am all races because there is the queer in me in all races.) I am cultureless because, as a feminist, I challenge the collective cultural/religious male-derived beliefs of Indo-Hispanics and Anglos; yet I am cultured because I am participating in the creation of yet another culture, a new story to explain the world and our participation in it, a new value system with images and symbols that connect us to each other and to the planet. *Soy un amasamiento*, I am an act of kneading, of uniting and joining that not only has produced both a creature of darkness and a creature of light, but also a creature that questions the definitions of light and dark and gives them new meanings. (102-103)

The new *mestiza* leaves no place for defeatism. She comes out of this self-creative process asserting new powers that ensure her wholeness, "all the lost pieces of [her]self come flying . . . magnetized toward the center. *Completa*" (73).

In Anzaldúa's work the subaltern woman can and does definitely speak: she assumes authority, voice, and thus control of the wor(l)d. Anzaldúa defends Chicano Spanish as a border/hybrid tongue, a language characterized by change and evolution, that creates new variants through the invention or adoption of words; it is a living language that fits the double condition of the people that speak it, a language "which they can connect their identity to, one capable of communicating the realities and values true to themselves—a language with terms that are neither *español ni* [nor] *inglés*, but both. We speak a patois, a forked tongue, a variation of two languages" (77). Chicanos and other Latino groups living in the United States appropriate and alter the language of the dominant culture making up a kind of syncretic variant, a hybridized formation that enriches both words and meanings. This creative interlanguage is the result of the need of people who do not originally belong in that culture to identify themselves as a distinct people. Their cultural distinctiveness is signaled in texts by the interspersion of English and Spanish, a way of drawing attention to their difference. In the earlier stages, the writers tended to gloss their texts for the benefit of non-Spanish speakers. Such glosses are not only a translation of individual words; their very existence within a written text does in fact foreground the reality of cultural distance.

In present-day Latina literature, a great majority of authors prefer the technique of what Ashcroft, Griffiths and Tiffin call *selective lexical fidelity* (*The Empire Writes Back: Theory and Practice in Post-Colonial Literatures* 67), leaving Spanish words untranslated and forcing readers who are not fluent in the language to be active in the reading process; they must infer meaning from the context or else look up in the dictionary those terms they do not understand if they want to fully grasp the meaning of the work. Readers are thus educated/trained in "border" literacy, or the ability to read border literature, an activity with a potentially counter-hegemonic effect since it entails "a kind of border crossing as well as a democratic thought process [that] avoids a single perspective, such as a middle-class, Western cultural bias [as well as it] takes a critical view of authority and supports the imaginative" (Hicks xxxi). Due to their education in schools where English was the only spoken language, most writers use Spanish sparingly, feeling as they do that they are more proficient in the "imported language" and consequently find it more natural to write in English. In some rare but significant instances, though, authors are reluctant to translate their works at all, inasmuch as they believe that their identity is bound up with language, which defines them and their experience, as well as consider that it is, and use it as, a powerful vehicle to signify and/or inscribe difference.

Coser y Cantar

Prida opens her bilingual play *Coser y Cantar*[8] with a note where she establishes the condition that the text "must NEVER be performed in just one language" (49). The short list of the dramatis personae hints at the reason of this specific requirement. The character(s), two but in reality only one, point(s) from the very beginning to the crucial duality that is going to be staged throughout the play. This duality only makes sense when one considers the character from her double subjectivity, conditioned to a great extent by language. The author has asserted elsewhere that language is actually the third character (qtd. in Feliciano 115). The character in the play will code-switch depending on the part of her reality that she brings to the fore and that informs who she is, with all her contradictions and ambiguities.

The female protagonist conveniently bears a simple identifier for a name, She/Ella (an Anglo and a Latina self, two sides of a personality), a pronoun in two languages that in its basic general quality universalizes the likewise ordinary (because commonplace) features of the immigrant/border woman who both belongs and does not to two cultures. She/Ella is involved in a process of transculturation and consequently suffers the tensions derived from the operation of two opposing forces: on the one hand, the assimilationist pressure of the dominant culture; and on the other, the desire to retain her own culture of origin. However, as the play shows, the latter can no longer be attained by just accepting its value system blindly, but by questioning the traditional cultural and societal constructs/beliefs that are detrimental to the woman's sense of self, and that insist on her subservience to patriarchal norms.

Coser y Cantar is ultimately about how to be a bilingual, bicultural woman without losing any part of one's identity or of one's mental sanity. Prida is concerned in this play with "the construction of the subject in process," focusing directly "on dualities and divisions inherent in hybrid spaces" (Arrizón 116). In the play, SHE/ELLA seeks to articulate her selfhood through "a verbal, emotional game of ping-pong" (Prida 49), played out as an internal struggle of her conflicting selves (ethnic and assimilated) to take control and establish supremacy over the other. The author situates the character in an apartment in Manhattan, divided into two ethnic territories that correspond in every instance to each of her fragmented subjectivities. Set, props and costumes show their respective juxtaposed socio-cultural realms:

> Stage right is ELLA's area. Stage left is SHE's. Piles of books, magazines and newspapers surround SHE's area. A pair of ice skates and a tennis racket are visible somewhere. Her dressing table has a glass with pens and pencils and various bottles of vitamin pills. SHE wears jogging shorts and sneakers.
>
> ELLA's area is somewhat untidy. Copies of *Cosmopolitan*, *Vanidades* and *TV Guías* are seen around her bed. ELLA's table is crowded with cosmetics, a figurine of the Virgen de la Caridad and a candle. A large conch and a pair of maracas are visible. ELLA is dressed in a short red kimono. (49)

Prida portrays her character(s) by parodying stereotypes that become, because so exaggerated, almost humorous. SHE has undoubtedly absorbed the Protestant work ethic, leads a healthier life, is tidier, more obsessed with order and more cultivated than ELLA, whose only reading material consists of some women's magazines and a television guide. Her space is taken up with objects that embody memories and absences, reminders of her culture that make her feel at home while not really belonging. A revealing stage direction introduces Act I: a recording by Olga Guillot is heard as ELLA sensually applies cream to her naked leg, brushes her hair and sings along with the record, "performing" in front of an imaginary mirror. In "See(k)ing the Self: Mirrors and Mirroring in Bicultural Texts," Judith Oster asserts that in texts written by bicultural, bilingual authors, characters look into the mirror confronting their fragmented subjectivity, seeking out "images and creat[ing] forms that integrate, or, at the very least, appear to have unity, in an attempt to give the lie to divisiveness and incongruency" (61). Characters seek coherence where/when only discrepancy between their outer and inner selves appears to exist. In the opening scene of the play, as differences gradually become more and more manifest, it becomes clear that the integration of the character's two selves is yet a utopia: while ELLA looks at herself "performing" in the mirror, her other self—SHE—does not return her look, but instead stares at her and, exasperated because she does not like that type of (Latin American) music, turns off the record-player. As could be expected, ELLA complains and scolds her for cutting her singing and acting off like that, reminding her that she never interrupts her when she imagines herself to be Barbra Streisand (51). Both Olga Guillot and Barbara Streisand represent Latin- and Anglo-American music respectively, functioning in the play as signifiers of the cultural modes at war within ELLA/SHE.

Food is another such signifier of cultural/ethnic difference. In "I Yam What I Yam: Cooking, Culture, and Colonialism," Anne Goldman argues that cooking can be a metonym for culture and that "to write about food is to write about the self" (169). In *Coser* ELLA resists the pressures of assimilation by cooking the recipes that she has probably learned from her mother in her home country. The elaboration and subsequent eating of a rich, succulent breakfast, "revoltillo de huevos, tostadas, queso blanco, café con leche [scrambled eggs, toast, white cheese, coffee with milk]" (51) become a way of reinforcing her ties to her cultural past and to her roots. Meanwhile, SHE, more concerned with body fitness, puts on a Jane Fonda exercise record and begins her workout exercises. The difference between the two is once again remarkable: "SHE: Do you have to eat so much? You eat all day, then lie there like a dead octopus. ELLA: Y tú me lo recuerdas todo el día, pero si no fuera por todo lo que yo como, ya tú te hubieras muerto de hambre [And you are reminding me of it all day, but were it not for all I eat you would have starved to death by now]. (*ELLA eats. SHE sips her orange juice*)" (52). SHE represses her appetite trying to conform to the physical model type in vogue in the US, only eats food without calories, and feels "violent, wild ... like ... chains, leather, whips" (63) after she has eaten. By contrast, ELLA prefers nourishment even if it means getting fat, eats out of nostalgia and feels "sexy. Romántica" (63) when she has satiated her more than physical (also cultural) appetite with typical filling, not precisely fat-free dishes of her home country. The way they relate to food seems to condition how they relate to their physical selves as well: SHE criticizes ELLA for her lack of emotional sophistication, whereas ELLA retorts that SHE is so aseptic and removed from her body that she does not even know any more how her own sweat smells (54). Their attitude toward sexuality also differs, SHE being more open-minded, liberated and promiscuous than ELLA, who is very sensual but has been raised in a more traditional education and therefore exerts more control over her sexual life.

In spite of all that separates them, they also have significant points in common: throughout the play both intersperse their ping-pong oppositional game with the search for a map. The map functions as a symbol of the uprooting and displacement that ELLA has had to undergo in her migration from Cuba to the United States. On the other hand, SHE's constant search for it implies that her sense of loss and alienation is greater than she will ever openly admit. Notwithstanding her apparent self-assuredness, she is tacitly asking to be guided through in her transculturation process in order to find the way into a cohesive self that may both *be* (whole) and *belong* without having to face any potential threat of personal annihilation. SHE's and ELLA's confrontations, a step closer to self-destruction after every individual battle for supremacy they fight, start to be finally resolved when they inadvertently switch language. Prida maintains that the switch "marks a change in their relationship, a tender moment. Instead of fighting, they're sharing, remembering, regretting" (qtd. in Feliciano 115). Just as they surmount the barrier of language, they begin to realize that control over mind and body, or knowing who is stronger of the two does not guarantee survival in a society where death is a ruling principle and a menace to everyone. At the beginning of the play SHE reads in the newspapers that three people have been shot for no reason at all, and comes to the conclusion that "no one is safe out there. No one. Not even those who speak good English. Not even those who know who they are . . ." (51). *Coser* ends with a new shooting and with other instances of violence against nature, "¡Y están cortando los árboles! . . . ¡Y echando la basura y los muertos al río! [And they are cutting down the trees! . . . and throwing the garbage and the dead into the river!]"; and against children, "They are poisoning the children in the schoolyard" (67). Their realization that they may well be next in this process of real (physical) destruction ultimately materializes their bonding, since both together and simultaneously feel prompted to search for the map once more, perhaps in a last attempt to find a secure place where she/they can be free and at peace with herself and with the world.

SHE/ELLA, self and other, must inevitably negotiate the terms of her identity. Self-affirmation will derive then from her understanding and acceptance of the two (paradoxical) halves that compose her ambiguous subjectivity. Prida asserts that *Coser* dramatizes these "convulsions of rejection and reconciliation," constituting an inextricable part of the process of transculturation, that she considers to be, though painful, nevertheless not negative: for, the moment SHE/ELLA accepts the other, "the Woman becomes a different person . . . a composite that accepts and reconciles dualities," a third woman who "is not the result of acculturation, which implies the melting pot concept" (qtd. in Feliciano 116) with its erasure of cultural idiosyncrasies, but rather a bicultural person who benefits from a much more "positive energy." With its balancing of polarities, biculturalism becomes in Prida's play a remedy to counter the self-estrangement and isolationism of fractured selves.

The House on Mango Street

Esperanza, the protagonist of Sandra Cisneros' *The House on Mango Street* (1984; this edition 1991, all page references are to this edition) learns early on in life that in order to live on the border she has to be an "amphibian," a term this Chicana writer employs to refer to herself as a bicultural woman (Mirriam-Goldberg 92). Like the character(s) in *Coser y Cantar*, the young woman narrator, in this hybrid book of vignettes halfway between prose and poetry, tries to define and come to terms with her subjectivity. Young though she is, she is aware that the main attribute of the subject is participation in language, and that to be a subject, or to have subjectivity, "one has to enter the language, and to enter the language is to become a signifier" (Frye 993).[9] Apart from the problems derived from her being a female in a patriarchal world, where the symbolic order of meaning is limited to males, Esperanza's access to subjectivity is further complicated by the language she is to use if she wants to be/come a signifier. In "My Name," one of the short vignettes that comprise her narration, she ponders on the transcendent importance of such a signifier in the bilingual/bicultural world she inhabits:

> In English my name means hope. In Spanish it means too many letters. It means sadness, it means waiting. It is like the number nine. A muddy color. It is the Mexican records my father plays on

Sunday mornings when he is shaving, songs like sobbing.
   It was my great-grandmother's name and now it is mine. She was a horse of a woman too, born like me in the Chinese year of the horse—which is supposed to be bad luck if you're born female—but I think this is a Chinese lie because the Chinese, like the Mexicans, don't like their women strong.
   My great-grandmother. I would've liked to have known her, a wild horse of a woman, so wild she wouldn't marry. Until my great-grandfather threw a sack over her head and carried her off. Just like that, as if she were a fancy chandelier. That's the way he did it. (10-11)

Esperanza realizes the importance of names/naming. Names are not only a series of letters joined together; names conjure up memories, recall sensations, and evoke feelings. Names also inscribe us in a culture and in a history, whether communal, personal, or both. Moreover, the role of tradition weighs heavily on names. Esperanza is linked to her familial genealogy through her name, which she has inherited from her great-grandmother. She fears that the fact that both share names may have a bearing on her development, and that it will mean that they will also share fates. Interestingly, the narrator/protagonist alludes to the Chinese horoscope and to her astrological sign that she likewise has in common with her ancestor. Both are horse women: strong, "wild," and self-assertive, characteristics that traditional and patriarchal cultures such as the Chinese or the Mexican do not consider appropriate for females, hence the haste to label such traits as bad luck. However, Esperanza sees through the lie; she is not willing to surrender to patriarchal constructs that define who she must be. Her great-grandmother had been finally subjected and forced to give up her self, condemned to be always looking out the window, probably regretting that "she couldn't be all the things she wanted to be" (11). Esperanza knows she has inherited her name, but she does not want to follow in her dramatic steps, or "inherit her place by the window." To counteract the pressure of her name, she wishes she could have one of her own choice, one that would better suit her subjectivity, "a name more like the real me" (11).
   Esperanza aims to redefine herself as "woman" in terms that are in opposition to basic tenets of the culture she has been raised in, a culture that confines women to the isolation of the home, and that has total control over their lives. Cisneros herself admits that, as a teenager, she felt that "[she] could not inherit [her] culture intact without revising some parts of it" (qtd. in Rodríguez Aranda 66). Besides the "schizophrenia" derived from "being a Mexican woman living in American society, but not belonging

to either culture" (66), she has to confront the misogyny embedded in her Mexican culture, where only two role models are available for women: La Malinche and the Virgin of Guadalupe. For women such as Cisneros and her protagonist the route to take is difficult, since there are no in-betweens (65). In an interview, Cisneros meditates on the dilemma the Mexican-American woman experiences on account of living between two cultures:

> I think that growing up Mexican and feminist is almost a contradiction in terms. For a long time—and it's true for many writers and women like myself who have grown up in a patriarchal culture, like the Mexican culture—I felt great guilt betraying that culture. Your culture tells you that if you step out of line, if you break these norms, you are becoming anglicized, you're becoming "the malinche," influenced and contaminated by these foreign influences and ideas.... Many writers are redefining our Mexicanness and it's important if we're going to come to terms with our Mexican culture and our American one as well. So it's a dilemma. I think my stories come from dealing with straddling two cultures. (qtd. in Satz 169)

She herself had a hard time with her family when she willingly diverted from the plan that traditional Chicano culture had designed for her, as it had for her foremothers before her: getting married and having children. Instead, she was determined to pursue an education, liked to read, abandoned her father's house, did not get married, and became a writer. Although her father and six brothers were upset because they thought that with her behavior she was rejecting (and betraying) her culture, she nevertheless persevered, convinced as she was that Latina women must accept their culture but not without adapting themselves as women (Rodríguez Aranda 66).

Like Cisneros, Esperanza transgresses the boundaries imposed on her by the traditional male-centered Chicano culture—with its gender constraints; and by the Anglo culture—with its triple alienating race, class, and gender constraints, intent on challenging and breaking consensual hegemony. She refuses to be what Paula Gunn Allen calls "las disappearadas (and desesperadas)" (304): invisible, muted, desperate and ultimately dead. She challenges the hegemonic power structure that underpins women's invisibility and their lack of agency by practicing with subtle forms of resistance and contrariness that she associates with masculine behavior: "I have begun my own quiet war. Simple. Sure. I am one who leaves the table like a man, without putting back the chair or picking up the plate" (89). Her strong, independent character makes her unsuitable to live under the rules of the traditional patriarchal home. In her narrative, Esperanza seems to agree with Caren Kaplan, who affirms, "[w]e must leave home, as it were, since our homes are often sites of racism, sexism and other damaging social practices" (194). In like manner, Anzaldúa observes that in order to find her true intrinsic nature, "buried under the personality that had been imposed on me," she had to leave "the source, the mother, disengage from my family, *mi tierra* [my land], *mi gente* [my people] . . . I had to leave home" (38). From her marginal position, the protagonist of *The House on Mango Street* envisages an alternative location where she can shape her self beyond patriarchal legacies, a "dynamic rather than a static site of power and signification" (Roberson 6), that she defines in terms that are far removed from what her gendered socio-economic and cultural reality actually dictates:

> Not a flat. Not an apartment in back. Not a man's house. Not a daddy's. A house all my own. With my porch and my pillow, my pretty purple petunias. My books and my stories. My two shoes waiting beside the bed. Nobody to shake a stick at. Nobody's garbage to pick up after.
> Only a house quiet as snow, a space for myself to go, clean as paper before the poem. (108)

Esperanza grows to be a writer for whom writing becomes itself "a location, a site for the construction of further spaces of power and knowledge, spaces that are also gendered" (Roberson 7). It is "a shamanistic process of transformation" (Yarbro-Bejarano 22), a strengthening, healing process that helps her come to terms with the negative aspects of her reality and with her inner conflicts of belonging. In one of her last vignettes, she confides that she likes to tell stories and that she is going to tell one about "a girl who didn't want to belong" (109). The narrator then recalls the different houses she lived in through the years, and the indelible impression left on her by the sad red house on Mango Street, "the house I belong but do not belong to" (110). Esperanza's house becomes a symbol of the ambivalent feelings of disaffiliation and belonging that her Chicano culture excites in her. She rebels against the laws and tenets of that culture that suffocate women, but is not willing to abandon it and simply become anglicized. For all the advantages that being on "the other side" may offer, she will not lose her Chicana identity, nor be exiled from her people, cognizant that "the inner expropriation of cultural identity cripples and deforms" (Hall 395). In the fashion of Anzaldúa's image of the turtle's shell (43; see also Reuman 35), she will take her "home" wherever she goes, for she has finally come to acknowledge the invisible bonds that inextricably entwine her life and creativity with Mango Street and its inhabitants. She understands that her privileged position as an intellectual makes her responsible for the fates of those who are less favored than her. She will use her writing as a socio-political weapon to denounce racist and economic oppression, as well as to expose the hegemonic ideological forces that forever keep women as passive sufferers of patriarchal domination. Esperanza's last words are significantly dedicated to all those "others" who dwell on the other side of the border, intended, like the meaning of her name in Spanish suggests, as a hope for a better future:

> One day I will pack my bags of books and paper. One day I will say goodbye to Mango. I am too strong for her to keep me here forever. One day I will go away.
>
> Friends and neighbors will say, What happened to that Esperanza? Where did she go with all those books and paper? Why did she march so far away?
>
> They will not know I have gone away to come back. For the ones I left behind. For the ones who cannot out. (110)

Esperanza gives voice to a self in process, engaged in a dynamic experience of exploration and discovery that leads to new understandings and relations. Her nomadic life, journeying in and out of Mango, breaking and crossing (geo)graphic boundaries, will enable her to remap the "cartographic, political, poetic, and psychic lines" that have become "destabilized, porous, redrawn" (Roberson 9) in her experience as a Latina woman. Living in the borderlands, at the juncture of cultures, in the in-between space of home and not-at-home-ness—Heidegger's *Unheimlichkeit*, that motivates "the reconstruction of the social and imaginative world" (Ashcroft, Griffiths and Tiffin, *The Empire Writes Back: Theory and Practice in Post-Colonial Literatures* 82)—will make Esperanza feel not a sense of disorientation or dislocation but rather of self-affirmation, (self-)empowerment and freedom. This social setting, "where peoples with different culturally expressed identities meet and deal with each other" (Clifton 24), is a plural, inclusive site of diversity and flexibility where the cultural hybrid/new *mestiza* can positively articulate her dual subjectivity, allowing contradictions to co-exist. As transpires from the literature of Latina writers, border women "are not decentered fragmented individuals" but subjects "who have begun to cohere a core identity by entering the transitional space between self and other," as Maggie Humm puts it (6).

"Child of the Americas"

In "Child of the Americas," a poem in *Getting Home Alive* (1986), co-authored by Puerto Rican-American Aurora Levins Morales and her Puerto Rican mother Rosario Morales, the former articulates the "core identity" Humm refers to, an identity that is realized positively through the celebration of diversity and *mestizaje*. Levins Morales draws power and strength from the meeting of the "many diaspora" that are blended in her multiple, fluid self. She avoids privileging any one single component as primary to her identity, thus affirming her non-unitary subjecthood, the legacy of a long history of forebears of whom she is a rich amalgam. In fact, the picture on the cover of the book depicts a patchwork quilt made with scraps of multi-chromatic material and different textures. Lourdes Rojas associates the verb *to knit* with the Spanish *tejer*, that comes from the Latin *texere*, a word that, as she points out, has the same linguistic root as *text(o)*. For Rojas, "the visual symbol (of the quilt) refers to both: a text made up of a variety of genres, co-authored by mother and daughter, who explore, in the text, the many and varied components or textures of their own histories" (171). In the last poem, appropriately entitled "Ending Poem," both Levins Morales and Morales subvert the Western hegemonic concept of racial purity, by bringing together their collective history and their individual experience as/at a crossroads, giving voice to a culturally syncretic identity that bridges seemingly disparate components, affirming their pluralism:

> I am what I am
> *A child of the Americas.*
> A light-skinned mestiza of the Caribbean,
> *A child of many diaspora, born into this continent at a crossroads.*
> I am Puerto Rican. I am U.S. American.
> *I am New York Manhattan and the Bronx.*
> . . .
> I am not African.
> *Africa waters the roots of my tree, but I cannot return.*
> I am not Taína.
> *I am a late leaf of that ancient tree,*
> and my roots reach into the soil of two Americas.
> *Taíno is in me, but there is no way back.*
> I am not European, though I have dreamt of those cities.
> . . .
> *Europe lives in me but I have no home there.*
> . . .

We are new.
They (women ancestors) gave us life, kept us going,
Brought us to where we are.
Born at a crossroads.
Come, lay that dishcloth down. Eat, dear, eat.
History made us.
We will not eat ourselves up inside anymore.
And we are whole. (212-213)

    As the poem so expressively illustrates, Levins Morales and Morales construct their identity out of fragments, but it is not fragmented or diffused. It is not born out of self-denial but of self-affirmation, of the assertion of their individual and collective history, in a dialogical process that inevitably encompasses "a rethinking of American identity" (Bost 201). Through their resistance against dominant ideologies, their transracial border-crossings and their cross-culturality, the authors make of hybridity the source of literary and cultural redefinition. They achieve in *Getting Home Alive* what political scientist Jane Flax identifies as the goal of psychoanalysis, feminist theory, and postmodern philosophy: "to understand and (re)-constitute the self, gender, knowledge, social relations, and culture without resorting to linear, teleological, hierarchical, holistic, or binary ways of thinking and being" (qtd. in Aigner-Varoz 51).

    Their life in the borderlands is imaginatively enriched by the distinct juxtaposed subjectivities that coexist, all of them contributing together to create a composite cohesive whole that poses what Bhabha calls an uncontainable "paranoid threat" because it "breaks down the symmetry and duality of self/other, inside/outside" (*The Location of Culture* 116). Searching for a de/territorialized, unmarked location, where they can challenge damaging essentialisms and transcend imposed conceptual boundaries, both mother and daughter have found a site that is pregnant with possibilities: the crossroads "where all points converge" (Rojas 176), where one "never belongs totally to one place, yet where one is able to feel an integral part of many places" (172), and where their alterity is no longer a form of absence but of signification. In consonance with their island of Puerto Rico, a land with an ambiguous political status—an "Associate State" whose territory both is and is not part of the United States, though it keeps its linguistic and cultural roots, Levins Morales and Morales make of the in-betweenness derived from their bicultural identity their (mobile) home.

Conclusion

The crossroads, as the hyphen (that represents this location visually), functions as what Fred Wah, in referring to code-switching, calls *synchronous foreignicity*, or "the ability to remain within an ambivalence without succumbing to the pull of any single culture" (62). The writers I have included here—and many others, such as Judith Ortiz Cofer or Julia Alvarez, I have not had the space to include—are themselves a crossroads, a bridge of/between two cultures. They and the characters they create are all women in transit, who find living on the border(s) to be a rich, self-empowering, freeing experience—though at times, because of the inevitable sense of disorientation that accompanies life in the liminal zone and the continual struggle that forever takes place there, it is not always a comfortable place to live in: Latina writers are definitely at war against dominant patriarchal attitudes that subjugate women, at the same time that they denounce the injustices that stem from all-pervasive, oppressive ideological practices that must be effectively confronted in order to force them out of women's (and also men's) lives. By contrast, they reveal themselves to be at home with "new affiliations that subvert old ways of being, rejecting the homophobic, sexist, racist, imperialist, and nationalist" (Saldívar-Hull, "Feminism on the Border: From Gender Politics to Geopolitics" 214).

With its decentering, subversive power, *mestizaje*, "founded on shifting components with no one defining center" (Bost 207, n2), turns out to be an essential concept for the cultural hybrid to engage in the necessary interrogation of, and to challenge, hegemonic assumptions based on racial and sexual differentiation as well as on monologic discourses of the nation. Even when *mestizaje* as a concept may eventually be considered as an exotic, attractive notion—likely, therefore, to be discursively appropriated and perhaps transformed by the center, it will still continue to find a way through/in the lives of many, working to create new worlds of confluence, and more enlightened and enlightening understandings.

Notes

[1] An American of Mexican descent.
[2] JanMohamed draws the distinction between the syncretic intellectual, who is "able to combine elements of the two cultures in order to articulate new syncretic forms and experiences," and the specular border intellectual who "subjects the cultures to analytic scrutiny rather than combining them; he or she utilizes his or her interstitial cultural space as a vantage point from which to define, implicitly or explicitly, other, utopian possibilities of group formation" ("Worldliness-Without-

World, Homelessness-As-Home: Toward a Definition of the Specular Border Intellectual" 97).

The Latina writers I include in this essay occupy both positionalities, since at the same time that they try to integrate their two dissimilar cultures into a dialogical, coherent whole—that I call *mestizaje* or hybridity—they do so critically: abandoning dichotomies, subverting hierarchies, and resisting domination.

Mestizaje, as I try to make plain in the text, is the word used by many critics and writers of Spanish/Latino origin to refer to hybridity. A *mestizo* would then be a half-breed, a person of mixed races. *Métis* or *hybrid* would be the equivalent in English.

[3] Pratt employs the term "contact zone" to refer to "social spaces where disparate cultures meet, clash, and grapple with each other, often in highly asymmetrical relations of domination and subordination, like colonialism, slavery, or their aftermaths as they are lived out across the globe today" (4).

[4] The appendix in the next chapter discusses *transculturation* further. Editor's note.

[5] La Malinche (*Malintzin* in Nahuatl), Hernán Cortés's interpreter and lover, bore a son to him, who became—at least symbolically—the first of the *mestizo* race (persons of mixed European and American Indian ancestry). For her alleged contribution to the Conquest, and for "selling" herself to a foreign power, she is cursed in Mexico as a traitor of her people. For a suggestive insight into this woman and her role in Conquest times, see Lanyon. For the construction of Malinche's legend as a traitor, see Cypess; Paz "Los Hijos de la Malinche" (The Sons of La Malinche); and Richard Rodriguez.

[6] Some voices utterly reject the idea of a heterogeneous culture, and the corresponding popular consensual view/fallacy that the color line is a feature of the past, long done away with and forgotten. Samira Kawash, for example, in her analysis of the black/white color line, argues that essentialized identities have been conveniently replaced by the so-called and more culturally accepted hybrid/diaspora/ borderland identities, terms that in her opinion enhance "such historical conditions as interaction, interdependency, cultural transformation, and movement." She highlights the efforts of contemporary cultural criticism to emphasize "the multiple ways in which the fixity, autonomy, stability, and separation of the racial categories of black and white are undermined, subverted, and destabilized" (2), when in reality critics are "confronted with a troubling discord between what we know as good essentialists, that culture is fundamentally heterogeneous, and what we see represented and reflected in everyday life, namely, that the color line is as intransigent as ever" (3).

[7] This line of thought has likewise been developed by feminist criticism in its analysis of women's subjectivity: Julia Kristeva's "subject in process"; Rosi Braidotti's "nomadic subjects"; and Teresa de Laureti's concept of "epistemology," a term that attempts to cover the notion of "the multilayered nature of subjectivity, as the process of interaction of self and other, in a multiplicity of relations of difference" (qtd. in Braidotti 299, n. 30), are just some representative examples.

[8] *Coser y Cantar* translates literally as "Sewing and Singing." The equivalent expression in English would be something like "plain sailing," such as in "it's plain sailing," when something is supposed to be very easy or safe. In the play it refers

to the words the mother of the protagonist used to talk about life, particularly a woman's life: "My mother told me once that life, especially the life of a woman, was plain sailing. And I believed her. But now I realize that life, everybody's, man's, woman's, dog's, cat's is really eating and shitting . . . in other words, the same old shit!" (Prida 57; my translation).

[9] Marilyn Frye argues that there is what she calls "a nice ambiguity" in the term *signifier*, "as between 'one who signifies' (a speaker) and 'that which signifies' (a word, perhaps a name)" (993). She points out that in Lacan's theoretical frame, both concepts are conflated, and thus to be "one who signifies" is to be "that which signifies," or, in other words, "to be a subject is to be a signifier . . . an element in a symbolic order" (993).

6
José María Arguedas and Vikram Chandra
Bridging Cultures, Living Translation[1]

Dora Sales Salvador

> "I wanted to belong."
> Meera Syal, *Anita and Me*

> "Here's ordinary human love beneath my feet. Fall away, if you must, contemptuous earth; melt, rocks, and shiver, stones. I'll stand my ground, right here. This I've discovered and worked for and earned. This is mine."
> Salman Rushdie, *The Ground Beneath Her Feet*

With boundaries tending to blur and fixed frontiers to lose significance, the contemporary world is characterized extensively by intercultural contacts. Thus, Spanish and especially English, literary languages that have also become *lingua francas*, are nowadays in touch with hundreds of other tongues previously marginalized or ignored outright. In this chapter, I focus on the narratives of two authors who are very different in both time and space, the Peruvian José María Arguedas (1911-1969) and the Indian Vikram Chandra (1961-), Spanish-language and English-language authors respectively, to argue that they live and create at the conflictive interface between cultures that are historically opposed to each other due to complex power relations.

More than thirty years after his death, Arguedas's[2] work is undoubtedly the best instance of transcultural literature in Latin American fiction. His writings represent the unavoidable, often tragic, bicultural blending of Andean and Spanish worlds in Peru, past, present and future. In the last few decades, there has been a new critical appreciation of this author's work and legacy, which is now very much part of the contemporary scene.³ Arguedas is currently considered one of the most important authors to speak out on issues such as the survival of native cultures and the dynamics between tradition and modernity. The significance and influence of his work, misunderstood during his lifetime and during the years immediately following his death, acquires its full meaning now, in our multicultural and globalized world.

The context of Arguedas's fiction is the semi-feudal socio-economic order that prevailed in the Andean highlands from the Spanish Conquest until recent times. However, while earlier writers had simplistically depicted a black-and-white confrontation between oppressive white landowners and a downtrodden indigenous peasantry, Arguedas was able to present a much more complex picture of Andean society. Furthermore, he has demonstrated that centuries of co-existence have brought about a process of transculturation and that, if the whites dominate socially and economically, it is the indigenous influence that predominates culturally and informs the worldview of the whites, despite their assumptions of cultural superiority. Thus, most of Arguedas's novels are very social-minded in character as they attempt to convey an overview of Andean society. Nonetheless, the main strand in his work draws on his personal experience to depict the clash of Peru's two main cultures at an individual level, by focusing on the experiences of a young boy—a boy who, evidently, is a narrative echo of Arguedas himself.

Chandra,[4] on the other hand, who is constantly shuttling between Bombay and Washington, D.C., is one of the new voices among the growing generation of Indians writing in English.[5] If one had to define Chandra's narrative in just one word, it would be *storytelling*. An enticing talent who proposes "yarns of yarns" to entertain audiences all over the world, he displays an untiring ability as storyteller, paying particular tribute to the Indian tradition of oral storytelling he appreciates so much. Since his début, he has explored fresh and emergent territories, showing the multifaceted nature of his narrative gift. At the same time, his literary project as a whole subsumes a deep understanding of the multiplicity of the socio-cultural life of India, past and present. Chandra is being more and more recognized as one of the main voices of Indian literatures in English.[6]

In the era of electronic communication, Chandra's prose manages to generate in the Internet-dependent reader an appreciation for traditional oral storytelling. In his work, one can notice how oral forms of literature are operating as distinct pre-texts in works explicitly written in English. As one's immediate reality becomes increasingly intertwined with global technology, this intercultural fiction seeks other ways of communication that are deeply human and are based on the art of oral storytelling and the voices of popular culture. Chandra's fiction shows that storytelling survives in modern India, but it also shows itself to be flexible, able to assimilate new elements (such as Western art) and change accordingly. Thus, by far, the Indian oral tradition of storytelling is the matrix of Chandra's narrative project. Chandra is a virtuoso creator of vivid descriptions that enliven smells, tastes, thoughts, feelings, how voices sound, how silences appear, and so on. In spite of the technical complexity of framing interconnected stories, his prose carefully introduces the reader into a calm, flashing, yet ever-changing narrative flow, constantly showing an ongoing dialogue between old and new forms. Hopefully, certain traditions survive in our paradoxical (post)modern times, and Chandra's fiction helps memory to be restored to its true abode. Although his literature belongs to the contemporary period, and indeed he employs certain present-day narrative resources, the seed of his prose lies in oral popular transmission, the texture of the great Indian epics, past memories reshaped and replenished in present times. For him, "tradition survives in odd and unexpected ways" (personal communication, 4 October 1997).

The narratives of both authors generate, above all, discourses of cultural mediation and meeting, as well as of emotional survival, resistance, and avoidance of polarization. Also, they are both aware of the role of translation as a bridge to understanding and as a way of living and creating.[7]

In the introduction to a collection of essays on the theme of being biracial and bicultural in contemporary North-American society (see e.g. Tsang), Claudine Chiawei O'Hearn finds that "racial and cultural identity becomes an inherent sum of who you are and what your experiences have been" (xiii). Indeed, ethnicity and race are neither fixed constructs nor measurable quantities, but ongoing negotiations constructed by juxtaposition. Nowadays, we are the witnesses of a bi- and multiculturalism that works in multiple directions and draws on the simultaneity of different times and presences. Out of this reality we find literatures, such as those written by Arguedas and Chandra, promoting a deep revision of what has been traditionally considered the canon of world fiction.

In this chapter I also wish to discuss the issue of *transculturation*.[8] Narrative transculturation allows Arguedas and Chandra to create a space for themselves in-between the two different worlds, cultures and languages they live in, bringing together the various strands they are made of, and interweaving knowledges, tongues, systems, worldviews, and inheritances. Avoiding rigid polarizations and binarisms, their fictions, without neglecting the emotional impact of the bicultural experience, account for the possibility and need of liminal spaces, interstices, cultural rhizomes, hybridity and cross-fertilization. The concepts of cultural dialogism, biculturalism, and transculturation are immensely useful in accounting for the emergence of artistic voices that seek to explore and negotiate their hyphenated identities, showing how it is indeed possible to stand by more than one culture and yet belong deeply and irrevocably to both.

In a world where unique, univocal and so-called pure identities do not really develop, one needs to be alive to two languages-cultures before attempting to build any bridge between them. This chapter aims to examine the inherent biculturalism in Arguedas's and Chandra's literary endeavors; to study, in a work of each, the interplay between cultures and also the undeniable life and richness of the traditionally marginalized cultural aspects of this encounter. The chapter focuses on the emotional clash of the bicultural experience and the counter-hegemonic force that springs from the mother culture, as fictionalized in Arguedas's *Los Ríos Profundos* (1958; this edition 1992, all page references are to this edition; translated into English as *Deep Rivers* [1978]) and Chandra's *Red Earth and Pouring Rain* (1995), respectively. These novels delve for the most part into the representation and construction of the self in a bicultural context. In this search, the greatest conflict lies in how to find an appropriate storytelling form, in terms of language, genre, and structure. The all-consuming question they raise is how to bring and hold together both one's inherited tradition and the baffling plural world the protagonists inhabit in the present.

It is worth mentioning that both Arguedas and Chandra clearly reject any attempt to fetishize the Andean or Indian past at the cost of ignoring the reality of cultural encounter and dialogue. What they argue is that there is indeed a past that should not be silenced, marginalized or manipulated by some univocal "official" account; there is a mother culture that demands its own voice. At the same time, integration versus disintegration, and the construction of cosmos within the experience of chaos (whether individual, textual, or cultural) somehow seem to be constants in Arguedas and Chandra's aesthetic and ideological projects. In Peru the political construction of "Indianness" has traditionally been a bipolar-bicultural one: Indian highlands - white and *mestizo* coast; white and *mestizo* cities - Indian countryside. Thus, although a variety of regional and ethnic fragments are being created and recombined across time, one can observe a strongly polarized construction of white and Indian ethnicities, which also gives way to an urban-rural opposition. Also in contemporary India, the linguistic, religious, ethnic and cultural diversities are huge. As Sunil Khilnani indicates, after independence the country has utilized the powers of the state and modern ideas associated with democracy to reconstitute the antique social identities of India—caste and religion—and to compel these re-formed identities to conform to the political scene (59). The main issue remains that of finding ways to deal with India's scale and multiplicity at all levels.

Biculturalism, Cultural Translation and "Translating Consciousness"

In any reflection on biculturalism, it is necessary to discuss first the concept of culture. For the purposes of this chapter one could venture that culture is a people's or society's way of life, including its rules of behavior; economic, social and political systems; language; religious beliefs, and laws. Culture is acquired, socially transmitted, and communicated in large part by language. It is a dynamic process, constantly being negotiated by those involved. As Paul Bohannan points out, a culture that cannot change is a dead culture, because innovation and transformation are a vital part of cultural dynamics (61). At the same time, as François Grosjean indicates, although bilingualism and biculturalism are not necessarily coextensive, many bilingual individuals are aware that in some sense they are also bicultural, and that biculturalism has affected their lives (157). One should also not forget that languages and cultures differ according to social position, status, and power relations. Thus, in any bilingual-bicultural situation, people tend to coexist in conflictual ways, in which interaction is usually asymmetrical and contentious. Cultures, like languages, come into contact in many different ways, but the main point to consider is the fact that there is not only a meeting of languages-cultures, but also a meeting of values, sensibilities and worldviews. In Frantz Fanon's words (as translated into English, in the 1986 edition), "To speak a language is to take on a world, a culture" (38).

Related to a complex realm between languages and cultures, the notion of cultural translation has a crucial role for Arguedas and Chandra, both in their literary projects and their living experiences. In this regard, Arguedas translates between languages and cultures to reflect the struggle of the Andean people to be heard in the space of a rapidly modernizing, increasingly national Peruvian society. John Landreau contends that through processes of translation and interpretation, the autobiographical element that is so present in Arguedas's fiction gains a collective, universal dimension. Landreau sees Arguedas as the "outsider" who employs his autobiographical experience as a living bridge between the Quechua- and Spanish-speaking worlds. The outsider is in fact a central figure in many of the author's stories and novels. Torn between languages and socio-cultural worlds, Arguedas's experience and fictional perspective are deeply contradictory. In both worlds, he is a participant and, at the same time, an outsider, an observer.

In this context of bilingualism-biculturalism, in order to properly tell an Andean story and represent the multiple voices and languages it contains, Arguedas had no other option but the difficult and very painful task of translating and mediating. As he puts it in "La novela y el problema de la expresión literaria en el Perú (The novel and the problem of literary expression in Peru)" he wrote in 1950 (published in the 1980 edition of *Yawar Fiesta*), "Realizarse, traducirse, convertir en torrente diáfano y legítimo el Idioma que parece ajeno; comunicar a la lengua casi extranjera la materia de nuestro espíritu. Ésa es la dura, la difícil cuestión"[9] (qtd. in Landreau 90). And yet, above all, "¡Se trata de no perder el alma, de no transformarse por entero en esta larga y lenta empresa! Yo sé que algo se pierde a cambio de lo que se gana. Pero el cuidado, la vigilia, el trabajo, es por guardar la esencia"[10] ("La novela y el problema de la expresión literaria en el Perú" 13).

Arguedas declared that he was not "an acculturated [person]," but a "happy demon" speaking "in Christian and in Indian, in Spanish and in Quechua" (*El Zorro de Arriba y el Zorro de Abajo* [The Fox from Above and the Fox from Below, 1971; this edition 1990, all page references are to this edition] 257; my translation). Quechua was his "mother tongue." In his writings we find a profound *consciousness* of his being a bilingual subject. For him Spanish was a learned language that he did not feel was his own. It was a language that produced in him a profound estrangement between word and reality, word and the perception of reality. In his battle with language,[11] Arguedas finally opted to translate the Quechua sensibility in correct Spanish, but still trying to convey Quechua thought patterns. He believed in the passionate word, a mythical living entity for which he could not find any Spanish equivalent. His wish was that his literary form would not adumbrate the cultural reality he wanted to communicate; he wanted both form and culture to become one. Margaret V. Ekstrom finds that in his attempt to express his views on biculturalism, Arguedas's greatest success was precisely his linguistic development.

In contrast, Chandra's plural linguistic knowledge is a typical feature within the complex multilingual situation of the Indian subcontinent:

> My mother tongue is Hindi. We speak it at home mixed with English, sometimes switching in the middle of a sentence. During my education, I've learned and, through disuse, lost many languages—Gujarati (could write and speak it, at one point); Sanskrit (could read and write); Punjabi (could write and speak). I have a smattering of Urdu, as many North Indians do, picked up from listening to ghazals[12] and watching movies (personal communication, 21 May 1997).

In contemporary India, the use of English as a literary language is part of a complex and open debate. Braj Kachru shows how English has provided a neutral vehicle for communication between contesting language groups (see *The Indianization of English. The English Language in India*; and *The Alchemy of English. The Spread, Functions, and Models of Non-Native Englishes*), while the writer Raja Rao in the foreword to his novel *Kanthapura* (1938) voices the challenge of the postcolonial writer to adapt the colonial language to local needs and realities: "One has to convey in a language that is not one's own the spirit that is one's own" (v). Perhaps, the appropriation of a second language is essentially a subversive strategy, for the adaptation of the standard language to the demands and requirements of the place and culture into which it has been appropriated amounts to a far more subtle rejection of the political power of the colonizing tongue. In Salman Rushdie's words, "to conquer English may be to complete the process of making ourselves free" ("Imaginary Homelands" 17); now "English has become an Indian language" ("Damme, This is the Oriental Scene For You!" 54). As Chandra remarks, writing in English is an advantage because this is the *lingua franca* of power, business, cultural exchange, and politics ("The Cult of Authenticity. India's Cultural Commissars Worship 'Indianness' Instead of Art" 187-188). And using this language in creative writing, he has forgotten nothing, given up nothing.

If Rushdie declares himself to be a "translated man," using translation as a metaphor of transportation across spaces or boundaries of any kind ("Imaginary Homelands" 17), Chandra's perspective, though related to Rushdie's, is more deeply rooted in translational principles. Chandra feels that "to live in Bombay is to be translating every second of every day, from a dozen languages and systems into each other" (personal communication, 11 November 1999). As a result, he writes in a wide range of voices—silenced, marginal, historical, mythical and daily argot— showing how easy it is to manipulate the past. He is very much aware of the role of translation in living and creating within a globalized, but intensely diversified world. In fact, Sujit Mukherjee believes that translation occupies a natural place not only in the literary sphere but also in the daily speech of India (127), while G. N. Devy regards translation as "origin" in the context of Indian literature written in English. From a broader vantage point, Devy considers that in postcolonial spheres, many literary traditions have their origin in acts of translation. In his view there are communities who possess what he names a "translating consciousness" (154-155) that exists in multilingual localities where a dominating colonial language has acquired a privileged status. In the works of Arguedas and Chandra, who may be viewed as displaying the "translating consciousness," translation is not merely a transposition of meaning or signs. It is more of an aesthetic than a linguistic enterprise, one that has a relevant bearing on literary history, theory, and criticism.

Los Ríos Profundos

Generally regarded as Arguedas's best novel, *Los Ríos Profundos* marks a break with his earlier work, for in it he abandons conventional realism in favor of a lyrical manner more appropriate for communicating the Andean magical-religious worldview, as well as the love and tenderness he learned as a child raised among the Quechua people. Another significant evolution in his style is his translating into the medium of Spanish the *sensibilité* of people expressing themselves in Quechua. Arguedas wrote in correct Spanish but managed to communicate Andean thought.

The novel portrays Peru immersed in a new paradigm, one of modernization and turmoil, and concentrates on the situation of a young boy pulled grievously in two different directions, the indigenous and the Western. Composing a representation of himself as a child, Arguedas mirrors his experiences through a re-creation of a boy's narrative voice and worldview. The novel raises an important issue, that of intercultural/bicultural children who, unable to cope with difference, desperately long to *belong* and be just like everybody else.[13]

Ernesto, the adolescent protagonist and main narrator of *Los Ríos Profundos*, is cut off from the beloved Indian world of his childhood when he is sent to a Church-run boarding school to receive the education that will supposedly equip and enable him to take his place in white society, to assume his "role" in it. Thus uprooted, he rejects the white world to which he belongs by birth and identifies affectively with the Indians among whom he had spent the happiest period of his childhood. As he tells the reader, "Los jefes de familia y las señoras mamakunas de la comunidad, me protegieron y me infundieron la impagable ternura en que vivo" (48).[14]

The Catholic Church-run school, whose value system is that of the landowning class it serves, stands as a microcosm of Andean society at large, and it is no wonder that Ernesto finds himself alienated in its oppressive atmosphere. Moreover, during the process of self-definition, the boy painfully feels a vast gulf between the world he longs for and the world he actually lives in. In spite of this, he is able to recharge himself emotionally by listening to Quechua music in the native quarter of the town, and by making trips into the countryside to renew his bonds with nature and his close friendship with the Pachachaca river: "¡Pachachaca! Puente sobre el mundo significa este nombre" (51).[15] These excursions become a

José María Arguedas and Vikram Chandra

magnificent vehicle for insights into Andean culture, for through them not only does the novel abound in observations on Quechua music, language, folklore and rituals, but conveys how magical-religious thought functions by showing it at work at the level of Ernesto's subjective experiences.

Music is a constant theme in Arguedas's fiction, regarded as a privileged space in which matter is transformed into meaning and emotion (Sales, "El intertexto musical quechua en el discurso narrativo de José María Arguedas: *Los Ríos Profundos, Haylli Taki*"). As William Rowe affirms, music functions as an indispensable element of Arguedas's vision of the world (114, 213). In the novel Ernesto's attachment to music is so intense that the boy wonders if the song of the *calandra* larks can be made of the same matter he is made of, and comes from the same widespread world of human beings he has been thrown into. At the same time, nature is understood as life itself. Indeed, Ernesto's relationship with music and his identification with the Pachachaca River provides some of the most beautiful passages in the book:

> Los ríos fueron siempre míos; los arbustos que crecen en la falda de las montañas, aun las casas de los pequeños pueblos, con su tejado rojo cruzado de rayas de cal, los campos azules de alfalfa, las adoradas pampas de maíz. Pero a la hora en que volvía de aquel patio al anochecer, se desprendía de mis ojos la maternal imagen del mundo. Y llegada la noche, la soledad, mi aislamiento, seguían creciendo. . . . Por eso, los días domingos, salía precipitadamente del Colegio, a recorrer los campos, a aturdirme con el fuego del valle. . . . A veces, podía llegar al río, tras varias horas de andar. Llegaba a él cuando más abrumado y doliente me sentía. Lo contemplaba, de pie sobre el releje del gran puente, apoyándome en una de las cruces de piedra que hay clavadas en lo alto de la columna central. El río, el Pachachaca temido, aparece en un recodo liso, por la base de un precipicio donde no crecen sino enredaderas de flor azul. . . . Yo no sabía si amaba más al puente o al río. Pero ambos despejaban mi alma, la inundaban de fortaleza y de heróicos sueños. Se borraban de mi mente todas las imágenes plañideras, las dudas y los malos recuerdos. . . . Durante muchos días después me sentía solo, firmemente aislado. Debía ser como el gran río: cruzar la tierra, cortar las rocas; pasar, indetenible y tranquilo, entre los bosques y montañas; y entrar al mar, acompañado por un gran pueblo de aves que cantarían desde la altura. . . . ¡Sí! Había que ser como ese río imperturbable y cristalino, como sus aguas vencedoras. ¡Como tú, río Pachachaca! ¡Hermoso caballo de crin brillante, indetenible y permanente, que

marcha por el más profundo camino terrestre!¹⁶ (68-71)

As Ernesto confusedly adapts to his new circumstances, his perspective is ambivalent. He is partially absorbed into white society, for though he feels he is different, he has inherited many of the attitudes of his class. His teachers and classmates embrace him mostly as one of their own, although he is sometimes referred to as "the little stranger" (87), "the fool" (47), or "the little Indian who looks white" (85). Furthermore, his experiences conspire to undermine his faith in indigenous values by calling into question their effectiveness in the world of the whites. Not only does he see the Quechua people marginalized and humiliated at every turn, but even the magical forces of nature seem to lose their power when they come into conflict with Western culture. In the latter part of the novel, however, a series of events occur that once again estranges Ernesto from the white world, forever consolidating his allegiance to the Quechua people. First the *chicheras* (female vendors of maize beer) challenge the established dominant social order by breaking into the government salt warehouses and distributing the contents among the poor. Then, following an outbreak of plague, the *colonos* (*hacienda* tenant laborers) shake off their servility and become mobilized. Believing the plague to be a supernatural being that can be destroyed only by religious means, they march on to town to demand that a special mass be said for them and force the authorities to comply with their wishes. In a triumphal climax, Ernesto and the Quechuas are able to convert their suffering into cultural resistance. In *Los Ríos Profundos*, the reader observes the emergence of a counter-hegemonic order represented by the *chicheras*, the *colonos*, Quechua music and rituals, and the Pachachaca River. These elements, ignored and marginalized by those who hold the power (the priest who is the school director, the owner of the farm property where the Quechua people work, the army that tries to repress the popular uprising), finally constitute a subversive paradigm, hegemonic in its own right.

The novel thus ends with a victory of the Andean population over the social order, a triumph that is paralleled on the internal plane by Ernesto's unreserved adherence to the Quechua ethos. His identification with the *chicheras* and the *colonos* against his own kind is much more than solidarity with the underprivileged, since his faith in the Quechua values he has been raised to live by depends on the outcome of the conflict between the two ways of life. In more than one sense, his personal salvation hinges on the ability of the Quechua people to assert the validity of their culture by asserting themselves socially. With the victory of the *colonos*, Ernesto's rooting is vindicated.

Nevertheless, the ending is somewhat problematic. Even if Ernesto appears to have resolved his inner conflict by embracing Quechua culture with complete faith in its effectiveness, he clearly faces a future full of tensions, since he must live by its values in the "alien" world of the whites.

The end may be regarded as the utopian vision of a dystopian reality. However, at the same time Ernesto's deep faith in Quechua culture reflects Arguedas's own confidence in the ability of that culture not only to survive, but, with increasing migration to the cities of the coast, to spread beyond its traditional geographical boundaries, to permeate and change the character of Peruvian society as a whole.

One of the most fascinating instances of Ernesto's bicultural existence, and of his profound affection for Quechua culture, comes when a classmate asks him to write a love letter for him because Ernesto has the reputation of writing like a poet. Ernesto starts writing for his friend, but suddenly the clash between the writing and the oral spheres makes him stop. He remembers the Quechua girls he liked and for whom writing would make no sense at all. The impossibility to express in written Spanish what he can only feel in oral Quechua becomes an insuperable abyss. At the end, in an emotional and painful moment, he decides to write the letter *in Quechua*, though in the novel, intended for Spanish-speaking audiences, it is fictionalized-translated into Spanish. Later, Ernesto will give the letter to his friend. And for that purpose, the letter will be already written in Spanish. It is thus assumed that Ernesto *needs* to express his feelings in Quechua. This is his only way to compose a love letter that he will later have to translate:

> Pero un descontento repentino, una especie de aguda vergüenza, hizo que interrumpiera la redacción de la carta. Apoyé mis brazos y la cabeza sobre la carpeta; con el rostro escondido me detuve a escuchar ese nuevo sentimiento. "¿Adónde vas, adónde vas? ¿Por qué no sigues? ¿Qué te asusta; quién ha cortado tu vuelo?" Después de estas preguntas, volví a escucharme ardientemente.
>
> "¿Y si ellas supieran leer? ¿Si a ellas pudiera yo escribirles?"
>
> Y ellas eran Justina o Jacinta, Malicacha o Felisa; que no tenían melena ni cerquillo, ni llevaban tul sobre los ojos. Sino trenzas negras, flores silvestres en la cinta del sombrero . . ." Si yo pudiera escribirles, mi amor brotaría como un río cristalino; mi carta podría ser como un canto que va por los cielos y llega a su destino". ¡Escribir! Escribir para ellas era inútil, inservible. "¡Anda; espéralas en los caminos, y canta! ¿Y, si fuera posible, si pudiera empezarse?" Y escribí:
>
> "Uyariy chay k'atik'niki siwar k'entita" . . .

Esta vez, mi propio llanto me detuvo. Felizmente, a esa hora, los internos jugaban en el patio interior y yo estaba solo en mi clase. No fue un llanto de pena ni de desesperación. Salí de la clase erguido, con un seguro orgullo; como cuando cruzaba a nado los ríos de enero cargados del agua más pesada y turbulenta.[17] (83-84)

Red Earth and Pouring Rain

Storytelling defines *Red Earth and Pouring Rain*, where fiction intermingles with both history and myth, and embraces diverse interpretations of the past history of India, as well as a contemporary road trip crisscrossing the United States. Abhay, back home in India after attending college in California, is the link between these separate worlds. Disturbed and alienated, he shoots and seriously wounds an old white-faced monkey which has been stealing food and clothes from his parents' garden for years. As a result of the wound, the monkey turns into a Brahmin poet named Sanjay. Deprived of human voice all the same, Sanjay the monkey uses a typewriter in order to communicate. Three praised Hindu deities arrive on the scene, Yama (king of the dead), Hanuman (ape-god protector of poets) and Ganesha (elephant-god of wisdom), and a vital contract is signed. Sanjay will live only if he is able to entertain an audience with his storytelling, which must be interwoven with the storytelling of Abhay and his parents, the retired teachers Ashok and Mrinalini Misra. All their voices, together with those of the many characters who inhabit the book, shape Chandra's multifaceted story of stories, spiraling across centuries, countries, cultures and feelings. As a sort of literary "zapping," the slippery interrelation between the stories is used as both a creative and critical practice, a strategy for communicating meaning across cultural boundaries. The interaction of the two main orally framed narrative branches, Sanjay's epic past and Abhay's postmodern road-movie present, subsume a meeting of languages, styles, values, and identities.

The cultural ethos and worldview of Chandra's novel clearly show his dislike of Western logic, with its tribute to self-interest and reason. This attitude is epitomized at one point by the criticism of Aristotle's *Poetics*, and, more specifically, of its insistence on emotional sameness and its clean and straight stipulations—so different from traditional Indian discourse where "narratives entwine and break into each other" (*Red Earth and Pouring Rain* 335). Indeed, the contrast between Aristotelian poetics and Indian aesthetics, Cartesian clarity and Indian curlicues, British rationalism and Indian mythological beliefs, and Western discipline and Indian meditation is a major subtext in the novel.

Sanjay is the persona who returns from the past, reincarnated as a monkey, in order to recount the history of India through the story of his own life and his brother's, Sikander, a soldier, at the tail end of the Mughal Empire (1526-1857) and the Indian Mutiny (1857-1859). Paradoxically, Sanjay returns to restore precisely what he lacks, a voice, which he acquires by composing his story in English, the tongue he paid so much to master. And each time he gives birth to a story, he scores a victory against Time. Thus, by reconstructing the past in the present and with an eye to the future, Chandra's text symbolically becomes a vehicle of timelessness. Moreover, Sanjay's endeavor embodies the tragic and painful process of learning the colonizer's tongue and its written transmission. For Sanjay, using the typewriter means, in fact, transcribing voice, with all its hues, tones and accents. For him, storytelling is life itself. The last words he pronounces during his human existence constitute an encouraging message in defense of cultural diversity and understanding:

> . . . you children of the future, you young men and women who will set us free, may you be happy, may you be faultless, may you be soft as a rose petal, as hard as thunder, may you be fearless, may you be forgiving, may you be clever and may you have unmoved faith, may you be Hindustani and Indian and English and everything else at the same time, may you be neither this nor that, may you be better than us, I bless you, may you be happy. (580)

Abhay's narrative, on the other hand, accounts for his experiences as an Indian student in the United States and introduces the contemporary view of a cosmopolitan migrant split between Indian and American cultural values. Noticing that his memory is fragmentary and feeling as if he were in a film and were expected somehow to react (57), Abhay considers his life a sort of broken mirror, "some of whose fragments have been irretrievably lost," as Rushdie puts it ("Imaginary Homelands" 11). Abhay's experiences in the U.S. are contradictory and somewhat dizzying. Subjected to a strictly monolithic version of history and culture that consistently misrepresents what he knows and feels to be skewed, Abhay senses while in the U.S. a bitterness he is not able to cope with, a strange feeling of loss that is evidently characteristic of his bicultural situation. In the following passage, we find an interesting moment when Abhay wants to react, to say something, but feels that words do not suffice. The picture he gives us is highly evocative:

> This feeling of being in a film hung over me even later, when I sat at the back of a classroom and listened to a fellow named Lin

talk about Asian revolutions. The British, he was saying, changed India for the better with their efficient railroads and efficient administration and so on, and for a moment I felt that I should be saying something, but then, sensing my face flush, full, somehow, of the realization that whatever I said wouldn't make any sense, would sound crazy, I opened a notebook and doodled instead, and at the end of the period I found that I had drawn birds and airplanes soaring across the page. (57)

Later, returning from abroad, Abhay becomes aware of the cultural features of his homeland and those traces that shaped him. He relearns his mother culture, which he finds essentially multiple.

Above all, Abhay rediscovers the importance of storytelling as a daily ritual that is part of life. In his confusing situation, Sanjay's return and lesson is a legacy of endurance and coherence. His encounter with Sanjay, and Sanjay's storytelling help to dissipate his existential confusion, and lead him to reembrace his culture, the meaning of his existence, his place in the world, and his personal *dharma*.[18] And so, in his voice, the storytelling circle starts again:

> I will tell you a story that will grow up like a lotus vine, that will twist in on itself and expand ceaselessly, till all of you are a part of it, and the gods come to listen, till we are all talking in a musical hubbub that contains the past, every moment of the present, and all the future. (617)

The novel also reflects the bicultural tension between the vernacular and English voices during colonial times, together with the clash between oral and written transmission. Literacy already existed in India before the Europeans' arrival; what the West brought to India was printing technology. In *Red Earth and Pouring Rain,* Sanjay and his brother Sikander are sent to Calcutta to become apprentices on the Markline Orient Press. There, by chance, Sanjay has to work on the printing of a book written by an English missionary,[19] who gives a false account of the death by immolation of Janvi, Sikander's mother. Confronted with this manipulation, Sanjay feels insulted and obtains a slightly modified duplication of the font used to print the book. He inserts into the English book a subversive message in Hindi that reads, in the author's own translation, as "This book destroys completely. This book is the true murderer" (354). When Markline tries to find the font, Sanjay literally swallows all the letters, which later on will be expelled from his body.

Sanjay learns in the course of his life what the power of transmission is and also the real value of speaking. Thus, "As the years passed, Sanjay wrote less and less; the act of putting words on paper became more and more a lie, an oppressive betrayal of life itself, and therefore one day he found himself unable to write at all" (454). In his human life, Sanjay acknowledges that although English is a necessary vehicle for communicating, it cannot substitute for his most beloved words, it is not his own:

> Sanjay moved his head, shut his eye, tried to speak, but found his throat blocked tightly by something as hard as metal; he did not know what it was he wanted to say but knew he couldn't say it, what was possible to say he couldn't say in English, how in English can one say roses, doomed love, chaste passion, my father my mother, their love which never spoke, pride, honour, what a man can live for and what a woman should die for, how in English can one say the cows' slow distant tinkle at sunset, the green weight of the trees after monsoon, dust of winnowing and women's songs, elegant shadow of a minar creeping across white marble, the patient goodness of people met at wayside, the enfolding trust of aunts and uncles and cousins, winter bonfires and fresh chapattis, in English all this, the true shape and contour of a nation's heart, all this is left unsaid and unspeakable and invisible, and so all Sanjay could say after all was: "Not." (344)

Later, Sanjay is on the verge of dying, after a tough fight against the British, in the wake of the Mutiny. But he needs to hold on to life, to gain immortality, mainly because he still has to fulfill his *dharma*. The deity Yama asks him for what is most holy and precious to him. In response, Sanjay opens his mouth, tears his tongue out by the roots, and offers it to Yama. In this way, literally and symbolically, Sanjay sacrifices his mother tongue in order to speak English; in other words, to be able to communicate with the colonizers on an equal basis. So, when he later travels to London, he speaks English *without a tongue*, painfully acknowledging that, "Vernacular is not a matter of tongue alone, a man had to die and leave behind his native earth to speak a new language" (553).

Red Earth and Pouring Rain is a novel about migrancy: about foreigners in India and Indians abroad. It is also much more. Indeed, as a literary genre, it is more than just a novel (as Chandra himself put it in a lecture entitled "Finding a Form" he gave in Spain in 2000). In this cultural narrative knot, Chandra unifies and unravels the threads that tell the (hi)story of India, past, present and future. According to Rushdie, the truest eye may now belong to the migrant's "double vision" ("Imaginary Homelands" 19), which is clearly depicted in *Red Earth and Pouring Rain*.

Its form, the way in which stories change and dive into each other, emerges from the flux of the traditional Indian epics,[20] the *Mahabharata* and the *Ramayana*,[21] Chandra's most beloved literary referents and the first stories he remembers absorbing, which his mother and aunts used to tell him when he was a child. This type of spiraling narrative, full of juxtapositions and unexpected meetings, is an ancient traditional Indian form in which storytelling displays a circling structure that consciously avoids linearity.

So, Chandra, emotionally attached to the Indian epics, follows this traditional form to tell modern versions of everyday life, to reflect the possibility of its survival in a transnational sphere, in spite of the spread of Western individualism and its values. His literary poetics is centrifugal, going from the inside towards the outside, from his own cultural forms to those with an international currency. The entire novel symbolizes the entanglement and knotting of cultures in our contemporary world. Its entwined texture is often as confusing and dizzying as jet lag or zapping, and as puzzling as the very experience of crossing cultures. But it is not really that complex. Mainly, it turns out to be a soft sensory journey into storytelling.

Components of Biculturalism: Western Rationality vs. Eastern Magic"?

I will now focus on a critical debate related to the works of Arguedas and Chandra, concerning the non-Western component of their fictions and the allegations that the latter may be "traditional," and therefore "inferior."

First of all, in my opinion no Latin American novel has come near the intensity with which Arguedas has portrayed the indigenous and bicultural people in *Los Ríos Profundos*, depicting their dual surroundings, profound knowledge of good and evil, tragic sense of life as beautiful and yet undermined by sorrow; and the deep love they feel for each other, for nature, and for the whole universe. In Arguedas's view, indigenous Andean culture is not a static reality; on the contrary, it is pregnant with ideas of change, hence in a process of continuous redefinition with regard to its complex relationships to tradition and modernity. Thus, the tendency to view Arguedas's world as an "archaic utopia," as Mario Vargas Llosa does (see his *La Utopía Arcaica: José María Arguedas y las Ficciones del Indigenismo* [The Archaic Utopia: José María Arguedas and the Fictions of Indigenism]), is erroneous and indefensible.

Arguedas read and interpreted modernity from within Andean cultural reality. In the view of many authoritative critics who have devoted their lives to the study of Arguedas's work (see, among others, the works of Columbus; Giménez Micó and José Antonio; Lienhard; Rama; Rowe;

and those gathered in Sandoval and Boschetto-Sandoval) and in my view as well (see Sales, "Identidad étnica, traducción cultural y oralidad en las narrativas de José María Arguedas y Vikram Chandra [Ethnic identity, cultural translation and orality in the narratives of José María Arguedas and Vikram Chandra]"; and "El intertexto musical quechua en el discurso narrativo de José María Arguedas: *Los ríos profundos, Haylli Taki* [The Quechua musical intertext in the narrative discourse of José María Arguedas: *Deep rivers, Haylli Taki*]"), Vargas Llosa's interpretation of Arguedas's life and fiction is too simplistic, mainly because he ignores the complexities of Arguedas's appropriation and use of Quechua knowledge and oral culture. Vargas Llosa sees Arguedas as a nostalgic Arcadian writer who innocently dreams of the return to an archaic Andean past, thus rejecting modernity and "progress." Indeed, Vargas Llosa seems to believe in a binary opposition between "modern" (rational) culture and "primitive" (mystical) culture. And so, in his viewpoint, despite a brilliant novel such as *Los Ríos Profundos*, Arguedas is ultimately a primitive and clumsy writer who represents the Andean world in an unrealistic utopian and mythical manner. Moreover, Vargas Llosa cannot assume that any "serious intellectual" would consider the Quechua oral tradition as a primary source for the construction of a modern and "good" Peruvian literary work. In his opinion, Arguedas writes intuitively, without relying on any sophisticated literary technique; thus he evidently "lacks" what only European and North-American novelists could have given him.

Clearly, Vargas Llosa's contention shows a narrow-minded vision of what literature and culture are. For him, the "primitive" Quechua culture cannot serve as the foundation of any "modern" literature. However, the major difference between what Vargas Llosa poses and what Arguedas really achieved is that while the former focuses his arguments on narrative technique, the latter was only concerned with feelings. What Arguedas did was to reject the notion that the knowledge embodied in Quechua oral culture—its music, rituals and myths—is inferior to, or less valuable than, the knowledge associated with writing and reading in the Western tradition. His conception of literature is, for critics and readers alike, a fascinating and profoundly precious legacy.

In the field of contemporary Indian literature written in English, there is a current debate somewhat different from Arguedas's case but certainly related to it. As Chandra himself explained in his "Finding a Form" lecture, there are Indian voices, such as those of Amit Chaudhuri and Pankaj Mishra, to name but two, who complain that certain postcolonial Indian authors, in order to depict "Indianness," choose to write in English. They also resort to "magical" subject matter and a non-linear narrative mode that conspires to avoid "real" India. These critics see magic as unreal and illogical, and as being constructed for exportation to the West. They plead instead for realism. To illustrate, Chaudhuri asserts that after the publication of Rushdie's *Midnight's Children* in 1980, Indian fiction in English edged out what Chaudhuri considers to be the "real" India, its indigenous languages and contemporary traditions. In Chaudhuri's opinion, a phenomenon has since emerged that conceptualizes both the postcolonial novel and Indian writing in English as texts in which multiplicity, polyphony, and propensity towards magic, fairy tales and fantasy are seen to be indicative of a non-Western mode of discourse and apprehension, with "Indianness" assigned only to that form. In his view, to "celebrate Indian writing simply as overblown, fantastic, lush and non-linear is to risk making it a figure for the subconscious, and to imply that what is ordinarily called thinking is alien to the Indian tradition— surely an old colonialist prejudice" (5-6). Chaudhuri finds that a close and fixed dichotomy was formed, which set thinking, morality, and reality in opposition to sub-consciousness, amorality and fantasy—conceptualized as defining elements of the "Indian" novel. He complains that "real" traditions, histories and languages have no presence in the hybrid post-*Midnight's Children* Indian novel in English, a sort of stereotype created for Western consumption.

In reply to this, Chandra retorts that there is much magic *and* much reality coexisting daily in contemporary India. As he puts it, "India *is* full of elephants and snakes and mysticism, and also cell phones and nuclear weapons and satellites" ("The Cult of Authenticity. India's Cultural Commissars Worship 'Indianness' Instead of Art" 197). Chandra knows that somehow we all live within our own mythologies and allegories; so, faced with rigid positions, he would ask, "how *real* is realism?"

Chandra acknowledges that one of his concerns in *Red Earth and Pouring Rain* was precisely the irony derived from the juxtaposition and interweaving of narratives and forms, both magical and real. For him, the sacred is present in everyday experience in many different ways. He also takes into account the tendency to melodrama in Indian popular culture. For him, popular culture and its multiple forms are very much alive and should not be considered as inferior (personal communication). Rachel Dwyer finds that Chandra belongs to a new generation of Indian writers who have a great affection for Hindi cinema, considering it as a cultural expression of emotion rather than as an object of parody. For Dwyer, this younger crop has a more complex understanding and acceptance of popular culture (105).

In *The True Story of the Novel* (1996) Margaret Anne Doody maintains that the conventionally assumed separation of Romance and Novel was an eighteenth-century product, England's solution for safeguarding the literary canon from anything "foreign" to the dual projects of imperialism and Enlightenment.[22] I believe that this break necessarily enforced a narrow definition of realism for the novel. Thus, what Ian Watt describes in *The Rise of the Novel* (1957; this edition 1972) is, in reality, the rise of the *English realistic* novel, not only of realism as the genre's hallmark but of the beginnings of "prescriptive realism" in the form. Thus realism, as traditionally posed by such "official" accounts as that of Watt's, is chiefly constructed around the notion of a congruent and unified individual subject, homogeneous and consistent, balanced and rational. From this angle critics could consider Chandra as a "primitive, fantastic" author, as Arguedas is in Vargas Llosa's view.

Conclusion

The debate regarding the fictional poetics of Arguedas and Chandra crudely posits their narratives as "magical" or "unrealistic" literature as opposed to "serious realism." This perspective has to do with the role of prescriptions in art; prescriptions that tend to be restrictions concerning the configuration and preservation of the academic canon, of a cohesive nationalistic identity, or of any other constriction that aims at controlling and selecting artistic production. This debate is also deeply rooted in the bicultural approach fostered in this chapter. While Arguedas and Chandra attach themselves, both emotionally and creatively, to popular culture (both past and present), Vargas Llosa and Chaudhuri anchor themselves in academic disquisitions and labels, and black-and-white definitions. In their opinion, Arguedas and Chandra cannot recount "real Peru" and "real India" by means of their "unrealistic" forms.

Emotionally, as a sign of the identity they deeply feel inside and defend as their own, Arguedas and Chandra attach themselves to certain features taken from their mother cultures. Quechua music and direct communication with nature are the traits that enable Arguedas to represent his indigenous identity. At the same time, the fictional re-elaboration and reshaping of the Indian storytelling tradition constitutes a chief element in Chandra's work. And yet, both Arguedas and Chandra assume the multiplicity of the worlds they inhabit, revealing an extraordinary cultural intertextuality in their fictions. They tell stories that challenge the formal criteria of the conventions of the novel as defined in the Western tradition,[23] and reshape it by virtue of their bicultural-multicultural experience. The main narrative levels of language, structure and worldview are created at the intersection of systems, as polysystem theory would aptly explain.[24]

In their works, strictly generic classifications collapse. Arguedas translated oral genres such as songs, tales and myths, as well as mythical uses of language, into the structure of literary genres such as the novel, the short story and the essay. Chandra's working idea is storytelling, the texture of the oral tradition of multiple stories, interspersing and completing each other, together with the Hindu worldview existing and persisting in Indian daily life, past and present. In their affections, there is obviously one culture, one language associated with intimate identity and the sense of belonging, that mother language-culture through which one sees and feels the world. And in fact, as seen in their fictions, their sense of cultural affiliation is deeply attached to their mother cultures. So, they are able to use Quechua and Hindu traditions as creative forces that reveal alternative ways of knowing. Their narratives show how possibilities arise for the intertwining of myth and history as forms of consciousness.

The respective commitments of Arguedas and Chandra to Quechua and Hindu sources and knowledge are both intellectual and emotional. Arguedas hoped that the cultural traumas of invasion and usurpation could be reassessed in new ways, opening up positive perspectives for the future of his beloved Peru. Hence, the importance of trying to find points where modern industrial technology and culture come together with magic, nature, and pre-industrialized culture. In Chandra's fiction one can always observe how Hindu principles (*dharma, karma*[25]) work through the lives of the characters, whether they live in colonial times or in the modern contemporary metropolis of Bombay. Tradition and modernity are not seen as irreconcilable.

Arguedas wanted to believe that out of the melting pot of Peru a new "Indianized" national culture would emerge. He was convinced that the Quechua people and culture could not only survive, but also become the foundation of an original and all-together national culture; that of a unified country where "all bloods" would have a voice, and those voices would be heard. More than thirty years after his death, the situation is still one of overt conflict and confrontation between those who rule and the silenced Quechua and *mestizo* communities. In India, the rise of strong nationalisms and critics' obsession with finding a "true" form to recount the country is starting to create discussions among Indians, due to the "anxiety of Indianness" among them. More than half a century after independence, it seems that this young democracy still has to learn to deal with its ancient diversity and cultural dynamics.

Ernesto, Sanjay and Abhay are interstitial characters living between two cultures and two languages, and as such they act as bridges between two worlds. Being aware of the fact that they are crossing borders, all three of them at times sense that they live in deterritorialized spaces and feel a deep sense of alienation. For them, the social process by means of which culture is learned and transmitted is an experience that is absolutely plural; an experience that may sometimes be damaging, but that is always cross-cultural, immersed as they are in a complex web of relationships. They have to learn to grow up while confronted with racism and force—their development involves the power of memory and its reconstructing component, sometimes healing and sometimes painful. In more than one sense, both *Los Ríos Profundos* and *Red Earth and Pouring Rain* are "rite of passage" novels that stop at the point of change, when a new stage is about to begin in the liminal characters' evolution and growth.

In my view, *Los Ríos Profundos* and *Red Earth and Pouring Rain* are peculiar instances of "resistance literature," in the sense propounded by Barbara Harlow. Not because they are engaged with a particular political ideology—quite the contrary. They defend absolute freedom of mind and spirit, being very much aware of the exploitation of knowledge by hegemonic forces interested in creating a distorted historical record. Their texts explore the multiplicity of cultural roots and the problems in cross-cultural communication. And both are able to overcome difficulties as they propose dialogic constructions of the self, by means of their counter-discourses and their defense of cross-fertilization. Always in touch with the wide ocean of historical, mythical, and personal memory, they espouse a dynamic reading of culture that fosters social process and mobility and promote transcultural modes of communication and living. In that sense, they are not only writing back to any center, but mainly *writing beyond*, towards a new future, perhaps towards the "universal garden of many-coloured flowers" imagined by Ngugi Wa Thiong'o (*Moving the Centre: The Struggle for Cultural Freedoms* 24).

Usually, biculturalism leads to a sort of dual conception, a kind of polarization hard to overcome, a cultural dichotomy. As Bharati Mukherjee felt in the colonial context of her childhood, "biculturalism was a fixed context between two cultures of opposing values: *ours* and *theirs*" (172). Yet, in a world where, "everywhere is so made up of everywhere else," as Pico Iyer, reminds us (11), what remains clear is that there is no return to a pristine origin. The task at hand would seem, therefore, to consist in striving for a "beyond," in going beyond fossilized discursive positions, traveling from one space to another, from one temporality to another. I suggest that the richness present in the writings of Arguedas and Chandra consists in their ability to go beyond. They live in a contact zone (Pratt 4) beyond borderlands, moving within the "bicultural context" on a journey of continuous discovery. Their gaze goes global, towards universalism.

Appendix

Transculturation

Ortiz

Transculturation, from the cultural reflection drawn by the Cuban thinker Fernando Ortiz on the anthropological sphere, and the application that the Uruguayan critic Ángel Rama carried out specifically referring to Latin American literature, is useful not only for Latin American processes, but also for those coming from many other spaces constituted after an intercultural-bicultural confluence: it is a meeting which subsumes interlinguistic (vernacular languages vs. colonization languages) and intersystemic contacts (oral cultures vs. written cultures). On the trail of a "cultural turn" that diverse disciplines manifest nowadays (literary theory, comparative literature, linguistic studies, communication studies, translation studies, etc.), I consider that transculturation does not only help as a rich descriptive frame; above all, it can also become a sound theoretical and critical basis in the field of comparative literary criticism.

Ortiz questioned the term *acculturation* because, in his view, it failed to account for the complexity of the process of cultural convergence and change in Cuba in particular, and all of Latin America in general. In these contexts, culture was not only being modified by external input, but also lost. Moreover, and above all, new cultural phenomena were being created. Thus, in 1940, Ortiz proposed the alternative of *transculturation* in order to try to account for the complexity of cultural contact and emphasize not only the outcome of that junction, but the process by means of which it modifies one or both of the cultures in touch.

The concept was introduced into the English-speaking criticism, mainly postcolonial criticism, by means of Gustavo Pérez Firmat's *The Cuban Condition: Translation and Identity in Modern Cuban Literature* (1989); and more widely, by Pratt's *Imperial Eyes: Travel Writing and Transculturation* (1992), an insightful study on travel writing as an ideological apparatus of empire.

Transculturation enhances the reciprocal effect of the process of interaction, showing that it is a two-way path that, moreover, can result in new creations. Hybridization could be one of the characteristics deriving from that process, but it is not the chief feature of the process itself. Transculturation is certainly related to mixing, but it is mainly a communicative dynamic that helps going beyond the polarized dialectics between the dominant culture and the dominated one, the global and the local, acting as a bridge between them.

Rama

Re-reading Ortiz in order to develop the notion of narrative transculturation in the large space of Latin American fiction, Rama recovered and rethought the concept of transculturation in *Transculturación Narrativa en América Latina* (Narrative Transculturation in Latin America, 1982). From an anthropological conception of literature, Rama applies Ortiz's reflections creatively by taking as center of analysis what he names *"regionalistas plásticos"* (plastic regionalists), authors who truly achieved an anthropological and aesthetic success: writers such as Arguedas (Rama's central focus, being regarded as the chief representative of narrative transculturation), Juan Rulfo, Augusto Roa Bastos, Gabriel García Márquez and Joao Guimarâes Rosa, who—in different degrees—revitalized the inner culture of their region with their narration. And yet, Rama also considered the cosmopolitan transculturation of authors such as Juan José Arreola, Jorge Luis Borges, and Julio Cortázar.[26] A very relevant point is the fact that the Uruguayan critic already introduces into this intercultural sphere the notion of *resistance* to any asymmetrical relationship, when he stresses that the concept of transculturation, "revela resistencia a considerar la cultura propia, tradicional, que recibe el impacto externo que habrá de modificarla, como una entidad meramente pasiva o incluso inferior, destinada a las mayores pérdidas, sin ninguna clase de respuesta creadora"[27] (Rama 33).

Rama emphasizes the creative force implied in the transitivity between cultures, even when these hold dissimilar power positions: he believes that the form that springs out of an intercultural encounter, the transcultured one, is not only a sum of different elements, nor an imposition that deletes all the own features that define a dominated culture. Because there is originality in that form, certain independence, freedom, a new phenomenon, a creation, Rama assumes that the transcultural process is related to a selective and inventive ability, part of the neoculturation posed by Ortiz, to a capacity to work with both cultural worlds at the same time. In this sense, there will be losses, selections, rediscoveries and new formations. In his study, Rama analyses these transcultural deals in the areas he considers to be the main levels in the literary process: language, narrative structure and worldview.

Bhabha

Above all, transculturation shows its main interest in, and attracts attention to, the *process* of "culturation." It goes beyond the diverse consequences (e.g., loss, displacement, adaptation, syncretism, and hybridity) of the evolution that the process brings about. This is related to a necessary and helpful conception of culture as a living, malleable and active entity, and not of culture as either a static model or monolithic fetish. Moreover, the transcultural identity is not predicated upon the idea of the disappearance of independent cultural traditions, but rather on their continual and mutual development: some features are lost, and some others are gained, producing new forms even as older ones continue to exist.

Transculturation is a hybrid process that is constantly reshaping and replenishing itself. In this sense, I would associate it with Homi Bhabha's concept of "in-betweenness"—the powerful reassessment of the creative potentialities of the liminal spaces. In his reflections on culture and cultural criticism, Bhabha posits the relevance of hybrid cultural spaces, as well as the emergence of the interstices. He views culture as a site in permanent transition, where the inscription and articulation of in-between, interstitial passages in the middle of fixed identifications open up both the possibility of a cultural hybridity able to deal with difference and multiplicity, and the representation, without any assumed or imposed hierarchy, of this cultural hybridity. The main idea in Bhabha's contention, which is also the core of the concept of transculturation, could be summed up in his following statement: "we should remember that it is the 'inter'—the cutting edge of translation and negotiation, the *in-between* space—that carries the burden of the meaning of culture. . . . And by exploring this third space, we may elude the politics of polarity and emerge as the others of our selves" (*The Location of Culture* 38-39).

The Polysystem Theory

An interesting theoretical frame for the understanding of bicultural and/or transcultural literatures is provided by the "polysystem" theory developed by the Israeli theorist and critic Itamar Even-Zohar. Given the current intensity of the debate, the rapid developments, and hegemonic position of contemporary literary critical theory in the West, I believe that it is indeed important to examine the applicability of the theoretical structures and modalities outside the cultural tradition that produced them. In this respect, the advantage afforded by the Polysystem theory lies in its descriptive (and not prescriptive) semiotic nature, very useful for any cross-cultural reading.

According to the Polysystem theory, closely related to the dynamic functionalism of the Russian formalists (in their last stage) and the cultural semiotics of the Tartu School headed by Iuri Lotman, literature is not conceived as an isolated activity in society, regulated by laws inherently different from all the rest of human activities, but as an integral, often central and very powerful factor within the larger polysystem of the social and cultural context. Literature is basically understood as a dynamic, functional, stratified, open, semiotic system that is perceived as having the form of an institution. This literary polysystem, a system of systems, is structured by a network of main oppositions, such as primary vs. secondary literature, canonized or official vs. marginalized strata, and center vs. periphery. In this context, interference can be defined as a relationship between literatures or literary systems, whereby a certain literature may become a source of direct or indirect loans for another one.

However, borders are always moving, not only within systems, but also and mainly between them, as it is the case with transculturation. Thus, concerning literary production in general and cultural situations in particular, the polysystemic view allows us to understand, for instance, how, the successive concepts of literature are elaborated and how the genres, forms and models are constituted. The polysystemic view considers that there is a vast multiplicity of intersections between systems, and that it aims mainly to observe and account for them.

Taking into account that colonization in literature may be seen as the imposition of norms and models, the polysystemic viewpoint clarifies how cross-cultural/bicultural literatures, being installed at the intersection of literary systems, from East and West, re-adapt forms and genres. Within the transcultural polysystem, any polarization of periphery and center is rejected, replaced by a transfer dialogue that is literally and figuratively boundless with reference to both time and space. Surrounded by an intercultural reality, interference seems unavoidable. As Karl Kroeber believes, narrative has been the primary means by which most societies have defined themselves (3). And narrative is also the primary means by which socio-cultural boundaries may be crossed. So, the polysystemic theory reveals its usefulness regarding the exploration and study of the cultural dynamics in multicultural and multilingual societies, where, most times, the very opposition between central and peripheral, official and unofficial, colonizer and colonized represents the generative force of literature and culture. Even-Zohar argues that literary systems differ from culture to culture; thus, intersystemic interactions are also intercultural, and the transfer between systems enters into the realm of transculturation.

To conclude, transculturation, the in-between third space, and the transfer of intersystemic dynamics emerge as productive critical concepts for the borderline experience of intercultural contact, both in life and in fiction, where the negotiation of differences, sometimes incommensurable, creates a complex tension that could also grow into a strategy of cultural survival: beyond polarizations, against the grain of the rhetoric of binarism, from a creative in-between transcultural intersystemic space of communicative bridging.

Notes

[1] First of all, I would like to express my deepest affection to Vikram Chandra, for his absolute generosity; all my gratitude to Gönül Pultar, for believing in this work and offering very useful suggestions, and María Jesús Martínez Alfaro, a sincere friend who provides me with interesting information and better conversation. Thanks to all of them. Also, these pages are dedicated to José María Arguedas, very much alive in the hearts of his readers.

The research carried out for this essay was financed by the Generalitat Valenciana, Spain. FPI00-07-210.

[2] José María Arguedas Altamirano was born in the southern Andean town of Andahuaylas, to Víctor Manuel Arguedas, an itinerant lawyer from Cuzco, and Victoria Altamirano, a lady from a distinguished upper-class family; and was introduced into a world shaped at the crossroads of modernization's thrust into Peru. He painfully lived from within the basic cultural dichotomy of the country: indigenous versus non-indigenous languages and cultures.

As a young boy, he accompanied his father on many travels through diverse towns in the southern Peruvian Andes, and would later portray its landscape and people in a powerful language, displaying their lyrical and magical-mythical visions of the world. When his mother died in 1914, Arguedas was only three years old. That event shaped his life, forever. In fact, Arguedas always recalled that he was the product of his stepmother, who hated and despised him as much as "her" Indians, and so decided that he should live with them. Thus, he spent his childhood largely at his stepmother's *hacienda* (farm property) among the indigenous servants who cared for him with the greatest tenderness and love. Quechua, he always claimed, was his native-mother language; and not only as a child but as an adult also, he saw the world from the Quechua magical and mythical viewpoint. Thus, the indelible scars of hate (on the side of his stepmother) and love (from the Quechua people who brought him up) would motivate his coming to terms with reality and creativity in a never-ending struggle with language; a struggle that, indeed, embodies his very life.

Arguedas was born white but was sentimentally Indian. His heart, soul and mind were Quechua; only his physical appearance and social position were white and Western. The fact that he was not born into that Quechua world to which he felt he deeply belonged by emotional attachment was a source of constant suffering. That frustration would later grow up into the aching acknowledgement that the dream of rescuing his beloved Andean world and culture through the creation of a national *mestizo* project was doomed. He loved the Quechua world, its language, culture, myths, rituals, with absolute *warma kuyay* (Quechua expression referring to child's love). Thus he dedicated his entire life to creating a bridge between those opposed worlds that coexisted within himself. He studied literature and anthropology at San Marcos University in Lima, and later became a professor of Quechua and ethnic studies there. As novelist, storyteller, poet, folklorist, ethnographer and educator, Arguedas wrote extensively. And yet, he never considered himself to be a professional writer—he saw his writing as the very embodiment of his life, and as a means of portraying the reality he knew, lived and suffered.

Arguedas wrote as a spokesman of the indigenous Quechua-speaking Andean world, setting out to correct the distorted stereotyped image of the Indian presented by earlier fiction. Though his own portrayal is somehow still the view of an outsider, being a Spanish-written work for a non-indigenous public, it offers a deep insight into the Quechua mentality, deeper than anything published before. The reader is shown that the basis of Quechua culture is a magical-religious view of the world that regards the earth not merely as something to be conquered and exploited, but as a unified cosmic order animated by supernatural forces and linked in a universal harmony. In his early fiction Arguedas's success in communicating that worldview was somehow restricted by his continuing reliance on a conventional realist manner. Moreover, in his first writings he portrayed a closed rural sphere. But from *Los Ríos Profundos* (1958, translated into English as *Deep Rivers* [1978]) onwards, he evolved a more effective lyrical-magical style. Artistically, too, he faced the problem of translating into the alien medium of Spanish the sensibility of people who express themselves in Quechua. His initial solution was to modify Spanish in such a way as to incorporate the basic features of Quechua syntax and thus reproduce something of the special character of indigenous speech. But these experiments were only partially successful, so subsequently he opted for a correct Spanish skillfully reshaped to convey Andean thought-patterns: "Yo, ahora, tras dieciocho años de esfuerzos, estoy intentando una traducción castellana de los diálogos de los indios (I am, now, after eighteen years of efforts, trying a Spanish translation of the Indians' dialogues)" ("La novela y el problema de la expresión literaria en el Perú" 16, my translation).

In terms of location, Arguedas's work evolves from the small indigenous communities, villages and towns of the Andes, to more complex geocultural spheres, as shown by the spatial and narrative distance that goes from *Agua* (Water, 1935) to the posthumous *El Zorro de Arriba y El Zorro de Abajo* (The Fox from Above and the Fox from Below, 1971). In the stories of *Agua* and the short novel *Diamantes y Pedernales* (Diamonds and Flint, 1954), the universe is perceived as an unavoidable dichotomy; in *Yawar Fiesta* (Yawar Feast, 1941) and *Los Ríos Profundos* (Deep Rivers, 1958), the Andean rural world is seen as opposed to the coastal white cities, but they are dialogically related; in *Todas las Sangres* (All the Bloods, 1964) and *El Zorro de Arriba y el Zorro de Abajo* Arguedas echoes the painful, contradictory and absolutely necessary approach between these two worlds.

[3] The essays collected by Sandoval and Boschetto-Sandoval are part of this new stage in the research on Arguedas's work, revisiting his writings from diverse, and recent theoretical and critical methodologies.

[4] Born in New Delhi, Vikram Chandra completed most of his secondary education at Mayo College, a boarding school located in Ajmer, Rajasthan, a desert state in the north-west of India and the traditional home of the Rajput warrior

clans. After a short stay at St. Xavier's College in Bombay, Vikram went to the United States. There, he graduated from Pomona College, in Claremont (near Los Angeles), in 1984 with a *magna cum laude* BA in English, specializing in creative writing. Then, he attended the Film School at Columbia University in New York. In the Columbia University library he chanced upon the autobiography of Colonel James "Sikander" Skinner, a legendary nineteenth-century soldier, half-Indian and half-British. When he read the translated version of Sikander's autobiography, originally written in Persian, he began to consider "the large interpolations and excisions made by the translator" (personal communication, 17 September 1999). The deep and reflexive reading of this book became the true inspiration for Vikram's first novel, *Red Earth and Pouring Rain* (1995). He left film school halfway to begin work on the novel. But art was not unknown to Vikram, who was deeply influenced by his mother's passion for writing. Of her, Kamna Chandra, a successful screenplay writer in the Indian film industry, Vikram would state that he could not remember a time when she was not creating.

Red Earth and Pouring Rain was composed over six years. During that time, Vikram supported himself on the writing programs at two American universities, working with well-known North-American contemporary authors: John Barth at Johns Hopkins University, where Vikram obtained an MA, and Donald Barthelme at the University of Houston, where he received an MFA. While writing his novel, Vikram taught literature and writing, and also worked independently as a computer programmer and software and hardware consultant. His diverse clients included oil companies, non-profit organizations and the Houston Zoo. Finally, *Red Earth and Pouring Rain* was published in 1995 by Penguin/India in India, Faber and Faber in the United Kingdom, and Little, Brown in the United States. It was received with outstanding critical acclaim and was awarded the *David Higham Prize for Fiction* and the *Commonwealth Writers Prize for the Best First Published Book* in 1996.

Chandra's second work, a collection of short-stories, *Love and Longing in Bombay*, was released in 1997, by the same three publishing houses that had published his novel. Two of these stories first appeared in the *Paris Review* and *The New Yorker*: "Dharma" in *The Paris Review* (1994), which won the Discovery Prize in 1994, and "Shakti" in *The New Yorker* (1994/1995). The book won the *Commonwealth Prize for the Best Book for the Eurasian Region* in 1998. This brilliant collection is a tribute to the multilayered beauty of Bombay, old and new, its peoples, its stories. As in Chandra's first work, the five stories gathered here are linked by a powerful oral storytelling frame (see Sales, "*Love and Longing in Bombay*, by Vikram Chandra: Forever Listening"). In *Love and Longing in Bombay*, Chandra leaves behind the anticolonial core and intercultural encounters of his novel and centers on present-day Indian reality and underworlds, starring Bombay, his own city, India's financial and commercial centre.

At the moment, Chandra spends his time shuttling between Bombay, his home, where he writes, and Washington, DC, where he teaches creative writing at George Washington University. He is working on his third book, a new novel, a detective story about cops and gangsters, initially set in Bombay. As a sort of foretaste, in a special issue of *The New Yorker* (June 23 and 30, 1997) he has already published "Eternal Don," which will be the first chapter of his forthcoming work.

Furthermore, he continues to nurture one of his most beloved projects: writing a film script, because cinema is a very well-known world for him, coming from a filmmaking family of producers, directors and script-writers. His film background is a starting point one should never forget in looking at his work.

[5] The novel *Red Earth and Pouring Rain* (1995); and the collection of stories *Love and Longing in Bombay* (1997).

[6] He has been included in the volume compiled by R. K. Dhawan in order to celebrate post-independence Indian writing (see in that volume Das; and Sales, "Vikram Chandra's Transcultural Narrative: *Red Earth and Pouring Rain*, Much More Than a Novel"; and "Vikram Chandra's *Love and Longing in Bombay*: The Order of Emotion"; and "Vikram Chandra's Constant Journey: Swallowing the World").

[7] The distances between Arguedas and Chandra bring an enriching flavor to the field of intercultural comparative literature (see Sales, *Identidad étnica, traducción cultural y oralidad en las narrativas de José María Arguedas y Vikram Chandra* [Ethnic identity, cultural translation and orality in the narratives of José María Arguedas and Vikram Chandra]). Delving into the field of comparative literature is, above all, an act of freedom. And this feeling becomes more intense when the work material is intercultural, as posed by, among others, Bassnett, *Comparative Literature: A Critical Introduction*; Miner; and Mohan.

[8] The concept originally comes from the anthropological studies developed in Cuba by Fernando Ortiz, being later applied to literary studies by Ángel Rama. See the appendix for an extended discussion of transculturation.

[9] "To realize oneself, to translate oneself, to transform a seemingly alien language into a legitimate and diaphanous torrent, to communicate to the almost foreign language the stuff of which our spirit is made. That is the hard, the difficult question" (my translation).

[10] It's a question of not losing one's soul, of not transforming oneself wholly in this long and slow endeavor! I know that something gets lost in exchange for what is gained. But the concern, the watchfulness, the work aim at preserving the essence (my translation).

[11] So far, the best study on Arguedas's literary language is that of Alberto Escobar.

[12] A "ghazal" is the same as a *gazel*. See the note on that term in chapter three. Editor's note.

[13] It would be worthwhile to analyse comparatively Arguedas's novel and Meera Syal's *Anita and Me* (1996), which is also the account of a bicultural formation, the portrait of a childhood caught in the clash between two cultures. The main difference, very interesting for comparative-contrastive purposes, is that Syal's tone is comic and funny — and does not cover at all either the seriousness of the topic or the pain of some of the experiences. Other novels of interest dealing with the subject of growing up in a bicultural-multicultural context are, for instance, Maxine Hong Kingston's *The Woman Warrior* (1976) taking place in the U.S., and Hanif Kureishi's *The Buddha of Suburbia* (1990) taking place in the U.K. All these texts, very different in substance and concern, explore how children confront the fact of being bicultural and having to face ethnic stereotyping.

[14] "The family chiefs and the older women, the *mamakunas* of the community,

protected me and instilled in me that kindness in which I live and which I can never repay" (*Deep Rivers* 42).

For the translations (of the quotations) in English I use *Deep Rivers* (1978), the published English translation of Arguedas's novel, though, as John C. Landreau indicates, it is sometimes inadequate (108). Landreau is a reliable voice on this score, precisely because he has carried out for years a study of the issue of translation in Arguedas's work.

Before writing this chapter, I had only worked with the original text, and certainly I myself have noticed shortcomings in Frances Horning Barraclough's translation, but have finally opted to use it because it is the version English-speaking readers have access to. In any case, I provide my own translation where no published English version is found.

[15] "Pachachaca! Bridge over the world is the meaning of this name" (*Deep Rivers* 44).

[16] The rivers were always mine, the bushes that grew on the mountain slopes, the village houses with their red roofs streaked with lime, the blue fields of alfalfa, the beloved valleys filled with maize. But at the time I'd return from the courtyard, at dusk, this maternal image of the world would fall from my eyes. And at nightfall my feelings of loneliness and isolation grew more intense. . . . That was why I dashed out of school on Sundays to go walking through the fields until I'd become dazed by the fiery heat of the valley. . . . Sometimes I managed, after hours of walking, to reach the river. I would come to it just as I was feeling sore and exhausted, and would contemplate it as I stood on the side of the great bridge, leaning against one of the stone crosses that are set up on top of the central pillars. A smooth bend of the river, the awesome Pachachaca, appeared before me, winding round the base of a cliff on which only blue-flowered vines were growing. . . . I didn't know if I loved the river or the bridge more. But both of them cleansed my soul, flooding it with courage and heroic dreams. All of the mournful images, doubts, and evil memories were erased from my mind. . . . For many days afterward I felt alone, completely isolated. I felt I should be like the great river, crossing the land, cutting through the rocks, undetainably and serenely flowing through mountains and forests, and entering the sea accompanied by a huge nation of birds that sang from the heavens. . . . Yes! I must be like that clear imperturbable river, like its conquering waters. Like you, Pachachaca! Handsome, glossy-maned steed, who runs undetainably and unceasingly along the deepest earthly roads! (*Deep Rivers* 60-63).

[17] But a sudden discontent, an intense feeling of shame, made me interrupt the writing of the letter. I laid my arms and head down on the desk; with my face hidden, I paused to listen to those new feelings. "Where are you going, where are you going? Why don't you continue? What has frightened you; who has cut short your flight?" After asking these questions I went back to listening to myself eagerly. "And what if they knew how to read? What if I could write to them?"

And they were Justina, or Jacinta, Malicacha, or Felisa, who had neither long hair nor bangs, nor wore tulle over their eyes. Only black braids, and wildflowers in the bands of their hats... "If I could write to them my love would flow like a clear river; my letter could be like a song that goes through the sky to reach its destination" Writing! Writing for them was useless, futile. "Go; wait for them on the

roads and sing! But what if it were possible, if it could be started?" And I wrote:
"*Uyariy chay k'atik'niki siwar k'entita*"...
This time my own sobbing made me pause. Fortunately, at that hour the boarding students were playing in the inner courtyard and I was alone in my classroom. I wept from neither sorrow nor despair. I left the classroom erect, with a certain pride; as proudly as I had swum across the rivers in January, when they are laden with the heaviest, most turbulent waters. (*Deep Rivers* 74-75)

[18] *Dharma* is a Sanskrit word denoting (besides the teachings of the Buddha), "the principle or law that orders the universe," and "individual conduct in conformity with this principle," as well as "the essential function or nature of a thing," in both Buddhism and Hinduism; and "individual obligation with respect to caste, social custom, civil law, and sacred law," in Hinduism (*The American Heritage Dictionary of the English Language*). Editor's note.

[19] This (fictional) book, written by (the fictional) Reverend Francis M.A. Sarthey, is entitled *The Manners, Customs, and Rituals of the Natives of Hindoostan: Being Chiefly an Account of the Journeys of a Christian Through the Lands of the Hindoo, and his Appeal to all Concerned Believers*.
The significance of travel writing as a subjective production of empire has been put forward by Mary Louise Pratt in *Imperial Eyes: Travel Writing and Transculturation* (1992).

[20] As an introduction to the great Indian epics, see the overviews provided in Blackburn *et al.*; Dimock *et al.*; and Nayak.

[21] For the texts of these national epics, see e.g. Rajagopalchari for the *Mahabharata*; and *The Ramayana of Valmiki*. Editor's note.

[22] At this point it may be also interesting to consult Firdous Azim, who provides a powerful feminist and anti-imperialist account of the development of the novel, a perspective that has been traditionally silenced.

[23] It is worth mentioning that Doody's study redefines the novel as a multicultural form whose origins could be traced back not only in Europe, but also in Africa and Asia.

[24] See the appendix for a discussion of this concept.

[25] *Karma* is a Sanskrit word, and a "basic concept common to Hinduism, Buddhism, and Jainism. The doctrine of karma states that one's state in this life is a result of actions (both physical and mental) in past incarnations, and action in this life can determine one's destiny in future incarnations (*The Columbia Encyclopedia*). Editor's note.

[26] I would like to underscore the fact that the two trends of transculturation, descriptively named "regionalist" and "cosmopolitan," are not opposed paths, but complementary projects that are dialogically interrelated.

[27] "[I]t is resistant to the consideration that one's own culture, the traditional one, that which receives an external impact that will modify it, is just a passive or even an inferior entity, destined to the greatest losses, without any kind of creative response" (my translation).

7
From Hybrid Original to Shona Translation
How *A Grain of Wheat* Becomes *Tsanga Yembeu*

Katrina Daly Thompson

Introduction

One of the most prevalent issues in African literary studies today is what is known as the "problem of language": which languages should African writers use, colonial or indigenous ones? Perhaps the most famous answer to this question is the one put forth by Kenyan author Ngugi wa Thiong'o in his 1981 *Decolonising the Mind* (this edition 1994, all page references are to this edition):

> The existence and the continuing growth of poetry [read: literature] in African languages, clearly and unequivocally so in orature (oral literature), make it manifestly absurd to talk of African poetry in English, French or Portuguese. Afro-European poetry, yes; but not to be confused with African poetry which is the poetry composed by Africans in African languages. (87)

Accordingly, Ngugi himself, initially an English-language author, switched mid-career to Gikuyu.

Yet more important than Ngugi's decision to write in an African language was his recognition of the role translation plays in facilitating intercultural communication in Africa. After writing his first Gikuyu novel, *Caitaani Mūtharabainī* (1980), Ngugi translated it into English as *Devil on the Cross* (1982), and saw it translated into Swedish, Norwegian and German. For him, however,

> more important has been the translation of the novel into Kiswahili under the title *Shetani Msalabani* [1982], a direct communication

between Gikuyu and Swahili languages. Indeed I see this kind of communication between African languages as forming the real foundation of a genuinely African novel. A novel originally written in Ibo could find itself translated into Yoruba and vice versa. A novel written in Dholuo or Maasai could find itself translated into two or three or more Kenyan languages or into African languages outside Kenya. There would thus be a real dialogue between the literatures, languages and cultures of the different nationalities within any one country—forming the foundation of a truly national literature and culture, a truly national sensibility. Within Africa as a whole there would be the foundation of a truly African sensibility in the written arts. This will also have the added effect of enhancing the art of translation, which would be studied in schools and colleges (another career open to graduates!), and this necessarily would mean more rigorous and committed study of African languages. Each thing will be feeding on every other thing, in a dialectical sense, to create a progressive movement in the African novel and literature. (*Decolonising the Mind* 84-85)

I quote Ngugi at length here not only because I share his enthusiasm for African languages and for translation, but also because in this passage he unwittingly positions translation as the very solution to the problem of language choice in African literature.

In 1987, Charles Mungoshi, a Zimbabwean playwright, poet, novelist and short story writer, translated Ngugi's English-language 1967 novel *A Grain of Wheat* (*AGW*; this edition 1986, all page references are to this edition) into Shona, the language of 80 percent of Zimbabweans, creating a new text called *Tsanga Yembeu* (*TY*).[1] Mungoshi's decision to translate a text by Ngugi reflects a deliberate attempt on his part to realize Ngugi's vision of an African literary scene founded upon African languages and cultural interchange, bringing African literature to African people through African languages.

In comparing the two texts in this chapter, I reconstruct the translation strategies Mungoshi uses to transfer aspects of culture from English, Swahili and Gikuyu (in Ngugi's text) into Shona. I argue that through creative translation strategies, Mungoshi transforms a multicultural text (English, Swahili and Gikuyu) into a mono-cultural (Shona) one. I go on to argue that Mungoshi's translation strategies may be fruitfully understood through my conception of the "trickster translator," which draws upon the trickster figure of African and world folklore. The idea of the trickster translator is especially relevant to the relationship between colonial and colonized languages. Since most postcolonial literature in English can be conceived of as bicultural or multicultural, it is interesting to see what happens when such a text is translated by a trickster translator who upends the relationship between the two (or more) cultures at hand.

Translation as a Meeting Ground of Cultures

Much of the existing literature on translation includes prescriptive rules about translating, and it is those prescriptions that a translator must balance with his/her personal strategies when transferring a text from one language to another. Gideon Toury demonstrates that even when a translator does not study these rules explicitly, s/he is aware of the translation norms of his/her culture that influence—and are influenced by—theory (53-69).

A review of the literature reveals an emphasis on prescribing fidelity (or mimesis) over creativity for translations of African literature into European languages—but not for translations in the opposite direction, i.e. the translation of European literature into African languages. Translation theorists who work with African texts tend to privilege fidelity and respect for the source text over originality and the creation of a new text in the target language, and this bias is evident in the terminology they use. For example, Paul Bandia dubs the respective strategies *source-text oriented* or *hypertextual* translation on the one hand, and *ethnocentric* translation on the other (58). By *hypertextual*, he means a translation such as the one Anthony Appiah describes as *thick translation*, which is "translation that seeks with its annotations and its accompanying glosses to locate the text in a rich cultural and linguistic context" (Appiah, "Thick Translation" 817). In place of *fidelity* and *originality*, Philip A. Noss applies the terms *foreignizing* and *domesticizing* (269), using African ideophones[2] as his textual examples:

> Will the ideophone be brought to the reader, that is, will its meaning be communicated according to the generic constraints of the receptor literary tradition? Or will the reader be brought to the ideophone in the hope that through the foreign element of the ideophone, he/she will not only decipher the meaning but will in a small way encounter the literary and cultural context of the source language expression? (270)

Because Bandia, Appiah and Noss work primarily with translations intended for "Western" readers, they privilege the cultural richness of their African source texts. All three want to ensure that African texts, even those originally written in French such as those with which Bandia works, do not get absorbed into the hegemonic English language and lose their (multiple) African identities. Gayatri Chakravorty Spivak, although she works with Indian rather than African languages, expresses the same concern in "The Politics of Translation":

> In the act of wholesale translation into English there can be a betrayal of the democratic ideal into the law of the strongest. This happens when all the literature of the Third World gets translated into a sort of with-it translatese, so that the literature by a woman in Palestine begins to resemble, in the feel of its prose, something by a man in Taiwan. (182)

Respect and concern for the status of the source texts is understandably important when translating from the language of the colonized to the language of the colonizer. Bandia, Appiah, Noss, Spivak and others seem to agree that, as Mary Snell-Hornby puts it, "the original function of the source text in its culture" should be preserved (qtd. in Bandia 57). That this should be so was especially important in the (recent) past when "translation was . . . a one-way process, with texts being translated *into* European languages for European consumption rather than as part of a reciprocal process of exchange" (Bassnett and Trivedi, "Introduction: Of Colonies, Cannibals, and Vernaculars" 5; emphasis theirs).

In bringing ideas from one language into another and thereby creating new metaphors, the translator transforms his/her culture. When the flow of ideas is, however, from colonial culture and language to colonized culture and language, a movement that already threatens African languages and cultures, a translator whose agenda is to preserve the cultural richness of African texts must proceed with caution. "The fact that . . . translation mixes two or more cultures . . . implies an unstable balance of power, a balance which will depend to a great extent on the relative weight of the exporting culture as it is felt in the receiving culture," writes Javier Franco Aixelá (52). The translator is thus placed in the ambiguous role of having to decide which aspects of the foreign culture s/he is to invite into the target one. Susan Bassnett suggests that, "if literature belongs to a nation, then in certain circumstances translation can be perceived as a theft, as a violation of the right of a language to keep its own literature to itself" ("The Meek or the Mighty: Reappraising the Role of the Translator" 13). Viewed in this way, the African translator who translates *into* an African language can be seen as a thief, a Robin Hood who steals from the colonizer. But it must be remembered that Africans had European literature forced on them in school during colonialism, and that in many African countries a Europhone educational system continues today. So, rather than simply "stealing" European literature by importing it into Africa, an action that would only be complicit with the current "Western" focus of the book market, both local and global, a culture may utilize translators in order to "import" European literature. Providing an example from Kenya, where readers have largely accepted as Swahili literature Julius Nyerere's Swahili translations of Shakespeare's plays, Alamin M. Mazrui writes that "[a] translator could be a kind of 'linguistic guerrilla' capable of bringing new literary gains to Third World peoples engaged in cultural battles against the imperialist North" (2-4). Thus, if originality and creativity are valued over fidelity, European literature may be transformed into African literature by means of translation.

The recent move toward postcolonial theory within translation studies marks an attempt to account for the power differentials that exist between languages. "The status of a language in the world is what one must consider when teasing out the politics of translation," Spivak suggests ("The Politics of Translation" 191), because, as Bassnett and Harish Trivedi explain, translation "rarely, if ever, involves a relationship of equality between texts, authors, or systems" ("Introduction: Of Colonies, Cannibals, and Vernaculars" 2). Just as the African writer must be concerned with the politics of language, the postcolonial translator must be concerned with the politics of language in translation.

Most published postcolonial theory on translation is focused on texts from colonized (often referred to as weak, minority, or third-world[3]) source languages to colonizing (or strong, dominant, first-world) target ones, and thus places great importance on the translator's duty to provide his/her readers with contextual understanding of the source language and culture.[4]

On the other hand, one of the most striking postcolonial theories put forth concerning translation from a language of a colonial culture to that of a colonized one is that based on Brazilian translator Haroldo de Campos' comparison of translation to cannibalism (see Peres Vieira). Discussing the transformative potential of translation in de Campos' terms, Else Riberio Peres Vieira explains that in translation, as in cannibalism, "foreign input, far from being denied, is absorbed and transformed" (98). Creative transformation, rather than faithful translation, means that foreign input can be absorbed with a difference, and not in a neutral act of repetition.

As Bassnett's, Mazrui's, and Peres Vieira's articles demonstrate, postcolonial theories focusing on translation from colonial languages to languages of colonized cultures often discuss translation in terms that could be considered negative: thievery, guerrilla warfare, cannibalism.[5] However, none of them relies on the potentially negative connotations of the words they use to describe translation; rather, viewing the translator as thief, guerrilla or cannibal captures the ambiguity inherent in the translator's position: s/he wants to import certain aspects of the source culture into his/her own through translation, but because of the colonizing history of the source language and culture,[6] s/he is compelled to do so selectively.

Mungoshi's translation of *A Grain of Wheat* into *Tsanga Yembeu* is a powerful example in support of theories regarding the translator as thief, guerrilla, cannibal, and, I argue, trickster: *Tsanga Yembeu* demonstrates that Mungoshi, a translator from a colonized culture, translating from a colonial language into the language of the colonized, is more creative in the target language than faithful to the source text, culture(s) and language(s). One view of translation holds that the translator's aim is a beneficent one: to share the source text and its culture with the target audience who might not otherwise have access to the text because of its language. The fact that, in Zimbabwe, many (perhaps most) potential Shona readers are literate in English, and thus have no real "need" for the Shona version, suggests that mere beneficence is not Mungoshi's motivation as a translator. This is not to say that Mungoshi has no positive feelings for Ngugi's original. On the contrary, Mungoshi builds a deliberate link to Ngugi, a sign of respect and admiration for the Kenyan author and an acknowledgement of the literary merit of *A Grain of Wheat*. But my examination of the translation reveals that Mungoshi's relationship to the source text is much more ambiguous than his respect for Ngugi would suggest: Mungoshi's translation strategies waver between respectful fidelity and creative transformation. In Bandia and Appiah's terms, Mungoshi is ethnocentric, refusing to provide the hypertextual material that the reader needs to have access to in order to understand fully the source cultures of Ngugi's novel. In Noss's terms, Mungoshi domesticates the text. In my own terms, Mungoshi is a trickster translator, a concept on which I elaborate below (for a more extensive discussion, see Thompson).

Translating *A Grain of Wheat* into another language, as in translating any text, requires knowledge of the source language and culture. But what is the source language and culture of *A Grain of Wheat*? Although written predominantly in English and therefore reaching a largely "Western" audience, the culture the novel describes is neither that of the United Kingdom nor that of the United States.[7] Despite Ngugi's choice to write it in English, the novel takes place in Kenya and depicts Kikuyu characters speaking African languages, Gikuyu and Swahili. How does Mungoshi translate such a bicultural—indeed multicultural or hybrid—text? The goal of this chapter is first to answer this question by reconstructing Mungoshi's translation strategies in the production of *Tsanga Yembeu*.[8] How does Mungoshi transfer aspects of culture from English, Gikuyu and

Swahili into Shona? I demonstrate that he does so by domesticizing the foreign cultures, translating Shona-centrically, and creating a new text in the Shona language.

Mungoshi's Translation Strategies

I have compared Mungoshi's version to Ngugi's original, seeking out textual examples that are representative of Mungoshi's translation strategies.[9] In all cases I found that Mungoshi exhibits a spectrum of translation strategies that range from extreme fidelity to extreme creativity. However, the most interesting points of comparison are in narrative structure, metaphors and figures of speech.[10] Each of these elements is a powerful carrier of culture, be it English, Gikuyu or Swahili; and all three reveal most clearly the nature and degree of Mungoshi's creative translation. It is these three elements I address below.

Narrative Structure
While Ngugi's decision to use Gikuyu as a means to reach his people came late in his career,[11] there are signs of his concern with the identity of his audience as early as *A Grain of Wheat*. Kofi Owusu comments, for example, on Ngugi's use of the second-person singular in the novel "to suggest shared experience" (2), such as when the narrator asks the reader, "You remember the Wednesday, just before Independence?" (*AGW* 202). The suggestion of shared experience is double-edged, though—for it both includes those who *do* share, and excludes those who do not. By addressing the reader directly, Ngugi makes a gesture towards including the reader in his narrative, but simultaneously reminds the same reader that s/he is not in fact included, since his/her answer to the question is likely to be, "No, I do not remember that Wednesday."[12] The dynamic relationships established among reader, narrator, and the novel's characters help create a space that allows Ngugi to comment on his various audiences and their interpretations of his novel. Deeply embedded in history, *A Grain of Wheat* is itself an interpretation, Ngugi's reading of Kenyan history from a Kikuyu perspective. However, Ngugi does not provide a historical background for his reader. Despite writing the novel in English, he privileges the Kenyan reader by expecting the non-Kenyan reader to craft his/her own sense of the historical events upon which *A Grain of Wheat* relies.

Mungoshi's decision to translate Ngugi seems a natural one, given Ngugi's popularity among Zimbabwean readers and the historical backdrop of *A Grain of Wheat*. Flora Veit-Wild's 1989 survey of Zimbabwean writers found that Mungoshi and Ngugi were the top two "favorite authors after school years."[13] The reason for Ngugi's popularity in Zimbabwe may well be not only his stance on African language literatures, but also his treatment of Kenyan history in most of his novels. That history, as it is embedded in *A Grain of Wheat*, bears a number of similarities to Zimbabwe's own history. In fact, on the back cover of Mungoshi's translation is written:

> Bhuku iri richaburitsa pachena kuti hondo yokusunungura Kenya haina kusiyana neChimurenga chakasunungura Zimbabwe. Kudeuka kweropa reKenya kuchakuridzira vaverengi kuti vaongorore nokufungisisa kuzvipira kwevana veZimbabwe muChimurenga chavo. Izvo zvichajekesa pfungwa dzavo pamusoro peramangwana renyiko ino. (This book makes clear that the war to liberate Kenya was not unlike the *Chimurenga*[14] to liberate Zimbabwe. The spilling of Kenya's blood will urge readers to observe and to remember to pass these things on to the children of Zimbabwe in their *Chimurenga*. Doing so will enlighten the future leaders of this country.)[15]

Clearly, the intention of *Tsanga Yembeu*'s publishers was to draw a comparison between Kenyan and Zimbabwean histories. While Zimbabweans may read *A Grain of Wheat* in the original, its events remain Kenyan and therefore foreign—a feeling, as I suggest above, that Ngugi may have intended for his non-Kenyan readers. When one reads the novel in its Shona translation, however, its connection to events in Zimbabwe becomes clearer, through the very fact that its events now occur in Shona rather than in a combination of English, Gikuyu and Swahili. As Ngugi himself suggests in *Decolonising the Mind*, reading in a second language, such as English, for the Shona reader is a "cerebral activity," whereas reading in one's mother tongue is "an emotionally felt experience" (17). Mungoshi creates this emotionally felt experience for his Shona readers, connecting them to a Kenyan history that parallels their own.

As Toury reminds us, translation often serves the purpose of filling a "gap" in the target culture (27).[16] African literatures, like any target culture's literature, can benefit from translation as it provides new perspectives on subjects that have not yet been dealt with in the literature of the target language. Terence Ranger pointed out such a gap in Zimbabwean literature in 1985, just a year before Mungoshi published his translation of *A Grain of Wheat*:

> [T]hough political leaders and others called for a "people's history" the new [Zimbabwean history school] books did not really deliver it. Admirable as they were as a corrective to the old

colonial history, they focused mostly on the states and aristocratic achievements of the past and on the continuities of the nationalist struggle in the twentieth century. The experience of workers and peasants was largely missing. (viii)

Interestingly, the Shona language has no word for *peasant*. But Mungoshi's translation of Ngugi's "peasants" as "the majority of the people" (*TY* 19) demonstrates the importance of peasants to Zimbabwean history. As historical fiction bearing similarities to Zimbabwe's recent experience with war and subsequent independence, Mungoshi's translation of *A Grain of Wheat* may help bridge this gap of missing peasant history, at least in the aesthetic imagination of its Shona readers.

Like the translation of Ngugi's focus on peasant history, the translation of his non-linear style also serves to fill a gap in Shona literature. As breaks in the text marking internal discontinuity indicate, *A Grain of Wheat* is a text comprised of multiple chronologies and multiple interpretations. In a recent interview, Ngugi contrasts this narrative structure with his previous work:

> In *Weep Not, Child* and *The River Between*, the form is linear, the narrative unfolds from point A to point B to point Z. When we come to *A Grain of Wheat*, we get multiple narratives and time frames shift. . . . It's like I wanted to see how the same events looked at different times . . . looked at by different characters located in different times, from multiple centers. ("A Conversation with Ngugi wa Thiong'o" 2)

Mungoshi maintains the narrative structure of Ngugi's novel; the storyline remains the same, complete with flashbacks and multiple versions of the same event. In mimetically preserving *A Grain of Wheat*'s structure, Mungoshi interprets Ngugi's narrative structure as being essential to the novel. He seems to hold, along with Ngugi, that there is no single interpretation of events, a view as relevant to Zimbabwean history as it is to that of Kenya.

Discussing novels written in Shona, Chirikure Chirikure writes that,

> most . . . Shona novels are written in the third person, omniscient author style. The story is presented with events following their chronological order. . . . While this style is handy . . . it has been over-used by Shona writers. . . . The novel can begin with the middle then go to the beginning—or any other way—as long as the story will come out logically. These kinds of experiments are

lacking in our Shona literary circles, resulting in our readership being flooded with works which are similar in style. (6-7)

Ngugi's novel meets the criterion that Chirikure is searching for in Shona literature. Mungoshi uses faithful translation of *A Grain of Wheat*'s internal structure to introduce Ngugi's innovation into the literature of his own language, and in doing so creates a new style in Shona literature.

Metaphors
Ngugi uses metaphors skillfully in *A Grain of Wheat* to add to characterization, to setting, and, in the case of Biblical metaphors, to the overall meaning of the novel. Metaphors may be the most difficult kind of language to translate because "they are literally untrue (and . . . must therefore be taken as evidence for meanings which are not directly encoded in them)" (Fabb 251). That encoding of meanings is a culturally and contextually bound process. Here is an exemplary passage, with a number of figures of speech, including culture-specific metaphors:

> Our people, is there a *song sweeter* than that of freedom? Of a truth, we have waited for it *many a sleepless night*. Those who have gone before us, those of us spared to *see the sun today*, and even those to be *born tomorrow*, must join in the *feast*. The day we hold *Wiyathi in our hands* we want to *drink from the same calabash*—yes—drink from the same calabash. (*AGW* 23)[17]

Compare Mungoshi's translations of Ngugi's metaphors, and his addition of new ones:

> Ko, nhai veduwee, mati imi pane chimbo chinganakidze here kupinda *chimbo chi chorusunguko*? Kubvira riini takachimirira *tichishayiwa hope*? Saka vose vakaenda kare, nesu *takasiyiwa kunze* kuti tirione ranhasi navose vacha*zvarwa mangwana*, tose tinosungirwa kupembera pamwe chete. Musi worusunguko rwedu ndiwoka musi watinofanirwa *kusanyimana*, ndiwo musi *wokunwa tichiravana mukombe mumwe chetewo*. (Tell me, our people, do you say there is a song which pleases more than this *song of freedom*? How long have we waited for it *without sleep*? So those who went long ago, and we who *remain outside* so that we might see it[18] of today and those who will be *born tomorrow*, all of us are obligated to celebrate together. The day of our freedom will be the day on which we should not *deny each other food*; it is the day of *drinking in turns from one cup*). (*TY* 27)

As this passage reveals, Mungoshi always attempts to capture at least the figurative meanings of Ngugi's metaphors, even if their literal meanings are not carried over into Shona; he never abandons the meaning of Ngugi's original. Mungoshi has at least six distinct strategies for handling the translation of metaphors, as this passage shows, ranging from the extremely mimetic to the extremely creative (cf. Toury 82-83).

One of the most elaborate examples of the translation—and creative transformation—of metaphor in *Tsanga Yembeu* occurs through Mungoshi's word-play on the Shona word *rungano*, which traditionally meant *story, fable,* or *folk-tale,* but in modern usage has come to also mean *history*. For example, in Chapter Three, Gikonyo explains to Mugo, "He [Kihika] will live in our memory, and history will carry his name to our children in years to come" (AGW 28). Mungoshi translates: "Achagara mundangariro medu uye *rungano* rwenyika yedu ruchatakura zita rake kuchizvarwa chose chichatevera (He will live in our recollections and the story/fable/folk tale/history of our country will carry his name to the whole generation which will follow)" (TY 33; emphasis added). While the emphasis on the open-ended interpretability of history is an important part of Ngugi's *A Grain of Wheat*, it becomes even more powerful in the Shona version because of Mungoshi's play on the word *rungano*.

In some parts of the novel, Mungoshi refuses to translate the word *history,* leaving it in italicized English instead; because of this, *rungano* becomes all the more associated with fiction when it *is* used. For example, Mungoshi translates one sentence as, "Vaitaura nezvehondo, zvamabhuku pamwe nezve*history* (They spoke about the war, about literature, and about *history*)" (TY 75). If there is no word for *history* in Shona, or at least in Mungoshi's *Tsanga Yembeu,* then all history becomes *rungano,* fiction.

Mungoshi extends the recurrent sewing images and references to cloth, thread, and weaving found in *A Grain of Wheat* as metaphors for speech and storytelling by linking them to *rungano*. The narrator of *A Grain of Wheat* explains, "The woman cleared her throat, an indication that she was about to take up the thread from Warui" (AGW 23). Mungoshi translates: "Mudzimai akabvisa makororwa pahuro pake zvichiratidza kuti aida ku*rwu*simudzira par*wa*kanga *rwa*siyirwa naWarui (The woman let out a croak from her throat to show that she wanted to pick *it* up where *it* had been left by Warui)" (TY 27; emphasis added). The unspecified *it* in Mungoshi's translation is marked by class 11[19] subject and object markers -*rwu*- and -*rwa*-, markers that seem to refer not to the *thread* of Ngugi's original, which would be *shinda* (class 9) or *kashinda* (class 12), but to *rungano*. Mungoshi further links *rungano* and *history* to cloth in the next example: "Kihika unrolled the history of the tribe," Ngugi writes (AGW 18), using the word "unrolled" to create an image of history as a long tapestry that can be physically handled. Mungoshi translates this sentence faithfully (*TY* 21), using *rungano* as a replacement for *history*, thus adding the connotations of fiction. Mungoshi's translation creates an image of *rungano*, rather than simply *history*, as Ngugi's tapestry.

Through the linkage of *rungano* to Ngugi's sewing imagery, Mungoshi ensures that *rungano* is recalled when subsequent sewing imagery is used, so that it is no longer necessary to repeat the metaphor. For example, when Mungoshi translates Gikonyo's asking himself "And who had thought of life as a thread one could continue weaving into a pattern of one's choice?" (AGW 132) as "Ko, iye akambenge afunga kuti upenyu kashinda kaunorudunura uchiruka patani yako yaunoda ndianiko? (Tell me, who is it who had thought that life is a little thread which you can unstitch, weaving your pattern which you like?)" (TY 165), the reader is reminded of the fictionality of history, including life histories. Mungoshi's addition of *rungano* as a metaphor thus invites us to read history as fiction, embedded in a novel that already invites us to read fiction as history.

The Ideophone as a Figure of Speech

Toury cautions the translation critic to proceed not only from source to target text, but also from the latter to the former, lest s/he overlook segments that exist only in the translation (83), as when Mungoshi adds metaphors. Following Toury's instruction, one finds that, in addition to metaphors, *Tsanga Yembeu* contains a figure of speech which does not occur in *A Grain of Wheat*: the ideophone.

The Shona ideophone, like those of many African languages, is a part of speech akin to onomatopoeia except that it can also refer to imagery other than sound. It is usually introduced by *kuti* (to say), so that the sentence "Ndati tseketu tseketu (I said 'budging a heavy object')" would mean, "I budged a heavy object." In *Tsanga Yembeu*, one finds the following ideophones, among many others: "n'ai (shining brightly for a short time)" (342), "changinja (seizing)" (23), "divi (happening unexpectedly)" (28), "nde-e (taking a prolonged look [of anger or curiosity])" (33), "vai (shining, glittering, flashing)" (75, 137), and "tindindi (entering; entering water gently, going deeper and deeper; lying dead; or beginning something difficult)" (26). Note that none of these examples represent onomatopoeic ideophones, although those exist in Shona as well. Their meanings are, in fact, far more complex and specific than mere sound symbolism. Mungoshi uses ideophones like these on virtually every page, usually during narration rather than dialog.

It is important to realize that the use of ideophones is Mungoshi's stylistic choice, not a requirement of Shona semantics or syntax.[20] For example, rather than using the verb *kuparadza* (to destroy), Mungoshi coins the ideophone *paradze* to translate Ngugi's "Destroy that, and the white man is gone" (*GW* 111): "Kungoti ichocho icho paradze, muchena wose kana kuzombomuona zvakare (That way over there, to say 'destroying,' is to never see the white person again)" (*TY* 137). Mungoshi's translation of Ngugi's straightforward English into ideophonic Shona must be seen as an intentional strategy, used "to achieve vivid and arresting description" (Fortune 5).

Shona ideophones, George Fortune explains, "may be used in a narrative or speech at certain points where a special lively style and special vividness" are desired. "Here they have considerable rhetorical effect. They are used to express emotion or excitement. . . . Stylistically, too, they rank higher than onomatopoeia [does in English]" (5). He goes on to indicate that an ideophone is:

> the right word for the complete situation, or its important aspects, at the right pitch of vividness. . . . With them one is in a special realm of *spoken art*. . . . They attempt to be a vivid re-presentation or re-creation of an event in *sound*. (6)

Fortune's emphasis on the use of ideophones in speech and storytelling suggests that Mungoshi's addition of Shona ideophones into his translation accomplishes several things. First, it creates the impression that *Tsanga Yembeu* is a *rungano*, a Shona oral tale. Second, it marks Mungoshi as a skilled storyteller. And third, it creates a more interesting, lively, vivid text for a Shona reader. Noss suggests, in fact, that the use of ideophones in an African story imply that the story is an eye-witness account (268), a strategy that would further transform Ngugi's account of Kenyan history into a Zimbabwean version of those events.

The "skilled storyteller" Mungoshi, who displays creativity in translating a multicultural English-language text into an African language, becomes the quintessential "trickster translator" who *transforms* a multicultural text into a purely Shona one. I elaborate below on my conception of the trickster translator, demonstrating its particular relevance to the translation of texts concerned with colonizing and colonized languages.

The "Trickster Translator"

According to Joseph Campbell, the trickster has been important to "almost all non-literate mythology" (qtd. in Hynes and Doty, "Introducing the

Fascinating and Perplexing Trickster Figure" 1). Borrowed from the oral tradition, the trickster has made his way into written literature as well. Recent literary scholars have called attention to postmodern and postcolonial fiction's appropriation of the trickster, and have appropriated the trickster as a metaphorical figure for the author. Others have highlighted the necessity for critics themselves to act as tricksters (See, e.g., Gates; Bal 138; and Monsma 86). Those who study tricksters, often anthropologists, have long noted the trickster's capacity as a verbal artist (see, e.g., Doueihi 287). Many folkloric tricksters, in fact, highlight their verbal skills by serving as translators.

Building on the metaphors of author as trickster and trickster as translator, I reverse the analogy, viewing the translator as trickster, one who transforms a text in one language into a text in another, while simultaneously concealing that such a transformation has taken place. Following from my examination above of Mungoshi's strategies of translation of *A Grain of Wheat* in the creation of *Tsanga Yembeu*, I now examine the "trickster translator" strategies he deployed.

Seeing the translator in this way highlights the act of translation as creative as well as mimetic, explores the translator's ambiguous relationship to the source text author, and gives recognition to the translator, too-often ignored in the study of literature. My conceptualization of the trickster translator allows the examination of literary translation from the theoretical perspective of an indigenous African tradition, that is, through the metaphor of the trickster, an important African folkloric figure. But since the trickster is not only an African figure, the theory of translator as trickster may be applicable to other traditions as well.

An important similarity between trickster and translator is the role of each as metaphor-maker. "As the embodiment of disparate domains, trickster is analogous to the process of metaphor, the incorporation of opposites into a new configuration" (Stewart 62). Similarly, in translation, "new metaphors are born, and the usual perceptions of the world are revisioned creatively" (Hynes and Doty, "Historical Overview" 20). Willis Barnstone notes that the English words *metaphor* and *translation*, when traced back to their respective Greek and Latin roots, have the same meaning: "carrying across" (15); and concludes that "translation is the activity of creating metaphor" (16). It seems appropriate, therefore, to translate the trickster himself into metaphor, creating the trickster translator.

I rely on the general idea of the trickster, just as I refer to the hypothetical translator—any one who translates a text from one language to another—in a general way, while at the same time acknowledging that there is no single translator, no single trickster. The comparison between translator and trickster draws on recurring features of multiple trickster figures from a number of cultures because "the trickster is always more than can be glimpsed at any one place or in any one embodiment" (Hynes 35). Although T.O. Beidelman wonders whether "[t]he category of trickster may be merely the product of a series of false translations" (175), many anthropologists have researched trickster figures worldwide and discovered significant similarities among them. Stories of one trickster in particular, Esu-Elegbara (or Legba) of the Yoruba people, have traveled throughout the African diaspora, so that he can no longer be considered an exclusively African trickster (Gates 5).

While the Shona words for "trickster" (*gube, chinyange, gore*) are mostly derogatory in that they suggest deceit, some Shona words for translation do acknowledge the Shona translator's trickster nature. A number of words for "translator" in Shona, some distinct and some morphologically related, reflect the different roles a translator may take on, the different strategies available to him or her. One type of translator is the *mududziri*: "one who explains," a noun related to the verb *kududzira*, "to explain, interpret or translate." Another type of translator is the *muturikiri*, "interpreter, translator," a noun derived from *kuturikira*, "to interpret, to translate, or to solve a riddle." Both *mududziri* and *muturikiri* depict a translator on the more faithful, respectful and mimetic end of the spectrum. Nevertheless, the words also suggest that even faithful translation involves interpretation. A third word for the translator is *mupinduri*, "one who answers, one who translates, or one who turns something over," a noun related to the verb *kupindura*, "to turn over, to answer or reply, to change or translate," a more creative kind of translating. *Kududzira* and *kupindura* are, in fact, the words used by the publishers on the cover of *Tsanga Yembeu* to describe Mungoshi's work, one connoting a faithful translation and the other a creative one—a subtle acknowledgement of the ambiguous nature of Mungoshi's translation. A fourth Shona term for translating is *kushandura*, that means, "to change or alter something's size, shape or nature, to translate," a word that perfectly reflects the transformative and creative power of translation. Mungoshi himself uses *kushandura* on the first page of *Tsanga Yembeu* to explain his work. From this word I have formed the noun *mushanduri*, which, although infrequently used, would be the Shona equivalent of the "trickster translator."

Above all, the trickster is both an imitator and a transformer. "The trickster is the master of metamorphosis," William Hynes has written (37). In his folkloric form, the trickster imitates the opposite gender, pretends to be a Koranic scholar, and mimics the voice of the nanny goat. He is able to physically transform himself and others in terms of gender, shape, and size. He brings the dead to life. He upsets power relations, changing the divine to profane and back again. Accordingly, a trickster translator—such as Mungoshi—both imitates his source text, translating faithfully, and transforms it, translating creatively.

In several traditions, one of the trickster's most important transformative powers is the ability to transform messages linguistically. Robert Pelton suggests that West African trickster figures represent "the constant possibility of transformation and thus of life itself." One trickster in particular, Legba, is imaged as not only a transformer, but literally as a translator. "From the beginning, he is the master of languages, the bearer of messages among his brothers, and the translator of Mawu's purposes for all." The Fon people of Benin address Legba as an intermediary for their High God Mawu-Lisa, and Legba translates for her, as a "divine linguist" (96, 113, 72). Likewise, Legba's Nigerian cousin Esu-Elegbara translates and interprets religious texts as they pass from the god Ifa to the Yoruba divining priest (Gates 9).

If the trickster is a messenger and linguist of the gods, then seeing the translator as a trickster leads to yet another analogy: the source author as god and the target language reader as humankind. The trickster translator must mediate between these two. Hynes proposes that this role, too, can be defined as a mimetic one: "the trickster can be both a messenger and an imitator of the gods. Admixing both divine and human traits, he can slip back and forth across the border between the sacred and the profane with ease" ("Mapping" 39-40). The translator, too, mixes traits, those of the author (the "divine") and the reader (the "human"), reminding us that translation is both creative and interpretive, and that all reading is translation; "every act of reading, writing, and interpretation of a text . . . leads us directly to the art and activity of translation" (Barnstone 19; cf. Paz, "Literature and Literalness" 195).

It is precisely the translator's position between source language author and target language reader that recalls the trickster, whose "position midway between the gods and humans allows him to function as cultural transformer" (Hynes 40). As a reader, the trickster translator interprets the source author's text. As an author, he brings his interpretation of the text to bear on his translation as he rewrites, creating his own, new text.

Mungoshi as Trickster Translator

When Mungoshi plays the role of faithful translator, he serves as Ngugi's reader, reading *A Grain of Wheat* and relating it in turn like a messenger, word for word, form for form, to his Shona readers. However, since Mungoshi's reading brings with it his own interpretation of the novel, he also plays the role of divine author. In this role, he becomes creative, using his own images and metaphors rather than Ngugi's, using Shona greetings and terms of address rather than ones that reflect the form of Ngugi's Kenya-specific language, adding vivid ideophones where they do not exist in the original.

Just as Legba mediates between heaven and earth, the translator becomes a mediator between his/her source text and an audience who reads—whether by necessity or by choice—in a language other than the source text. S/he is like the trickster who "becomes a mediator by means of a lie that is really truth, a deception that is in fact a revelation, and a conspiracy that should have been no secret" (Pelton 79). The translator's lie is his/her presentation of the translation as "original," a practice Juliane House calls *covert* translation. Mungoshi translates covertly when he subjugates his own name to Ngugi's but simultaneously domesticates the novel so that it reads as if it were originally written in Shona; without foreignness, few traces of the original's multiculturalism and multilingualism remain. "The [covert] translator's task is, in a sense, to cheat, and to be hidden behind his feat, the transmutation of the original" (House 114). While House uses the term "covert" translations somewhat disparagingly, that is an attempt to instruct the translator how *not* to translate, my claim is that trickster translators are always wavering between the covert and the overt translation, at one moment concealing the source text, at the next revealing it. This wavering is reflected in Mungoshi's inconsistency as he moves across the fidelity spectrum, in some cases translating with almost complete respect for Ngugi's text and in other cases translating with complete creativity, as he does with Shona ideophones.

The translator's presentation of his/her translated text as the original is only in part a lie, since, as Willis Barnstone, Jorge Luis Borges and Christopher Francis Hasty remind us, the translation can never repeat what comes before. His/her deception, then, is a double revelation, first of the source text to those who do not read the source language, and second of the very process of translation. In the trickster's corresponding act lies the "greatest metamorphic feat: that of transforming [the Fon High God] Mawu-Lisa's absence into transparent presence and of unveiling her/his creative purposes" (Pelton 80). The translator relates to his/her source exactly as the Fon trickster does to the High God; s/he transforms the absence of the source text into thinly veiled presence and reveals its creative purposes in a new language.

Precisely because of the translator's "betwixt and between" position, s/he has an ambiguous relationship to the author. Just as the trickster depends on the gods for the messages s/he is to deliver, for chronological reasons the translator is necessarily dependent on the writer who precedes him/her.

Regarding a text as a translation entails the obvious assumption that there is another text, in another culture/language, which has both *chronological and logical priority* over it: not only has such an assumed text assumedly preceded the one taken to be its translation in time, but it is also presumed to have served as a *departure point and basis for the latter* (Toury 33-34; emphasis added).

Because of the existence of an original, the translator, in one sense, can only create a copy, a frustration about which Pelton writes with regard to the trickster: "Legba finds his lack of independence and differentiation from his mother oppressive" (78). Legba's mother is Mawu-Lisa, the High God for whom he translates. Similarly, the translator lacks independence and differentiation from *his/her* literary "mother," the author whose text s/he translates. Barnstone reads the translator's lack of independence and the shame caused by this dependence as an extreme form of Harold Bloom's famous "anxiety of influence" or literary Oedipus complex (qtd. in Eagleton, *Literary Theory* 159). But an alternative theory for translation is Henry Louis Gates' notion of "Signifyin(g)": unlike Bloom's theory, which would position the translator as an antagonist to the original author, Gates' theory allows us to see the translator deliberately drawing on and revising the source text, in a respectful rather than antagonistic way, in order to create or draw attention to an intentional literary tradition. In sync with Gates' theory of respectful revision, some postcolonial theorists have suggested that the strong traditions of oral storytelling and retelling and the relatively recent onset of literacy in the "Third World" means that ownership through authorship is relatively less important than it is in the "Western" literary tradition (see, e.g., Bassnett and Trivedi, "Introduction" 2, 8). In cultures with strong oral traditions, this theory suggests, verbal artists are constantly revising the creations of those who precede them, without a sense of antagonism toward their precursors, and this tradition of respectful revision carries over into written literature. As a trickster, the translator oscillates between Bloom and Gates' theories, at times oppressed by his/her reliance on a precursor and yet all the while deliberately creating links to that precursor. Tricksters thrive on ambiguity, so the translator trickster's equivocal relationship with Bloom and Gates' theories makes perfect sense.

Reading a translator like Mungoshi through Bloom's "anxiety of influence" theory, one can see that, though relying on the text of his precursor, Mungoshi conceals *A Grain of Wheat* in order to reveal—indeed, highlight—his own text in Shona. Pelton relates a Fon myth used to explain the High God's distance from earth, a situation caused by Legba's tricks. However, he writes, "[i]f he pushes her away from the earth, he is using the force that she shared with him to do so" (78). Analogously,

Mungoshi pushes the source text away from his readers in order to focus their attention on the translated text. One of the clearest ways Mungoshi conceals Ngugi's *A Grain of Wheat* is by translating Ngugi's code-switched words into Shona. In doing so, he focuses the Shona reader's attention on the (sometimes incorrect) meanings of Ngugi's Swahili and Gikuyu words, rather than on the foreignness they bring to the English original.

Conversely, Gates' theory would suggest that although Mungoshi attempts to conceal his source, paradoxically he is always revealing it. "[I]f he [Legba] helps to make Mawu . . . the god-who-went-away, at the same time he himself embodies her presence in the new space created by her withdrawal" (Pelton 78). Every word in the translation signifies not only something in the target language, but also, by definition, refers back to the source language text. The source text "is ever-present, because the translation, without *saying* it, mentions it constantly or else turns it into a verbal object that, though different, reproduces it" (Paz, "Literature and Literalness" 188). The trickster translator's text becomes a *supplement*, in Derrida's sense, to the original text: "a progressive implicating of, *and* a gradual distancing from, the origin" (Derrida, *Of Grammatology* 200; emphasis added). Even Mungoshi's translation of the *A Grain of Wheat*'s title suggests *Tsanga Yembeu*'s constant pointing to the original text. Its very translation, its very existence in a language other than English, places it at a distance from the original, but it is always understood as *A Grain of Wheat*, as the title page indicates by equating the two. The fact that most literate Shona can also read English effectively dissolves the binary opposition between *A Grain of Wheat* and *Tsanga Yembeu*. Mungoshi's translation of such a well-known novel, one published and available in Zimbabwe, in fact invites comparison of his version to Ngugi's original. Of this possibility Brian Harris writes: "Those of us who *are* bilingual and who want to study the translation can also 'restore' both versions, or at least parts of them, in our minds simultaneously, and consider them together" (qtd. in Toury 96). The bilingual reader's ability to read both texts together, as two parts of one *bi-text* (Harris, qtd. in Toury 96) also questions the very existence of an original.

As Mungoshi's translation demonstrates, the amount of distance the translator places between him/herself and his/her source, or the extent to which s/he translates covertly, depends on the historical relationship and power dynamics between the source and target languages s/he translates. That is to say, the translator may feel a greater need to appear original when translating between two languages and cultures with a history of inequality and degradation between them. For this reason, the trickster is an apt metaphorical figure for those who translate from a colonial language into the language of a colonized culture. Pelton comments on

"Legba's unflagging movement from center to periphery and back again" (98), noting Legba's reenactment of the Fon capacity for negotiating the entrance of imported notions into their own developed culture. In the world market, English is a central language and Shona a peripheral one, making the movement between these two languages an important one for a Zimbabwean translator.

Conclusion

My examination of literary and cultural norms in *A Grain of Wheat* and *Tsanga Yembeu* has demonstrated that Mungoshi, like most translators, is an inconsistent and idiosyncratic one. Whether presenting the text, dividing it, setting up its internal narrative structure, translating authorial commentary, or transferring aspects of culture such as proper names, political terminology, terms of address, code-switching, or metaphors and figures of speech, Mungoshi uses a number of contradictory and inconsistent strategies. In a number of cases, as I have illustrated elsewhere (see Thompson), Mungoshi translates respectfully, with extreme fidelity to Ngugi's *A Grain of Wheat*. The internal narrative structure of *Tsanga Yembeu* is the aspect most faithful to Ngugi's *A Grain of Wheat*. Mungoshi's mimesis of this aspect of Ngugi's text suggests not only his respect for the source text and author, but also his desire to carry such stylistic innovations over into Shona literature. Despite Mungoshi's extreme fidelity to a number of aspects of *A Grain of Wheat*, in a larger number of cases he exhibits creativity in his translation. And even within the translation strategies I have labeled "creative," one finds a range of creativity in *Tsanga Yembeu*.

Most creatively, Mungoshi uses addition, supplementing *A Grain of Wheat* with his own work. Sometimes these supplements add very little to the text, such as when Mungoshi forms new sections or new paragraphs where they do not exist in the original. At other times they dramatically change and enhance Ngugi's novel. Mungoshi's most creative transformations of *A Grain of Wheat* are his additions of the *rungano* metaphor and of Shona ideophones. On the one hand, the *rungano* metaphor, by linking itself to Ngugi's sewing imagery and metaphors, strengthens the novel's existing emphasis on the constructedness and interpretability of history. The Shona ideophones, on the other hand, transform *A Grain of Wheat* into a Shona oral story, Mungoshi and Ngugi together into master storytellers, and the novel itself into an eyewitness account. Thus the Shona reader feels as if s/he is there, an effect that plays on the history and fictionality of the events depicted in *Tsanga Yembeu*.

After examining Mungoshi's strategies for a number of literary and cultural norms and witnessing his inconsistency, how can one reconcile the fidelity evident in some of Mungoshi's strategies with the creativity found in others? In some cases Mungoshi exhibits the utmost respect for Ngugi as author and owner of *A Grain of Wheat*. His very decision to translate Ngugi over other African writers who use English suggests Mungoshi's respect for and agreement with Ngugi's stance on "the politics of language" and a deliberate linkage of translation to the debate over language in African literatures. Moreover, Mungoshi's respect for Ngugi's work is also evident in his use of *A Grain of Wheat* to fill a gap in Shona literature (both stylistically and in its historical content), rather than writing a text of his own that might have served the same purpose.

The answer is that despite his evident respect for Ngugi and for *A Grain of Wheat*, Mungoshi becomes the author of a new text, rewriting *A Grain of Wheat* into *Tsanga Yembeu*, in many cases without concern for the language or form of the original. In these cases *Tsanga Yembeu* becomes an original novel, and Mungoshi its author. At the same time, Mungoshi's fidelity to some aspects of the original text and his subjugation of his own name to Ngugi's in the presentation of the text, work to conceal the changes he has made.

Although Mungoshi's translation strategies may be inconsistent, clearly they result in a novel that is far more original than the translations described (and prescribed) by those translation theorists who privilege fidelity over creativity. Unlike most translations *from* African languages *into* European ones, *Tsanga Yembeu* is not source-text oriented or hypertextual; it does not provide a "thick" translation with explanations of culture-specific items from English, Gikuyu or Swahili. Mungoshi does not preserve the original function of the source text in its culture, since, as Ngugi has noted, *A Grain of Wheat* is a text disconnected from its culture—whether "its culture" is read as African because of its subject matter, or as European because of its language.

On the other hand, seen from another angle, in the context of African literature, Mungoshi is the "trickster translator" who complicates the belief that the development of indigenous-language literatures marks a complete rejection of European literatures, languages, and their influence.

Ngugi, after writing four novels in English, including *A Grain of Wheat*, argues for the sole use of African languages in African literature as a means of decolonization. Dambudzo Marechera, on the other hand, rejected indigenous Zimbabwean languages, Shona and Ndebele, on the grounds that their use promotes a romantic return to the past. Translation from English into an African language disturbs both of these notions through a deliberate transformation of the colonial into the African. Brian Street notes that "[T]o question everything would lead to anarchy; to preserve everything would lead to stagnation; the conflict is presented, and the balance is achieved, in the trickster tales" (qtd. in Hynes and Doty, "Historical Overview" 19). Likewise, the trickster translator achieves a balance between the questioning of all colonial languages and a preservation of all indigenous ones, by breaking the taboo against mixing the two. Compare this notion to Hynes's description of the trickster:

> The trickster quite regularly brings gifts essential to human culture, usually by breaking a central taboo established in the divine order. . . . Because it is the trickster who breaks the taboo, while conveying the benefits of this act to humans, the appropriate consequent punishment is deflected from humankind. Thus, the cosmic boundaries are preserved while a crucial power slips across to human use. ("Mapping" 40)

Analogously, the African translator brings new literatures, metaphors, ideas, and other cultures to the target language culture, by breaking the "taboo" of language choice. Because it is the translator, rather than the African author, who breaks the taboo, the potential "punishment" of having one's language choice questioned by critics and readers is deflected from the author. In this way, the trickster translator simultaneously disrupts and renews the target language society.

Mungoshi as trickster translator or *mushanduri*, brings a fresh look at peasant history and a new style of narrative to Shona literature, by interpreting, turning over, answering, and transforming Ngugi's *A Grain of Wheat* into a Shona novel.

Mungoshi's translation is (without, I hope, any negative connotations) an ethnocentric text, one that prioritizes Shona language and culture over English. *Tsanga Yembeu* allows Shona readers access to an African novel written in English without requiring them to use the language of Zimbabwe's colonizers. It is a transformed text that, although no longer multicultural in the sense of Ngugi's original, truly exists at the meeting ground of cultures. Through this act of transformation, Mungoshi responds to Ngugi's call for African language literatures and also to the call for a trans-African literature.

Notes

[1] Unlike Ngugi who turned to literature in his mother tongue rather late in his career, Mungoshi began writing in both Shona and English early on. In fact, Rhodesian publishing policies required Zimbabwean writers to use Shona, so

under colonialism Mungoshi published outside of the country when he wrote in English. Due to this forced use of Shona, Mungoshi claims not to share Ngugi's strong commitment to his mother tongue as a medium for literary expression. In an interview with Flora Veit-Wild, he explains, "I felt more myself when writing in English because I knew it wouldn't be published in Rhodesia. In Shona, you would always look out to compromise" (qtd. in Veit-Wild 287). In 1969, he published *Makunun'unu Maodzamwoyo* (Deep Considerations of a Rotting Heart) in Rhodesia, which won the first prize in the Literature Bureau Competition for the best Shona novel of the year (Veit-Wild 297). Three years later he published a collection of short stories, *Coming of the Dry Season* (1972), in England. Rhodesian publication laws created a clear geographical divide between the audiences of his Shona work and his English work. In 1975, he published two novels, *Waiting for the Rain*, his best-known English work, and *Ndiko Kupindana Kwamazuva* (How Days Pass). In 1980, the year of Zimbabwe's independence, his first play appeared, *Inongova Njakenjake* (It Pulls Each in His Own Direction). It is unclear to what extent Mungoshi's publisher, the Zimbabwean branch of Longman, was controlled by the Rhodesian Literature Bureau at that time, since their address on the title page of *Inongova Njakenjake* is listed as "Salisbury, Zimbabwe," a linking of the colonial capital with the postcolonial nation. Yet one can assume that Mungoshi's decision to write in Shona was not entirely forced on him, because he continued to write and publish in Shona after independence, coming out with *Kunyarara Hakusi Kutaura?* (Is to be Silent not to Speak?) in 1983, and his Shona version of Ngugi's *A Grain of Wheat* in 1987. Since then he has published predominantly in English, including, significantly, one translation from Shona into English.

² The *ideophone* is discussed later in the chapter.

³ These terms tend to be used interchangeably in postcolonial theory. For my part, I use *colonizing* and *colonized* throughout, except when referring explicitly to another author's terminology.

⁴ See, for example, most of the essays in Anuradha Dingwaney and Carol Maeir, eds., *Between Languages and Cultures: Translation and Cross-Cultural Texts* (1995), especially Dingwaney's "Introduction: Translating 'Third World' Cultures"; Maier's "Toward a Theoretical Practice for Cross-Cultural Translation"; bell hooks's "'this is the oppressor's language / yet I need it to talk to you': Language, a place of struggle"; and Dingwaney and Maeir's "Translation as a Method for Cross-Cultural Teaching." Postcolonial translation theory in this vein suggests "a conceptualization of translation as a cross-cultural activity in which the goal of immediacy or readability is tempered by a simultaneous willingness—even determination—to work in difference" (Dingwaney and Maeir, "Translation as a Method for Cross-Cultural Teaching" 304), a framework similar to those put forth by Bandia, Appiah, Noss, and Spivak.

⁵ One is reminded of the famous Italian description of translation, *"traductor, tradditore"* (translator, traitor), a maxim expressing the notion that even the translator who attempts to be faithful can never replicate the original with total mimesis (Barnstone 259).

⁶ Theorizing about the transformation of literature from a European language into an African one becomes even more complex when one considers that not all literature in European languages is European literature. Ngugi wa Thiong'o's *A*

Grain of Wheat is an example of such a literature. Complicating my analysis of *Tsanga Yembeu*, therefore, is the question: how does the fact that Ngugi's novel also comes from a colonized culture affect Mungoshi's need to protect the target culture from the cultures embedded in the source text? In forcing one to examine this question, Mungoshi's translation of Ngugi's bicultural "Afro-European novel" (in fact a multicultural "Swahili-Gikuyu-English" novel) highlights the complexity of the interaction between languages and cultures in Africa.

[7] Ngugi wrote later, "After I had written *A Grain of Wheat* I underwent a crisis. I knew whom I was writing about but whom was I writing for? The peasants whose struggles fed the novel would never read it" (*Decolonising the Mind* 72).

[8] My aim in doing so is to provide a descriptive rather than prescriptive discussion of Mungoshi's translation. In other words, I do not evaluate his translation "as good or bad according to a fixed theory of what constitutes equivalence between two texts" (Kruger and Wallmach 2), because no such fixed or unified theory exists. Rather, I analyze the techniques he uses to transfer elements of English, Gikuyu and Swahili cultures from the source text into Shona. When I do refer to Mungoshi's translation as differing from Ngugi's original, I do so not to claim that Mungoshi has made an error; rather I work from the assumption that his strategies are deliberate.

My methodology is based on a combination of the methods outlined by Alet Kruger and Kim Wallmach in "Research Methodology for the Description of a Source Text and Its Translation(s): A South African Perspective" (1997); similar methods suggested by Toury in *Descriptive Translation Studies and Beyond* (1995); and the terminology used by Javier Franco Aixelá in "Culture-Specific Items in Translation" (1996).

[9] Because a descriptive translation study can never compare two texts in their entirety, I have chosen a set of dimensions that represent the literary norms of the source text and a set that represent aspects of culture in the two texts. In a much longer version of this chapter (Thompson, "A Trickster Translation: How *A Grain of Wheat* Becomes *Tsanga Yembeu*" [1999]) I examined the literary norms of the two texts—presentation of the text, division of the text, internal narrative structure, and authorial commentary (Kruger and Wallmach 5)—as well as cultural dimensions—proper names, political terminology, terms of address, language variety, and metaphors and figures of speech (cf. Kruger and Wallmach 5).

[10] For example, an examination of the metaphors and figures of speech of both texts shows that not every word or concept in Ngugi's version has an equivalent word or concept ready and waiting for it in Shona. With what strategies does Mungoshi handle these cultural gaps?

[11] Although perhaps best known for his 1981 decision to write only in Gikuyu, Ngugi wrote *A Grain of Wheat* while he was still an active part of the tradition he calls "the Afro-European Novel" (*Decolonising* 71). He began his literary career with two earlier English language novels, *Weep Not, Child* (1964) and *The River Between* (1965), both of which, like *A Grain of Wheat*, concern Kenya's colonial history. Ten years after *A Grain of Wheat* appeared, Ngugi wrote two works: *Petals of Blood* (1977), which marked "seventeen years of involvement in Afro-European literature"; and *Ngaahika Ndeenda* (with Ngugi wa Mirii; translated into English by the authors as *I Will Marry When I Want*), a play that began his work as a Gikuyu

language writer (Ngugi, *Decolonising* 27).

[12] Although Ngugi "gives the impression that he is writing on behalf of, and communicating with, his people" (Owusu 2), his choice of English ensures that most of his readers are not in fact Kikuyu.

[13] Ngugi also became quite well known in Zimbabwe around the same time Mungoshi was translating *A Grain of Wheat*: the Kenyan novelist gave presentations on "The Language of African Theatre" and "The Language of African Fiction" at the University of Zimbabwe in 1984; a reprint of *A Grain of Wheat* was published by Zimbabwe Publishing House in the same year; and his *Decolonising the Mind* was published by them in 1987.

[14] *Chimurenga* is the Shona word used for the freedom struggle. Since most Zimbabweans use the word even in English, I have left it untranslated throughout.

[15] All translations from Shona to English throughout the chapter are mine.

[16] This is not to suggest that African cultures need translation because they do not have literary traditions of their own; on the contrary, they have strong ones.

[17] I have underlined the figures of speech in these examples to draw the reader's attention to these rather than other differences between the original and the translation.

[18] According to Shona grammatical rules the class 5 infix 'ri' could refer to *zuva* 'sun' but its referent is not explicitly stated.

[19] References to class refer to the Bantu noun class system. Unlike Romance languages, which have three noun classes (masculine, feminine, and neuter), Bantu languages (including Shona, Swahili and Gikuyu, as well as hundreds of others) have up to twenty-one noun classes. Each class takes agreements with other parts of speech such as verbs, adjectives, and so on. Thus an infix that might be translated as "it" could refer to a specific noun in one of these noun classes, providing a linguistic clue as to what "it" is intended.

[20] "Most things can be expressed in either way, either verbally or ideophonically" (Fortune 4-5), and most ideophones have morphological relationships with specific verbs.

PART III

HYBRIDITY AND INTERCULTURALITY

8
Hybridity and the Artist in *Out of Africa*

Rachel Trousdale

Few critics have paid serious attention to the work of Isak Dinesen (the pen name of the Danish writer Karen Blixen).[1] Critics who do discuss her work generally do so from a particular political standpoint: feminists such as Susan Hardy Aiken and Sara Stambaugh, and postcolonial critics such as Abdul R. JanMohammed (see his *Manichean Aesthetics: The Politics of Literature in Colonial Africa*) use her work to illustrate political points. These standpoints can provide excellent starting positions for a reading of Dinesen's work, but they are by no means the whole story. My aim in this chapter is twofold. First, I would like to initiate a discussion of Dinesen that, while it incorporates the political reality of her life, focuses on her artistic transformation of, and escape from, that reality in her 1937 memoir *Out of Africa* (*OA*, this edition 1989).[2] Second, through this discussion of Dinesen, I want to demonstrate a new approach to reading what I call hybrid literature—literature that incorporates elements of varied cultures, and that creates out of those cultures a new world. For Dinesen, and others like her, the role of the artist is in fact to produce hybridity: a creative self-fashioning using all materials that come to hand.

The term *hybrid* has a number of semi-overlapping definitions. Robert J. C. Young does an excellent job of tracing its early, unfortunate associations with nineteenth-century race theorists in *Colonial Desire: Hybridity in Theory, Culture and Race* (1995). For Homi K. Bhabha, on the other hand, hybridity is a form of resistance, whereby the colonized challenges the authority of the colonizer (*The Location of Culture* 117). Neither of these definitions exactly fits the phenomenon I discuss in Dinesen. She is not interested in the children of interracial unions, nor does she resist either European or African power, since she sees herself as a representative of both. The hybrid community of the farm resembles Mary Louise Pratt's "contact zone" (4) with the addition that in a hybrid community there is a deliberate effort on all sides to combine the conflicting cultures. This is to some extent what Salman Rushdie describes when he talks about writing "his" India in "Imaginary Homelands" (10); he is not concerned with accuracy of fact so much as accurate representation of emotion and tone, and in order to achieve the one is ready to allow great departures from the other.

The story of *Out of Africa*, in as much as there is one, focuses on a number of artists, who survive—and enjoy—the contradictory demands of colonial Kenya by re-inventing themselves to incorporate elements of European and African cultures. While the main tale told in *Out of Africa* is about Dinesen's losing her coffee farm through bad luck and bad management, the bulk of the work consists of descriptions of a European colonist's life in British East Africa. Dinesen came to Africa with her husband, Baron Bror Blixen, and remained on the farm after their divorce. While the best-known parts of the book (which were adapted for Sydney Pollack's 1985 film of the same name) involve Dinesen's British lover, Denys Finch-Hatton, she reserves the greatest part of *Out of Africa* to writing about the Africans who work on the farm, and presenting herself (the colonist, landowner, anthropologist, and amateur doctor) as a large part of their lives. The African and European populations contribute to Dinesen's collection of artists, whose willingness to adapt to the demands of society paradoxically allows them to be most fully themselves. Among these artists are the narrator herself, whose ambiguous position as both storyteller and character makes her the most explicitly invented person in the work; Emmanuelson, an exiled Swedish actor; and Kamante, Dinesen's Kikuyu chef. I discuss below how, by re-inventing themselves through the appropriation of a culture different from their initial one, these three artists become hybridized in *Out of Africa*.

The Narrator–Dinesen

It is never quite clear from the text of *Out of Africa* precisely who the narrator is. The reader knows from the content that this is a woman, although the English and American (but not the Danish) editions of the book were both published under a male pseudonym.[3] The reader hears pieces of her name or names scattered throughout the volume—she is Msabu (synonymous with "Memsahib," a title rather than a name) when someone wants a favor from her; Baroness Blixen when she signs a formal document regarding blood-payments or when speaking to the ragged fugitive Emmanuelson; Tania to Berkeley Cole; and Jerie to the old women of the farm. But she never names herself except in quotation marks. The reader never reads her full name—Tania Blixen, Karen Blixen—anywhere in the work, and never hears, so to speak, Denys call her anything at all, although we know from both Judith Thurman (168) and Parmenia Migel (69) that he nicknamed her Titania. Dinesen's apparent project in *Out of Africa* is not to describe herself at all, but rather to describe the world of her farm and its occupants. Their names are more important to the story than hers; her story is told only as a frame narrative for theirs.

Or so Dinesen would have the reader believe. The reader naturally realizes that she is in fact telling him/her only about herself. For the farm is Dinesen's true self-representation. She *is* her fictional farm. And thus *Out of Africa* is explicitly what Paul de Man describes when he writes that autobiography "may contain lots of phantasms and dreams, but these deviations from reality remain rooted in a single subject whose identity is defined by the uncontested readability of his proper name," adding that in autobiography, the name "is made as intelligible and memorable as a face (68, 76)." The work opens with the main subject: "I had a farm in Africa, at the foot of the Ngong hills." This is all the identity the author wants. Every scene in *Out of Africa* is self-representation, from which the reader learns Dinesen's true name. Like a character in a fairy tale, she goes by many pseudonyms; only by learning her real name does the reader have any power over her. It is this identification that most strikingly marks *Out of Africa* as fiction.

The invention of self is directly tied to the reinvention of community. Dinesen presents a picture of her farm as it *should* have been: a community of Africans and Europeans, each identifiably a member of a particular "tribe" (Kikuyu, Somali, Danish, English), and yet each dependent on the others. Dinesen's revisions of reality in her memoir are in the service of her representation of a hybrid community—which is both an extension and definition of her persona as an artist.

If Dinesen is to belong anywhere, it must be a place she has invented for herself. That place is the farm, which is made of hybrids of truth and fiction, of autobiography and self-invention, and of African and European cultures. She uses colonial African culture to approximate a version of older Europe: she establishes a feudal society among people who remind her of "ancient Icelanders," or "the very poor people of Europe." Through her African farm, Dinesen lives out her fantasy of "cut[ting] a figure at the time of the plague of Florence" (*OA* 383, 123, 217), creating a hybrid society with the appropriate cultural conditions to allow her to tell her stories.[4] She is not in a state of limbo—or at least not until the farm is sold. For Dinesen, the purpose of hybridity is to create a place where she is comfortable—which is to say, her farm. *Out of Africa* presents the farm as a hybrid construction, made up of apparently incommensurable elements to form a functioning whole. This is what Dinesen would call a "unity."

Dinesen describes her idea of a unity in her late memoir *Shadows on the Grass* (*SG*, 1960; this edition 1989, in the same volume with *OA*):

> In order to form and make up a Unity, in particular a creative Unity, the individual components must need be of different nature, they should even be in a sense contrasts. Two homogeneous units will never be capable of forming a whole, or their whole at its best will remain barren. Man and woman become one, a physically and spiritually creative Unity, by virtue of their dissimilarity ... A number of perfectly similar objects do not make up a whole ... An orchestra is a Unity, and may be perfect as such, but twenty double-basses striking up the same tune are Chaos. (377-378)

For Dinesen, unity is impossible without difference, and hybridity is not only an artistic device but also a necessary element in real life; it is a kind of love affair. She distinguishes between a "unit" and a "unity"; a "unit" is a piece of a whole, incomplete in itself, whereas a "unity" is an assemblage of diverse units. The example she uses—man and woman—is telling: a unity is in fact indispensable to productivity. The "barren" union of like units is biologically incapable of creating anything new. Unities need not be on the heterosexual model, however: the "orchestra" is a unity of dozens of unlike instruments—more a figure of a society than of a marriage. Dinesen describes the workings of a unity as an "interaction between those who can be made one *by reason of their incongruity*" (*OA* 16, emphasis added). Dinesen's insistence on the need for an unlike other condemns mono-cultural societies (like the one she left in Denmark) as unproductive—neither "physically" nor "spiritually" creative. A unity saves one's "horizon" from being "restricted," as Dinesen, in a letter to her mother, says it must be in Denmark (*Letters from Africa* 67). In *Shadows on the Grass* Dinesen writes that, "the introduction into my life of another race, essentially different from mine, in Africa became to me a mysterious expansion of my world." Her "voice" becomes "fuller and richer in the duet" (378). Encountering difference and entering into a unity expand the self and make art (the "song") better.

It is Dinesen's very difference from the Africans, which allows her to feel she belongs in Africa. If she thought she were the same, her presence would be redundant. She substantiates this feeling with a series of stories about her encounters with and emotional responses to Africa. She finds the most important evidence that she belongs where she is in her own sense of well-being: "In the highlands you woke up in the morning and thought: Here I am, where I ought to be" (*OA* 4). This sense of comfort is reinforced by a response Dinesen imagines in Africa:

> If I know a song of Africa, I thought, of the Giraffe, and the African new moon lying on her back, of the ploughs to the fields, and the sweaty faces of the coffee-pickers, does Africa know a song of me? Would the air over the plain quiver with a colour I had had on, or the children invent a game in which my name was, or the full moon throw a shadow over the gravel of the drive that was like me, or would the eagles of Ngong look out for me? (*OA* 75)

Dinesen implies that her love of Africa is reciprocated, and that this perceived mutuality draws her into a unity with its landscape itself. The passage is in the form of a question—"does Africa know a song of me?"—but some of the responses she looks for (a shadow by moonlight, the children's game) are so probable that the other, stranger responses are made to seem possible. She does not claim complete knowledge for either party: she knows "a song" of Africa. A "song" is a single artistic representation, not an expression of complete understanding. But she imagines these responses to her presence—from the rather terrifying image of the air taking on the color of her clothing to the much more plausible idea that a shadow could resemble her—as an acknowledgment of her right to be there. She knows—has made—a song of Africa, and Africa responds by making a song about her: she and Africa, she claims, take turns representing each other. If the children accept her into their play-world, then she has become a part of everyday life; if the air takes on the color of her clothing, then she has become a part not only of everyday life but also of the very atmosphere. Conversely, Africa has become *her* atmosphere, outside of which she will not thrive. (She does not mention in *Out of Africa* her extended trips to Europe, except by reference to her return voyages.) While Africa, the real place with the real people, has not invited Dinesen in nor imitated her clothing, "Africa," the place Dinesen creates in her memoir, has. A sense of belonging may be impossible without a degree of deliberate self-deception—as Dinesen implies by her use of the word "song"; songs are not truths. Dinesen reinvents herself in order to best reflect Africa—and to be reflected by it.

Dinesen is not the only one to feel linked to the landscape; the common experience through the land turns the farm into a real community. The same force that makes Dinesen's loss of the farm certain—drought—is also the force which ties the farm's tenants together. When the long rains fail,

> we were all merged together into a unity, so that on another planet

we shall recognize one another, and the things cry to each other, the cuckoo clock and my books to the lean-fleshed cows on the lawn and the sorrowful old Kikuyus: "You also were there. You also were part of the Ngong farm." That bad time blessed us and went away. (*OA* 264)

Everyone on the farm, from the comparatively rich settler to the poorest squatter to the very inanimate objects, is "merged together" by the terrible drought. The cuckoo clock and the books, objects which are at first mysterious to the Africans (the young boys used to come in every day at noon to watch the cuckoo) become a necessary part of the landscape, just as the cows do. The people and things that "belong" in Africa (cows, Kikuyus) become kin to the European settler and her belongings because of their mutual suffering. Through this acquired kinship, the European and African people and things become part of an interdependent community—hence, for Dinesen, the blessing.

The wording of recognition is important: "You also were part of the Ngong farm." Not *on the farm* or *living at the farm*, but "part of"; every object, animal, or person on the farm is a necessary piece of it. The phrase "You also were there" echoes Matthew 26:69, "Thou also wast with Jesus of Galilee" and Mark 14:67, "And thou also wast with Jesus of Nazareth," both of which appear in the scene where Peter denies Christ—a denial Dinesen writes about in "The Deluge at Norderney," one of the stories in her *Seven Gothic Tales* (1934). The Biblical allusion stresses allegiance: to deny one's part of the farm would be a terrible betrayal and cowardice. Both Biblical verses stress place: the accusations against Peter would be less precise without the "of Galilee" and "of Nazareth." The *Out of Africa* passage, too, emphasizes the place: "the Ngong farm." The people on the farm are "blessed" by the bad time because it binds them together, and because, unlike Peter, they do not deny their allegiance. All the occupants of the farm are brought into a unity by the lack of rain.

This connection, which appears to include everyone on the farm, is an identity. Everyone on the farm will recognize everyone else on the farm because, after the drought, they have a shared experience. The occupants of the farm are "blessed" by the "bad time" because it, and it alone, forges a real connection between them—makes them into a "we." The shared experience makes difference secondary, and allows people from different backgrounds to complement each other. The reader may object that the other occupants of the farm have not agreed to join a "we"; Dinesen's response would be that she was not consulted either—the "we" was forced on everyone by the drought. Unequal as the society she presents is, all are similarly powerless in the face of the drought. This helplessness is,

Hybridity and the Artist in *Out of Africa*   175

to Dinesen, a unifying force.

At times, Dinesen's identification with Africa is less baldly phrased and thus more plausible. In the wake of a tragic shooting accident, an old woman is accused of witchcraft, and Dinesen thinks in Swahili as she considers the accusations:

> I had by now become used to the idea of witchcraft, it seemed a reasonable thing, so many things are about, at night, in Africa. "This old woman is mean," I thought in Swahili, "she uses her arts in making Kaninu's cows blind, and she leaves it to me to keep her grandchild alive, on a bottle of milk a day, from my own cows." I thought: "This accident . . . [is] getting into the blood of the farm, and it is my fault. I must call in fresh forces, or the farm will run into a bad dream, a nightmare. I know what I will do. I will send for Kinanjui." (134-135)

By thinking in Swahili, she is able to contemplate the possibility of black magic. Witchcraft becomes "reasonable" as Dinesen internalizes her surroundings. The solution to the problem is not to think in a European language and dismiss the possibility of witchcraft, but to think in Swahili, a language spoken by the people who have made the accusation. The trouble is Dinesen's "fault" because she is not sufficiently assimilated to know how to deal with a witch. But she can recognize the problem and act to solve it. The farm, which in this passage resembles a single, physical entity, with "blood," is in danger of becoming fragmented and disembodied: it will turn into a "nightmare," a non-physical, bloodless, hideous thing. It is in order to ensure the possibility of thinking of the farm as a single body—a community—that she calls in Kinanjui, the chief of the Kikuyu.

By sending for Kinanjui to arbitrate the dispute, Dinesen legitimizes the possibility of witchcraft. She undercuts her own authority (taking the problem to a higher court) while simultaneously reinforcing it (she knows which court to go to). And she does so through a new system: Kinanjui is not a "real" chief, but one set up by the British. He is not a British authority, but neither is he exactly a traditional Kikuyu authority, either. And Dinesen thinks in Swahili, the lingua franca, not Kikuyu, the native language of her laborers. She does not simply join the old Kikuyu society—such a thing would be impossible. But by thinking in Swahili, she is able to think in the proper mindset: the language allows her to handle the accusations of witchcraft with the right degree of distance.

This entry into a new mindset would be impossible without some fluency in Swahili. Although Dinesen's Swahili is imperfect, she is able to have substantive conversations in it. Most settlers, Dinesen complains, do not speak more than kitchen Swahili, which is really "a kind of English" (*Letters* 8).[5] Dinesen herself almost fails to improve her linguistic ability because of European prudery. She describes an emblematic example: her Swedish tutor, in a fit of embarrassment, claims that there is no Swahili word for nine, because it "has a dubious ring" (*OA* 262).[6] The tutor says that the Swahili numbers skip from eight to ten, simply in order to avoid saying a word, which might offend someone who spoke Danish. This piece of misinformation causes Dinesen to spin a series of fantastic, unfounded speculations about the minds of the Africans. By mislearning Swahili, Dinesen is actually led away from understanding African culture. The linguistic lesson is also moral: she must not make the same kind of mistake, and import inappropriate European resonances into African speech.

But in some places, those resonances do exist. Successful hybridization depends on finding a single common element and building on it. Dinesen does not reserve the possibility of cross-cultural unities to herself. The characters in *Out of Africa* are often dramatically hybridized: their personalities, talents and beliefs are assembled from pieces of several civilizations. These are the people who are able to reinvent themselves — Dinesen's fellow artists. Within the fictional world of *Out of Africa*, they understand each other not only through a common culture but also through their shared experience of self-invention. This shared experience is the basis of a growing community.[7] People who reinvent themselves in *Out of Africa* tend to be doubly artists: their work (Emmanuelson's acting, Kamante's cooking) and their lives are both artistic.

Emmanuelson

Dinesen's house acts as a meeting ground between civilizations not only for herself and her friends but for some varied wanderers, the most striking of which is Emmanuelson, the Swedish tragic actor. Emmanuelson appears one evening asking for a night's lodging. He has been driven out of Nairobi by some unspecified trouble with the law and is on his way, on foot, to Tanganyika. The journey "was not a possible thing to do for anyone," as the trip through the Masai Reserve involves walking ninety miles with no water through lion-infested country. The Masai, in fact, have just been up to the farm "to complain" about the lions, and "had asked me to come out and shoot one for them" (*OA* 190) — a fact Dinesen mentions to further emphasize not only the dangers of the Reserve but her own close ties with it. Despite Dinesen's warnings, Emmanuelson answers that he will continue on to Tanganyika. Dinesen's response to Emmanuelson's determination is to invoke a complex set of European figures:

> It seemed that I was to take the part of the High Priest who presents the goat alive to the Lord, and sends it into the wilderness. I thought that here we needed wine. Berkeley Cole, who generally kept the house in wine, some time ago had sent me a case of a very rare burgundy, and I now told Juma to open a bottle from it. When we sat down for dinner and Emmanuelson's glass was filled he drank half of it, held it towards the lamp and looked at it for a long time like a person attentively listening to music. "*Fameux,*" he said, "*fameux*; this is a Chambertin 1906." It was so, and that gave me respect for Emmanuelson. (*OA* 191)

Dinesen as High Priest presides over the sacrifice of the scapegoat, turning Emmanuelson into the Christ figure his name suggests. Emmanuelson, as we shall see, is a "sacrifice" for a community of aesthetic experience. Despite his dubious appearance, Emmanuelson's ability to identify a rare burgundy, as much as his determination to reach Tanganyika, gives Dinesen respect for him. In this sense, Emmanuelson's identification of the wine, "this is a Chambertin 1906," is akin to Christ's "this is my blood": the wine is a communion wine, because it is through the identification of the Chambertin that Emmanuelson and Dinesen first understand and appreciate each other. Both have been trained to appreciate the same things, and both consider this training to be important. Like the aristocrats in Dinesen's "Babette's Feast" ("Babettes Gaestebud" in the Danish original, 1952; this English edition 1988), they are uniquely qualified to appreciate a particular sort of art.

Metaphorically speaking, the wine *is* Emmanuelson's blood: knowledge of this sort makes him who he is. Emmanuelson is not only an actor, he is a trained audience; appreciation of food and wine on the level that Emmanuelson and Dinesen both value is a highly rarefied and expensive form of knowledge, which is all the more incongruous on a coffee farm in Kenya, where no Chambertin ought to appear at all. But Emmanuelson's privileged knowledge will not help him in Kenya. He can identify wine, but he cannot drive a tractor, which makes him useless not only to the surrounding farmers but to Dinesen herself, who has no place for an actor on her farm. Emmanuelson's abilities have not adapted to Kenya's demands. Moreover, the statement "this is a Chambertin 1906" is in fact the opposite of Christ's "this is my blood": Emmanuelson's identification of the wine is an identification of another, of something external. The Chambertin 1906 is a commodity to be appreciated, not, after all, a piece of the self. It may act as a symbol of artistic sensibility that Dinesen considers inherently valuable, but it is not a vehicle of salvation. Emmanuelson is a scapegoat, an outcast from society, who has committed unnamed crimes. A decrepit, parodic Christ figure, he goes to Tanganyika with "empty" hands in "a long black overcoat such as nobody wears in Africa" (*OA* 191); he is entirely a stranger in the land. With his remarkable courage and complete uselessness, he is at once a true sacrifice and a mockery of one.

The next morning, Dinesen drives Emmanuelson the first ten miles of his way. "I did not like to see him step straight from the threshold of my house into his uncertain fate," she writes. She drives him to the borders of the farm, across the river that marks the boundary of the Masai reserve. She does this, she says, because she wants "to be, myself, somewhere within this comedy or tragedy of his," but it also serves the function of seeing him directly into the wild, rather than allowing his adventure to begin while he is still in the safer borderland of the farm. The farm's hybrid status, between the African and European civilizations, does not allow Emmanuelson to face dangers while still within its boundaries. She gives him money borrowed from her major-duomo Farah, some sandwiches, hard-boiled eggs, and a bottle of the Chambertin 1906 "since he appreciated it. I thought that it might well be his last drink in life" (*OA* 194). Emmanuelson carries the wine of their mock communion with him into the unknown.

In these scenes Emmanuelson continues to appear as an equivocal Christ figure.[8] When Dinesen wakes him in the morning, he "looked like one of those legendary corpses whose beards grow quickly in the earth." This is the imagery of resurrection, but a resurrection, which leaves the subject corpse-like. And rather than achieving apotheosis, he is immediately sent out into the wild. Dinesen drives him to "the other side of the Mbagathi River," where he gets out of the car and walks away. The newly-risen sun is "dull and red: like the yolk of a hard-boiled egg" (*OA* 195). The hard-boiled sun echoes the hard-boiled eggs in the package Dinesen has given Emmanuelson. The eggs are food for Emmanuelson's journey and a figure of birth and renewal; the trip across the Masai reserve will be a rebirth for Emmanuelson, which will be more effective than his grotesque, zombie-like resurrection that morning. But like all rebirths in Dinesen's work, it will be grueling. The red sun is threatening, for it will do its own boiling, heating the plains across which Emmanuelson must walk. This is rebirth by fire; nothing gentle or easy is worthwhile in Dinesen's world.

As Dinesen watches him walk away, she decides that he is still performing:

> I believe that the dramatic instinct within him was so strong that

Hybridity and the Artist in *Out of Africa* 179

he was at this moment vividly aware of being leaving the stage, of disappearing, as if he had, with the eyes of his audience, seen himself go. Exit Emmanuelson. Should not the hills, the thorntrees and the dusty road take pity and for a second put on the aspect of cardboard? (*OA* 195)

Emmanuelson's "dramatic instincts" are strong enough to affect his own consciousness—he is "aware of being leaving the stage"—and Dinesen's, who has been trained to understand those instincts herself. Even though he may very well be going to his death—Exit Emmanuelson—he remains an actor. This is of a piece with his recognition of the Chambertin; his whole life follows his artistic training. But here his training does not work: the thorn trees clearly do not become cardboard—they do not even "put on" its "aspect." Africa refuses to become less real in order to suit his needs. Emmanuelson, so un-adapted to Africa, evokes no response from the landscape. He does not manage the feeling of communion Dinesen has with the farm. The land will not imitate an imitation; it cannot parody itself. Dinesen knows that Emmanuelson has not transformed Africa into the set of his private play: the passage is in the subjunctive. It would be entirely unnatural for the African landscape to "take pity" on anyone, especially if that pity required it to somehow become a representation of itself. Emmanuelson himself expects no pity. But he has what he needs—an audience. The landscape makes no compromise, but Emmanuelson sets off content because Dinesen is there to make compromises instead. Dinesen here emphasizes Emmanuelson's *non*-hybridization—and that his failure to adapt to Africa is likely to kill him.

But despite Africa's unwillingness to be reduced to cardboard, Emmanuelson successfully crosses the Masai reserve, and eventually sends back the money Dinesen has lent him. It turns out that Emmanuelson is adapted to Africa in an unforeseeable way. He writes to Dinesen that he has entertained the Masai by pantomime and lived with them for some months. Emmanuelson and the Masai understand each other, despite their total lack of any shared language:

> It was fit and becoming, I thought, that Emmanuelson should have sought refuge with the Masai, and that they should have received him . . . [The Masai] . . . would have recognized at once in the lonely wanderer in black, a figure of tragedy; and the tragic actor had come, with them, into his own. (*OA* 196-197)

Emmanuelson ends up creating his own hybrid society among the Masai, one even stranger and more dramatic than that on the farm. His inappropriate talents come in handy after all. The details of his aesthetic training are still useless—the Masai have no interest in Chambertin—but his artistic outlook finds a common ground. Emmanuelson and the Masai agree that tragedy is "the fundamental principle of God" (*OA* 196); their kinship lies not in language or in interests but in an understanding of how the world works. That single shared attitude allows communication despite all other differences. Emmanuelson's "sacrifice" allows him entrance into a community of artistic appreciation. He, Dinesen, and the Masai all have similar attitudes: they are appreciative audiences confronted by the same spectacle—Emmanuelson's courage—to which they react in the same way.[9] Emmanuelson proves the possibility of communication across apparently insuperable cultural boundaries. He is drawn to Dinesen's farm and then to the Masai because he will be understood in both places.[10] Emmanuelson, too, is looking for a place where he belongs.

Emmanuelson's story grows more interesting when compared to its counterpart in the letters. Dinesen writes to her mother on Sunday, February 12, 1928, that "a pathetic personage, a Swede, Casparson" (*Letters* 340) came to the Ngong farm that Friday asking for help. Casparson is on his way to Tanganyika, on foot: "It is an absolute impossibility, it is 230 miles, most of the way without water" (*Letters* 341). Dinesen reports that she gave him dinner and "it was really very pleasant," but that he resisted her attempts to talk him out of the dangerous trip. She then says,

> I drove him to Farah's duca at half-past five and gave him a parcel of food and a bottle of beer, ten shillings, and my blessing, but he looked pitiful when he started off along the road; he did not even have a blanket, only a big overcoat, and no luggage at all. I sent him to Nepken and doubt if he will get any further than that; surely Nepken will be able to explain to him that it is impossible . . . of course I could have driven him to Nepken, but I thought it wiser to let him get some experience of walking tours in this country before he got there so that he can change his mind before leaving the last human habitation behind and going off into the desert. (*Letters* 341-342)

These are very significant differences from *Out of Africa*. First of all, Dinesen reports giving Casparson a bottle of beer, not a bottle of wine. Whatever they may have drunk that night at dinner, Casparson did not take a bottle of rare burgundy with him into the Masai Reserve. Olga Anastasia Pelensky, noting this discrepancy, writes that "for Isak Dinesen, life was not to be distinguished from the ceremony of the stage, and was lived intensely only when it was arranged artistically" (107-108).

Although this does not seem like an explanation for the discrepancy, we can accept Pelensky's judgment with a little alteration. Dinesen, writing her memoirs, gives Casparson the stage he wanted. She does this not only as a favor to him, but because it seems artistically appropriate. If he is the accepted sacrifice, the scapegoat, her literary aesthetic demands that he should be accompanied by precious wine. However, Dinesen *is* aware of the difference between life and "the ceremony of the stage"; her fictional Emmanuelson's theatrical disappearance is, as we have seen, problematic. Dinesen does not retroactively *believe* that she gave Casparson the wine, as Pelensky's analysis half implies; instead, she believes that she *should* have, to preserve both his persona and her own. We are not reading "life lived artistically," but memory artistically constructed.

In the second deviation from the *Out of Africa* version of the story, Dinesen does not drive Casparson across the river. Instead, she sends him to her neighbor Nepken, and has him go on foot so that he will know what he is in for. This is very different from "I did not like to see him step straight from the threshold of my house into his uncertain fate." Both versions place emphasis on some form of compassion for the wanderer, but the compassion is expressed in very different ways. Where the version in the letter has a certain pragmatic logic to it, the version in *Out of Africa* is nothing but a symbolic gesture. Dinesen seems to deny her own original common sense in order to improve her story. Her deliberate placement of the fictional farm on the outposts of "civilization"—in the letter, Nepken has the dubious honor of being "the last human habitation," a statement which both changes Dinesen's location and entirely overlooks the presence of the Masai—is emphasized by this change, and thus so is her personal involvement with Emmanuelson's journey. Also, oddly, the distance has changed: in *Out of Africa*, it is ninety miles to Tanganyika, whereas it is two hundred and thirty in the letters; the reason for this discrepancy is not clear (for more on Dinesen's relative veracity in letters and memoirs, see Lee; Thurman 165-166; and Pelensky 86-87).

There are several motives for these transformations. To start simply, the *Out of Africa* version makes a better story. The gift of wine is a grand gesture, almost as grand and impractical in its way as Emmanuelson's decision to set off across the Masai Reserve for Tanganyika. It ties the narrator to his grandeur, gives her a piece of it. Having him simply walk to a nearby farm is nowhere near so dramatic. More importantly, though, in the *Out of Africa* version Dinesen's farm is a springboard into the unknown. The Ngong farm is the doorstep; one gets there from Nairobi, the "civilized" world, and one leaves it for the Masai Reserve. The hybrid community lies between the extremes of African and European culture: it gives the traveler an opportunity to acclimatize. It is on Dinesen's farm that Emmanuelson stops to collect himself; she is the transitional point. Dinesen plays Charon and ferries him across the river.

Kamante

Emmanuelson is an artist who transforms the world around him, but he only does so temporarily, in transit. Far more interesting is the case of a hybrid person who lives permanently on the farm: Dinesen's cook, Kamante, who goes from a wild, alienated creature to a mature artist, through a series of tremendous acts of self-invention and self-hybridization.

When Dinesen first meets the nine-year-old Kamante, he is "the most pitiful object that you could set eyes on." He has a small, stunted body, and his legs are "covered with deep running sores from the thigh to the heel." Kamante is entirely a creature of the wild: "Rarely, rarely, have I met such a wild creature, a human being who was so utterly isolated from the world, and, by a sort of firm deadly resignation, completely closed to all surrounding life" (*OA* 21, 24-25). This is not an idyllic, Rousseauan state of nature: young Kamante's wildness does not connect him to the land. Instead, he is only separate from humanity. In his wild state, he is Dinesen's exact opposite. While she believes she is firmly part of a community, Kamante is utterly alone, alienated from both human society and the nature which surrounds it.[11] Kamante's initial alienation springs from his suffering, and is itself akin to a disease or deformation: it is unhealthy and unusual for anyone to be so alone. Only when Dinesen offers Kamante a glimpse of a different culture and a vehicle for self-expression does hybridity and its paradoxical partner, the artist's distance from society, save Kamante from utter isolation.

Even as a young boy, Kamante is probably too estranged from society to ever come back into a normal position in the Kikuyu world:

> ... in his early life something in him had been twisted or locked, and now it was, so to say, to him the normal thing to be out of the normal. He was aware of this separateness of his, himself, with the arrogant greatness of soul of the real dwarf, who, when he finds himself at a difference with the whole world, holds the world to be crooked. (*OA* 31)

Kamante is entirely too used to his outside position to change it. His "separateness" and "arrogant greatness of soul" both mark and cause his alienation. These characteristics give him a certain familial relationship to Dinesen. Kamante is Dinesen's mirror image. Like her, he is apart from his original society; like her, he nonetheless must learn to navigate it; and like her, he takes pride in whatever sets him apart. Most importantly, as we shall see when Kamante's cooking is discussed below, he is an artist: this fact makes his distanced observation of his surroundings productive instead of simply painful. For Dinesen, an artist does in small what a society does on a larger scale, synthesizing pieces of old cultures into a new one; the artist, however, as a single individual, remains separate from the culture he or she has created.

But if Kamante is a mirror image of Dinesen, he must be a disturbing one. For his "arrogant greatness of soul," which Dinesen admires and in which she recognizes something of herself, is that of "the real dwarf"—of a freak. Kamante is not a "real" dwarf, only dwarf-like—and this, perhaps, is even worse, because his strangeness is increased by his attitude. Kamante "holds the world to be crooked" based upon his own physical and psychological "deformity." That Kamante's oddity, his "eccentric[ity]" (*OA* 30), in which Dinesen takes so much pleasure, springs from something to be described as a disease or malformation implies a good deal about Dinesen's own nature and limitations. Her separateness, too, can be read as a deformity; the value of artistic distance is called into question.

Dinesen tells Kamante to come to her for treatment. He does so, but she is unable to cure him and sends him to the mission hospital. He returns some months later, at Easter. With "a strong sense for dramatic effects," he appears at Dinesen's house with the old bandages still on his legs, which he unwinds, the better to show his healed legs. This rebirth at Easter identifies Kamante as another Christ figure—the difference being that while Dinesen borrows images of sacrifice for Emmanuelson, with Kamante she uses images of resurrection. Kamante's suffering is ended; he is reborn by his trip to the hospital. Kamante's sense for dramatic effects, too, links him to Emmanuelson, and Dinesen can identify with Kamante because of it. After he has displayed his healed legs, Kamante announces "that he was now a Christian. 'I am like you,' he said" (*OA* 29). Kamante's rebirth includes not only a new body but also a new religion, and a new approach to other people at the same time: it is now possible for him to be "like" someone.

Kamante's physical healing allows him to become partially socialized. His rebirth is a rebirth into society. He starts work in Dinesen's house, in regular contact with many other people. However, because he was healed, through Dinesen's intercession, by missionary doctors, he has also converted to Christianity, and thus is re-estranged from Kikuyu society. Just as Kamante's legs will always remain stick-thin, so his former "wildness" will always leave a slight distance between him and the rest of human society. First his illness and then his conversion have made him irrevocably strange.

So, although he makes an announcement to the contrary, the newly Christian Kamante is not "like you" in any obvious way. Dinesen is puzzled by what he means:

> ... once or twice I tried to catechize him, but then he explained to me that he believed what I believed, and that, since I myself must know what I believed, there was no sense in questioning him. I found that this was more than an evasion, it was in a way his positive program, or confession of faith. (*OA* 48-9)

Kamante's "confession of faith" is a complex problem. He does not mean that he believes that Dinesen knows the truth and that therefore he trusts her judgment; he does not mean that she must once again take the role of high priest. Instead, he means that he has finally entered a community, and it is a community of which she is a member. She has only to consult her own sense of community, he thinks, to know what he believes. He is "like you." But Dinesen, inevitably, does not agree. She reports Kamante's misunderstandings of Christian doctrine with amusement, as when he tells the other children "that a Christian might at any moment put his heel upon the head of the largest snake and crush it" (*OA* 59). Nevertheless, Kamante's oddity as a Christian implies Dinesen's oddity as an African. While as a young boy Kamante misunderstands Christian references to snakes, Dinesen herself blithely accepts her tutor's false claims about the Swahili numeral system; each, in an attempt to join the other's culture, makes ludicrous mistakes. Dinesen—while of course retaining her power as settler and storyteller—suggests by her likeness to Kamante that she must seem as strange to the Kikuyu in her semi-assimilation as Kamante does in his.

Despite Dinesen's condescension, Kamante and Dinesen both still see their religion as a form of kinship—although in different ways. For the young Kamante, Christianity makes him "like you," that is, makes him somehow the same as his employer. For Dinesen, Kamante seems to be kin not in his likeness but in his strangeness: neither of them belongs in their own societies. Although their religious understandings may differ profoundly, each one sees that they have something in common.

One of the most important changes in Kamante, from Dinesen's point of view, is his willingness to break old Kikuyu taboos, which he had previously observed—particularly the fact that "after Kamante had become a Christian he was no longer afraid to touch a dead body" (*OA* 52). Kamante becomes a new sort of person: a Kikuyu without the Kikuyu taboo against touching the dead. For Dinesen, this means that he is in a position not only to help her (which of course is one of the primary effects of the change) but also to help the rest of the people on the farm: the removal of corpses is necessary for public health. Only Kamante is willing to help her move bodies. This is at once a further alienation from his original society and a productive adaptation to new conditions. Hybridity makes him flexible. Moving dead bodies together links Dinesen and Kamante all the more firmly, as do their prayers for a woman in childbed. Together they watch the spiritual boundaries of the farm, and shepherd people across them, just as Dinesen sees travelers off the physical boundaries of the farm.

But Kamante is much more than a sidekick. He is also an artist. After trying him in several jobs, Dinesen eventually teaches him to cook for her—an art form, it is important to note, that Dinesen took very seriously.[12] While it is Dinesen who does the teaching for her own purposes, Kamante learns more than she is able to teach. She may look at him with "something of a creator's eyes," but Kamante escapes her creation. He turns out to be a great artist in the kitchen—at the top of the artistic hierarchy Dinesen and Emmanuelson have been trained to appreciate. His talent for European cooking is amazing, as much for its incongruousness as for its power. "Nature had here taken a leap and cut away from the order of precedence of faculties and talents, the thing now became mystic and inexplicable, as ever where you are dealing with genius." "Nature" is responsible for Kamante's "genius"; when he cooks, he is closest to his natural state. The state of nature is not isolation on the plains but creation in the kitchen. Kamante is a "genius" rather than simply an able pupil because he transforms Dinesen's teachings. He is beyond her understanding: "I could not make clear to myself how or indeed why he worked as he did" (*OA* 30, 34, 36). Where Kamante once thought that, as a Christian, he must be comprehensible to Dinesen, it turns out that, as an artist, he is "inexplicable."

He seems to know everything about French cooking already:

> The great tricks and tours-de-force of the kitchen were child's play to his dark crooked hands; they knew on their own everything about omelettes, vol-au-vents, sauces, and mayonnaises. (*OA* 35)

Kamante's talent is inborn and incongruous. His hands are "dark" and "crooked," emphasizing his racial strangeness and semi-deformity. But alien and deformed as they are, these same hands know *"on their own"* how to do everything Dinesen tries to teach him. French cooking is suddenly an integral part of this Christian Kikuyu's nature. The "trick" and "tour-de-force" alike become simplified: they are instinctual rather than artificial. Here artifice and nature meet, a generic hybrid (much like the memoir-novel *Out of Africa* itself). The phrase "child's play" makes the process of cooking into a naturalized game: children's games have already figured in *Out of Africa* as extensions of the landscape. The "great[ness]" of the cooking becomes childlike, too. Kamante makes the art innocent. (This is in stark contrast to Dinesen's previous chef, Esa, an old man who is poisoned by his young wife.) But Kamante's innocence is not foolishness: it is a kind of freedom. Some of Dinesen's methods he simply ignores:

> He scorned all complicated tools, as if impatient of too much independence in them, and when I gave him a machine for beating eggs he set it aside to rust, and beat whites of egg with a weeding knife that I had had to weed the lawn with, and his whites of eggs towered up like light clouds. (*OA* 35)

As anyone who has ever beaten eggs knows, Kamante takes the difficult way of doing things. His "scorn" of machines makes his cooking entirely dependent upon his own muscle and ingenuity (for it takes a great deal more skill, as well as strength, to beat eggs by hand than with an egg beater). Kamante's "impatience" with the "independence" of tools is a form of independence in its own right; he sets himself outside of Dinesen's control by refusing the gadgets she offers him. By cooking in his own way, Kamante himself becomes more than a tool to Dinesen: he separates himself from her purposes, even while he cooks in the way she wants him to. By insisting on his own methods, Kamante consolidates his control of his art form—it is entirely his own.

Robert Langbaum writes, "[i]f the capacity for our most civilized accomplishments can be found in nature—as they are in Kamante's genius ... then those accomplishments acquire an absolute value and a civilization can be judged by the extent to which it is congruent with nature" (137). Dinesen, in short, finds validation of her own culture in Kamante's ability. Her assessment of his cooking is an act of self-justification, and, as such, unpalatable. But it is also, in its way, a mark of respect. Kamante, by far the most foreign person in *Out of Africa*, is the one who most resembles Dinesen; she is drawn to and frightened by him.

But Dinesen and Kamante's approach toward each other's cultures only goes so far. Despite his great talent, Kamante himself does not, she says, understand "the real meaning" of his art, and he feels "nothing but contempt" for European cooking. Kamante's hybridity is only partial—as is Dinesen's: she is scornful when he offers her "a Kikuyu delicacy" like "a roasted sweet potato or a lump of sheep's fat" (*OA* 37).[13] Neither party has all the necessary talent and training to appreciate the other fully—the hybridization is incomplete. Their mutual incomprehension, however, strikes Dinesen as "moving" (*OA* 36); she is as mystified by Kamante's understanding of some of her wishes as she is by his failures to understand others. By cooking with talent and scorn Kamante registers his kinship to and independence from Dinesen; she must acknowledge that she has not created him after all. He is almost entirely self-made, out of a set of wildly varied elements.

Kamante's artistic insight is most useful to Dinesen outside of the kitchen. In his opinion of Dinesen's own art, Kamante forms a deeper interplay of African and European cultures than in his Christianity or even his cooking. One day, he expresses doubt that the book she is writing, which will eventually become *Seven Gothic Tales*, can be a very good book, because the pages do not hold together as they do in Dinesen's copy of *The Odyssey*. Dinesen explains that with some expense, her book can be made to resemble the one Kamante holds—that is, to hold together in a hard binding—and then tells him the story of Polyphemus.[14] Kamante is interested, and asks Dinesen to tell him Odysseus' word for "*Noman*," the name Odysseus uses to trick the Cyclops. Dinesen tells him the Greek word "*Outis*." Kamante asks if she must write about the same story, and Dinesen answers that "people can write about anything they like. I might write of you," an explanation which despite its claim of difference implies that writing *The Odyssey* and writing about Kamante are not so very far apart. Kamante, taken aback, asks what she would write about him. Dinesen suggests that she might write about his early life, and asks what he thought about before she found him on the plain. He answers, "'*Sejui*—I know not.' 'Were you afraid?'" asks Dinesen, and Kamante says that, "all the boys on the plain are afraid sometimes." Dinesen asks of what, and he answers, "Of Outis . . . The boys on the plain are afraid of Outis" (*OA* 47).

This marvelous story contains several important kinds of hybridity. There is first of all the linguistic mixing: Kamante and Dinesen must have been speaking Swahili, so the word for "Noman" that we read in *Out of Africa* cannot be the same that Dinesen used in telling Kamante the tale. The only words we have in the original form from the conversation are *sejui*, "I know not," and *Outis*, the Greek original Kamante asks for. These words are to some extent synonyms. They are single words for a complex concept of absence: *a thing which I cannot describe because I do not know it* and *a person whose name denies his personhood* are similar concepts. When Polyphemus cries out that Outis has stolen his sheep, he might as well answer the question "who was the thief?" with the word "Sejui" as with "Outis"; the effect would be the same.

The initial cultural mixture is Dinesen's construction, because she chooses to tell Kamante about that particular Homeric episode, and because of her decision to write about it—a decision which naturally highlights her own status as heroic wanderer; her book is to resemble *The Odyssey* in more than simply having a hard cover. The second mixture, however, is Kamante's, when he adopts Odysseus' language to claim, "with a little wry grimace" (*OA* 47) that the boys are afraid of Outis. Kamante's answer is a pun: the boys will admit to being afraid of no man, but they are in fact afraid of the place where no men are—the emptiness of the plains. Kamante's almost-joke about Outis describes a familiar fear with a new word, and makes sense of both, and simultaneously identifies the joker with the trickster-hero Odysseus and with the deformed Cyclops: Kamante sees his kinship with all the characters in the story—a feat which Dinesen herself only occasionally manages. Janet Handler Burstein writes that "[f]or most characters in the stories, awareness of oneself as both self and 'other' depends partly upon one's sensitivity to the symbolic meaning of experience, and partly upon one's openness and vulnerability to forces outside the self" (617). Kamante demonstrates his sensitivities in this scene. He can make subtle shifts between cultures, using each to illuminate the other, just as Dinesen herself does throughout *Out of Africa*. Dinesen and Kamante each enter the mindset of a new civilization by learning its language. Kamante is more than just a foil to Dinesen here; he is a colleague. While Dinesen never abandons the master's position, she sees in Kamante a like-minded interest in bridging cultural gaps. Kamante is "like her" after all: like all Dinesen's artists, and hybrid artists everywhere, he creates himself out of all the available materials. The work of a cross-cultural artist is to find kinship where none is evident, to create shared communities, and in the process to become most truly him/herself.

Conclusion

Out of Africa's hybrid artists combine African and European words and art forms to create their own identities, and in so doing enter into an artistic community which supercedes all other communal allegiances. By virtue of their deliberate self-creation and their loyalty to their hybrid art forms, Dinesen, Emmanuelson, and Kamante are more "like" each other than they are like anyone else. The core identity of the self-hybridizing artist is hybridization itself.

Notes

[1] The author of *Out of Africa* and the *Seven Gothic Tales* has many names. I refer to her by her primary, half-invented pseudonym, rather than any of the other names her friends, publishers, critics, and biographers have used: Karen Blixen, Pierre Andrèzel, Tanne, Tania, and Titania.

[2] Unlike the Western narrator described by Edward W. Said who, according to Said, omits personal statements, "shed[ding] ... [his/her] purely autobiographical and indulgent descriptions in favor of descriptions on which Orientalism in general and later Orientalists in particular can draw" (*Orientalism* 157), Dinesen's memoir is intensely personal, and, as I show, makes some attempt to find out what its characters (if not their originals) are thinking—because as residents of her farm, their thoughts affect her. But in its personal nature, Dinesen's picture of the farm performs a radical transformation of the sort Sidonie Smith suggests when she writes that the female autobiographer "may transform herself and cultural stories generally by shifting generic boundaries so that there is neither margin nor center" (59). Dinesen's boundary shift, in fact, turns margins *into* center, with her farm as the prime example. In effect, Dinesen is what Said describes as an Orientalist in that whatever attempts she makes to represent Africa on its own terms are secondary to her use of "Africa" for her own nostalgic purposes. It should be clear, though, that she treats Denmark and Paris in exactly the same way.

[3] The Danish edition was published under the author's real name, Karen Blixen; the British and American editions preserved the pseudonym, Isak Dinesen, which she had already used for *Seven Gothic Tales* (1934).

[4] It is by now a critical commonplace to remark that Dinesen closely resembles Walter Benjamin's "storyteller." See Landy; and Benjamin.

[5] Dinesen is far more scornful of the British colonists in her letters than in her memoir.

[6] The word for "nine" in Swahili sounds like the Danish word "to pee." I thank Lena Ahlin and Vera Kutzinski for help in finding this information.

[7] Similarly, when the farm is hit by a terrible drought, the shared experience of waiting for rain turns the farm from an assemblage of people into a durable, interconnected community.

[8] It is surprising that Robert Langbaum, who discusses the Biblical resonances of *Out of Africa* in *The Gayety of Vision: A Study of Isak Dinesen's Art* (1965) does not discuss Emmanuelson's Christ imagery.

[9] Dinesen's admiration for the Masai is not without a tinge of something disturbing.

In *The Africa That Never Was*, Dorothy Hammond and Alta Jablow write that British colonists in general tended to idealize the Masai, seeing in them a reflection of British aristocratic values:

> One can understand the cult of Masai worship only by recognizing that the bases of British perception rest upon a concept of aristocracy partly defined in terms of feudal values and partly in those of nineteenth-century gentry. Aristocracy becomes associated with a somewhat curious syndrome of traits: disdain for the tradesman, impassioned interest in

domestic animals, appreciation of the value of pedigree for man and beast, disciplined self-possession as well as marked self-assurance, and above all, a chivalric preoccupation with warfare. British adulation of the Masai is based on their seemingly upper-class attitudes. (165)

Dinesen's view of the Masai, in this context, is neither unusual nor comfortable.

[10] Robert Langbaum suggests that Emmanuelson goes to the farm in search of an audience (124).

[11] Kamante himself indicates that he was "left alone with no one to help me" (Gatura and Beard 32).

[12] Cooking is the artistic center of Dinesen's story "Babette's Feast," and one of the three careers—the others being writing and caring for the insane—which Dinesen considered upon her final return to Europe.

[13] For an interesting viewpoint on British accounts of Africans and food, see Youngs 54-80.

[14] Nobody has yet studied Dinesen's memoirs as a re-write of *The Odyssey*. A glance at the Homeric references in *Out of Africa* suggests a complex pattern of homecomings—Dinesen to Africa, Dinesen to Europe, Denys to the farm, etc. Dinesen's association with Odysseus marks her as a hero-wanderer, a storyteller, and a liar—all poses she embraces throughout *Out of Africa*.

9
Myth and Magic in the Fictional Worlds of Salman Rushdie's *Haroun and the Sea of Stories* and Maxine Hong Kingston's *Tripmaster Monkey*

Kuldip Kaur Kuwahara

> "And in the depths of the city, beyond an old zone of ruined buildings that looked like broken hearts, there lived a happy fellow by the name of Haroun, the only child of the storyteller, Rashid Khalifa, whose cheerfulness was famous throughout that unhappy metropolis, and whose never-ending stream of tall, short and winding tales had earned him not one but two nicknames. To his admirers he was Rashid the Ocean of Notions, as stuffed with cheery stories as the sea was fill of glum fish; but to his jealous rivals he was the Shah of Blah."
> Salman Rushdie, *Haroun and the Sea of Stories*

> "I'm writing a play for you, Nanci," said Wittman. "Wait for me while I write for you a theater; I will plant and grow for you a pear garden." Then she did look at him—he's wonderful. She stopped in her tracks to look up at him. She took his upper arm with her two hands. "I'll write you a part," he said, "where the audience learns to fall in love with you for your ochery skin and round nose and flat profile and slanty eyes, and your bit of an accent."
> Maxine Hong Kingston, *Tripmaster Monkey*

It would not be too far-fetched to assert that traditionally the Western mind has looked to the magic of the East with both awe and skepticism, and also with a sense of wonder as well as hesitation. The power of reason associated with the Enlightenment is, after all, still with us in the West just as myth-making and magical thinking are still with us in the East. This, despite all the shifting geographical boundaries associated with the rise and fall of empires, the expanding and shrinking of colonial powers, and, most recently, the growth of regionalism and internationalism.

In *Myth, Literature, and the African World* (1976) the Nigerian poet, dramatist, and literary critic Wole Soyinka points out that to the African mind, myth-making and magical thinking are not a form of escape, as has often been assumed in the West, but a way of capturing the very essence of experience. In his play *The Lion and the Jewel* (1963), Soyinka explores the power of Yoruba myth to recreate the reality of cultural conflict through the magic of song, dance and pantomime. As an entire world comes alive, the spectators are immersed in the experience of not only watching a play, but also participating in it as viewers turned into actors and actresses. The writer at play extends the stage of life to include all players in the business of living, dreaming, laughing and thinking. Soyinka thus challenges the logic-driven Western mind to experience the Nigerian world through myth and magic, which provide not an escape from life but capture the very essence of it through art.

The art of writing a play or creating a fictional world of winding tales that magically involves the reader in a reality that goes deeper than reason is certainly not the exclusive domain of the East, the West or the rest. Speaking and writing at a time of globalization and cross-cultural traffickings, it is particularly challenging to postcolonial and postmodern readers of contemporary world fiction to respond to writers such as Salman Rushdie and Maxine Hong Kingston. Riding the waves of multiculturalism, both Rushdie and Kingston draw on a complex range of East-West cultural contexts to create new meanings. To read Rushdie's *Haroun and the Sea of Stories* (1990) and Kingston's *Tripmaster Monkey* (1989; this edition 1990, all page references are to this edition) is to enter two distinct yet connected worlds. Rushdie, born in India and now living and writing in the West (first in the U.K., then in the U.S.), conjures up the magic of myth-making to address a very real question: What is the use of stories spun out of pure fiction? Born in the U.S., Kingston returns to the myths and legends of her Chinese ancestors to reconstruct an Asian-American writer's dream of staging an epic production of interwoven Chinese stories and folktales. Essentially, both Rushdie and Kingston explore the magic of playing with words in different worlds. Preoccupied with the art of fiction, these writers bridge East and West as they examine the reality of living in several cultures at once through abstractions and fictions.

Bridging East and West

Wandering between two worlds, Rushdie makes real, through his fiction, the life of the imagination. According to him, the artist's only reality is the one he creates for himself through his unique perspective. At the same time, he raises disturbing questions related to the artist's courage to tell the truth as he sees it and despite censorship. In *Haroun and the Sea of Stories*, the reader catches a fascinating glimpse of yet another dimension of biculturalism in world fiction. Rushdie, writing in the West, draws on his Eastern roots that connect with the art of story-telling in *The Arabian Nights* as well as the Sanskrit epic, *The Mahabharata* (for a recent edition in English, see Rajagopalchari). He both mocks and applauds the fiction-maker's art and poses the compelling question: How is the imagined different from the real?

As an Asian-American, Kingston turns to her Chinese roots to explore the identity of her fictional hero, Wittman Ah Sing, in the multi-ethnic city of San Francisco. Though named after America's quintessential poet, Wittman also bears a striking resemblance to Monkey, the trickster-saint of Chinese legend who helped bring the Buddhist scriptures from India to China. The Monkey stories of Chinese, Japanese and Indian folklore are based on the Sanskrit epic *The Ramayana* (see *The Ramayana of Valmiki*) as well as the Chinese classic *The Journey to the West* (see Kherdian for a recent retelling). Kingston draws on this background in *Tripmaster Monkey*. Her novel is an indictment of twentieth-century American society's preoccupation with superficial stereotyping of minority cultures. Wittman, the quintessential American hero, transcends race and class in American society as a triumphant artist at play. We catch him in the very act of writing an epic as American in its mythic proportions as it is Chinese in essence.

If Rushdie's Haroun poses questions about the identity of the true artist and the essential nature of true art, Kingston's Monkey explores the relationship of the individual and society, of the dilemma facing the Asian-American hero as his roving eye "takes it all in." As an artist, the hero transcends life's pettiness to suggest how art can shape life to create an alternate reality based on compassion and respect for all races.

Haroun and the Sea of Stories

In *Haroun and the Sea of Stories*, Rushdie juggles impossible fantasies with the realities of fictional creation. A self-conscious artist, he plays with both the ideal and real worlds. Challenging the Platonic dichotomies of Western philosophy, he deploys the syncretic powers of the artistic imagination. Weaving an intricate pattern of complex references, Rushdie draws on the magic of *The Arabian Nights* as well as (Frank Baum's) *The Wizard of Oz* (1900) to affirm Schiller's theory of the play drive. Rushdie develops his narrative around the Eastern concept of life as a *lila* or life as a game with all its players, both winners and losers. He conjures up the magic of the genie, as well as the sparkling Scheharazade outwitting the King for a thousand and one nights with a thousand and one stories. At the very beginning of the novel, Haroun asks his father Rashid, the poet, this rather Platonic question: What is the use of stories that are not even true? In true fairy-tale fashion, the novelist waves his magic wand to conjure up the world of stories and storytelling. In true Platonic fashion, Rashid Khalifa, is symbolically banished from the Republic when his mouth opens and no story comes out. Haroun had "often thought of his father as a Juggler, because his stories were really lots of different tales juggled together, and Rashid kept them going in a sort of dizzy whirl, and never made a mistake" (16). Where did all his stories come from, Haroun wondered:

> It seemed that all Rashid had to do was to part his lips in a plump red smile and out would pop some brand-new saga, complete with sorcery, love-interest, princesses, wicked uncles, fat aunts, mustachioed gangsters in yellow check pants, fantastic locations, cowards, heroes, fights, and half a dozen catchy, hummable tunes. "Everything comes from somewhere," Haroun reasoned, "so these stories can't simply come out of thin air . . .?" (16-17)

Playing with the form of the novel, and of mirrors reflecting mirrors, Rushdie takes his fictional characters on a breathtaking, fantastic journey to the very source of poetic inspiration. When Khattam-Shud attempts to poison the Ocean of stories, Haroun, feeling stunned, blurts out:

> "But why do you hate stories so much? . . . Stories are fun . . ."
> "The world, however, is not for Fun," Khattam-Shud replied. "The world is for Controlling."
> "Which world?" Haroun made himself ask.
> "Your world, my world, all worlds," came the reply. "They are all there to be Ruled. And inside every single story, inside every Stream in the Ocean there lies a world, a story world, that I cannot Rule at all. And that is the reason why." (161)

Khattam-Shud goes on:

"We are going to plug the Wellspring itself, the Source of Stories, which lies directly beneath this ship on the ocean-bed. As long as the Source remains unplugged, fresh, unpoisoned, renewing Story Waters will pour upwards into the Ocean, and our work will only be half-done. But when it's Plugged! Ah, then the Ocean will lose all its power to resist my anti-stories, and the end will come very soon. And then, water Genie: what will there be for you Guppies to do, but to accept the victory of Bezaban?" (162)

As the action develops, stories triumph over anti-stories with Haroun and his friends' discovery of the very source of all Stories:

The Source of Stories was a hole or chasm or crater in the sea-bed, and through that hole, as Haroun watched, the glowing flow of pure, unpolluted stories came bubbling up from the very heart of Kahani. There were so many Streams of Story, of so many different colours, all pouring out of the Source at once, that it looked like a huge underwater fountain of shining white light. (167-168)

If political control and the rhetoric of Empire can lead to anti-stories, only the truly free artist can explore the truth and tell it through the magic of story-telling. Rushdie thus explores the notion that one can be a true artist only if one is free to realize oneself by looking deep within the creative self to discover a moment of truth untouched by political and social considerations.

Tripmaster Monkey

In *Tripmaster Monkey* Kingston writes a picaresque account of the hero's adventures as an aspiring playwright who imagines himself to be an incarnation of the legendary Monkey King of Chinese myth. Kingston's novel is about a young male's search for community in America. Wittman struggles with the central question: How to live? The novel is as much about what disconnects, isolates and alienates individuals from each other as it is about what connects and creates harmony, empathy and compassion for fellow human beings. In his search for identity and community, and through his artistic endeavors, the hero, Wittman Ah Sing, articulates the question: Where do I belong?

Like Rushdie's Haroun, Kingston's Monkey plays with life and art. In both these fictional works, the artist triumphs through his ability to create ideal magical worlds that would reshape and give meaning to life. When

Nanci accompanies Wittman home, she learns what follows:

> "So this is where you live," Nanci said, looking down into one of his cartons, not touching the poems, just looking. "See that trunk over there?" He pointed at it with the toe of his boot. Books, papers, his coffee cup sat on its lid; a person could sit on it too, and it became a second chair. "That's the trunk I told you about. Proof, huh? Evidence. It exists. It became a theatrical trunk; it used to be a Gold Mountain trunk." It was big enough for crossing oceans, all right. It would take a huge man to hoist it onto his back. The hasps and clasps were rusty (with salt sea air), and the leather straps were worn. Big enough to carry all you own to a new land and never come back, enough stuff to settle the Far West with. And big enough to hold all the costumes for the seventy-two transformations of the King of the Monkeys in a long run of The Journey to the West in its entirety. "My great-great-grandfather came to America with that trunk." "Yes," said Nanci, "I recognize it." Every family has a Gold Mountain trunk in their attic or basement. "I can't die until I fill it with poems and play-acts," said Wittman. (29)

After Nanci leaves, Wittman "jumped off the table to the mattress, trampolined off that to the Gold Mountain trunk and onto the chair." His monkey-like movements reflect his self-image as the incarnation of a present-day King of the Monkeys:

> Elongating his chimp-like torso, he stretched for a look at himself in the built-in mirror on the door . . . "Bee-e-een!" he yelled . . . which is what Monkey yells when he changes. He whipped around and began to type like mad. Action. At work again. (33-34)

Thus we see Wittman turned monkey turned artist making the world spin in the "palm of his hand." At this point the narrator boldly intrudes to announce to the reader:

> Our Wittman is going to work on his play for the rest of the night. If you want to see whether he will get that play up, and how a poor monkey makes a living so he can afford to spend the weekday afternoon drinking coffee and hanging out, go on to the next chapter. (35)

In Wu Ch'engen's version of the Monkey story or "The Journey to the West" (see Kherdian for a recent retelling), the mythical monkey is born of a magical rock. As the Buddhist priest Hsuan-tsang makes his journey to India, which is situated west of China, and returns with the sacred scriptures, he encounters several obstacles. The magical Monkey helps him overcome both supernatural and physical obstacles. It is the story of a pilgrimage with the religious connotations all such journeys have, a journey in search of spiritual salvation. Kingston weaves her narrative within this structural framework of myth and magic and brings alive a compelling work of fiction. Just as the society in which Monkey travels—no matter how spiritual it may seem to be—is also a satire of earthly society with its bureaucracy and unreasonable ritual, Kingston's *Tripmaster Monkey* mocks social inadequacies that are obstacles in the path toward self-realization. Wittman Ah Sing monkeys around with his script until he is free to partake in an ironic celebration of community at the novel's conclusion: "To drums and horns, the dragons and lions were dancing again, a bunny-hopping conga line that danced out of the house and into the street. Wittman's community was blessing him, whether he liked it or not" (340).

Conclusion

While in *Haroun and the Sea of Stories* Rushdie is deeply engaged with the whole question of art and the relevance of the life of the imagination and the power of words to create new meaning, in *Tripmaster Monkey* Kingston addresses questions about ethnicity through the myth and magic of the writer's art. *Haroun and the Sea of Stories* ends on a note of triumph. The source of poetic inspiration unplugged, the writer is free to open his mouth and continue to tell his tall, winding stories. In *Tripmaster Monkey*, Kingston plays with words to examine multi-ethnic layerings that define American society. Through the use of magical realism, she explores mythical structures to create community even as she gives voice to distinct cultural sensibilities and endless possibilities in a complex world. Kingston creates a central character who struggles to write an epic, rich in irony and paradox, to define the nature and value of the aesthetic experience, challenge existing social patterns and create new patterns of possibility.

In the spirit of artistic freedom, Kingston and Rushdie move freely across different worlds and historical moments in time to play with time past as well as time present. In bridging East and West, as well as historical time zones, they challenge the contemporary reader to re-trace and bridge vast cultural divides that, at the highest level, are one.

10
"Cracking India"[1]
Tradition versus Modernity in Attia Hosain's *Sunlight on a Broken Column* and Manju Kapur's *Difficult Daughters*

Nadia Ahmad

Introduction

The 1947 Indian Partition lingers as a pivotal moment in the modern world, not so much for its political significance in the emergence of the sovereignties of India and Pakistan, but for its lasting impression of monstrosity and horrific emotional duress. Arguably, before the Indian Partition, the twentieth century had not experienced such a massive and excruciating migration of people.[2] A body of fictional explorations has arisen since, in response to this tumultuous period, and also in an effort to define the inner turmoil and social complexes that have been plaguing the subcontinent. It is naturally significant to observe why these phenomena occurred in terms of the novel form that allows one to go beyond mere historical accounts. What is even more interesting, however, is to examine the use authors have made of the events of Partition and the proclamation of national independence as a backdrop to probing the social, political, and economic issues that have been foregrounded by these very events. It must be underscored that Partition is not a bygone event, but a contemporary phenomenon that continues, along with attitudes toward interweaving aspects of religion and culture on the one hand, and the relationship between tradition and modernity on the other, to influence the politics of identity in South Asia.

Arguably, Partition and the fiction describing it are very much an attempt at reconciling problematic configurations of tradition and modernity. The events leading up to Partition and the response to it were not so much a hope for independence as a desire for modernity. Any reading of Partition or Indian independence reveals the picture of an on-going struggle between tradition and modernity, especially when modernity in Western terms is defined as excluding religious belief. Postcolonial theory has taught us that this Western understanding of modernity is problematic, or turns out to be inapplicable, when exercised on non-Western constructs; because to ignore the role which established culture and religion play in the social structure of a people is to shatter its ideological virtues.

When one looks at the conflicting notions of modernity the novelists whom I will deal with here mimetically engage in, it becomes evident that one group in particular experienced the severest kind of trauma: women. They prove to be the ultimate sufferers because woman's body is constantly the site of self-definition, which entire cultures make a site of contestation, especially within the South Asian literature depicting Partition. This chapter focuses on Attia Hosain's *Sunlight on a Broken Column* (1961; this edition 1992, all page references are to this edition), with an additional, briefer look at Manju Kapur's *Difficult Daughters* (1998), two works of fiction with women protagonists that put on stage, so to speak, Muslim and Hindu India, respectively. I argue that in both novels the difficulties arising from Partition and its aftermath are framed within the binary opposition of tradition versus modernity, representing Indian/Eastern and British/Western cultures, as two antagonistic poles affecting the lives of the characters, and especially the women protagonists. In examining the novels, I analyze the ways in which the writers demonstrate the concepts of tradition and modernity, as represented in the spheres of religion and culture, to be problematic and fluid in connotation, but also manipulated in the politics of identity deriving from and complicated by Partition. I start, however, by discussing the significance and use of Partition literature to better contextualize my readings of the two novels.

The Significance and Use of Partition Literature

Within the past decades, several works of fiction, of substantial and not so substantial quality, have been surfacing in European and American libraries, bookstores, and college reading lists on the subject of the 1947 Indian Partition. This newfound interest in Partition literature arises from multiple constraints and systems. Indo-Anglian Partition and post-Partition works of fiction are part of an emerging genre of postcolonial literature,[3] that aims to cope with the intimate concerns of people against the backdrop of nationalism and religious fervor by linking the political with the personal. For the most part, the great majority of South Asians are still experiencing an enduring trauma from the events of Partition because the emotional and psychological problems related to them were never fully addressed in a public way or even considered an issue.

As Mushirul Hasan points out:

> The history books do not record the pain, trauma and sufferings of those who had to part from their kin, friends, and neighbors, [nor] their deepening nostalgia for places they had lived in for generations, the anguish of devotees removed from their places of worship, and the harrowing experiences of the countless people who boarded trains thinking they would be transported to the realization of their dreams, but of whom not a man, woman or child survived the journey. (48)

Accompanying the birth of the two nation-states, communal riots flared up not only in large cities but also in remote villages. Hindus, Muslims, and Sikhs slaughtered each other by stopping trains to and from India and Pakistan and slitting the throats of the passengers.[4] They raped women and murdered children in the fields. Property was seized from migrating groups. Civil tension continued mounting for several months. More than 75,000 women were raped, kidnapped, abducted, and forcibly impregnated by men of the "other" religion. Thousands of families were split apart, homes burnt down, and villages abandoned (Butalia 35). Some women were so embarrassed by the sexual humiliation they suffered that they refused to return home. The destruction of families through murder, suicide, broken women, and kidnappings caused grievous post-Partition trauma. "Refugee camps became part of the landscape of most major cities in the north," as Urvashi Butalia writes in *The Other Side of Silence: Voices from the Partition of India*; however, as the same author points out, "a half century later, there is no memorial, no memory, no recall, except what is guarded, and now rapidly dying, in families and collective memories" (35). The focus of Butalia's observations is the women who were forgotten, together with what they went through—as the form of their contributions to independence. Such disregard for women's memories is an indication of the disparity between their sufferance and the treatment they later received.

Moreover, the communal hatred is difficult to pinpoint: was it the result of a tension already existing between the native groups, or was it rooted in a British propaganda that turned the South Asians against each other? Indians, who had only one month earlier been chanting such slogans as "Hindu, Muslim, Bhai, Bhai,"[5] began using slurs to address one and other. Entire generations of differing but interconnected religious groups were shattered in a matter of weeks or even days. As Butalia points out:

> The transformation of the "other" from a human being to the

enemy, a thing to be destroyed before it destroyed you, became the all-important imperative. Feelings, other than hate, indifference, loathing, had no place here. Later, they would come back to haunt those who had participated in violence, or remained indifferent to its happening. (56)

The heart of the matter is not determining what groups created such and such a situation because in point of fact, all sides contributed to the physical, emotional and sexual violence. Undoubtedly, the emphasis should now be placed on how the groups might learn to reconcile with each other. Thus, the purpose of Partition literature can be seen as steps toward conflict resolution because accusations, threats, insecurity and fears are prevalent among those who were and continue to be traumatized by the events surrounding the independence movement.

The two nations and their peoples are searching today for a way to come to terms with a difficult history. The continuing impact of unresolved geo-political issues illustrates the lack of closure of the Partition episode: even after Partition several issues remain unsettled, particularly in Kashmir. The British may have abandoned Indian soil, but foreign Western powers, particularly the United States of America, continue to wield considerable influence in the area. Western countries still maintain an upper hand in South Asian policy because they supply arms. And, while with the advent of urbanization people have started moving into urban centers, causing the collapse of the village and family units, Hollywood films and sit-coms along with large multi-national corporations such as Coca-Cola and McDonalds have infiltrated the social scene, creating an ever-widening gap between tradition and modernity. This may appear to be an oversimplification of recent social developments, but it is symptomatic of the crippling effects of modern multi-national capitalism.[6]

Therefore, given this fraught situation, it appears that only the novel, with what I would call its "subjective objectivity," can be "trusted." The novelist creates a discourse to bring these past and current issues to the forefront of society. At the same time, the novels I will discuss below engage the issues of independence and Partition, using these as a means to explore other issues, which then emerge as the larger picture to the devastation that followed in the wake of the bloody birth of nations. The fragmentation of cultural syncretism leads to the conflation of religion and culture. The novelists suggest that this was disastrous for South Asia, especially with the confused approach to "modernity." Since it is impossible to sort out the historical, political, and economic intricacies associated with Partition, history seems incapable of examining the full implications of Partition trauma; hence, the necessity of fiction.

Examining Partition from a literary perspective provides keener insight into the vacillating experiences of individuals and the collective vicissitudes of nations. The novel form creates a discourse for understanding the sentiments of various sides of the tale because the author is not bound by a sense of "historical objectivity." Anita Desai in her introduction to Hosain's *Sunlight on a Broken Column* writes, "To read [Hosain's] novel and short stories is to become aware of the many and varied threads that go to make up a rich and interesting life as well as the doubts and struggles and contradictions it contained" (ix). The fiction writer has the unique ability to produce a greater comprehension of the events because he or she places racial, religious, socio-economic, and political biases in front of the reader to present a rounded narrative account of Partition. Even though the narrator and characters in the text may not be free from bias, they can still offer a broader range of the emotional and personal ramifications inherent in, and penetrating, the social fabric. In short, the novel form provides us with a unique understanding of the ideology of the nation in a way that is distinct and different from the typical historical approach to South Asia.

Tradition versus Modernity

The notion of modernism creeps up—indeed strikes one—repeatedly in Partition literature. Characters in *Sunlight on a Broken Column* and *Difficult Daughters* illustrate the effects of modernity in its triumphant moment (though not without an accompanying sense of alienation): individual social simulacra promote a syndrome for the modern, which becomes a vehicle for not only self-empowerment but also self-aggrandizement.

Understanding the linguistic origins of "modernity" may help situate the term in the context of the two novels examined in this chapter. *Modern* signifies pertaining to the present time; contemporary; not antiquated or obsolete; characteristic of contemporary styles of art, literature, or music that reject traditionally accepted or sanctioned forms and emphasize individual experimentation or sensibility (*Webster's Encyclopedic Unabridged Dictionary of the English Language*). A "modern person" is thus one whose views and tastes are considered as being so. The word arrives into the English language by way of the Latin adverb *modo*, which means only, merely, lately (of the time), just now. The word *modernus* derives from the original ablative singular of *modus* (*mode*) added to *-ernus*, the adjectival suffix of time (*The New College Latin and English Dictionary*).[7] This etymological excursus is important because it introduces the element of *time*: it is time that propels movement and, therefore, evolution. In the context of literature, modernism refers, especially in the twentieth century (in which both novels take place), to the character, tendencies, or values that adhere to or sympathize with the modern; modernism rejects or diverges from the past and takes form in any of the various innovative movements and styles (*Webster's Encyclopedic Unabridged Dictionary of the English Language*).

I will now examine the narrative and thematic concerns of *Sunlight on a Broken Column* and *Difficult Daughters* in order to show why modernity becomes problematic within the context of post-Partition India. As a semi-autobiographical story set in the 1930s during the waning moments of British rule in India, *Sunlight on a Broken Column* focuses on the life of a young aristocratic Muslim girl, Laila, on the verge of becoming a woman, who is dealing with both independence politics and her own, personal struggle to balance tradition and modernity. While her relationships with her peers and relatives provide a framework for exposing/discussing the issues of Partition, her inner conflicts lay bare her position vis-à-vis tradition as symbolized by the Islamic religion. Laila does not tolerate any sort of hypocrisy, whether it is found in feudal, religious, or modernist relations. Noticing the fragmentation of (her) culture and tradition, as she seeks to find a place for herself, she deals with her questions and doubts by working herself into a position that leads to a subtle realization of the spirituality of Islam. Likewise, in *Difficult Daughters* the story hinges on the tension between tradition and modernity. The author presents a young woman from Amritsar who struggles with family duty, educational aspirations, and an illicit relationship with a college professor during Partition. Kapur suggests that the root of all present-day evil is this tension between tradition and modernity, while religion and inter-religious conflicts become a subtext in the gender war. *Difficult Daughters* was published in 1998 in the shadow of Hindu nationalism, and offers a disguised critique of religious communalism and of the pretensions of nationalism. Again, both novels provide a backdrop for dramatizing issues of tradition and modernity during a particular moment of crisis, Partition.

Sunlight on Broken Column

In nationalistic discourse, the word "modern" becomes problematic because it serves as an umbrella term for the self-justification of ideas that promote an individual subjectivity through rationalism, modern science, and technological progress. However, this equation simultaneously brackets off the spiritual and the religious as "irrational." This shift, I suggest, is antithetical to the Eastern worldview, which is basically spiritually oriented.

In *Sunlight on Broken Column*, Laila's relatives, Aunt Saira, Kemal, and Saleem, have the following conversation:

> "Things have changed so much. But you must learn what your position in life is, and where you belong," [Aunt Saira sighed].
>
> "We were left in no doubt about that on quite a few occasions in England—we coloured people," Kemal smiled.
>
> "I like my position in life," laughed Saleem. "It is very comfortable. When I was young I thought otherwise, but that was adolescent masochism which I mistook for Marxism. Mind you, I still appreciate its principles, but I am no Lenin and can establish no Soviets..."
>
> "Linen serviettes" Aunt Saira frowned. "I do not know what you are talking about."
>
> "How fortunate you are, mother. Oh, brave old world!" Saleem laughed and kissed his mother.
>
> She smiled happily and kissed both her sons. (Hosain 178)

This conversation expresses a preoccupation, if not an obsession, with the modern age, which the characters are struggling to define. Rhetorical theory argues that the rhetor, the speaker, is able to affect his/her audience by anticipating and controlling the audience's reaction, and eliciting a specific, controlled response.[8] Trained in modern education, which is equated with "England," Saleem and Kemal illustrate the concept of the dialogic. From their words and their revealing smiles, they plan their acts to obtain a specific response from their mother. The conversation indicates that for the two young men, to transform themselves through modern education and European principles, i.e., Marxism, constitutes an inner struggle, as they can only "appreciate" (and not appropriate) Marxist principles.

Interestingly, Marxism is a way of analyzing/solving the problems of the feudal system, by which the young men's family earns its wealth. Thus, a definite tension emerges because of the conflict between the traditional source of this money and the modern philosophical principles Saleem and Kemal uphold. These two are unable to reconcile the incompatible aspects of this issue, and often project their confusion in the way they treat their mother. Indeed, in their smirks and witty putdowns the two brothers appear rather cynical toward her. In this, are they being truly "modern," or are they, on the contrary, merely exhibiting filial impiety? If the latter, I suggest that Hosain points here to an act having graver consequences: she taps into religious ideals concerning disrespect to parents, considered an enormity in Islam.[9] In a well-known Hadith, the Prophet Muhammad is reported to have said that Paradise lies under the feet of the mother. Moreover, it is said in the *Quran* that:

> Your Lord decrees that you shall worship none but Him and treat your parents well, and if one or both of them reach old age with you, say not "Uff!" to them nor upbraid them, but speak noble words and lower the wing of humility to them out of mercy, and say, "O Lord, have mercy on them, as they raised me when I was young." (Chapter 17, verses 23-25)

I wish to advance that if saying "Uff!" to one's mother or father is not permitted, then mocking and belittling them is also in the realm of what is prohibited within the context of Muslim Indian tradition. Most religions and cultures sustain the ideal of showing respect to parents; the Hindu worship of the goddess as mother also expounds the high sanctity of the maternal role. The "modern" phenomenon of rebellious children and filial impiety is adverse to the traditional model of the parent-child relationship in India, while in modern Western societies, with their emphasis on the individual, the child must rebel against its parents in order to grow up.

Arguably, Saleem and Kemal's "cleverness" reflects a feeling of personal insecurity on their part. If they were confident about their espousal of Western principles, they would not need to make humorous remarks about them. They are, in fact, not truly convinced of their validity, since these principles are at odds with their Indianness. Hosain suggests a bit of hypocrisy here.

Trapped between two worldviews, the young men cannot reconcile being both shut off from the English on account of racial prejudice, and misunderstood by unlettered folk "back home." The irony that emerges in the passage is due to the author's suggestion that modernity for these characters is only a façade; the modern (Indian, postcolonial, Eastern) person in the novel only "thinks" that his/her situation is better. In reality, his/her condition is not necessarily "improved." To illustrate, the distance that separates the sons from their mother is the result of their being sent to England to study.

This distancing between characters occurs in other instances in the novel as well. For example, Uncle Hamid would like Saira and his children to be "modern" in their education and thinking, and Zahra's husband wants her to appear "modern" in her clothing and manners. Yet what does modernity really mean for these characters as they go about trying to be "modern"? At best, they have achieved only a superficial level of modernity, apparent in their academic degrees, apparel, and talk. And yet, it would be difficult to consider this kind of "modernity" as substantive. I would suggest that within the universe of the novel, these characters ultimately feel disconnected to the (real) modern world and therefore disillusioned.

In Laila's case, the question invariably arises as to whether she is traditional or modern, or to what extent she is either one. She herself reflects: "I felt I lived in two worlds; an observer in an outside world, and solitary in my own—except when I was with friends at College. Then the blurred, confusing double image came near to being one" (Hosain 124). This duality in her personality and her acceptance of hybridity represent a confused sense of identity. Exposed to "modernity," she cannot relate wholly to her Muslim tradition any more; but at the same time, she is hesitant to wholeheartedly accept the modern system of education and all that it entails. Meanwhile, Laila does not feel comfortable adopting the new *social* system of modern India (that is basically Western/British in character) because it conflicts with the ideals of her tradition. Trying to reconcile tradition and modernity creates tension in her. She also doubts that she will achieve inner satisfaction through her studies because she questions the value of the modern educational system as a means to liberation.

Nadira, one of Laila's peers, exemplifies what Laila views as the difficulty of attempting to preserve a Muslim heritage from the Mughal Indo-Islamic world. Laila finds that Nadira's "visions of the greatness of the Islamic world in the past were blurred," for her, Laila, "by its decadence in the present" (Hosain 125). While Laila brings forth mimetically what for many seems to be a valid complaint concerning the "decadence" of the Islamic present, the question that must preoccupy us is what she means by her concept of "the Islamic world." Is it the religious or the cultural aspect?

The notion of adhering to religion *per se* is problematic for some people in parts of South Asia, and maybe everywhere, to the extent that Islam is seen solely as a religious ideal, with mores, and standard codes of conduct—and not as (also being) a cultural expression that needs to be preserved. This issue is compounded when the scholarly aspect of the *din* (way of life[10]) escapes the concern of the people and is replaced by the preservation of an Islamic *culture* separate from *din*. Orthodox Islam does not in fact espouse a separation of culture and religion; it defines cultural practices within the scope of Islamic methodology. That is, Islam is an overarching social construct in which the cultural elements are subsidiary. However, ignorant of or oblivious to this configuration, material capitalism in essence dilutes the notion of religion into a cultural entity that is distinct from actual Islam—which in fact encourages moderation in material as well as religious affairs: practitioners can very well find concordance and balance between the material and the spiritual, avoiding either extremes. So, within the context of material capitalism (i.e., from the perspective of Western modernity), Muslim Indian culture comes to signify the way in which people eat food, celebrate weddings,[11] mark death, etc.; in short, a set of specific customs and rituals. The problem with this narrow understanding is that the concept of Islam becomes associated with these "external" elements[12] when in point of fact Islam strives to distance itself from material excess.[13] In other words, this specific problem is rooted in how Islam is perceived: a particular cultural norm versus the totalizing *din*.

In contrast to Laila's quandary, the sense of alienation that Saleem and Kemal, who have apparently opted to repudiate "tradition," are shown to experience in the novel is mimetically indicative of the ills of emerging modernism in Indian society. Yet, since variant forms of modernism exist in South Asia, it is essential to single out the particular one evoked in the novel. The standard model of European modernism in the colonies was a capitalistic system, maintained by imperialist bonds.[14] The colonized in this system could easily be subjugated if they were convinced that their former tradition inhibited forward progress. At the same time, it was impossible for them to forsake tradition altogether. Looking back on the early Anglo-Indian encounters, the systematic attempt of the British to anglicize Indians is obvious, if not out and out blatant. Lord Thomas Babington Macaulay in his famous "Minute on Education" in 1835 helped devise "an Indian elite, junior allies in imperial progress: 'a class of persons, Indian in blood and colour but English in taste, in opinions, in moral and in intellect.' The elite, in turn would assist in guiding India to a better future" (qtd. in A.S. Ahmad 121). Macaulay's vision symbolizes European humanism in South Asia: he sought to encourage the natives to abandon centuries-old languages, values, and customs at the spur of the moment. This sentiment had been pervading colonial India, but Macaulay was one of the first Victorians to enunciate it. As Akbar S. Ahmad notes, "Simply put, the more like an Englishman an Indian thought and behaved the higher he scored on Macaulay's scale. A paradox lies at the heart of the matter: the more English the Indian becomes, the more alienated he is from his own people and the culture, which he is meant to represent" (A.S. Ahmad 121). European humanism, which is the basis of colonialism, degenerates into racism when the civilized nations impart the doctrine of humanism to the colonized. I advance that the predicament of the fictional characters Saleem and Kemal should be contextualized within such "modernism."

The debate over tradition—that appears in *Sunlight on a Broken*

Column in the form of Islamic heritage and North Indian customs—and modernism is part of an age-old intellectual argument. The process of colonization entailed several hundred years because of the intellectual might of the Muslims, who were considered the greatest threat to imperial rule, particularly in the case of the British Raj. The British realized this strength and set about to win Muslim support.[15] It would be far-fetched to assume that only military superiority conquered them. Syed Muhammad al-Naguib al-Attas asserts in *Islam and Secularism* (1978) that there was at first a confrontation between Western and Islamic fronts on the historical, military, and social level; and that the conflict was moved to the intellectual level later. Once the colonizers conquered the Muslims militarily, they set about to weaken what empowered the Muslims: their intellectual strength. The confrontation between Islam and the West is a permanent one because the challenge is not to Western Christianity, but to the entire system of metaphysics, which results in the conviction among some Muslims that Christians do "not believe [in] anything."[16] Al-Attas finds that the dispute between "you and them" is a perpetual clash between Islam and the Western worldview.[17]

Thus, the tension between Aunt Saira and her sons is due to a clash of worldviews evident through the sons' disrespect toward their parents, that is a lack of *adab*.[18] Eastern cultures place a high degree of importance on *adab*, especially in connection with behavior toward the mother. Disregarding this principle metaphorically, through however seemingly inoffensive, insignificant smirks and witty putdowns, signifies in *Sunlight On a Broken Column* a collapse of *adab*. I would like to suggest that it is modernity that causes this dramatic change because it shifts the focus from respect and proper conduct (as forged and sustained by the collective in Muslim India) to the individual, who can more easily abandon these ideals.

Difficult Daughters

Difficult Daughters creates a space where the issue of woman and modernity can be discussed openly. Yet there prevails throughout the novel a bitter tone regarding the social and gender constructs that arose as a result of modernity—which becomes an ambiguous proposition, since, along with its promise of "liberation," it can also entrap as a tool of patriarchy and colonialism. The female protagonist, Virmati, creates a scandal in her family when she falls in love with "the Professor," an already married man, who places her in his home alongside his wife and helps her obtain higher education in Lahore. Virmati is being exploited by a patriarchal system (the Professor) through the mode of colonialism (English literature) and Indian nationalism. Kapur presents her main characters as symbolic of figures of the Indian Partition.

On a personal level, the character of Virmati represents female naiveté and passivity because she is easily taken advantage of by the Professor and is abused on an emotional level. After a miscarriage:

> Virmati became better. But not less dull. One abortion and one miscarriage. She was young, she told herself, years stretched before her. Years of penetration, years of her insides churning with pregnant beings.
>
> God was speaking. He was punishing her for the first time. Maybe she could never have children. She had robbed her own womb earlier, just as she had robbed another woman of her husband. Ganga's face, swollen with hate and fear, had followed her everywhere, the venom concentrated in the gaze of her evil eye. Maybe that was why Kishori Devi had taken all those precautions.
>
> The brief time she had been in perfect health, but, preoccupied with shame, she had violated her body. The time for a child lay in the future. Now she felt she was left with nothing. Her job could not sustain her, and flaunting Harish seemed a pathetic gesture, signifying her emotional poverty. (227-228)

Virmati realizes the importance of her body and how she, as a woman, is perceived when she violates it. The *gharr-bahir* (home - outside world) dichotomy in the novel can only be understood by realizing how greatly women's personal lives and relationships were impacted by the way they preserved their modesty or not. The "shame" motif continuously appears in the novel because it is a cultural and religious virtue. Virmati's feeling of guilt arises because she feels she has incurred divine wrath. She is trying to achieve a level of modernity through education and social mobility, but she finds herself stumbling on traditional values that haunt her efforts to grasp female agency. Her inner conflict is very much the issue of reconciling tradition and modernity.

The author relates episodes such as the one above to the larger political issues of the era in order to allow for a critique of politics and Indian independence. Another force at work in the novel is religious communalism, which vehicles the tension deriving from self-definition based exclusively on religion and nationalistic grounds. At a broader societal level, Kapur uses the novel to criticize the politics of Partition and post-Partition events, especially contemporary Indian issues. The

Bharatiya Janata Party,[19] the political wing of Indian/Hindu nationalism, is a phenomenon of the 1990s, which gained momentum in part as a response to the communal tensions that arose after the 1992 Babri Masjid demolition.[20] At the same time, the discourse of Hindu nationalism professes to be a celebration of the nation reaching back to the moment of birth, Partition. Kapur critiques the formation of nationhood by mapping Virmati's relationship with the Professor against the political background. Virmati feels she should exhibit the ambitions of Hindu nationalism apparent in her friend Swarna:

> Virmati stared at Swarna. What a girl! Her opinions seemed to come from inside herself, her thoughts, ideas and feelings blended without any horrible sense of dislocation. She was committed, articulate. Would the Professor want her to be like Swarna? She didn't want to do anything that would alter the Professor's underlying love for her. Maybe she could be more like Swarna from the inside, secretly. (123-124)

In one sweeping stroke, the narrator reduces Hindu nationalism by narrowing it to an attempt to win male approval in a basically patriarchal situation. At one point, Virmati is admiring this other girl's assertiveness, but in the meantime she is shaping/restricting her own views according to the manner a male authority figure would perceive her affiliation with Hindu nationalism. And Hindu nationalism itself is being equated with an underlying patriarchal system. The mixed message here suggests a serious flaw in Hindu nationalism and in the way that it is constructed because it works within the existing patriarchy that can further limit the woman's sphere.

The critique also takes the overt form of reevaluating "modernity" by looking at the patriarchal system. The question posed is, how "modern" can Hindu nationalism and the colonial education system be in a patriarchal system? There is even a collusion of patriarchy with colonialism, which appears through the English literature the Professor teaches. Swarna herself indicates she was studying English Honours in Lahore when she became active in Indian politics. The presence of English language and literature carries a foreboding association to colonialism. Through modern education, patriarchal elements of colonialism can further subjugate women. In the election for senior studentship at Lahore College for women, Swarna's rival was a Muslim student, Ashrafi, who had been "persuaded" by the principal (122), understandably British and probably male. The actual contest for the election was not even Hindu and Muslim, but was more along the lines of colonial authority and patriarchy.

Even though Swarna wins, she remains a pawn of the interests of Hindu nationalism.

Difficult Daughters is a disguised critique of religious nationalism that takes the form of a nationalism that equates being Indian with being Hindu and generates communal tension. I would suggest that the novel argues that instead of creating a feeling of communal harmony and societal unity, Indian nationalism creates an antagonistic discourse, turning past friends into enemies because of political, national, and religious affiliations. Swarna tells Virmati:

> What a baby you are Viru! So many things are deeper than friendship. In this case it must have been religious identity, maybe Muslim fear and insecurity. They must have told her she would be disloyal to the Muslim cause. I didn't want to stand against Ashrafi, but my group said we had to win this election if it was the last thing we did. So you see, ultimately I too put something before friendship. (123)

In the novel, the construction of Hindu nationalism is problematic on multiple levels. Firstly, it can destroy friendships, which should neither be evaluated as an abstract concept nor devalued as a merely particularistic bond. Kapur inserts this thematic to question the ethics of the nationalist movement, formed by party affiliations. The difficulty lies in what "the group" wants as opposed to the individual. The reader is expected to ponder the claim that "So many things are deeper than friendship" and, one senses, is expected to disagree with Swarna. The narrator often associates religious communalism with nationalism and regards them as resulting from patriarchal and colonial structures. The novel portrays the "modern" Indian as being pushed into a false dialectic of self-definition based on nationality and religion when having to decide between tradition and modernity, a choice that definitely entails culture and religion.

Conclusion

Evidently, the term "modern" is problematic because of what it signifies. Yes, the phenomena of improved technology, education, and communication that it has come to denote can potentially benefit people irrespective of their social positions. At the same time, however, modernity from the European imperialist perspective is a self-justification for colonizing countries pursuing nationalist and capitalist enterprises at the expense of the native populations.

At the same time, by virtue of being "modern," the contemporary perspectives of fictional narratives are estranged from the past and create a latent sense of uneasiness. The Indo-Anglian writer offers alternative views of modernity: in the end, s/he feels it contributes to a feeling of disillusionment with the self, others, and the nation form.

Along the same lines, through the process of recollection, fiction is able to do also what history and historiography fail to do; just as an ideological understanding of the Muslim view of women replaces the estrangement of women through modernity. To leave out the work of remembering is to discount the personal and emotional element of Partition trauma. History constrains memories in its futile attempt to be objective, but it is humanly impossible to achieve absolute objectivity. Yet the "new" historiography of Partition is attempting to counteract the traditional mode to relating historical events. Besides authors such as Urvashi Butalia and Mushirul Hasan, novelists such as Hosain, Kapur and others[21] are trying to recover overlooked fragments of experience by looking at a different kind of "history"—one based on memoirs, interviews, and women's testimonies. The novels *Sunlight on a Broken Column* and *Difficult Daughters* provide a backdrop for dealing with issues of Partition that were overlooked in the traditional historiographical processes of narrating it. Hence, fiction proves to be an important alternative medium for coping with experiences of trauma and gender because, as a basically subjective tool, it is often better at dramatizing testimony than history.

Notes

[1] *Cracking India* (1991) is the title of a novel by Bapsi Sidwa.

[2] "The Partition of the subcontinent led to one of the largest ever migrations in world history, with an estimated 12.5 million people (about 3 percent of undivided India) being displaced and uprooted. In Punjab, the province most affected by the violence and the killings, 12 million Hindus, Sikhs, and Muslims were involved, and [the] migration of 9 million people began overnight in an area the size of Wales. In the north Indian state of Uttar Pradesh (UP), nearly 4,000 Muslims a day boarded the train to Pakistan until 1950" (Hasan 47).

[3] *Postcolonial literature* essentially refers to works arising after a period of colonialism. The date a nation obtains independence would determine what constitutes that nation's postcolonial literature. Thus, for India and Pakistan, the era of postcolonial literature begins after 1947, whereas for some Latin American countries "postcolonial" works can date back to the nineteenth century. However, the indication is significant not only historically, but also because it suggests a shifting mind-set toward colonialism, that is reflected in the fiction.

[4] "By far the largest proportion of refugees—more than ten million of them—crossed the Western border which divided the historic state of Punjab, Muslims

traveling west to Pakistan, Hindus and Sikhs east to India" (Butalia 3).

⁵ "Bhai" means *brother* in Hindi. "Bhai, Bhai" refers to the bond of trust and affection as between brothers. I am indebted to Kuldip Kaur Kuwahara for this information. Editor's note.

⁶ It is important to note that the global marketplace and speculative finance have become capitalism's dominant forms, displacing its earlier industrial and monopoly stages. In *Postmodernism, or, The Cultural Logic of Late Capitalism*, Fredric Jameson writes that

> there have been three fundamental moments in capitalism, each one marking a dialectical expansion over the previous stage. These are market capitalism, the monopoly stage or the stage of imperialism, and our own, wrongly called postindustrial, but what might better be termed multinational, capital. . . . [L]ate or multinational or consumer capitalism . . . constitutes . . . the purest form of capital yet to have emerged, a prodigious expansion of capital into hitherto uncommodified areas. . . . [it] eliminates the enclaves of pre-capitalist organization it had hitherto tolerated and exploited in a tributary way. One is tempted to speak in this connection of a new and historically original penetration and colonization . . . (35-36)

⁷ Middle French *moderne* is from the Latin term *modernus*.

⁸ One must understand the role of the rhetor in comparing the monologic and dialogic theories.

Mikhail Bakhtin argues that the importance of the communicative function of language is often underestimated, if not ignored. For him, language philosophers, and their understanding of exactly who the speaker is and of his/her capacity as a speaker are to blame: they regard language from the speaker's standpoint only, as if there were just *one* speaker who does not have any *necessary* relation to *other* participants in speech communication. Apparently, the monologic listener does not realize the importance of what is being said because s/he merely absorbs the information in a robotic way. The emphasis of the communicative approach is on the speaker, who is seen as an independent entity within the speaking-circuit.

The monologic model is accurate, in terms of defining the speaker, but it fails when taken as the whole system of communication. Therefore, Bakhtin is not invalidating Saussure's claim; he is merely developing the other half of Saussure's speaking-circuit. According to the Russian language philosopher, when the listener perceives and understands the meaning (the language meaning) of speech, s/he simultaneously adopts an active, responsive attitude towards it. The perception and understanding of the speaker and his/her subject force the listener to take an active, responsive attitude towards it. Because this process occurs simultaneously with that which is being said, the speaker must be aware of this phenomenon, and act accordingly, anticipating the response of the audience and even, in some instances, controlling it.

⁹ "The Prophet (Allah bless him and give him peace) said, 'Shall I tell you of the worst of the enormities . . ?' and one of those he mentioned was undutiful behavior to one's parents" (Ibn al-Naqīb 655-656).

[10] This would encompass the totality of the Islamic philosophy and teachings. Editor's note.

[11] In *Sunlight on a Broken Column*, the depiction of Zahra's wedding emphasizes sheer luxury and extravagance:

> Later, when Zahra was married, there was little of the ceremonial, spread over many days of feasting, music and dancing, that coloured and brightened the secluded life of the community; yet it was stripped to the bare bones of its Islamic reality, as a simple contract.
> Once again the house at Hasanpur was crowded, but keyed to a brighter note. The zenana stirred and vibrated with movement and noise as guests and maid-servants and children and groups of village women milled around, their voices raised and shrilled with sheer excitement. For every woman and girl there was an excuse to wear the richest of clothes and jewels, and the whole house spilled with gem-set colours and throbbed with the rhythm of the *mirasins*' gay marriage songs, and the insistent beat of their drums. (Hosain 112-113)

Perhaps Hosain is merely showing how upper-class Indian aristocrats reduce culture to ostentatious displays—whether or not they are Muslims.

[12] Western eyes may see Zahra's lavish wedding as representing in the novel "Islamic reality"—that is reduced thus to an image of Islamic culture that is itself part of Indian "tradition," that appears, not only "decadent" in the extravagance displayed, but also, inimical, e.g. in Saleem and Kemal's terms (to Marxism, and therefore metaphorically, within the fictional universe of the novel), to "modernity" by Western standards.

[13] The Prophet Muhammad is reported to have said: "Beware of going to extremes for those before you were only destroyed by their excessiveness."

[14] The colonizers staked their claims in the colonized countries because of monetary interests. According to Marx, imperialism is the highest form of capitalism. Moreover, capitalism has the capacity to integrate economic and socio-political elements within the colonial construct for self-interest. This system inverts the natural order when everything changes shape.

[15] Francis Robinson explains:

> At this time [late nineteenth century] the British felt Muslims to be the greatest threat to their rule. They had failed to reconcile the former rulers of India to their government; the Mutiny uprising of 1857 was seen to confirm this. In 1870 they decided that the safety of the Raj demanded that they find ways of attaching powerful Muslims to their side. This policy was developed just at the time that Saiyid Ahmad Khan was striving to reconcile his co-religionists to Western knowledge and British rule. His initiatives received much official encouragement. Arguably Aligarh College would never have been founded, and may not have survived, but for the government support, which ranged from land made available at derisory rates to personal donations from viceroys. His All-India Muslim Educational Conference, which from 1886 drew

Muslims together from all over India for the first time, operated within the framework of government approval. He himself was given the most unusual distinction, for an Indian at the time, of being knighted.

Aligarh College and the Educational Conference were the institutional bases on which the All-India Muslim League, the spearhead of Muslim separatism, was founded in 1906. The first office of the League was at Aligarh; its first secretary was the College secretary. The first major campaign of the League was to demand separate electorates for Muslims, and extra representation in those areas in which they were "politically important," such as the UP, in legislative councils which Viceroy Minto and Secretary of State Morley were developing for India. With some misgivings the British were persuaded and these privileges were granted in the Council reform of 1909. Thus a separate Muslim identity was enshrined in India's growing framework of electoral politics. When in 1919 and 1935 the franchise was extended and further powers devolved, separate electorates were continued and the principle of Muslim separateness confirmed. (41)

[16] The Arabic word *aamna*, which is translated as *belief* or *to believe*, has a different connotation than the English word. *Aamna* signifies belief in Allah and is reserved only for that particular belief. While in English it is possible to say, "I believe in Marxism," *aamna* cannot be applied in such a case. This linguistic nuance illustrates the clashing worldviews of the European and the Islamic.

[17] As to the intellectual cause of the decline of Muslims, he considers that the basic problem is reduced to the single evident crying of the loss of *adab* (see his *Islam and Secularism*).

[18] Proper conduct. Editor's note.

[19] The Bharatiya Janata Party (BJP; "Indian People's Party"), one of the largest political parties in India, is the successor party of the BJS (founded by Syama Prasad Mookerjee), which merged itself into the Janata Party in 1977. The BJP was formed as a separate party in 1980 after internal differences in the Janata Party resulted in the collapse of its government in 1979. The BJP was the dominant component of the National Democratic Alliance which formed the government headed by A.B. Vajpayee, with Lal Krishna Advani as the deputy prime minister, before the general elections in 2004 which saw Sonia Gandhi's Congress Party as victor.

The BJP has close ties to the Hindu nationalist Rashtriya Swayamsevak Sangh (RSS) organization and is considered by many to be responsible for inciting Hindu-Muslim riots in a number of occasions. The BJP considers itself to be a Hindutva party and defines Hindutva not in terms of religion but as Indianness. According to the party this is in consonance with the root meaning of the word Hindu by which the Arabs referred to all people inhabiting India. However the BJP is considered by some to be a Hindu-fundamentalist or even a Hindu-fascist party (http://www.fact-index.com/b/bh/bharatiya_janata_party.html). Editor's note.

[20] The Babri Masjid was a mosque built in 1528 in honor of the first Mughal emperor Babur in Ayodhya, Uttar Pradesh, in northern India. It is alleged that Babur destroyed an existing temple at the site, which many Hindus believe was the temple built to commemorate the birthplace of Rama, a mythical figure

who Hindus believe was an incarnation of Vishnu (regarded as a major god in Hinduism and Indian mythology) and ruler of Ayodhya. The mosque was used by Muslims as a prayer site until 1947, when Hindu activists, who wished to see it replaced with a Rama temple, broke in and placed statues of Rama inside the mosque. Following this, the state government ordered the mosque sealed. In 1986 the mosque was reopened by a lower court at the request of the Hindu nationalist Vishwa Hindu Parishad (VHP, "World Hindu Council") to allow Hindus to worship there. In 1990, Lal Krishna Advani, a top member of the Bharatiya Janata Party (BJP) began a campaign tour (a *rathayatra*, or "chariot-journey") to build support for a Rama temple at the mosque site. The VHP also negotiated with the All India Babri Masjid Action Committee (AIBMAC), an organisation created to represent the interests of Muslims in the mosque, over the site, each presenting evidence to the court of their claims to the site.

The mosque was destroyed on December 6, 1992 by a crowd of nearly one million activists (*karsevaks*) of the VHP and other associated groups such as, allegedly, the BJP. The destruction occurred at the end of Advani's *rathayatra*, and there is some evidence that it was pre-planned by Hindu nationalist groups. Following the destruction of the mosque, communal riots broke out between Hindus and Muslims across India, including in Mumbai (Bombay), which is a largely secular and cosmopolitan city. It is generally accepted that the campaign to build the Rama temple and the destruction of the mosque was responsible for the BJP's meteoric rise to power. Since then, the AIBMAC has been campaigning to have the mosque rebuilt at the same site, while the VHP has been moving forward with plans to build a Rama temple there.
(http://www.fact-index.com/b/ba/babri_mosque.html). Editor's note.

[21] Other such authors are, *inter alia*, Sidwa with *Cracking India* and Khuswant Singh with *Train to Pakistan* (1956).

11
Rabindranath Tagore, Cultural Difference and the Indian Woman's "Burden"

Sriparna Basu

> "I had thought that the island of England was so small and the inhabitants so dedicated to learning that, before I arrived there, I expected the country from one end to the other would echo and re-echo with the lyrical essays of Tennyson; and I also thought that wherever I might be in this narrow island, I would hear constantly Gladstone's oratory, the explanation of the Vedas by Max Mueller, the scientific truth of Tindall, the profound thoughts of Carlyle and the philosophy of Bain. . . . But I have been very disappointed in this."
>
> Rabindranath Tagore, *Europe Probashir Patra* (Letters of a European Sojourn)

In a spate of recent critical debates, the 1913 Nobel literature prize winner Rabindranath Tagore has emerged as an icon of multiculturalism, with his work supposedly marked by a fluid interchange between Indian and Western identities. A consensus has emerged that the Bengali author dissociated himself from nationalism, the dominant trend in the cultural politics of his time, to become a pioneering proponent of "universal humanism," that grappled with the intricate question of decolonization and the birth of the transnational/plural/hybrid subject, and that also marked the beginning of a dynamic interaction between Indian and Western modes of thought. *Gora* (1910; this edition 1961, all page references are to this edition, identified parenthetically as *G*), one of Tagore's most influential novels, has been a centerpiece of this debate; with its principal character Gora, an Irish foundling adopted by Indian parents, seen as articulating precisely such a hybrid identity: one that resists incorporation in terms of nationalism or imperialism. "Since many anticolonial critiques of culture equate universalism with imperialism," writes Lalita Pandit,

> it is important to remember that Tagore's universalism is different . . . it refers to a moral/intellectual/emotional discipline based on the principle of empathy. The imperialistic notion of universalism, in contrast, is nonempathic, fixed, and hegemonic. . . . Tagore's universalist philosophy developed as an antidote to this annihilating, nonassimilative, separatist universalism. . . . Tagore's Gora does not only incorporate the contradictions of caste and race; this hybrid figure makes the dividing lines between the nation and the world *blurry*. (emphasis added, 207-208)

According to this reading of Tagore, imperialism is aligned with nationalism, both of which are opposed by Tagore's assimilative and multicultural version of universalism that seeks, in place of the imposition of hegemony, artistic and human empathy. Shyamal Bagchee makes a similar case when he places Tagore's poetic and artistic discourse merely at the margins of cultural nationalism. In arguing his case, Bagchee adopts a dangerously essentialized view of the relationship between literature and nationalism, when he writes, "A poet *as a poet* does not care much for the notion of a nation. Exceptionally clear in his disapproval of exploitation and colonizing, and loud in his praises of liberty and freedom, Tagore found the idea of a nation to be unappealing" (142).[1]

I argue in this chapter that, far from being "blurry," a dividing line between the Indian nation and its others is clearly marked in Tagore's writings, and that what often takes place in them is an agonistic back-and-forth that marks a contest between hegemonies, that is a veritable clash of cultures. Tagore's texts—rather than weaving together and moving fluidly between multiple and disparate cultural selves in postmodern fashion, as recent critical work will have it—are bicultural in a way that recognizes the intractability of cultural difference. Thus, despite the assertion of many critics, Tagore may end up privileging a form of cultural nationalism, even though the presence of the West as cultural nationalism's "other" is also strongly marked in his work. In fact, universalism itself may be reclaimed in Tagore's text as a *national* trait, and bespeaks a structured and programmed interaction between India and Europe.

As is known, women are often the ground for the formation of cultural identity. In the case of colonial India, women are "a central symbol in reciprocally constituting the identities of colonizer and colonized alike," as Barbara Metcalf has pointed out (19). The Tagorean feminine subject, premised upon self-restraint and the sublimation of destructive erotic and political passions, emerges as a significant marker of cultural identity.

Tagore's idyllic feminine has a nurturing quality which he hopes will find expression in nationalist discourse, leading to a form of cultural nationalism that is more authentic than political nationalism's aggressive assertions of identity. His writings harbor a significant conjunction between militant nationalism and transgressive sexuality. What I find salient is not a rejection of nationalism, but an unresolved tension between (a sublimated, "Eastern" style) cultural nationalism and (the formal, "Western" mode of) political nationalism in which Tagore's effort to preserve feminine aesthetic expressiveness at the expense of female sexuality gives rise to acute dissonances in the rhetoric of his novels. This chapter looks at how the Tagorean feminine subject, founded upon self-restraint and the sublimation of destabilizing erotic and political passions, emerges as a bearer of cultural nationalism. I foreground first the aporias present in this discourse, through a reading of his accounts of visits to Europe, and of his essays on the relationship between East and West; and then examine three major fictional works: *Gora*, *Ghare Baire* (The Home and the World, 1916; this edition 1961, all page references are to this edition, identified parenthetically as *GB*), and *Char Adhyay* (Four Chapters, 1934; this edition 1961, all page references are to this edition, identified parenthetically as *CA*).

East and West: The Providential Encounter

In a diary entry on the occasion of a visit to Europe in 1890, Tagore records the following parable:

> A clever fox once invited a wise stork to a feast. Upon arrival at the banquet, the stork found enormous plates full of sweet and appetizing foods. After some polite remarks the fox said, "Brother, let us commence." No sooner had he said this that he started wolfing down the food. The stork knocked against the plates with his long beak but could not lift the food to his mouth. Giving it up at last he began to contemplate, with his customary gravity, the stretch of water by which he lived. The fox, I suppose, looked at him meaningfully as he said, "brother, you are not eating. You came all this way in vain. The feast has not been up to your standards." ... The next day the fox went at the stork's invitation, to find that various appetizing victuals had been arranged in tall vessels. They provoked the fox's greed, but he could not reach inside the vessels with his mouth. Without wasting time, the stork used his long beak to commence his meal. The fox licked the

vessels from the outside and obtained one or two morsels of food, but had to return home hungry . . .

If the Britisher is a fox, then we have to return hungry after merely surveying the delicacies displayed on his silver platter, and if we are meditative storks, then the fox does not even see well what lies within our deep stone vessels—he has to return content with a whiff of its odor. (Tagore, "*Europe Jatrir Diary* [European Diary]"[2] 400-401)

Tagore makes it apparent that this parable is to be read as an allegory of the East-West encounter. It is, however, difficult to read into it a message of universalism, or a hybridization and fusion of Eastern and Western selves; it emphasizes rather the separateness of cultures. In E.M. Forster's *A Passage to India* (1924), India's landscape figures as constituted of uncanny, disquieting spaces that can never quite acquire coherent representation in discourse: Forster's narrative brings to the reader's attention the liminality of an "other" world that is ghostly and impenetrable; it can lure, but refuses satisfaction. Despite Adela Quested's best efforts, India remains beyond her reach. Tagore's visit to Europe as retold through the parable of the fox and the stork parallels Adela's experiences of cultural alienation in India; it is a view, from the other side, of the Orient/Occident divide. In a manner reminiscent of Tagore's parable, *A Passage to India* also recounts the incompatible menus of Anglo-India: "Julienne soup full of bullety bottled peas, pseudo-cottage bread, fish full of branching bones, pretending to be plaice, more bottled peas with the cutlets, trifle, sardines on toast . . . the food of exiles, cooked by servants who did not understand it" (48-49). Anglo-India's menus register in gastronomic terms the limits of cultural intimacy, just like the mutually incompatible platters on which the fox and the stork serve up their repasts.

It is noteworthy that in Tagore's version it is the fox, representative of the Britisher, who initiates contact between them; while the stork, representing the Indian, responds to the former's ambiguous overtures. Neither the fox's cleverness nor the stork's wisdom and gravity are accidental attributes—they were largely the terms in which Tagore conceived the difference between India and the West. Both in his novels and discursive essays Tagore cast Indians as deficient in material civilization, political organization and general canniness, but also as possessors of an ancient spiritual wisdom. The Hegelian assumption that the people of each nation express a different world-historical principle seems to guide Tagore's many statements on nationalism.[3] For him, the particular world-historical principle embodied by the Indian people is that of spirituality, which entails a rejection of politics:

... the teaching and example of the West have entirely run counter to what we think was given to India to accomplish.
...
... here is India, of about fifty centuries at least, who tried to live peacefully and think deeply, the India devoid of all politics, the India of no nations, whose one ambition has been to know this world as of soul, to live here every moment of her life in the meek spirit of adoration, in the glad consciousness of an eternal and personal relationship with it. (*Nationalism* 13)

In this reading, India lives by and embodies an ancient spiritual wisdom, which runs counter to the "national carnivals of materialism" indulged in by Western peoples (*Nationalism* 141). Rather than resembling a Western nation, Tagore sees India as a meeting ground of all nations, thus fulfilling the purpose of preserving the universal:

... if it be true that the spirit of the West has come upon our fields in the guise of a storm it is all the same scattering living seeds that are immortal. And when in India we shall be able to assimilate in our life what is permanent in Western civilization we shall be in the position to bring about a reconciliation of these two great worlds.... [T]he history of India does not belong to one particular race but is of a process of creation to which various races of the world contributed—the Dravidians and the Aryans, the ancient Greeks and the Persians, the Mohammedans of the West and those of central Asia. At last now has come the turn of the English to become true to this history and bring to it the tribute of their life, and we neither have the right nor the power to exclude this people from the building of the destiny of India. Therefore what I say about the Nation has more to do with the history of Man than especially with that of India. (*Nationalism* 26-27).

Indian history had been reconstructed in colonial historiography as an unending series of invasions from outside, commencing from an imputed "Aryan" invasion and culminating in the contemporary British domination of India. Thus "conquerability" appeared as a principal feature of Indian society in Orientalist discourse, albeit combined with a touch of recalcitrance, as repeated incursions from outside failed to produce any fundamental changes in its civilization.[4] This combination of pliancy and recalcitrance are stereotypically feminine characteristics; the passage quoted above also registers India as a feminine and erotic presence. Tagore characterizes the West as a forceful male presence in India "scattering living seeds" and regenerating Indian civilization; contact with it is like a fated encounter to which India must surrender herself. He transfigures the colonial presence in India into the story of a romance, with the English bringing to it "the tribute of their life."

Tagore thus transforms the "conquerability" trope of colonial historiography into a myth of universal assimilation, where it is India's role to receive and synthesize elements from all cultures. What is being played out in India, therefore, is not merely the history of a nation; it has to do with no less than the "history of Man." In Tagore's vision of the encounter between India and other cultures India becomes a nurturing feminine figure, simultaneously self-effacing and self-aggrandizing, accepting tribute from and nursing elements from all cultures that come to her shores. In the battle for hegemony between Indian and Western cultures, it is the "spirit of the West," likened to a forceful storm, that scores; but the Indian pole that ultimately wins by absorbing and incorporating the West.

If Tagore's vision of cultural assimilation transforms the West and the English into figures of exoticism, in keeping with the nature of exotic desire, the scene of East-West eroticism is shadowed by interruptions, absence, and failure. While there are intimations in Tagore's work of a providential encounter between England and India, its physical embodiments turn out to be grotesque and perverse. In Forster's *A Passage to India*, the enigma of India is figured through the Marabar caves: they look romantic from a distance, but proximity to them brings disenchantment and disorientation. In a reversal of the exotic trope, Tagore experiences intimacy with Europe through its literature, but finds a closer encounter with it to be disorienting and estranging. Contrary to his reputation as a universal humanist, Tagore observed that, "an international feast is possible only on the field of literature" ("*Europe Jatrir Diary* [European Diary]" 400-401).

On his first trip to Europe the young Tagore reported that "some laughed in our faces, while a few shouted—'*Jack, look at the blackies!*'" (*Europe Probashir Patra* [Letters of a European Sojourn] 252).[5] On the way back from his second trip Tagore found a beefy Englishman regaling his lady friend with anecdotes of how Indian *punkah*[6]-pullers could be made to work through the night with kicks and blows from a stick:

> Suddenly a hot spear struck me. Those who make conversation with women in this manner are eminently capable of kicking a weakling native, a pathetic specimen of humanity, into the other world. I too am of that insulted race, how could I bear to sit and eat at the same table and occasionally smile at him? (*Europe Jatrir Diary* [European Diary] 404)

As in the case of Forster, sublimated erotic relationships are rudely interrupted by the realities of colonial rule, which effect a grotesque desublimation of the cultural encounter. Tagore's *Crisis in Civilization*, written in 1941 towards the end of his life, sounds out the same themes as his youthful European diaries, and reflects a tone of painful disillusionment:

> I naturally set the English on the throne of my heart. Thus passed the first chapters of my life. Then came the parting of the ways accompanied by a painful feeling of disillusion when I began increasingly to discover how easily those who accepted the highest truths of civilization disowned them with impunity whenever questions of national self-interest were involved.
>
> There came a time when perforce I had to snatch myself away from the mere appreciation of literature. As I emerged into the stark light of bare facts, the sight of the dire poverty of the Indian masses rent my heart. . . . And yet it was this country whose resources had fed for so long the wealth and magnificence of the British people. While I was lost in the contemplation of the great world of civilization, I could never remotely imagine that the great ideals of humanity would end in such ruthless travesty. (6-7)

Thus romantic attraction for the West has to take a back seat as it confronts the reality of a despotic desire articulated by colonialism, and "the parting of the ways" is akin to a painful divorce between lovers.

Tagore's novels clarify further the thematics of the providential/dystopic encounter and failed erotics between Europe and India, and of femininity as the ground for an ideological negotiation of these issues. The early *Gora* marks a relatively optimistic mapping of this terrain, in which women are seen as bearers of universal values. Tagore's vision considerably darkens in *Ghare Baire*. *Char Adhyay*, written during a later stage of the nationalist movement, articulates an apocalyptic vision in which politics and sexuality, home and world, India and the West are brought into destructive juxtaposition; this collapsing of boundaries is shown to lead to a collapsed self. This last novel is testimony to the death of Tagore's universal humanism.

Gora: the Nurturing Mother

In *Gora*, the circumstances of Gora's birth and adoption may be seen as an allegory of a providential meeting between East and West, a reading of which helps delineate the character of Tagore's cultural nationalism. Gora was born of Irish parents, and orphaned as an infant during the Mutiny of 1857. He was consequently adopted by Anandamoyi, the childless wife of Krishnadayal, a Hindu Brahmin in the service of the imperial government. According to Anandamoyi, speaking to Krishnadayal:

> One day in a dream I saw myself offering a basket of white flowers while worshipping the deity—but when I looked again there were no flowers in the basket, in their place was a flower-like snow-white child; I cannot tell you what I felt when I saw it, my eyes filled with tears—but just when I was about to snatch it into my lap I awoke. Within ten days I found Gora—God's gift to me. How could I give him up to anyone else? I must have held him in my womb in my previous life, at the cost of great pain, which is why he has come now to call me "Mother." Just think how strangely he came to us! Fighting and bloodshed raged all around us, we went about in fear of our lives—when deep at night that white woman came to take shelter with us, you were too afraid to take her in, but I put her in the cowshed unknown to you. That night she delivered the baby and died. Would the orphan boy have lived if I hadn't taken care of her! What did you care? You wanted to hand him over to a padre. Why a padre? Is the padre his parent, or did he save his life? Was such a way of getting a child less wonderful than giving birth to him myself? Whatever you say, unless He who gave to me my child takes him away from me, even if I die I will not give him up. (G 23-24)

Anandamoyi is a nurturing mother figure here, allegorically representative of India as the motherland. Although Gora is born orphaned, he does not lack a mother. Anandamoyi's acceptance of Gora as God's gift at the agonistic moment of the Mutiny is a reminder of the dual character of East-West relations as envisioned by the Tagorean problematic: the providential encounter occurs in the midst of bloodshed and violence.

However, Anandamoyi and Krishnadayal, who has retreated into orthodox Brahmin ritualistic practices, dissent on the issue of Gora's adoption. By keeping Gora instead of giving him up to the local padre, Anandamoyi subverts her husband's will. Born at the moment of the Indian Mutiny, Gora is the son of invaders on Indian soil. As Anandamoyi reminds Krishnadayal, despite his Brahmin pride, his ancestors have had to place themselves at the service of various "invaders": "if you are of such high lineage, and the elect of God, why has He made you grovel in the dust before the Pathans, then the Mughals, and now the Christians?" (G 24). Anandamoyi's act of adopting and raising Gora may therefore be interpreted as a passage from a motif of invasion and conquest to one of assimilation: mother India accepts all who come to her as her own. In a victory for cultural nationalism, Gora can now be raised Indian, setting the stage for his realization at the end of the novel: "Mother, you are my mother. The mother I had been in search of was all the time sitting in my room at home. You have no caste, you make no distinctions, and have no hatred—you are only the image of our welfare. It is you who are my India" (G 350).

The cultural nationalism articulated through the figure of Anandamoyi struggles against dual hegemonic possibilities, fighting a battle on two fronts. On the one hand Anandamoyi wrests Gora away from the padre, who would have returned him to his racial origins. But on the other hand, Anandamoyi also goes against the exclusivist nativism represented by Krishnadayal, who would have Gora turned out of the household (and also, symbolically, from the larger Indian "family") as an outcaste.

From his early childhood, Gora manifests a national consciousness, and, through his forceful word and example, eventually gathers around himself a band of followers. Through his energetic actions, Gora asserts allegorically the Tagorean notion of the regeneration of the East by the "spirit of the West." Gora derives something from both nature and nurture: while he brings vigor and charisma to a colonial milieu which appears lacking in these qualities, through Anandamoyi's tutelage he acquires a spiritual center of being as well as devotion to the cause of the nation, which Anandamoyi figuratively represents.

Gora's acceptance of the feminine principle of spirituality and restraint that Anandamoyi and later his fiancée Sucharita represent may be seen allegorically as the triumph of the East. While Gora represents the forceful masculinity of the West that appears as an essential element of colonial romance, this masculinity needs to be softened and humanized by the spirituality of the East, present in Anandamoyi's and eventually Sucharita's influences on Gora. The Gora/Sucharita couple thus represents the possibility of an ideal synthesis of Eastern and Western values that Tagore dreamed of. If this is taken to be indicative of Tagore's universalism, it is, however, premised upon an extremely essentialized version of East/West difference, in which the West represents vigor and power, while the East stands for spirituality and nurturance. It may also be noted that the Tagorean synthesis circumscribes gender roles, and is based on an essential difference between masculinity and femininity—the West/East difference maps on to a masculine/feminine difference. The reason Gora is paired with Sucharita rather than her sister Lolita is that the latter is too much like Gora himself—forceful, passionate, direct, lacking restraint—thus impugning the principle of femininity. Moreover, the West/East synthesis happens best on Indian soil. Upon the discovery of his true identity at the end of the novel, Gora tells Sucharita's and Lolita's father Pareshbabu: "This dawn, with my mind absolutely bare, I have been born into the very lap of India—after so long I have fully realized what is meant by a mother's lap" (G 349). The reference to Gora's mind made "absolutely bare" suggests that Gora begins with a clean slate, his mind purged of all other influences, ready to accept the inscriptions of the East.

The name *Anandamoyi*, signifying a tranquil bliss in its female incarnation, connects the character Anandamoyi semantically to the blissful harmony associated with the private sphere and an idyllic home.[7] Gora's image of Sucharita is close to this relationship with Anandamoyi, but it is not quite the same. When Gora is in prison after a clash with the colonial police, Sucharita's image comes to haunt him:

> At one time Gora had avoided Sucharita. . . . But during his days of confinement in gaol the memory of Sucharita could not be kept at bay. There had been a time when the fact that there were women in India hardly entered Gora's mind. Now he had made a new discovery of this truth through Sucharita. The sudden revelation of such a great and ancient fact made the whole of his strong nature tremble as though from a blow. . . .
> . . . he did not then regard Sucharita as a special individual, but rather as an idea. The womanhood of India was revealed to him in the figure of Sucharita. He regarded her as the manifestation of all that made the homes of India sweet and pure, loving and virtuous. . . . He thought to himself that she was the nation . . . The misfortunes of the country are insults to her, and since we are indifferent to those insults, our manhood is shamed today. (G 240-243)

While Gora perceives Sucharita here as the nurturing feminine who safeguards the space of home, his worshipping her as the image of the nation contains, however, the potential for a more overt sexuality as well as militant nationalism. Through her modesty and self-effacing character, Sucharita holds these passions in check. But what if the erotics implicit in Gora's attitude towards Sucharita as well as in his relationship to the nation were to be desublimated and receive overt expression? We turn to exactly this situation in *Ghare Baire*, where cultural nationalism is placed in sharper tension with political nationalism, and the clash of cultures becomes explicit.

Ghare Baire: The Home and the World or the Fire Next Time

Ghare Baire is a critique of political nationalism, and may therefore seem to conform to the dominant construction of Tagore as a universal subject placing himself outside the logic of nationalism. The attitude of political nationalism is conveyed in the novel through the figure of Sandip, a leader of the *swadeshi* movement.[8] Nikhilesh is a friend who went to college with Sandip, but they come from different backgrounds: Sandip is of urban lower middle class origin, Nikhilesh a feudal landlord. When Sandip comes to stay at Nikhilesh's rural estate, he is seen as an outsider and interloper, introducing urban-style politics and eventually breaking up the sanctity and harmony of his friend's home. Nikhilesh is made to formulate a critique of Sandip's model of aggressive nationalism, a critique confirmed by subsequent narrative events when Sandip triggers violence between Hindus and Muslims on the estate, and riots break out, with Nikhilesh falling victim to them.

Seeing *Ghare Baire* in those simple terms would be to miss out, however, on the brand of cultural nationalism that Nikhilesh himself articulates. Certain subtle affinities between Sandip and Nikhilesh emerge, which bring out the mutual imbrication of cultural and political nationalism, and which would have to be elided in any reading of the novel as a critique of nationalism. A careful reading of *Ghare Baire* shows that *both* Sandip's political nationalism and Nikhilesh's cultural nationalism are irredeemably bicultural, caught between Eastern spirituality and Western modernity, and that the unresolved tension between them contributes to the tragedy at the end of the novel.

Sandip adheres to *realpolitik*, emphasizing craft and force as the only valid means of obtaining political power. His political aggressiveness is also shown to be linked to sexual aggressiveness. He does all he can not only to win over Bimala—wife of his friend and host Nikhilesh—to the cause of *swadeshi*, but also to seduce her and make her his mistress:

> Today you are the nation's voice to me.... I can only stay here and be the instrument for passing on your ardor to the whole country, this I can confidently assert.... You are the Queen Bee of our hive; we will surround you on all sides and continue our work, but the vitality for our work will be yours, therefore it will lack purpose and joy if you are far from us. (*GB* 430-431)

Bimala is referred to by members of her household as *Chhoto Rani* (Youngest Queen). Sandip, in effect, offers her an extension of this role by conceiving the nation as a family, over which she can preside as its "Queen

Bee," thus reconfiguring the "world" as "home." In the erotic transference that takes place here, Bimala effectively anthropomorphizes the nation. Sandip muses, apropos of her:

> Who says *Satyameva Jayate*?[9] Infatuation [*moha*] will win in the end. The Bengali understood this when he conceived the image of the ten-handed goddess astride her lion [Durga], and spread her worship in the land. Bengal must now create a new image to enchant and conquer the world. (*GB* 494)

Here Sandip turns around a quotation from the *Upanishads* to emphasize a modern sense of the contingency and constructedness of truth. Sandip's gods and goddesses are under the impact of post-Darwinian evolutionism:

> "Evolution is at work amongst the gods," says Sandip. "The grandson has to remodel the gods created by the grandfather to suit his own taste, or else he is left an atheist. It is my mission to modernize the ancient deities. I am born the savior of the gods, to emancipate them from the thralldom of the past." (*GB* 519)

In "modernizing" traditional deities and setting up Bimala as an erotic icon, Sandip combines Hinduism, Darwinism and social constructionism. His nationalism is marked by the presence of the discontinuous, the heterogeneous and the exotic, and amounts to a modern "invention of tradition" that consciously re-inflects and politicizes traditional religious practices and meanings.[10] Sandip evinces an awareness of nationalism's bicultural, split subjectivity:

> It is not that I do not at all understand Nikhil[esh]'s point of view; that is where my danger lies. I was born in India; the poison of its spirituality runs in my blood . . .
>
> This is exactly how such curious anomalies happen nowadays in our country. The refrains of our religion run concurrently with those of our nationalism . . . the result is that none of them gain clear definition. . . . It is like performing with an English military band, side by side with our Indian *shehnai*.[11] (*GB* 460)

At this instance Sandip likens the existence of discordant elements within nationalist subjectivity to the playing of English martial music along with the incompatible *shehnai*, a flute-like instrument on which mellow or melancholy notes are usually played. Despite his appeal to the emotional power of Hindu goddesses, he urges that "the western military style" prevail as their means, which does not help resolve the incompatibilities he perceives between the traditional identity of "our religion" and the imported concept of "our nationalism." Sandip's nationalism is thus ambivalent and bicultural, striving to appropriate such exotic and "foreign" elements into the Indian self as English military music.

In Nikhilesh's eyes, Sandip's overstepping of limits and the principle of erotic excess that animates Sandip's variety of nationalism have also invaded the home and disturbed conjugal relations. Subsequent to Bimala's alienation from him, Nikilesh reflects that,

> [w]e have so fanned the flames of the love of men and women as to make it overpass its rightful domain, and now even in the name of humanity we cannot bring it back under control. We have turned the lamp of the house into a fire in the house. We cannot indulge it any more, but need to turn away from it. (*GB* 465)

Traveling down the path of erotic excess could cause the "lamp of the house" (Sucharita in *Gora*, the housewife as companion and domestic helpmate) to turn into a "fire in the house," triggering an apocalypse. Such an apocalypse indeed takes place at the end of the narrative, confirming Nikhilesh's diagnosis: Sandip's activities, encouraged by Bimala, trigger riots in the countryside, resulting in Nikhilesh's implied death.

In place of Sandip's brand of political nationalism, Nikhilesh propounds his own version of constructive *swadeshi*, whose objective is to produce the goods needed by the "nation within the nation" rather than boycotting or making bonfires of foreign goods (*GB* 416). As opposed to the excessive and Dionysiac impulses released by Sandip's *swadeshi* initiatives, Nikhilesh emphasizes an economy of "thrift," and to this end strives to give Bimala lessons in political economy. In keeping with this notion of thrift, Nikhilesh also attempts to reform his own household. While his elder brothers led lives of aristocratic excess and died of drink at a young age, Nikhilesh, in keeping with social reformist ideals, educates his wife and induces her to come out of *purdah* (seclusion in the home). In keeping with his emphasis on *swadeshi* thrift Nikhilesh sets up his drawing room, where he receives important guests—in particular Europeans—with indigenously produced items. He thus uses an ordinary brass-pot for a flower vase, in preference to a more expensive stained glass vase of European make. Prior to her *swadeshi* days, Bimala had objected to its use, wondering whether Europeans might consider their couple to be lacking in refinement, and Nikhilesh had replied:

"If they do, I will pay them back by thinking that their civilization does not go deeper than their white skins . . . that brass pot is as unconscious of itself as those blossoms are; but this thing protests its purpose so loudly, it is only fit for artificial flowers." (*GB* 472-473)

Nikhilesh's reply reiterates a cultural nationalist trope on Western civilization and East/West difference. Western civilization is understood to be fixated on material details, on external particulars and on artifice, while the East is projected as the site of spontaneity of being and the probing of spiritual inner depths. The indigenously made brass pot projects this organic spontaneity of being (like the blossoms), while the European vase, like Western civilization, self-consciously proclaims itself and is fit only for artificial flowers.

Curiously, while Nikhilesh projects to visitors and outsiders a cultural nationalist identity, the inner recesses of his household witness a transaction with the West. In dressing and educating Bimala, Nikhilesh draws on Western outfits, Western fashions, Western manners, thus eliciting adverse responses from other members of his traditional household. Bimala narrates that,

> [t]he many colored garments of modern fashion with which my husband loved to adorn me—those jackets, *saris*, blouses and petticoats roused the jealousies of his sisters-in-law: "more show than beauty! Isn't she ashamed to make a shop window of herself!" . . .
>
> [My grandmother-in-law] did not like all the attire that my husband purchased from European shops and decked me out with. . . . But by and by even her tastes changed. Thanks to the present age, she reached the state when she could not pass an evening unless her granddaughter-in-law read her stories from English books. (*GB* 411-415)

Bimala's account is testimony to the ways in which the colonial economy had reached into and begun to restructure homes, changing tastes and desires in ways considered transgressive by traditional members of a Hindu household.[12] While Bimala lives in *purdah*, cut off from transactions with the outer world, her dress suggests to the sisters-in-law a shop window, locating her in the extraterritorial space of the marketplace. Their exclamation "more show than beauty" resembles Nikhilesh's own observation on the European vase as more artifice than substance. The restructuring of tastes and desires by the colonial economy occurs in ways antithetical to the logic of *swadeshi*. When the *swadeshi* movement begins, Bimala considers burning the sizable wardrobe of foreign-made clothes she has accumulated, but is prevented from doing so by Nikhilesh. According to him, burning them would be equivalent to setting fire to the home (*GB* 417). Nikhilesh thus considers the West and Western influence to be an integral part of his home. While Nikhilesh criticizes Sandip for asserting a heterogeneous identity, he speaks from a subject position that is no less split and bicultural.

Nikhilesh invests in Bimala's education in a fashion similar to his investment in her clothes. He hires Miss Gilby, an English governess, to be her teacher and companion, although this too draws criticism in the household. Drawing on Western models, Nikhilesh also wishes to break the codes of *purdah* and introduce his wife to the outer world. However, when Bimala does emerge from seclusion and is attracted to Sandip, Nikhilesh finds this a more difficult proposition to swallow:

> I longed to find Bimala fully blossomed in all her knowledge and love and power in the world.
>
> But the thing I did not take into account was that if one would find a person freely revealed in truth (*satya*), one must give up definite claims on that person. Why did I fail to think of this? . . . It was because I placed the fullest trust upon love.
>
> I was vain enough to think that I had the power in me to bear the sight of truth in its awful nakedness. (*GB* 428)

Nikhilesh differentiates his position from that of Sandip's brand of *swadeshi* in that he takes his stand by *satya* (truth) rather than *moha* (infatuation). In accordance with this position, he is driven to discover the truth of his relationship with Bimala. However, when he finds the truth he seeks—that Bimala may leave him if given the choice—it is hard to acknowledge. He finds truth in a transcendental sense to be inflected by the truth of desire, or *moha*—the "love" he places "the fullest trust upon."

Nikhilesh's confusion serves to dramatize the contradictions of his bicultural identity. In keeping with his determination to "modernize" his household and reconstitute his relationship with Bimala on the lines of the companionate marital model, he does away with *purdah* and insists that Bimala should choose him of her own free will. While encouraging Bimala's crossing of the threshold between East and West, home and world, he does not register the full implications of Bimala's Westernized modernity. Bimala's desire for the world implies that she can no longer be regarded as belonging to the culturally sanctified space of home, thus reinstating the home/world, East/West dichotomy.

Nikhilesh's ambivalence about modernity is also apparent in his romance with his widowed sister-in-law, who is uneducated and embodies the values of the traditional Indian woman. Although Nikhilesh is interested in proving himself to be different from his brothers through his investment in companionate marital monogamy, the reader finds Bimala suspecting that Nikhilesh's relationship with his sister-in-law is not entirely innocent:

> Her talk and jests were inclined towards the perverse. . . . [T]hat is why she laid various traps in the path of her brother-in-law. I feel ashamed to admit that I feared even for a husband like him. . . . My sister-in-law would occasionally cook for him herself and very affectionately invite him. . . . He would accept her invitation every time with a smile, and it . . . seemed to me that something of men's restlessness came out in this. Even if I had a thousand engagements, I would make some excuse and accompany him to my sister-in-law's room. (*GB* 411-412)

Nikhilesh's sister-in-law entered his family at the age of nine, when Nikhilesh was six. Ketaki Kushari Dyson has written about the anomalous situation of child brides married to adult young men in large families such as Tagore's own, at a time when the young men were being exposed to psychosexual stimuli mediated by Western romantic literature. In such a situation, the younger men were likely to adopt as companions the spouses of their elder brothers.[13] That Bimala's suspicions about Nikhilesh's intimacy with his sister-in-law are not unfounded is apparent from Nikhilesh's own testimony later in the novel. Nikhilesh testifies to an idyllic childhood in which his prime companion was his sister-in-law, subsequent to which,

> as we grew up, our mutual joys and sorrows took on deeper tones of intimacy. How we quarreled! . . . and when Bimala came between us, these breaches seemed as if they would never be mended, but it always turned out that our inner affinities proved more powerful than the wounds on the surface. So has a true [*satya*] relationship grown to be unbreakable between us, from our childhood till now, and its branching foliage has spread and broadened over every room, balcony, terrace and garden of this great house. . . .
>
> I could see at once that the little differences she used to have with Bimala and me, about money and property matters, did not proceed from any sordid worldliness, but because she felt that

her claims in regard to this one relationship of her life had been overridden. . . . Bimala also had felt that my sister-in-law's claim over me was not based merely on our social connection, but went much deeper; and she was jealous of these ties between us, reaching back to our childhood. (*GB* 539-540)

In this passage Bimala is repeatedly perceived as coming in between Nikhilesh and his sister-in-law; and who, of the two women, has a more primary claim on his affections remains ambiguous. If Bimala serves the Western paradigm of companionate marriage, Nikhilesh's sister-in-law stands in for his primary affective and filial roots, the space of "home" in which he perceives a certain foundational truth or *satya*. Nikhilesh's attitude towards both women thus embodies a split desire. Bimala is a product of Nikhilesh's imported tastes, and embraces the world and the West. She carries the inscription of Nikhilesh's exotic desire for the West, while his sister-in-law embodies the virtues of tradition/home/fidelity/ the East. The latter is invested as a space of transcendental truth (*satya*), breaking down Nikhilesh's frequently asserted opposition between truth and desire, *satya* and *moha*.

Nikhilesh does not regard Bimala's association with Sandip in the same light as his own intimate relationship with his sister-in-law. Nonetheless, this unfixing of the boundaries of "home" renders its meaning radically fluid, ambiguous and unstable, giving rise to the tragic conflicts in which the characters of *Ghare Baire* are enmeshed. Nikhilesh's home is itself a terrain of checkered desire, unable to achieve successful equilibrium or resolution between contradictory cultural poles.

This sense of checkered and conflicted desire is captured by the recurring and ambiguous imagery of fire in the novel, which signifies both passion and its purgation. Present in the *swadeshi* bonfires of foreign cloth, fire represents the passions of a new age. Thus Bimala says of Sandip, engaged in erotic worship of her: "I could not be sure whether he was a person or a living flame. . . . You cannot take shelter behind the walls of decorum when the fire dazzles the eyes and makes destruction beautiful" (*GB* 454). Bimala perceives fire as an element that is simultaneously destructive and beautiful; it also signifies an elision of the boundaries between home and world. As the burning of foreign cloth also signifies to Nikhilesh a setting fire to the home, as mentioned above; the riots which signal Nikhilesh's injury/death are visible from his home as tongues of flame on the horizon.

Near the end of the novel, Bimala says of herself: "I have passed through fire. What was inflammable has been burnt to ashes; what is left is deathless" (*GB* 547). At this point fire becomes an element of purgation, as she is left passionless and bereft of her desires. The image evoked by Bimala is that of a *sati*, who braves the funeral pyre to be reunited with her dead husband. Through this act, emblematic of Indian tradition, she hopes to resolve the crisis of home and world by effacing her sexuality/desire and renouncing the world. The end of the narrative draws a profound blank; with Nikhilesh's injury, the way back home appears barred, and Bimala is left poised in a moment of eternal waiting. Fire, which renders fluid and combustible the boundaries between home and world, East and West, creates dangerous contradictions which are close to bringing about a cessation of self.

This dissolution of self and the note of blankness on which the novel ends, also signal the death of Tagore's universal humanist subject. Both Bimala and Nikhilesh had started out with the promise of reconciling within themselves the opposed poles of East and West, home and world. Bimala's attempts to step out of the home, however, result in catastrophe. While critiquing Sandip's brand of political nationalism, Nikhilesh's own attempts at implementing *swadeshi* also turn out to be hopelessly quixotic, and his isolation is palpable when he rides out in a similarly impracticable and single-handed attempt to quell the riots on his estate. Nikhilesh's own version of cultural nationalism is marked by a desire for appropriating the West, which works to undermine his investment in the home as an inner sanctum untainted by the world. The transcendental truths that his version of cultural nationalism is thought to articulate may be shown to be as enmeshed in sensuous particulars as is Sandip's political nationalism.

Unlike the optimistic ending of *Gora*, which held out the possibility of inaugurating a universal subject through Gora's successful return home, the way back home for the protagonists of *Ghare Baire* is barred. While it was possible in *Gora* to project the home as a center of the nation, home appears as a dislocated metaphor in *Ghare Baire*. It is a space that does not reassure; on the contrary, infiltrated by a clash of cultures and by the world, it has been rendered unstable and treacherous. The loss of meaning that ensues makes the existence of a universal subject able to reconcile cultural contradictions an increasingly remote possibility. This crisis of universal humanism reaches a crescendo in *Char Adhyay*, to which I now turn.

Char Adhyay: Apocalypse Now

If the narrative of *Ghare Baire* gains in tragic stature by structuring its events around the gradual disappearance of "home," Tagore's novella *Char Adhyay*, written in 1934 after the onset of the anti-British revolutionary terrorist movement in Bengal, describes a world where "home" has long been submerged within a maelstrom of politics and is not available as an independent point of reference.[14] *Char Adhyay* also correlates the collapse of the home to a breakdown in feminine nurture. In *Char Adhyay*, politics is a terrain of the malleability of *satya* or transcendental truth. Yet home, as the place where a benign feminine influence could help nurture the (male) subject of universal humanism devoted to upholding *satya*, is simply unavailable as an alternative space for articulating a critique of politics.

While *Ghare Baire*'s narrative is driven by Bimala's stepping outside the home, *Char Adhyay*'s plot turns around the young and beautiful Ela, who lives independently and joins the revolutionary terrorist movement. However, Ela's origins are shown to be already marked by a breakdown in nurture: her mother is an unsympathetic figure who cannot make a good "home." The novella begins as follows:

> Ela could remember that her initiation into life took place in the midst of revolt. Her mother Mayamoyi had a tendency towards obsession; her behavior could not proceed along the broad path of proper judgment or consideration. With the unrestrained blasts of her erratic temper she would agitate the household every now and then, punish unjustifiably, suspect without reason ... speaking the unadulterated truth [*satya*] could be called a vice of the daughter. She was punished most for this reason. (*CA* 877)

The narrative establishes therefore an early link between what happens in the home and the political macrocosm. The "revolt" in the midst of which Ela's early life unfolds also describes the political conditions of revolt against colonial rule. While revolts in both spheres may be seen to arise out of a lack of nurture, these conditions are duplicated within the revolutionary terrorist movement. Although what impels Ela to join the revolution is its promise of an extended family, something that has been missing from her life so far, it is Ela's erotic identity, rather than her identity as mother and nurturer, that receives the most emphasis among the revolutionaries. Indranath, their charismatic leader, makes her take a vow never to marry, as she is "betrothed . . . to the nation" (*CA* 880, 895). This sets up a contrast to *Gora*, where it is the woman's role as universal mother and nurturer that receives most prominence. As sons of a universal mother, male patriots may return to her lap and thereby cure their alienation. In relation to a universal erotic icon that cannot be associated with any particular man, however, male patriots are constituted as competitors, and Ela becomes a locus of their exotic desire. This is a key element of *Char Adhyay*'s critique of the direction in which militant nationalism has been developing. However, as one will see, even the novella's sympathetic characters, Ela and her lover Atin, are caught up in a network of exotic desire.

The Nikhilesh - Bimala - Sandip triangle in *Ghare Baire* is reproduced in *Char Adhyay* as the Atin - Ela – Indranath triangular relationship, with a difference. As Ela is "betrothed . . . to the nation," and not to her lover Atin, Indranath—as the leader of the nationalist organization of which both Atin and Ela are members—has more authority over her than Atin has. Indranath may be seen as a further development on Sandip in *Ghare Baire*, in terms of the use to which he puts Ela within the movement. Indranath explains to Ela the matrix of male heterosexual desire that animates nationalism as follows:

> It's not work I want of you, I do not even let you know many things about our work. It is hardly possible for you to know of the fire that lights up the hearts of the boys at the touch of your fingers when you anoint their foreheads with the blood-red sandal-paste of initiation. The dry rewards I have to offer cannot evoke the same quality of work. . . . Where desire works, I put woman on a pedestal. . . .
>
> Only the incurably immature revel in calling their country "Mother." Our country is not the mother of senile infants. She is *Ardhanarishwara* [a god who is half male and half female]—her realization is in the union of man and woman, but such union should not be enervated by imprisonment within the cage of a household. (*CA* 885)

Indranath enunciates here a political technology of sex, in which sex is regulated and administered to achieve a maximization of desired political effects. According to Michel Foucault, the "technology of sex" is a key element in the emergence and development of those apparatuses of supervision, administration and intervention that have constituted the foundation of "culture" and society in Europe since the eighteenth century (see his *The History of Sexuality: An Introduction*;[15] this edition of the translation 1990, all page references are to this edition). Likewise, Indranath extends a network of surveillance and administration throughout his movement, in which sex is a key tool.[16] His brand of erotic politics is opposed to the "natural" order of nurture proposed by *Gora*. Hence, it also implies a negation of home, which could inhibit the proliferation and saturation of the discourse of the nation by sex. Ela's performance of political tasks within the movement is not of great importance; neither is she expected to perform the role of a nurturer and "mother." Rather she figures as an erotic icon, bringing into play the libidinal energies of male patriots and channelizing them into the movement.

While Sandip had made a similar use of Bimala in *Ghare Baire*, it is significant that unlike Sandip, Indranath evinces no trace of any personal attraction for Ela, but rather engages in a fully conscious production of her as image. Indranath had initially been a scientist who had been denied advancement in his career because of his association with a political suspect. An element of "scientific" disinterestedness and detachment may be discerned in the impersonal and clinical manner in which he administers Ela's image for the purpose of furthering the cohesion of his group. While Sandip had been viewed as transgressing *dharma* (a term encompassing both physical and moral order) because of his adoption of a utilitarian and ends-oriented morality, Indranath takes this point of view to an extreme, severing politics from all expressions of personal emotion and regarding it solely as a domain for the deployment of technique and administrative rationality.

Given Indranath's extreme position, even achievement of political goals is no longer the point; what matters, rather, seems to be the perfection of technique, and the attitude of impersonality that this entails. As Indranath tells one of his followers:

> I called you in the midst of the impossible, not for results, but to prove your valor. My temperament is impersonal. I accept ungrudgingly the inevitable.... With the dispassionate and scientific attitude I acknowledge a terminal patient must die. . . . Perform action without waiting for results ["Karmanyevadhikaraste ma phaleshu kadachana": a phrase from the *Bhagavad Gita*]. (CA 890)

Indranath presses into service here the disinterestedness prescribed by the *Bhagavad Gita*. Like Sandip, his project is a bicultural one, in which there is a negotiation between East and West. He combines the spirituality of the *Gita* with knowledge of European sciences, for which he had gained a reputation during his long sojourn in Europe (CA 881).

The figure of Indranath condenses Tagore's fears about encroaching apparatuses of modern state power and supervision, which exercise what Foucault has designated (as rendered into English) as "bio-power" (see 135-159 for an explication of this notion), or a form of power that "brought life and its mechanisms into the realm of explicit calculations and made knowledge-power an agent of transformation of human life" (143). Indranath represents, in other words, the death of erotics, and its replacement by the impersonal and "scientific" eye of the modern state. *Gora*'s vision of the nation as an extension of home cannot be validated by the modern state, which reaches into the home and destroys its autonomy, making it the target of administration and supervision.

Nikhilesh's closest counterpart in *Char Adhyay* is Atin. Like Nikhilesh, Atin is an introverted, poetically gifted young man from an aristocratic background. However, Atin may more properly be designated as Nikhilesh's ghost, arising from the ruins of the past and signaling the end of the world. In a world from which erotics has been exiled, desire is a ghostly presence, and Atin's attraction towards Ela resides at the edges of imaginative consciousness. As in *A Passage to India*, Atin and Ela are unable to access desire freely but remain caught up in its echo:

> [Atin]: "The days that do not rise to the height of fulfillment are doomed to such ghostly wanderings on the horizon of the might-have-been. Our union can only be in that mirage of a bridal chamber. I've come to invite you to it—your [revolutionary] work may be disturbed."
>
> "Bother the work!" said Ela . . . "I'll light the lamp."
>
> "No, don't. Light can show reality. I want to take you along the unlighted road to the imperceptible. It's now almost four years since I was crossing the river at Mokameh on the ferry steamer. I was still holding to the broken remnants of my debt-ridden ancestral fortune. Luxurious tastes still clung to me like the cloud colors of declining day. Clad in a silk tunic, a scarf of old gold silk neatly folded on my shoulder, I was sitting alone in a cane chair on the first class deck. . . . You had cast in your lot with the people as a deck passenger. . . . The brown of your sari is still vivid in my mind. . . . With strained naturalness you asked me, 'Why don't you wear *khadi*?' Do you remember? . . . The music of your voice thrilled me through and through. It struck me like a sudden shaft of light; as if some unearthly bird swooped from the sky and snatched up the rest of my days . . ." (CA 894-895)

Atin and Ela come from two different worlds, and this is what constitutes their exotic appeal for each other. Atin is the foppish aristocrat on the first-class deck, while Ela belongs to the party of the people. She is pictured on the crowded third-class deck, wearing a sober brown sari made of inexpensive *khadi*,[17] suggesting identification with the masses. Both Atin and Ela, however, are pictured in a moment of crossing, figured by the literal crossing of the river that they undertake. While the fortunes of Atin's aristocratic family are on the decline, Ela represents a rising bourgeois nationalism, soon to assume power.

Ela is attracted by the impression of an aristocratic individuality and fastidiousness conveyed by Atin, who is "not made to the measure of his surroundings" (*CA* 895). This constitutes Atin's difference from Nikhilesh: Atin is portrayed as being denied any sense of possession except that of self-possession. While Nikhilesh's identity had been firmly grounded in the feudal estate that he owned, Atin is pictured as holding on to the fragmented remnants of self, as he crosses over to the side of the third-class deck. Significantly, it is Ela who makes the first move between them, signifying the shift in power between classes as well as between genders. Ela brings Atin over to the side of the "masses" and the revolutionary terrorist movement, reversing Nikhilesh's moves in trying to found Bimala's identity on the basis of his own.

Atin and Ela's meeting symbolizes a meeting between a decaying past and an uncertain future, which condenses into a brief and precarious moment of desire, triggering in Atin's case a synaesthesia of the senses in which light, sound and a swooping bird mingle. The image of the swooping bird, "snatch[ing] up the rest of [Atin's] days," condenses desire, dispossession and death. Such desire may be embraced only at the cost of a vertiginous loss of self, culminating in death. By the end of the narrative Atin kills Ela, and his own survival is uncertain.

While Ela induces Atin to make common cause with the revolutionary extremists, he resents Ela's standing as erotic icon of the nation, which would render him just another one of Ela's many conquests. Thus he claims it was his "evil fate" that made Ela's "resolve plural" (*CA* 895). Atin points out that Ela, by standing in for the nation, is an object of exotic desire, and wishes to relocate Ela to the home, where a more fulfilling order of personal relations may be conceived. Atin thus constructs "home" as the place where Ela belongs according to an order of "nature" and where she should have invited him, rather than to the illusions of nationalism's collective home-making:

> At last the woman who is for real has manifested itself in you. It is quite apparent that you are a romantic whenever you appear on the stage of national salvation. Where there is home and hearth, with rice-milk and fish-head offered on plates of bell metal—at its center you belong, holding in your hands a fan of palm-leaves. Where there is the prick of the political goad, there you come by not guided by commonsense, but by unnatural means—hair undone, eyes rolling. (*CA* 910)

In *Ghare Baire*, where Nikhilesh educates Bimala and induces her to partake of the world in limited measure, there remains a possibility or at least a hope of bridging the gap between home and world, East and

West. In *Char Adhyay* home and world, East and West have become radically disjunctive and incompatible spaces, and women's participation in political matters is seen to be socially and erotically transgressive. The image of women in politics—"hair undone, eyes rolling"—suggests an uncircumscribed sexuality and Westernized promiscuity that is opposed by the very Indian image of a housewife with a "fan of palm-leaves," who fans her husband as he consumes the traditional meal that she has prepared for him. There is no hope, whatsoever, of bridging the gap between these two spaces.

Tagore thus implies in this novella that the radical incompatibility of East and West destroys any possibility of a universal humanist subject transcending the gap between cultures. In the case of *Gora* the world had to be mediated by the home; Gora could see in Sucharita an image of the nation. The sublimated erotics present in this construction has become, however, radically desublimated in *Char Adhyay*, leading to a breakdown in feminine authority and ownership of cultural identity. In *Gora* nurture is seen as a sublime quality in itself, enjoying an extra-political, moral authority, sustaining Gora's capacity for proclaiming the universal, however shot through with contradictions. In *Char Adhyay*, on the other hand, Ela's attempts at playing the role of universal nurturer are perceived by Atin as providing a cover for her seductive charm and political ambitions:

> Three years ago you celebrated my birthday . . . Your devoted "boys" were all there. . . . [Y]ou vigorously played the loving elder sister. Perhaps you thought a touch of jealousy would help in my reformation . . . I can still hear your honeyed accents . . . I was charmed, but still I could see that this overly amiable sisterhood was prompted by your overly pristine India. What an ideal *swadeshi* sisterliness. . . . [Y]our pose in those days savored of the ludicrous. (*CA* 917-918)

Ela can, therefore, no longer mediate the universal. Her efforts in this regard invite ridicule from Atin, who suggests that Ela drew considerable attention by performing a masquerade. Atin even suggests that by playing the role of nurturer, she infantilizes the receivers of her solicitude: "I won't stand it if you make me out a minor in need of your guardianship. Come down, rather, from your pedestal; look me in the face" (*CA* 909).

Although Atin may be placed in a line of descent from Tagorean heroes such as Gora or Nikhilesh, his actions constitute a betrayal of the ideals of universal humanism, transcendent subjectivity and Indian "spirituality," as he joins the extremists and participates in acts of violence and brutality at their behest. He even kills Ela, when ordered to by the organization. It is clear that he does not represent any autonomous or transcendent principle. Stripped of selfhood and bereft of hope, Atin is pictured as awaiting an apocalypse:

> Atin sat awhile in silent thought, looking inward. The last act of his life's drama had been brought on out of its time; the curtain would soon be rung down, the lights put out. His start had been made in the clear light of dawn, since when he had traveled very far.... The vision of beauty that had been revealed to him at the bend of the road by the goddess of his fortunes did not seem to be of this world.... [I]t occurred to him again and again that Dante-Beatrice had been reborn between them. It was the inspiration of history working within him that had made Atin, like Dante, throw himself into the vortex of political revolts. But where was the truth, the valor, the glory in it? From the mire of masked robberies and murder into which the movement had progressively been drawn, no pillar of light would ever rise to illumine the pages of history ...
>
> The daylight waned. The cicadas shrilled in the courtyard. The wheels of a distant cart creaked their agony. (CA, 906-7)

Significantly, Atin's voice merges in this passage with the narrator's, suggesting that there is continuity between the narrative vision and Atin's thoughts at this point. Ela had started out by telling the unadulterated truth (*satya*) but later became complicit with the nationalist terrorists' plotting. Likewise, Atin's start "had been made in the clear light of dawn," signifying his early promise of achieving creative transcendence. However, the "lights" would soon be "put out," as Atin has "destroyed his soul" (CA 907) and can no longer pursue humanist meanings.

This association is reinforced by the reference to Dante, thought of as being at the origin of Renaissance humanism. Dante played a prominent role in the politics of his native city-state, Florence, from which he was exiled upon the defeat of the political faction he supported.[18] In contrast, Atin suggests that the historical and political role he plays is undistinguished and insignificant, compared to that of Dante Alighieri's; nor can he turn his political defeat into an occasion for creative insight, as Dante did by writing the *Commedia* (later called *Divina*) in exile. While the relationship between Atin and Ela had the potential of being the equivalent of the Dante-Beatrice relationship, which had helped Dante achieve the transcendent subjectivity of the *Commedia*, there is no prospect of a similar outcome in the case of Atin and Ela. The passage ends with a sense of gloom and foreboding through its use of apparently disconnected images, suggesting a world fraught with contradictions where meanings are radically dispersed.

Afflicted by an unnamed but fatal disease, Atin exhibits signs of degeneracy in the very final episode of the novella. The schizophrenia of the bicultural subject emerges in the erotic and political death he visits upon Ela. Atin terminates the history of dispossession in his relationship with Ela by a final act of possession, killing Ela:

> Ela seized Atin's feet, telling him: "Kill me Ontu [Atin], with your own hands. I couldn't wish for better fortune than that." She got up from the floor and, kissing him again and again she said, "Kill me now." She tore open her blouse. . . . "Don't let unclean hands touch my body, for this body belongs to you."
> Atin caught hold of her arm and pulled her to the bedroom . . .
> "I've brought medicine that'll put you to sleep."
> "What's the use of that, Ontu [Atin]? Let the last bit of my consciousness be for you. . . . Let me die awake, in your arms. Let our last kiss be eternal, Ontu, my Ontu." (CA 923)

The logic of the text suggests a sadomasochistic dynamics whereby Ela must expiate, through her death, her entry into political space, where she rendered herself an object of the public gaze and thereby erotically available. That sadomasochistic dynamics is fulfilled in this passage, which destroys the possibility that the gap between disparate cultural and personal worlds can be bridged. In standing for the radical incompatibility of home and world, politics and the imagination, *Char Adhyay* testifies both to the termination of Tagore's dream of an ideal synthesis of East and West, and to the death of the subject of universal humanism.

Conclusion

In an interesting omission on their part, critics who stress Tagore's universal humanism that transcends cultural barriers privilege his early *Gora*, while excluding from their analysis any consideration of the later *Char Adhyay*. Readings of Tagore that dwell entirely or primarily on *Gora* and exclude *Char Adhyay* cannot do justice to the range of Tagore's texts, nor clarify how the problematic terrain of plural cultural subjectivities articulated by *Gora* are re-examined in his later fiction. *Ghare Baire* brings to a crisis the aporias constitutive of this terrain, while *Char Adhyay* spells the definitive collapse of the subject of universal humanism. The acute cultural tensions and clash of hegemonies that find expression in these texts are played out around the figure of the Indian woman who, as in the case of Bimala in *Ghare Baire* or Ela in *Char Adhyay*, are made to assume sacrificial identities in a narrative effort to resolve those tensions.

Notes

[1] The view of Tagore as "universal humanist" unsympathetic to nationalism is something of a critical commonplace. According to Indrani Mitra, "Rabindranath remained for the most part fervently committed to a universal humanism" (245). Sabina Sawhney states that "it is out of [Gora's] 'vast negation' [when he discovers his true identity at the end of *Gora*] that Tagore finally creates his desired image of a true Indian—one who refuses to accept any barriers between himself and the rest of humanity. . . . The shifting margins of cultural displacement experienced by Gora finally confound any hermetic or authentic sense of a 'national' culture" (100).

[2] Published in volume 10 of the 15-volume *Rabindra Rachanabali* (1961), Tagore's Bengali collected works. All translations from this edition are mine, although sometimes adapted from available English translations.

[3] Hegel asserts in his *Philosophy of History* that "in the History of the World, the Idea of Spirit appears in its actual embodiment as a series of external forms, each one of which declares itself as an actually existing people. . . . Spirit, clothing itself in this form of nature, suffers its particular phases to assume separate existence; for mutual exclusion is the mode of existence proper to mere nature. These natural distinctions must be first of all regarded as special possibilities, from which the Spirit of the people in question germinates, and among them is the Geographical Basis" (79). While Tagore does not explicitly cite Hegel, he may have picked up Hegelian ideas from his Latin teacher in England, according to whom "in each age one dominant idea is manifest in every human society in all parts of the world" (see Tagore, *Reminiscences* 165-172).

[4] On the attributes of Indian society in colonial historiography, see Ronald Inden's *Imagining India* (1990). According to Inden, in its Indological version,

> India's history begins with the arrival there of the Aryans during the second millennium BC. No sooner, however, had India reached her full flower under the Mauryas in the fourth century BC, as an oriental despotism, than she—and recall that India is often considered feminine—began her decline. This downward turn was exacerbated (if not actually caused) by the invasions of the Hellenes, Scythians, and Turks during the first and second centuries BC, and the first century AD. Although there was a renascence under the Guptas in the fourth and fifth centuries AD, the decline that set in after the intrusions of the Huns in the sixth century was never reversed. . . . It is worth pausing over this feature of conquest. It became an important part of the discourses on philology, ethnology, and world history in the nineteenth century. . . . But India was remarkable, for the repeated conquests of that subcontinent did not bring an end to her

civilization or even, for that matter, produce any fundamental change in it. (54-55).

[5] Italicized words are in English in the original.

[6] A large fan used in India, made of a frame covered with canvas hanging from the ceiling by a rope which needs to be pulled to circulate air. Editor's note.

[7] A telling instance of Anandamoyi's restraint and lack of bitterness is provided in her reaction to Gora's arrest by the colonial authorities. When Lolita denounces the colonial magistrate's action, Anandamoyi

> smiled at her pungent remarks and said: "My dear, God alone knows what Gora's being in gaol has meant to me, but I can't bring myself to be angry with the *sahib*. . . . Gora has done his duty. The authorities are doing theirs. Those who are hurt by this will have to suffer. If only you will read my Gora's letter . . . he is not venting childish anger against anyone. He has weighed all the consequences of what he has done" (G 165).

Thus Anandamoyi sees hatred as an extreme reaction to Gora's arrest, and restrains herself.

[8] *Swa-deshi*, "of one's own country," was the name given to the protest movement in Bengal, lasting from 1905 to 1908, against the British plan of partitioning the province. Agitation principally took the form of boycotting British goods and making bonfires of clothes manufactured abroad.

[9] "Truth always triumphs"; a quotation from the *Upanishads*.

[10] For historical instances of such modern "inventions of tradition," see *The Invention of Tradition* (1983), edited by Eric Hobsbawm and Terence Ranger.

[11] A musical instrument.

[12] Women members of a Hindu household traditionally wore a single stretch of fabric or *sari*; hence the chemises, petticoats, blouses and jackets that Bimala wore, inspired by Western fashions, draw adverse reactions from traditional members of her household. On how transgressive such items of women's clothing such as the blouse, the petticoat and shoes were considered within a traditional context, see Chatterjee, "The Nationalist Resolution of the Women's Question" (240).

[13] Interestingly, Tagore's childhood companion in his own household was Kadambari Devi, the wife of his elder brother Jyotirindranath, whose marriage took place when Kadambari was nine and Tagore seven. When Tagore's own marriage to Mrinalini Devi, aged nine, was announced sixteen years later, Kadambari Devi committed suicide. Jyotirindranath himself was known to have preferred the company of Jnanadanandini Devi, wife of *his* elder brother Satyendranath. While Dyson suggests that Tagore's novella *Nashtanid* (The Broken Nest) portrayed a triangular relationship and its tragic consequences similar to the relationship that obtained between Jyotirindranath, Kadambari and himself, this argument could be extended to *Ghare Baire*, where Nikhilesh's relationship with his sister-in-law acquires similar overtones as that between Tagore and Kadambari (see Dyson 21-23).

[14] The period 1930-1934 was marked in Bengal by an upsurge in the revolutionary terrorist movement directed against the British. According to historian Sumit Sarkar, during this period,

Bengal remained a nightmare for the British because of terrorism. Though the new Governor Anderson was a specialist in repression ever since the Irish Civil War days, the number of terrorist cases was the highest ever (104) in 1932, before declining to 33 in 1933 and 17 in 1934. Two more white magistrates were killed in Midnapur, Governor Jackson was attacked at the University Convocation by a girl student . . . More than 3000 were detained at concentration camps in Buxa, Hijli, and Deoli, while the Chittagong prisoners were sent to the Andamans [a penal settlement in the Indian Ocean]. (323)

[15] The translation into English of *La Volonté de Savoir* (1976), the first volume of *Histoire de la Sexualité*. Editor's note.

[16] Thus Indranath commands Uma to marry Bhogilal when he finds out that she loves Sukumar, as Sukumar is more valuable to his movement and he fears that Sukumar's patriotic ardor will be deflected by marriage. Indranath has someone spy on meetings between Ela and her lover Atin, who always manages to interrupt them at the moments of greatest passion between them. He uses Ela as bait to draw Atin to the movement, and later dispatches Atin to kill Ela.

[17] *Khadi* is a coarse, homespun fabric. Gandhi's recommendation that nationalist volunteers wear *khadi* and spurn foreign-manufactured textiles was adopted widely.

[18] Dante Alighieri (1265-1321) was a prominent White Guelf and became involved in the strife between the Guelfs and the Ghibellines, and later between the White and Black Guelfs of Florence. When the Black Guelfs came to power Dante was, during an absence from Florence, condemned to exile. For a brief biography of Dante, see Sayers.

12
The Cultural Mirroring in-between Two Symbolic(s)
A Lacanian Reading of John Okada's *No-No Boy*

Fu-jen Chen

Set just after the end of World War II, Japanese-American author John Okada's *No-No Boy* (1957) begins with protagonist Ichiro Yamada's return to the Japanese-American community in Seattle from a two-year prison term. A twenty-five-year-old Nisei (second generation Japanese American), Ichiro is imprisoned for refusing the draft and answering "No-No" on the loyalty oath to the two questions issued by the War Department in 1943. The first question asks: "Are you willing to serve in the armed forces of the United States on combat duty whenever ordered?" The other reads: "Will you swear unqualified allegiance to the United States of America and faithfully defend the United States from any or all attack by foreign or domestic forces, and foreswear any form of allegiance or obedience to the Japanese emperor, to any foreign government, power, or organization?"

Ichiro's double negative to both inquiries regarding his loyalty and combat duty makes him a traitor to the country and an outcast in the Japanese-American community. Moreover, he is labeled a "no-no boy." *No-No Boy* relates Ichiro's reunion with his family and a rapid sequel of encounters with friends, neighbors, and strangers. The succession of events portrays Ichiro's recovery from the trauma of being a no-no boy and the journey he embarks upon to re-establish an identity. His quest for a sense of self exposes the disfiguring effects of racism and the internment, not only on the individual psyche but also on the family as well as the community.

When first published in 1957, *No-No Boy* was not only neglected by the American mainstream, but also unwelcome in the Japanese-American community. Its first edition of 1500 copies had not sold out when John Okada died in obscurity in 1971. The negative response to the novel surprised its publisher, Charles E. Tuttle, who had assumed that the

Japanese-American community "would be enthusiastic about it." On the contrary, they "were not only disinterested but actually rejected the book" (Chin, "Preface" to *Aiiieeeee* xxxix). In the afterward of the second edition in 1976 (all page references are to this edition), Frank Chin wrote that he "got the impression," that, moreover, "[Okada's] family was ashamed of the book."[1]

Thus, when Chin and other Asian-American writers rediscovered it in the mid-1970s, the novel had been ignored for almost two decades. The reasons behind the silencing of *No-No Boy* are social, political, and historical. It is not difficult to understand why the novel was ignored for almost two decades: it was published during a period in American history when the Japanese Americans could not wait to start over their lives; the American public sought to construct a national consensus against communism, while remaining unwilling to confront the fact that the nation once confined its own people in camps without legal reasons or procedures; and both the Japanese Americans and the American public refused to be reminded of the historical stain—the disgrace of the issue of "no-no"; the exposure of racial discrimination; and the blemish of the American spirit of democracy, freedom, and equality.

Ironically, since it was reclaimed as a classic of Asian American literature, *No-No Boy* has been widely written about and examined in scholarly journals, literary history books, anthologies and Asian American Studies, both at home and abroad.[2] Critics usually explore its political and historical tensions, within a socio-cultural context, by focusing on such issues as the struggle between Japanese nationalism and American assimilationism; generational conflicts between the issei (first generation Japanese immigrants) and the nisei; the predicament of dual identity in a binary opposition; and desire for literary articulations of political and social constraints.

Like many other classic ethnic American writings, the story *No-No Boy* recounts has been generally read as a "progressive" or "redemptive" journey —a passage from identification with "Japaneseness" to identification with "Americanness." Accordingly, from the 1970s through the 1980s, the novel was interpreted as depicting the fragmented protagonist's search for "wholeness"; and as ending with a "hopeful" note, illustrating the transformation of the protagonist from a "no-no" boy to one saying "yes" to the future, through a practice of excluding "Japaneseness" and including "Americanness" (see Chan *et al.*; Chin ["Come All Ye Asian American Writers of the Real and the Fake"]; Inada ["Of Place and Displacement"]; Kim; and McDonald).

In the critical readings since the 1980s, however, as an underlying subversive and problematic texture in the novel has been unearthed and highlighted, the interpretation of a process of redemption toward an optimistic ending has been questioned; and the protagonist's compulsive practice of exclusion of "Japaneseness" and inclusion of "Americanness" challenged (see Jingi Ling; Palumbo-Liu; Sato; Sumida; Yeh; and Yogi; see also Wang for the concept of "double consciousness"). Postcolonial theory in turn views *No-No Boy*, through the lens of a new diasporic or exilic identity in Asian-American writing, as a text "situated at the juncture of immigrant and ethnic literary tradition" (Ma 73). Nevertheless, all of these readings, whatever aspect or issue of the novel they may be taking up, presumptively situate it within the *American* context, perceiving the Japanese element as the Other of the hegemonic American. I wish to argue that this approach tends to ignore the wealth of psychoanalytic insight the novel offers, and to suggest that a bicultural approach to the novel—that would allow for an equitable focus on the Japanese element (without, of course, undermining the cultural, political and social themes of the novel, or depoliticizing the racial issues it brings up), coupled by a psychoanalytic examination taking into consideration both cultures—will afford yet another dimension of the text.

This reading will not only diagnose the psychic structure of mental illness that the novel portrays ethnic minorities in the U.S. (and among them especially the first generation immigrants) as being afflicted with—a theme that has to my knowledge so far not emerged in any interpretation; but also trace the stage of constructive subjectivity the protagonist undergoes, that is a realm where, to use Jacques Lacan's terms, two Symbolic(s) reign over the minority subjects. To that end, I propose below a Lacanian psychoanalytic examination of the novel, focusing, however, not on the protagonist, but on the character having made him into the "no-no boy": his mother, the first-generation immigrant caught in-between the two cultural Symbolic(s).

I start below with a brief rehearsal of Lacanian precepts that are of relevance to my analysis.

The Lacanian "Mirror Stage" and "Cultural Mirroring"

Lacanian Mirror Stage
In order to illustrate the emergence and formation of what he calls "Symbolic subjectivity," Lacan has developed the theory of the "mirror stage":
The infant between the ages of six and eighteen months, Lacan believes, sees its reflection in the mirror as a unified whole; that is, it sees the image of its body as a unified whole in contrast to the lack of coordination in

its real body. When there is no actual mirror, the infant is still able to see the "wholeness" as reflected in/through the behavior of an(other child or) adult, who functions thus as a "specular image."

Yet, the contrast between the wholeness of its image and its uncontrolled body gives rise to an aggressive tension in the infant. And, in order to resolve this aggressive tension, the infant turns to identify with the image. It also experiences a feeling of great joy, because when identifying with the visual gestalt of its own body, the infant succeeds in reassembling its scattered body into a unified whole and integrating its fragmentation into totality as well as unity.[3]

After transforming itself thus into the counterpart in the mirror, the infant gains an imaginary sense of mastery, but at the same time becomes alienated. This alienation, in turn, constitutes the ego, according to Lacan.

Thus, the infant's primal identification with the specular image forms the ego. The formation of ego indicates the achievement of the mirror stage. Specifically, the mirror stage is the turning point after which the infant anticipates a vision of totality out of its disjoined body.[4] It is also when the mirror stage is achieved, and its ego formed, that the infant is finally able to sense the difference between self and other, and see someone else as someone else.

But, warns Lacan, what the infant visualizes in the mirror is merely an ideal image, in anticipation of what it could be at some *future* date. The ego formed by identification with this ideal image is thus merely the *"ideal ego"* (emphasis added). What is to be noted is that as a projected image with which the infant identifies, the ideal ego presupposes a perfect fit between the infant and its virtual image, anticipating future mastery over the body, and functioning as a promise of future wholeness (*The Psychoses*[5] 137). Accordingly, the ideal ego is essentially a narcissistic formation, that is the result of a purely *"imaginary* identification" (emphasis added).

Once the infant has assumed the (idealized) image in the mirror, and appropriated this image as itself, believes Lacan, it turns towards the adult, who represents the big Other, to ask for the Other's ratification of the image. This stage in turn brings about what Lacan labels "symbolic identification."

While "imaginary identification" is an *intrapsychic* experience, with the infant having/identifying with an ideal image of itself, "symbolic identification" is an *intersubjective* relationship in which the child is imposed with an external entity. This is a development that leads to the formation, this time, of an ideal that requires the growing infant to comply with precepts put forth by others; in other words, to the formation of the "ego ideal" that requires the child to fulfill the dictates of laws or internalize the strictures of society.⁶

The transformation from the ideal ego to the ego ideal or the transition from imaginary to symbolic identification signifies, in Lacanian terms, a departure from the Imaginary order to the Symbolic order and from an Imaginary ego to a Symbolic subject.⁷

Though the infant's "progressive" passage to become a subject in the Symbolic seemingly indicates a natural order of development, Lacan never intends to offer a chronological sequence of developmental stages of "subjectivity."⁸ Thus, rather than a chronological development, the construction of subjectivity should be seen as a timeless and logical structure. In other words, instead of a moment in the life of the infant, the mirror stage represents a permanent structure of/within subjectivity, in which the subject is endlessly caught and captivated by his/her own image. As the mirror stage is understood as a timeless structure of subjectivity, and the formation of the ego is an endless process, the human being continuously identifies with successive "specular images" in life reflected back to him/her by parents, teachers, friends, colleagues, and so on.⁹

Bruce Fink depicts the transition from identification with the ideal ego to the ego ideal thus:

> [O]nce internalized, these various images fuse into a vast global image which the child comes to take for him[-] or her[-] *self*; new images being grafted upon the old. . . . [I]t is this crystallization of images which allows for a coherent "sense of self" and a great deal of attempt to "make sense" of the world around us involves juxtaposing what we see and hear with this internalized self-image: How does what happens reflect upon us? Where do we fit in? Is it a challenge to our view of ourselves? (*The Lacanian Subject* 37)

Cultural Mirroring

The identification with recurring images in life extends the mirror stage to the notion of "the cultural mirror" in the post-psychoanalytic paradigm of cultural study. Post-psychoanalysis, according to Richard Feldstein, features its use of "psychoanalytic principles in the service of cultural criticism, which critiques gender, class, race, ethnicity, age, and the heterosexist axes of power relations" (141).

In the post-psychoanalytic discourse, the cultural mirror is a process of mirroring in which the subject does more than internalize an image from the looking glass, but reconfigures him/herself in response to the circulation of the visual images produced by mass media. Dancers, sport stars, or a poem full of spatial imagery can manifest the "specular image" in the cultural mirror, either pictorially or verbally. Through the introjection of images that the subject appraises and re-appraises, the subject internalizes social, political, and religious values.

In fact, the concept of cultural mirroring may be found as early as in Frantz Fanon's *Peau Noire, Masques Blancs* (1952; in English translation *Black Skin, White Masks*, 1967, all page references are to this translation) in which he examines the psyche of the Antillean within the framework of Lacan's theory of the mirror stage. According to Fanon's application of this theory, the foundation for the Antillean knowing him/herself as a conscious unity is in the infant's identification with the specular image of its own body; i.e., with the *imago*, in Lacanian terms, of the black body first, and then with his/her further identification with the symbolic representation of the body. Therefore, the Antillean psyche is constructed through identification with the imaginary perception and the symbolic representation of the black body.

The dual identification with the imaginary perception and the symbolic representation of the body is the constitution of the Antillean psyche first through the family constellation and second the cultural constellation. For the family constellation, Fanon writes:

> in Europe and in every country characterized as civilized or civilizing, the family is a miniature of the nation. As the child emerges from the shadow of his parents, he finds himself once more among the same laws, the same principles, [and] the same values. A normal child that has grown up in a normal family will be a normal man. (141-142)

As the Antilleans grow up, however, in "abnormal" families, they may not become normal subjects, and, actually, many of them suffer psychologically. Fanon explains that the Antillean's abnormality stems from the radical incompatibility of the two constellations—the familial and the cultural constellations.

For the cultural constellation, he writes:

> every neurosis, every abnormal manifestation, every affective erethism in the Antillean is the product of his *cultural* situation. In other words, there is a *constellation* of postulates, a series of propositions that slowly and subtly, with the help of books, newspapers, schools and their texts, advertisements, films, radio [that] work their way into one's mind and shape one's view of the world of the group to which one belongs. (152; emphasis added)

Tragically, these two constellations offer different "laws," "principles," and "values." As the Antilleans are interpellated at once both by the familial and the cultural constellations, the conflicts of the two constellations traumatize the Antillean psyche. As the imaginary perception of the black body—*imago*—is restructured, rewritten, and overwritten by the symbolic representation of the body—*négre*—the Antilleans are unable to properly identify with the body *imago*. Fanon asserts that usually at around the age of twenty, the Antillean becomes aware of the conflict between the body *imago* and the *négre*: the former as the specular image is acquired through the familial constellation and the latter symbolizes "the no good," acquired through the cultural constellation.

The discrepancy between *imago* and *négre*, between the familial and cultural constellations, and between the imaginary specular image and the cultural mirroring is actually the gap between imaginary identification with the ideal ego and symbolic identification with the ego ideal.

Although the gap between the ideal ego and the ego ideal is inevitable, an extreme discrepancy between them will make difficult the transition from the imaginary ego to the symbolic subject and even cause psychological disorders. Fink notes that if "the images are too contradictory to fuse in any way," the crystallization of images or the sense of self will be in danger (*The Lacanian Subject* 37).[10] For example, Fanon diagnoses the Antillean neurosis caused by the gap between the familial and cultural constellations (namely, the gap between the ideal ego and the ego ideal). For the Antillean, the ideal ego and the ego ideal are located in two incompatible realms, so the mirror stage, instead of a mere "family" matter, is complicated by cultural, social, and racial differences.

A Regressive Passage to the "Real": The Mother's Psychosis in *No-No Boy*

Okada's *No-No Boy* illustrates how the construction of the psyche of the American ethnic minority group is complicated by involvement with culture and ethnicity. In the novel, the "mirror stage" cannot be simply applied as a stage that a child goes through in a nuclear family in a Western cultural milieu. In examining the formation of the ego of Japanese-Americans and their subjectivity, one has to take into account the cultural encounter of the two Symbolic(s)—Japanese and American—and the disparity between them. As identification with the ideal ego and the ego ideal shapes identity, the gap between the ideal ego and the ego ideal is critical to the racial minority.

Set immediately after the end of World War II, the novel shows mimetically that the social and political context in the U.S. of the 1940s did not allow for a multi-symbolic milieu. *No-No Boy* exposes how, although both of the Symbolic(s) (American and Japanese) truly existed and dominated the minority's psyche in their own ways, for political and social reasons, the juxtaposition of the two Symbolic(s) was blindly or deliberately misread as a mere cultural diversification (or aberration) under *the* exclusive and intact Symbolic—with one Symbolic as *the* exclusive and intact one, and the other as merely the *American* societal Other. As a result, the encounter of the two Symbolic(s) forcefully led to the negation of one of them. The Symbolic of Japan (indicated as Sj) was ideologically and politically marginalized. Psychoanalytically speaking, Sj was coercively reduced to the realm of the Imaginary by the Symbolic of America (indicated as Sa henceforth).

The reduction of Sj into the Imaginary makes the Name-of-the-Father,[11] to use Lacan's term, of Sj into the imaginary father. And according to Lacan, the reduction of the symbolic father to the imaginary father causes psychosis or perversion. Faced with the encounter between the two Symbolic(s), the first-generation Japanese immigrants can only make a choice of "either-or": to assimilate the new big Other, re-regulate their desire, and accept a new symbolic position assigned by the new Symbolic. Or they may decide to expel the Name-of-the-Father of Sa in order to keep Sj intact. On the second occasion, they continue to live up to the Symbolic Father of Sj that used to impose the law and regulate their desire, so that they can still keep having the desire of the Other as speaking beings of Japanese.

However, the act to expel the Name-of-the-Father of Sa, called "foreclosure" by Lacan, results in the absence of the Name-of-the-Father in the Symbolic. It is the absence of the Symbolic father that causes a psychological breakdown. When a subject forecloses the Name-of-the-Father, the subject is said to have a psychotic structure. Without assimilating the Name-of-the-Father of Sa, the Japanese immigrants, even though they are "normal" subjects, are still seen as "an inscrutable other" in the view of the Symbolic of America—the way they dress, the food they eat, the language they speak, and so on. In *No-No Boy*, the mother demonstrates how the first Japanese immigrants had tried hard to maintain Sj intact at the expense of gradual psychic disintegration. The mother represents a victim of psychosis caused by an act to foreclose the Name-of-the-Father of Sa within an enforced constitution of a single Symbolic. Her regression to psychosis, however, is not a common clinical development, but a cultural and psychoanalytic "acting out," as I discuss below.

While regarding his mother as a crazy woman, Ichiro cannot help but wonder:

> Was it she who was wrong and crazy not to have found in herself the capacity to accept a country which repeatedly refused to accept her or her sons unquestioningly, or was it the others who were being deluded . . . ? (104).

Ichiro's question points out the dilemma confronting the mother and other issei in the New World in which they are denied a subjective position. Americans are defined through a process of selective inclusion and exclusion, and issei are constantly rejected as aliens and outsiders. Much worse, as the Imaginary other without Symbolic representation of subjectivity, they may even be viewed as not adequately "normal" or less "humane." For example, the mother, who does not carry subjective signifiers in the new Symbolic, hardly speaks throughout the novel and is even viewed as a maniac. Without a voice like a Symbolic "speaking being," she is always referred as "the mother" instead of by her name. Her name—Kin-Chan—appears only in chapter 6 in which her husband recalls their lives in Japan. Indeed, only in Japan is the mother positioned as a Symbolic subject with a proper name; in the New World, she loses her voice as well as her name and is reduced to a limited set of Symbolic or stereotypical features—she becomes one of the living dead.

Reacting to racial oppression in the New World, the mother fanatically embraces Japanese nationalism. Because her original Symbolic identity is erased and a new Symbolic signifier in the New World is not granted, the mother has no choice but to "foreclose" the new Symbolic Master Signifier of America and, identifying with the Symbolic Father of Sj who becomes the Imaginary father in the New World, turn to embody the Name-of-the-Father of Sj. And as an embodiment of the Symbolic Father of Japan, or, put in another way, thinking of herself as possessing the Imaginary Phallus, the mother becomes from a Lacanian viewpoint a "Phallic Mother" or the "Maternal Phallus." As a phallic mother, the mother is observed by her son, Ichiro, to have the "phallic power": there is a "*power* [in her] and in the wiry, brown arms, a hard, blind, *unreckoning force*," and her thin arms "swabbed the green-painted wood with sweeping, *vigorous strokes*" (20; emphasis added). Besides, the mother is a rock: "the rock that's always hammering and pounding, pounding, pounding in her unobtrusive, determined, fanatical way" (12).

As the possessor of the Phallus, the mother usurps the role as head of the family at the expense of her husband who is coded as being childlike or feminine. The son calls the father "a baby," "a fool," "a woman," and even "a goddamned, fat, grinning, spineless nobody," and says of the mother that she "should have been Pa" (112). Besides, the mother has few feminine features since she *is* the phallus. Early in the novel she is introduced as "a small, flat-chested shapeless woman who wore her hair pulled back into a tight bun. Hers was the awkward, skinny body of a thirteen-year-old which had dried and toughened" (10).

While the mother is living as the embodiment of the Paternal Signifier reduced to the Imaginary Phallus, her Symbolic world amounts to the Imaginary domain in the New World. According to Lacan, psychosis is defined by the Imaginary and is even equated with the Imaginary (Jacques-Alain Miller 245). The mother turns out to be not only an Imaginary other but also a psychotic. For Lacan, psychosis involves the reduction of the Other into the other, and the collapse of the Symbolic into the Imaginary. More specifically, its reduction or collapse is caused by the absence of the paternal function. Lacan states, "It is an accident in that register and in what takes place in it, namely the *foreclosure* of the Name-of-the-Father in the place of the Other, and in the failure of the paternal metaphor, that I designate the defect that gives psychosis its essential condition, and the structure that separates it from neurosis" (Lacan, *Écrits* 215; emphasis added). Imprisoning herself in her psychotic universe, the mother forecloses the new Symbolic Father who fails to overwrite her psychic structure and does not establish a new ego ideal. The mother expels a given notion, thought, or memory just as she denies the fact that Japan has lost the war because "Japan could not possibly lose" (24). The mother, however, has not loosened her relationship with reality; rather, as a psychotic she has "built a fictitious ground in [her] relation to the Other" (Apollon 120) and "reduces reality itself to 'something that exists only in [her] head,' a 'product of the delirium of [her] brain'" (Zizek, *Enjoy Your Symptom* 130). Though she is diagnosed as a psychotic due to her act of foreclosure of the Symbolic Father, Lacan argues that for most of us, it is the psychotic who is rejected, repudiated, and sealed off.[12]

As Lacan defines psychosis in terms of the operation of foreclosure—the Name-of-the-Father is not integrated to the symbolic universe of the psychotic because it is "foreclosed"—the failure of paternal function clinically results in some psychotic phenomena. The most common psychotic phenomena are hallucination and delusion. Since the psychotic is unable to distinguish fantasy from reality, hallucinations, to him/her, are taken "to be what are most real in his[/her] experience" (Jacques-Alain Miller 246). Imprisoning herself in the Imaginary register, the mother lives up to the Imaginary father that is seen by her as omnipotent like God in religion or as mighty like Japan as a nation. She believes that Japan becomes unconquerable. Expecting Japan's glorious victory in the war, she is awaiting her eventual return to Japan. "Dried and toughened through the many years" of hardship in America, the mother saves her pennies for the day when the Japanese government will send ships to conquer America and to bring her home. Her delusions are further expressed in the letter she receives from "a friend in South America" (14):

> To *You* who are a loyal and honorable Japanese, it is with humble and heartfelt joy that I relay this momentous message. *Word* has been brought to us that the victorious Japanese government is presently making preparation to send ships, which will return to Japan *those residents* in foreign countries who have steadfastly maintained their faith and loyalty to our *Emperor*. The Japanese government regrets that the responsibilities arising from the victory compels them to delay in the sending of the vessels. To be among the few who remain to receive this honor is a gratifying tribute. Heed not the propaganda of the radio and newspapers which endeavors to convince the people with lies about the allied victory. Especially, heed not the lies of your traitorous countrymen who have turned their backs on the country of their birth and who will suffer for their treasonous acts. The day of glory is close at hand. The rewards will be beyond our greatest expectations. What we have done, we have done only as Japanese, but the government is grateful. Hold *your* heads high and make ready for the journey, for the ships are coming. (14; emphases added)

Jacques-Alain Miller states that "the psychotic subject may feel certain that someone is sending him[/her] messages" (246), and the messages the mother receives are the "Word" from "the Emperor," the Imaginary Father, who is omnipotent and all-powerful. Zizek also asserts that in the Imaginary order, a letter always arrives at its destination since "its destination is wherever it arrives" (*Enjoy Your Symptom* 10). Specifically, the letter that circulates in the dimension of the Imaginary always arrives at its destination insofar as one (mis)recognizes oneself as its addressee. Since the mother finds herself in the circuit of this letter and recognizes herself as the addressee, the categories of "you," "us," "those residents," "our," and "your" in the letter has always already included the mother. Thus, the letter will never go amiss.

Because the mother "foreclosed" the Symbolic Father or "is foreclosed" by it, she is unable to receive any message from the Symbolic realm. The mother misses the letters from her relatives in Japan who beg for money and food while the letters, to her, represent a Symbolic perspective of reality. Because the mother does not believe what is said about Japan in the letters, she is unable to receive the messages even though in the letters the addressee—she herself—is clearly indicated. These letters all fail to arrive at their destinations. As Zizek notes, "'A letter arrives at its destination' only with the subject entering the circuit of communication" (*Enjoy Your Symptom* 26). Because the mother refuses to recognize herself as the addressee and resists entering "the circuit of communication," she does not receive the messages in the letters. Zizek moreover points out that, "there is a subjective position within which a letter does not arrive at its destination, . . . within which the subject does not receive from the Other his[/her] own message in its true form: that of *a psychotic*" (*Enjoy Your Symptom* 26; emphasis added).

Although hallucinations or delusions are typical phenomena of psychosis, they are not criteria of psychosis, in that hallucinations and delusions are also common in neurosis. Fink argues that in Lacanian psychoanalysis, "[c]ertainty is characteristic of psychosis, whereas doubt is not," underscoring that "doubt is the very hallmark of neurosis" (*A Clinical Introduction to Lacanian Psychoanalysis* 84). Accordingly, the psychotic "speaks of [his/her hallucinations] with complete certainty which is not open to doubt" (Jacques-Alain Miller 246). In contrast to the neurotic who is always unsure, the psychotic knows and believes and follows what s/he believes. Clinging to the word from the Imaginary Father, the mother is very certain that Japan has won the war and insists that the claim of Japanese defeat is just "a trick of the American" (37). In his clinical study of psychotic patients, Willy Apollon also observes that, "most of the time such patients do not think they are sick, nor do they think they have any need for help" (128). In effect, the mother never thinks of herself as mad. When people call her crazy for believing in a Japanese victory, the mother states that "[t]hey do not mean it. They say it because they are frightened and because they envy my strength, which is truly the strength of Japan" (43). It is this "unshakable non-dialectical certainty" that characterizes the psychotic like the mother (Jacques-Alain Miller 247).

Another important characteristic of psychosis is a lack of "desire." In psychosis "desire is missing," or more specifically, the psychotic has "no properly human desire at all" (Fink, *A Clinical Introduction to Lacanian Psychoanalysis* 101). In the novel, since the Symbolic fails to overwrite the Imaginary in the mother's psychic structure and does not establish a "lack," the mother personally desires nothing from the Symbolic or, in other words, what the mother "desires"—Japan's glorious victory in the war—is considered "improper" or "abnormal" in the Symbolic order. Thus, the dialectic of desire never takes place in her psychic structure in view of the Symbolic. She is a woman without desire, or rather, without *proper* desire; with no desire, she never doubts or questions. Fink describes how the psychotic acts: "I cannot call into question my past, my motives, or even my thoughts and dreams. They simply are" (*Clinical* 101).

The mother's descent into psychosis consists of her regression from the Symbolic to the Imaginary. Once "[s]mall and proud and firm and maybe a little bit huffy, but good and soft inside" (177), the mother, named Kin-chan, was treasured by her husband in Japan, who recalled how wonderful it was when they made love, before they married, "in the darkness of the narrow corridor" (178) behind their parents' back. Also, her son remembers that "there was a time" when she was a mother who "used to smile a mother's smile" and told her son stories (15). Yet because she is not accepted as a Symbolic subject in America, she reacts to racism and injustice in the New World by isolating herself socially and psychologically. She becomes "a rock of hate" (21)—a nonsymbolizable object. Refusing to be "symbolized," she forecloses the Symbolic Father and turns all her hopes toward the Imaginary Father. Fanatically embracing the Imaginary Father, she embodies "Japaneseness" culturally, politically, historically, and socially. Thus, as stated above, she is the Phallus—the Maternal Phallus. The mother simply usurps the role of the head of the family and makes her son say "No."

Although initially her husband and sons do not question the position she has acquired, her domestic tyranny diminishes when the war ends. When her family can no longer tolerate her belief in the "strength of Japan" and denies her, the mother collapses, facing a psychotic breakdown finally. When her elder son Ichiro calls her a "crazy woman" as well as a "crazy mother," she "collapses limply to the floor" (43). When her second son, Taro, packs up and leaves home for the army, she cannot help but utter "a single, muffled cry which was the forgotten spark in a dark and vicious canyon and the spark having escaped, there was only darkness, but a darkness which was now darker still, and the meaning of her life became a little bit *meaningless*" (68; emphasis added). When her husband reads her a letter from a sister in Japan who writes to beg for food, describing the desperate situation in Japan after the war, and, moreover, divulging a secret only she and her sister shared in childhood, she is depicted with "a look which meant nothing, for the meaning was gone" (111). Her Imaginary world has fallen apart.

The mother's psychic regression from the Symbolic to the Imaginary is an "acting out" in Lacanian terms; more specifically, her passage to psychosis is a "cultural" acting out. According to Lacan, "acting out" is an act addressed to the Big Other: "[w]hen the Other has become 'deaf,' the subject cannot convey a message to him[/her] in words, and is forced to express the message in actions" (Evans 3). As she is excluded from the Other who plays "deaf" and does not grant her a subjective signifier or name, the mother inevitably suspends the dimension of the Other and escapes to the Imaginary. Her "acting out is . . . a ciphered message which the subject addresses to an Other" (Evans 3), and is an act that "embodies a certain reproach to the Other" (Zizek, "The Undergrowth of Enjoyment" 33). The mother's submission to the Imaginary is a reaction to the racial oppression around her. In order to survive, she has to act out and act for the Other. First embodying "Japaneseness" bodily and psychologically, she acts as the Maternal Phallus that has to be more "Japanese" than the Japanese. She acts just like another character in the novel—"Mike," a World War I U.S. Army veteran—who reacts to the evacuation during World War II by swearing that, "if they treated him like a Japanese, he would act like one" (98). Mike later becomes a protest leader in the camp and goes to Japan when World War II ends.

Even at the end, when her family forces her to accept the truth, the mother still strives to act out in order to prevent a psychotic breakdown. She develops certain symptoms—repeatedly lining shelves with cans and knocking them down. These repeated symptoms at least temporarily help keep her from a total psychotic breakdown. Symptom formation is the way the mother avoids madness because she can still "choose something (the symptom-formation) instead of nothing (radical psychotic autism, the destruction of the Symbolic universe)," and through identification with her symptom, "assure a minimum of consistency" (Zizek, *The Sublime Object of Ideology* 75), and "retain [her] coherence" (Zizek, "The Undergrowth of Enjoyment" 33).

After her Imaginary realm collapses in the face of the Symbolic Father, the mother's regression from the Symbolic to the Imaginary moves closer to the Real. After Taro leaves home for the Army and Ichiro looks for a job out of town, the mother stops eating and develops compulsive reactions. After a couple of days of begging her to eat, the father says, "Mama, eat or you will take sick. Eat or you will die" (175). His words become for her a message from the Real. On the Real level, Zizek argues that a letter that always arrives at its destination is the call of our fate: we will all die (*Enjoy Your Symptom* 20). Fink asserts that a psychotic "may see meaning in nothing, or find a purely personal meaning in virtually everything" (*The Lacanian Subject* 75). The mother initiates the move to pick up the letter of death as soon as she (mis)recognizes herself as its specific addressee. Responding to the message—the letter that "nobody can evade, that sooner or later reaches us" (Zizek, *Enjoy Your Symptom* 21), the mother goes to the bathroom and drowns herself in a tub full of water. The scene of her death is described thus:

> She was half out of the tub and half in, her hair of dirty gray and white floating up to the surface of the *water* like a tangled mass of seaweed and obscuring her neck and face. On one side,

the hair had pulled away and lodged against the overflow drain, damming up the outlet and causing the flooding, just as her mind, long shut off from reality, had sought and found its *erratic release*. (185; emphasis added)

On the one hand, the mother's final act, of committing suicide, is a "passage to the act" in Lacanian terms, a way to the total destruction of the Symbolic world, an exit from the Other into the realm of the Real. Her final act results in "a dissolution of the subject" that becomes "a pure object" (Evans 137). On another level, her act is an escape to the pre-Symbolic Real. Illustrated by the floating hair, the flooding, the bathtub, the erratic expression, the pre-Symbolic Real indicates the space Julia Kristeva labels "chora," the Greek word for the enclosed space, *womb*. A Buddhist believing in the notion of samsara,[13] the mother is returning to a figurative womb—the pre-Symbolic realm.

The mother's final act is an embrace of life as well as death, just as the Real is life and death because the Real is "not only the pale, frozen, lifeless immobility but also . . . the life substance in its mucous palpitation" (Zizek, *Enjoy Your Symptom* 22). The pre-Symbolic Real is the infant's body before it submits itself to the ways of the world, assimilates language, and agrees to become a user of letters, etc., and, furthermore, before it was "born" in the womb. Throughout the novel, the mother's withdrawal from the Symbolic, her identification with the Imaginary, and her final escape to the Real show a reverse subjective journey toward rebirth as well as annihilation.

Coda—in lieu of Conclusion

Who is crazy? The Mother? Or those so deluded that they fight for a country that never accepts them? Ichiro says of his mother: "Did it matter so much that events had ruined the plans which she cherished and turned the once very possible dreams into a madness which was madness only in view of the changed status of the Japanese in America?" (104). The mother did exhibit psychotic phenomena such as delusions, hallucinations, absolute certainty, the lack of desire, and the foreclosure of the Symbolic Father. The paternal signifier she forecloses, however, is the big Other, the American public. In her psychic structure the paternal signifier of the Japanese public still exists; that is, there is no "hole" in her psychic structure. She *did* desire, though her desire for Japan's victory is not "proper" in the view of the Symbolic of the U.S. mainstream. Her other psychotic phenomenon, certainty, can be viewed as an expression of her fanatic loyalty to Japan, like other people's patriotism during the war. Besides, what if Japan really had won the war, sending the ships to the West coast as the mother wished? What if her psychotic "delusions" or "hallucinations" had come true? The mother would then be perceived as more "normal" than any "yes-yes" Japanese Americans. One may suggest that although seen as a psychotic in the United States, the mother would be a "normal" subject in Japan.

The mother's madness, thus, is not defined by essential qualities, but by social and cultural contexts. Her madness is merely a failure to "accede [to] normality, *symbolic* normality" in the New World (Jacques-Alain Miller 245; emphasis added). Truly, she falls a victim to a denial of a possible amalgam of two Symbolic(s), to a negation of bi-symbolic operations, to a compulsive submission of one Symbolic to another, to a misdiagnosis of inter-subjective struggles as intrapsychic conflicts, and, ultimately, to a reduction of racial and cultural *differences* to an ethnic and multicultural *diversity*.

Appendix

Jacques Lacan
Mary Klages

For Lacan, the unconscious looks like a continually circulating chain (or multiple chains) of signifiers, with no anchor—or, to use Derrida's terms, no center. This is Lacan's linguistic translation of Freud's picture of the unconscious as this chaotic realm of constantly shifting drives and desires. Freud is interested in how to bring those chaotic drives and desires into consciousness, so that they can have some order and sense and meaning, . . . be understood and made manageable. Lacan, on the other hand, asserts that the process of becoming an adult, a "self," is the process of trying to fix, to stabilize, to stop the chain of signifiers so that stable meaning—including the meaning of "I"—becomes possible; although, of course, Lacan considers that this possibility is only an illusion, an image created by a misperception of the relation between body and self.

. . . Freud lists the three stages of polymorphous perversity in infants: the oral, the anal, and the phallic; it is the Oedipus complex and castration complex that end polymorphous perversity and create "adult" beings. Lacan creates different categories to explain a similar trajectory, from infant to "adult." He devises three concepts—*need*, *demand*, and *desire*—that roughly correspond to three phases of development, or three fields in which humans develop—the Real, the Imaginary, and the Symbolic. The

Symbolic realm, which is marked by the concept of desire is the equivalent of adulthood; or, more specifically for Lacan, the Symbolic realm is the structure of language itself, which one has to enter into in order to become a "speaking subject," in order to say "I" and have "I" designate something which appears to be stable.

Just as in Freud, Lacan's infant starts out as something inseparable from its mother; there is no distinction between self and other, between baby and mother (at least, from the baby's perspective). In fact, the baby (for both Freud and Lacan) is a kind of blob, with no sense of self or individuated identity, and no sense even of its body as a coherent unified whole. This baby-blob is driven by *need*; it needs food, it needs comfort/safety, it needs to be changed, etc. These needs are satisfiable, and can be satisfied by an object. When the baby needs food, it gets a breast (or a bottle); when it needs safety, it gets hugged. The baby, in this state of *need*, does not recognize any distinction between itself and the objects that meet its needs; it does not recognize that an object (like a breast) is part of another whole person (because it does not have any concept yet of "whole person"). There is no distinction between it and anyone or anything else; there are only needs and things that satisfy those needs.

This is the state of "nature," which has to be broken up in order for culture to be formed. This is true in both Freud's psychoanalysis and in Lacan's: the infant must separate from its mother [and] form a separate identity, in order to enter into civilization. That separation entails some kind of *loss*; when the child knows the difference between itself and its mother, and starts to become an individuated being, it loses that primal sense of unity (and safety/security) that it originally had. This is the element of the tragic built into psychoanalytic theory (whether Freudian or Lacanian): to become a civilized "adult" always entails the profound loss of an original unity, a non-differentiation, a merging with others (particularly the mother).

The baby who has not yet made this separation . . . exists in the realm of the *real*, according to Lacan. The Real is a place (a psychic place, not a physical place) where there is this original unity. Because of that, there is no absence or loss or lack; the Real is all fullness and completeness, where there is no need that cannot be satisfied. And because there is no absence or loss or lack, there is no language in the [realm of the] Real. . . . there is only complete fullness, needs and the satisfaction of needs. Hence the Real is always beyond language, unrepresentable in language (and therefore irretrievably lost when one enters into language).

The Real, and the phase of need last from birth till . . . when the baby blob starts to be able to distinguish between its body and everything else in the world [and] . . . shifts from having needs to having *demands*.

Demands are not satisfiable with objects; a demand is always a demand for recognition from another, for love from another. The . . . baby starts to become aware that it is separate from the mother, and that there exist things that are not part of it; thus the idea of "other" is created. (Note, however, that as yet the binary opposition of "self/other" does not yet exist, because the baby still does not have a coherent sense of "self"). That awareness of separation, or the fact of otherness, creates an anxiety, a sense of loss. The baby then demands a reunion, a return to that original sense of fullness and non-separation that it had in the Real. But that is impossible, once the baby knows (and this knowing . . . is . . . happening on an unconscious level) that the idea of an "other" exists. The baby demands to be filled by the other, to return to the sense of original unity; the baby wants the idea of "other" to disappear. Demand is thus the demand for the fullness, the completeness, of the other that will stop up the lack the baby is experiencing. But of course this is impossible, because that lack, or absence, the sense of "other"ness, is the condition for the baby becoming a self/subject, a functioning cultural being.

Because the demand is for recognition from the other, it cannot really be satisfied, if only because the six-to-eighteen month infant cannot *say* what it wants. The baby cries, and the mother gives it a bottle, or a breast, or a pacifier, or something, but no object can satisfy the demand—the demand is for a response on a different level. The baby cannot recognize the ways the mother does respond to it, and recognize it, because it does not yet have a conception of itself as a thing—it only knows that this idea of "other" exists, and that it is separate from the "other," but it does not yet have an idea of what its "self" is.

This is where Lacan's *mirror stage* happens. . . . Eventually, this entity the child sees in the mirror, this whole being, will be a "self," the entity designated by the word "I." What is really happening, however, is an identification that is a *misrecognition*. The child sees an image in the mirror; it thinks, that image is "*me*". But it is *not* the child; it is only an image. But another person (usually the mother) is there to reinforce the misrecognition. The baby looks in the mirror, and looks back at mother [who] . . . guarantees the "reality" of the connection between the child and its image, and the idea of the integrated whole body the child is seeing and identifying with.

The child takes that image in the mirror as the summation of its entire being, its "self." This process, of misrecognizing one's self in the image in the mirror, creates the *ego*, the thing that says "I." In Lacan's terms, this misrecognition creates the "armor" of the subject, an illusion or misperception of wholeness, integration, and totality that surrounds and protects the fragmented body. To Lacan, ego, or self, or "I"dentity, is always on some level a *fantasy*, an identification with an external image, and not an internal sense of separate whole identity.

This is why Lacan calls the phase of demand, and the mirror stage, the realm of the *imaginary*. The idea of a self is created through an Imaginary identification with the image in the mirror. The realm of the Imaginary is where the alienated relation of self to its own image is created and maintained. The Imaginary is a realm of images, whether conscious or unconscious. It is prelinguistic, and preoedipal, but very much based in visual perception, or what Lacan calls specular imaging.

The mirror image, the whole person the baby mistakes as itself, is known in psychoanalytic terminology as an "ideal ego," a perfect whole self who has no insufficiency. This "ideal ego" becomes internalized; one builds one's sense of "self," one's "I"dentity, by (mis)identifying with this ideal ego. By doing this, according to Lacan, one imagines a self that has no lack, no notion of absence or incompleteness. The fiction of the stable, whole, unified self that one sees in the mirror becomes a compensation for having lost the original oneness with the mother's body. In short, according to Lacan, one loses one's unity with the mother's body, the state of "nature," in order to enter culture, but one protects oneself from the knowledge of that loss by misperceiving oneself as not lacking anything—as being complete unto oneself.

According to Lacan, the child's self-concept (its ego or "I"dentity) will never match up to its own being. Its *imago* in the mirror is both smaller and more stable than the child, and is always "other" than the child—something outside it. The child, for the rest of its life, will misrecognize its self as "other," as the image in the mirror that provides an illusion of self and of mastery.

The Imaginary is the psychic place, or phase, where the child projects its ideas of "self" onto the mirror image it sees. The mirror stage cements a self/other dichotomy, where previously the child had known only "other," but not "self." For Lacan, the identification of "self" is always in terms of "other." This is not the same as a binary opposition, where "self" = what is not "other," and "other" = what is not "self." Rather, "self" *is* "other," in Lacan's view; the idea of the self, that inner being one designates by "I," is based on an image, an other. The concept of self relies on one's misidentification with this image of an other.

Lacan uses the term "other" in a number of ways . . . First . . . in the sense of self/other, where "other" is the "not-me"; but . . . the "other" becomes "me" in the mirror stage. Lacan also uses an idea of Other, with a capital "o," to distinguish between the concept of the other and actual others. The image the child sees in the mirror is an other, and it gives the child the idea of Other as a structural possibility, one which makes possible the structural possibility of "I" or self. In other words, the child encounters actual others—its own image, other people—and understands the idea of "Otherness," things that are not itself. According to Lacan, the notion of Otherness, encountered in the Imaginary phase (and associated with demand), comes before the sense of "self," which is built on the idea of Otherness.

When the child has formulated some idea of Otherness, and of a self identified with its own "other," its own mirror image, then the child begins to enter the Symbolic realm. The Symbolic and the Imaginary are overlapping, unlike Freud's phases of development; there is no clear marker or division between the two, and in some respects they always coexist. The Symbolic order is the structure of language itself; we have to enter it in order to become speaking subjects, and to designate ourselves by "I." The foundation for having a self lies in the Imaginary projection of the self onto the specular image, the other in the mirror, and having a self is expressed in saying "I," which can only occur within the Symbolic, which is why the two coexist.

. . .

For Lacan, the ideas of other and Other, of lack and absence, of the (mis)identification of self with o/Other are all worked out on an individual level, with each child, but they form the basic structures of the Symbolic order, of language, which the child must enter in order to become an adult member of culture. Thus the otherness acted out . . . by the distinctions made in the Mirror Phase between self and other, mother and child become categorical or structural ideas. So, in the Symbolic, there is a structure (or structuring principle) of Otherness, and a structuring principle of Lack.

The Other (capital O) is a structural position in the Symbolic order. It is the place that everyone is trying to get to, to merge with, in order to get rid of the separation between "self" and "other." It is, in Derrida's sense, the *center* of the system, of the Symbolic and/or of language itself. As such, the Other is the thing to which every element relates. But, as the center, the Other (again, not a person but a position) cannot be merged with. Nothing can be in the center with the Other, even though everything in the system (e.g., people) want to be. So the position of the Other creates and sustains a never-ending *lack*, which Lacan calls *desire*. Desire is the desire to be the Other. By definition, desire can never be fulfilled: it is not desire for some object (which would be *need*) or desire for love or another person's recognition of oneself (which would be *demand*), but desire to be the center of the system, the center of the Symbolic, the center of language itself.

The center has a lot of names in Lacanian theory. It is the Other; it is also called the *phallus*. . . . Lacan borrows again from Freud's original Oedipus theory.

The mirror stage is pre-oedipal. The self is constructed in relation to an other, to the idea of Other, and the self wants to merge with the Other. As in Freud's world, the most important other in the child's life is the mother; so the child wants to merge with its mother. In Lacan's terms, this is the child's demand that the self/other split be erased. The child decides that it can merge with the mother if it becomes what the mother wants it to be — in Lacan's terms, the child tries to fulfill the mother's desire. The mother's desire (formed by her own entry into the Symbolic, because she is already an adult) is to not have lack, or Lack (or to be the Other, the center, the place where nothing is lacking). This fits with the Freudian version of the Oedipus complex, where the child wants to merge with its mother by having sexual intercourse with her. In Freud's model, the idea of lack is represented by the lack of a penis. The boy who wants to sleep with his mother wants to complete her lack by filling her up with his penis.

In Freud's view, what breaks this oedipal desire up, for boys anyway, is the father, who threatens castration. The father threatens to make the boy experience lack, the absence of the penis, if he tries to use his penis to make up for the mother's lack of a penis. In Lacan's terms, the threat of castration is a metaphor for the whole idea of Lack as a structural concept. For Lacan, it is not the real father who threatens castration. Rather, because the idea of lack, or Lack, is essential to the concept of language, because the concept of Lack is part of the basic structuration of language, the father becomes a function of the linguistic structure. The Father, rather than being a person, becomes a structuring principle of the Symbolic order.

For Lacan, Freud's angry father becomes the Name-of-the-Father, or the Law-of-the-Father, or sometimes just the Law. Submission to the rules of language itself—the Law of the Father—is required in order to enter into the Symbolic order. To become a speaking subject, one has to be subjected to, one has to obey, the laws and rules of language. Lacan designates the idea of the structure of language, and its rules, as specifically paternal. He calls the rules of language the Law-of-the-Father in order to link the entry into the Symbolic, the structure of language, to Freud's notion of the Oedipus and castration complexes.

The Law-of-the-Father, or Name-of-the-Father, is another term for the Other, for the center of the system, the thing that governs the whole structure—its shape and how all the elements in the system can move and form relationships. This center is also called the *phallus*, to underline even more the patriarchal nature of the Symbolic order. The Phallus, as center, limits the play of elements, and gives stability to the whole structure. The Phallus anchors the chains of signifiers that, in the unconscious, are just floating and unfixed, always sliding and shifting. The Phallus stops play, so that signifiers can have some stable meaning. It is because the Phallus is the center of the Symbolic order, of language, that the term "I" designates the idea of the self (and, additionally, why any other word has stable meaning).

The Phallus is not the same as the penis. Penises belong to individuals; the Phallus belongs to the structure of language itself. No one has it, just like no one governs language or rules language. Rather, the Phallus is the center. It governs the whole structure, it is what everyone wants to be (or have), but no one can get there (no element of the system can take the place of the center). That is what Lacan calls *desire*: the desire, which is never satisfied, because it can never be satisfied, to be the center, to rule the system.

Lacan believes that boys can think they have a shot at being the Phallus, at occupying the position of center, because they have penises. Girls have a harder time misperceiving themselves as having a shot at the Phallus because they are (as Freud believes) constituted by and as lack, lacking a penis, and the Phallus is a place where there is no lack. But, Lacan finds, every subject in language is constituted by/as lack, or Lack. The only reason we have language at all is because of the loss, or lack, of the union with the maternal body. In fact, it is the necessity to become part of "culture," to become subjects in language, that forces that absence, loss, lack.

. . .

So, to summarize. Lacan's theory starts with the idea of the Real; this is the union with the mother's body, which is a state of nature, and must be broken up in order to build culture. Once one moves out of the Real, one can never get back, but one always wants to. This is the first idea of an irretrievable loss or lack.

Next comes the Mirror stage, which constitutes the Imaginary. Here one grasps the idea of others, and begins to understand Otherness as a concept or a structuring principle, and thus begins to formulate a notion of "self". This "self" (as seen in the mirror) is in fact an other, but one misrecognizes it as oneself, and calls it "self.". . .

This sense of self, and its relation to others and to Other, sets one up to take up a position in the Symbolic order, in language. Such a position allows one to say "I," to be a speaking subject. "I" has (and all other words have) a stable meaning because they are fixed, or anchored, by the Other/Phallus/Name-of-the-Father/Law, which is the center of the Symbolic, the center of language.

In taking up a position in the Symbolic, one enters through a gender-marked doorway; the position for girls is different than the position for boys. Boys are closer to the Phallus than girls, but no one is or has the Phallus—it is the center.

The Cultural Mirroring   271

One's position in the Symbolic, like the position of all other signifying elements (signifiers) is fixed by the Phallus; unlike the unconscious, the chains of signifiers in the Symbolic do not circulate and slide endlessly because the Phallus limits play.

Paradoxically . . . the Phallus and the Real are pretty similar. Both are places where things are whole, complete, full, unified, where there is no lack, or Lack. Both are places that are inaccessible to the human subject-in-language. But they are also opposite: the Real is the maternal, the ground from which one springs, the nature one has to separate from in order to have culture; the Phallus is the idea of the Father, the patriarchal order of culture, the ultimate idea of culture, the position which rules everything in the world.

Notes

[1] Chin reports that after Okada's death, his wife offered his manuscripts to the Japanese-American Research Project at UCLA, but the manuscripts were rejected and she was even encouraged to destroy the papers. Before Okada died of a heart attack in Los Angeles in 1971, he had almost finished the draft of his second novel in which he claimed to have a strong urge to "faithfully describe the experiences of the immigrant Japanese in the United States" before they speedily vanished (Chin, "Afterword" [to the 1976 edition of *No-No Boy*] 256-257). Yet, shortly after his death, his wife burned the draft of the story about the Issei as well as all other manuscripts and notes. *No-No Boy* remains thus Okada's only published work of fiction. See also Inada, "Introduction" [to the 1976 edition of *No-No Boy*].

[2] Part of the novel has been anthologized in *Aiiieeeee! An Anthology of Asian-American Writers* (1974, edited by Frank Chin et al.); *The Heath Anthology of American Literature* (1990, edited by Paul Lauter et al.); and *The Big Aiiieeeee!* (1991, edited by Jeffery Paul Chan et al.); introduced in *Columbia Literary History of the United States* (1988, edited by Emory Elliot et al.); as well as *The Columbia History of the American Novel* (1991, edited by Emory Elliot et al.); recognized in various series of Asian-American literary studies such as *Ethnic Literatures Since 1776* (1978, edited by Wolodymyr T. Zyla and Wendell M. Aycock); *Three American Literatures* (1982, edited by Houston A. Baker, Jr.); Elaine H. Kim's *Asian American Literature: An Introduction to the Writings and Their Social Context* (1982); *Frontiers of Asian American Studies* (1989, edited by Gail M. Nomura et al.); *Reading the Literatures of Asian America* (1992, edited by Shirley Geok-lin and Amy Ling); *An Interethnic Companion to Asian American Literature* (1997, edited by King-Kok Cheung); and Sheng-mei Ma's *Immigrant Subjectivities in Asian American and Asian Diaspora Literature* (1998). Besides, the novel is thoroughly examined in ethnic journals such as *Amerasia* (see Yeh) and *MELUS* (see McDonald), and in such mainstream journals as *American Literature* (see Jingi Ling); it has been, moreover, discussed in France (see Rigal-Cellard).

[3] Lacan describes the infant's moment of identification with the image as a

moment of jubilation (*Écrits* 1).

⁴ But it is deceived in the illusion that it has control over its own body when it actually does not.

⁵ This is the translation into English of book III of *Le Séminaire de Jacques Lacan*, a volume comprising a series of lectures given by Lacan at the École pratique des hautes études of Paris. Editor's note.

⁶ Slavok Zizek explains that, in contrast to imaginary identification through which "we appear likeable to ourselves" because the image we identify with represents "what we would like to [be]," symbolic identification is "identification with the very place *from where* we are being observed, *from where* we look at ourselves so that we appear to ourselves likable, worthy of love" (*The Sublime Object of Ideology* 105). The difference between imaginary and symbolic identification is the difference between "how we see ourselves and the point from which we are being observed" (Sarup 103)—namely, the difference between the ideal ego and the ego ideal, requiring one, as I mentioned above, to fulfill the dictates of laws or internalize the strictures of society.

⁷ The Symbolic realm is the equivalent of adulthood, while the Imaginary would be that of (the stage of) primary principle in Freudian terms. The appendix contains additional information on Lacan's precepts. Editor's note.

⁸ Instead of a linear process in time, subjectivity can be equally constructed in reverse, by retroaction, and anticipation.

⁹ That is why a "mirror" is actually not essential in the mirror stage for the infant, and one is always caught by successive specular images: throughout life, one keeps projecting and internalizing the image of one's "body" (or self) onto all other objects or subjects in the world around him/her.

¹⁰ Zizek finds that, "This gap between the way I see myself [namely, imaginary identification] and the point from which I am being observed to appear likeable to myself [namely, symbolic identification] is crucial for grasping hysteria" (*The Sublime Object of Ideology* 106).

¹¹ See the appendix for an explanation for terms such as this one. Editor's note.

¹² For a further discussion of psychosis in Lacanian terms, see Michael Walsh's "Reading the Real in the Seminar on the Psychoses."

¹³ The concept of reincarnation or rebirth. Editor's note.

13
Postmodern Blackness and Unbelonging in the Works of Caryl Phillips

Paul Smethurst

The dominant theme in British black author Caryl Phillips' work is belonging, or rather *unbelonging,* the condition felt by characters at odds with their environment. More specifically, his work articulates the "unbelonging" felt by immigrants and their descendants, something Phillips himself encountered while growing up in the U.K. He was technically a first-generation immigrant himself, although only an infant when he arrived from the British colony of St. Kitts in the West Indies. The irony of feeling distinctly not at home in the home country must surely have colored Phillips' literary imagination. It also drove him to research the history of the African diaspora and the history of the slave trade, both to understand his own identity and to provide the backcloth for most of his novels.

Themes of racism and unbelonging are common in the Commonwealth literature of the 1980s. Timothy Mo's *Sour Sweet* (1982), Joan Riley's *The Unbelonging* (1985) and V.S. Naipaul's *The Enigma of Arrival* (1987) all explored these themes, in predominantly realistic form. Yet, only in Phillips' first novel, *The Final Passage* (1985; this edition 1995, all page references are to this edition), is unbelonging given such direct expression. It was perhaps Salman Rushdie who first introduced postmodernism into the novel of unbelonging, and Rushdie's work has clearly been an influence on Phillip's later novels, as their postmodernist character attests.

A further distinction may be made between Phillips' work and that of many of his contemporaries. Riley's *Unbelonging* matches Phillips' novels for darkness and tragedy, but in the novels of Mo, Naipaul and Rushdie, the bitter experience of unbelonging is often sweetened by the comic pathos that arises from a bicultural artistic vision. In Mo's *Sour Sweet,* characters are bewildered rather than oppressed, and considerable comic pathos arises from the misunderstandings and mistranslations that arise. The sour/sweet motif is maintained by seeing from both sides of the cultural divide, and the stance of the novel is therefore bicultural. In the end, *Sour Sweet* charts a difficult but inevitable journey towards the assimilation of Chinese immigrants into the margins of British society. Any sense of alienation stemming from the systemic racism in British society in the 1980s is far more muted than in the novels of Phillips and Riley. Similarly, unbelonging in Naipaul's *The Enigma of Arrival* arises from the gap between the "real" England, and that of a literary imagination furnished by colonial education. In this semi-autobiographical novel, the Naipaul protagonist/narrator approaches this as an enigma, a puzzle that he attempts to work out through writing. The narrator seems less to suffer from this gap than be intrigued by it, and even to exploit it, such that the gap, rather than the unbelonging itself, becomes the matter of the novel. One senses that both Mo and Naipaul are writing from both the inside and the outside of British society.

The double identity of Commonwealth writers such as Mo, Phillips and Rushdie puts them in the category of "transnational" writers. Born across two cultures, their experience of the world is conditioned by existential in-betweenness and dislocated insideness. These are not abject exiles writing from the margins, but could be said to suffer from an excess of belonging, rather than an absence of it—although the quality of that belonging may not run too deep. Tim Brennan refers to an earlier generation of writers of international literature in English, including Isabel Allende, Bharati Mukherjee, Rushdie, Mario Vargas Llosa and Derek Walcott, as "Third World cosmopolitan celebrities" (2). However, for today's transnational writers, the term "cosmopolitan" fails to convey the complexities of their lines of belonging, or the multi-cultural nature of today's Western societies. Both Mo and Phillips are *post*colonial subjects, rather than colonial subjects. Unlike Brennan's cosmopolitan celebrities, they were born straight into postcoloniality and brought up in postmodernity. To call them Third World cosmopolitans seems doubly inappropriate.

Like Rushdie, Phillips has selected his own literary parentage, drawing freely from European and American, and African and Caribbean writers, as well as from the "cosmopolitan celebrities" themselves. Phillips declares that his influences include Toni Morrison and Rushdie (qtd. in Davison 94), and, as Morrison looks back to William Faulkner and an American tradition of slave narratives, and Rushdie speaks of Cervantes, Gogol, Kafka, Machado de Assis, and Melville as his literary parentage (see his *Imaginary Homelands* 21), Phillips claims kin to a remarkably polyglot family tree. In the geopolitical and literary sense, Phillips is dislocated, but well placed to orchestrate the polyphony and heteroglossia celebrated by M.M. Bakhtin over fifty years ago and recently "valorized in recent

North American criticism" (Brennan 3). In his novel *Crossing the River* (1993; this edition 1994, all page references are to this edition), the idea of a "multi-tongued chorus" heard across two hundred and fifty years of history, and across the boundaries of race and gender, pulls together the various narrative strands into a single story of survival and communicable empathy.[1] Here Phillips speaks not from one side, but from both sides of the river.

As Benedicte Ledent suggests, the postcolonial writer struggles to define him/herself in the historical drama of his/her people, but at the same time s/he must also be able to stand apart from the struggle and contemplate the flows of history. S/he needs to cross that river and watch the historical drama from the other shore, and yet s/he does not want to leave his/her people behind (62). A further complication is that for Caribbean writers, the historical drama of their own people is a drama of broken history—something that existed before the "middle passage," a memory on the fringe of consciousness.[2] In George Lamming's *In the Castle of My Skin* (1953; this edition 1986, all page references are to this edition), another semi-autobiographical novel, the narrator describes the attempt to locate this memory: "And what did I remember? My father who only fathered the idea of me . . . And beyond that my memory was a blank. It sank with its cargo of episodes like a crew preferring to scuttle to the consequences of survival" (3).

The realistic and partly autobiographical form of *The Final Passage* is not typical of Phillips' fiction. In his non-fiction (such as *The European Tribe* [1987; this edition 1992], *Extravagant Strangers: A Literature of Belonging* [1997]; and *The Atlantic Sound* [2000]), the history of black involvement in European culture is explicit; but in his major novels, Phillips interweaves history and fiction and uses postmodern narrative form to engage with issues of racism. The major theme in all his novels is the exile, marginalization, oppression and exploitation of black people; but increasingly, race and racism are explored through theories of non-essentialism in race, ethnicity and gender. The presence of such theories, and the novelistic form and style through which they are explored is the hallmark of Phillips' writing. I argue in this chapter that postmodern theory informs these ideas on race, and postmodern narrative informs the mode of expression, which I demonstrate by examining three works of fiction by him, *The Final Passage*, *Cambridge* (1991; this edition 1992, all page references are to this edition), and *The Nature of Blood* (1997).

The Significance of Postmodernism in Caryl Phillips' Novels

Probably the most relevant intervention postmodernism makes in the politics of race is the critique of essentialism, and the introduction of the decentred subject. The critique of essentialism, by deconstructing the link between race, or negritude, and the racist denotation of blackness as denigration, uncouples the politics of difference from the politics of racism. Postmodern blackness might be conceived less as a signifier of race, blood and ethnicity, and more as a floating signifier that attaches itself to any marginalized and oppressed subject. Here, the category "black" remains associated with the etymologically racist notion of denigration, but the denigrated subject is not necessarily black. Blackness, when removed from the essentialism of race, can attach itself to the dispossessed in general, to the unbelonging. But unbelonging is itself not a stable condition in the postmodern. In postmodern theories of space and place, the opposition between the rootedness of existential insideness and the rootlessness of existential outsideness are also deconstructed. For the postmodern, decentred subject, insideness and outsideness are dialectical, not binary opposites. Where the modern subject was threatened by rootlessness and alienation, the postmodern subject has learnt to feel at home in the complex inside-out and outside-in spaces of postmodernity. The postmodern subject, one might say, inhabits (is at home in) thresholds, margins, hyperspace and heterotopia. The firm, and delineated, ground of home, nation and identity are exposed as mythical constructions and the lumpy, misshapen world of postmodernity has become the norm.

While postmodern space and place become fluid, shadowy and mutable, identity, which attempts to map such spaces, is conditioned by dislocation and dispersed belonging. The key difference between this theoretical postmodern subject and the actual exile or immigrant is that for the former, the condition is confused but comic, for the latter it is invariably tragic. The element of compulsion and oppression, i.e. the politics of racism, is still there for the black outsider. The postmodern subject can afford to wallow in dislocated and dispersed belonging when his/her history speaks to him/her of security, belonging and shared identity. The postmodern may beckon towards globalism and pluralist societies, but the history of racial difference continues to drag one back into difference, division and conflict. One must be clear, therefore, that the idea of postmodern blackness posited here is theoretical, and its presence in novels such as those by Phillips must be seen in relation to strategies for understanding real historical and cultural conditions, not direct reflections of them.

The association between black identity politics and postmodernism is somewhat fraught because, as bell hooks points out, "as a discursive practice, it [postmodernism] is dominated primarily by the voices of white male intellectuals and/or academic elites who speak to and about one another with coded familiarity" ("Postmodern Blackness" 24). Phillips is Oxford-educated, and might feel more at home in the trendy restaurants of Oxford than the places where ordinary black folks hang out, in his home town of Leeds, or in downtown Brixton. But, if Phillips uses radical postmodernism to question the essentialism of race, he does so by calling attention to "those shared sensibilities which cross the boundaries of class, gender, race, etc., that could be fertile ground for the construction of empathy" (hooks, "Postmodern Blackness" 24). This idea of empathy is key to understanding Phillips' strategies. As hooks concludes in her otherwise skeptical approach to postmodernism, "the decentred [postmodern] subject can be the space where ties are severed or it can provide the occasion for new and varied forms of bonding" ("Postmodern Blackness" 31). My only adjustment to this conclusion in approaching Phillips' novels would be to replace the "or" with an "and."

What is always very much in evidence in Phillips' novels is the organization of the decentred subject, and in particular the refraction of black experience through other experiences of marginalization in class, gender and ethnicity. This strategy of postmodern blackness extends the experience of outsideness beyond racial categories. Black experience is thereby seen in a wider context of prejudice and dispossession. Postmodern blackness is a strategy through which black and white coexist within the same imaginative vision, held for a moment in the same bi-focal view. One strategy Phillips employs is to explore female experience through the lens of black experience, and vice versa—this is most successful in the realization of Emily in *Cambridge*. Such stereoscopic form is further developed in Phillips' later novel, *The Nature of Blood*, in which not only the lens of female experience but also that of Jewish experience are set beside that of black experience, giving three categories of difference: Jewish, black and female, each superimposed upon each other. Postmodern blackness is taken through and across the history of the Jews in a bold attempt to find resonance between the alterity of black and Jew in European history.

The Final Passage
The postmodern novel is an appropriate form for the transnational writer because it allows the presentation of unfixed or fluid identities and the juxtaposition of apparently unconnected times and spaces. The hallmark of Phillips' fiction is his use of multiple narrators, usually of more than one gender and more than one race or ethnicity, each of whom seems to connect, oddly, across different times and spaces. This is not simply

a matter of literary style, but a consequence of the transnational writer trying to retrieve lost (cultural) memories and simultaneously speak to the contemporary—a contemporary which is, largely, no longer monocultural. Furthermore, the contemporary, postmodern, world in which difference is erased through globalization (and yet reasserts itself in complex transnational geopolitics), is not, like the modern world, one of linear journeys in space and time. As if reflecting these spatial and temporal complexities, postmodern narrative invariably disrupts the linear flow of storytelling. Even in *The Final Passage,* which is, as mentioned before, predominantly realistic in form, Phillips uses disjunction as a narrative strategy. The experience of the post-war diaspora from the West Indies to England is presented as a disjointed journey.

The novel begins with a section called "End," which tells of a young family's emigration from a small Caribbean island to England in the 1950s; it then moves back in time to the "Home" episode which tells of life on the island for Leila, Michael and the baby Calvin; then it jumps past the passage to describe their arrival in "England," before returning to the "Passage" itself. The novel ends in "Winter" in England as Leila prepares herself, her son and her yet to be born child to return home. The story begins in *medias res,* but it remains unresolved at the end. The "final passage" of the title is ironic as the novel returns to a point of continuous rupture. Leila plans to take her family, minus husband who disappears, and minus mother who dies, back to her island home where some day, she imagines taking her children down to the harbor: "She would watch as they climbed into the small boat and made their way out to the ship and on to England to find a Michael, or men like him who might give them the answers they sought" (Phillips, *Final Passage* 204). Michael is the absenting paternal authority who is blamed for the disruption of the black family.

It is implied that the absent father is a common phenomenon in black families. The father who sold his children into slavery haunts *Crossing the River,* and the master who displaces paternal authority with colonial authority is presented in *Cambridge.* For Phillips, the idea of absent fathers is a consequence of the effect on the psyche of a man of African origin who, under slavery, had his children taken away from him by the master, acting as head of the family. This, suggests Phillips, "induces an irresponsibility," that may lead to the disruption of the black family (qtd. in Davison 95). Ironically, in *Cambridge,* the master is an absentee landlord, spending his time at the gaming tables of Europe. His place as head of the family is taken over by the estate manager and his daughter Emily, but, for reasons of class or gender, neither is able fully to assume the role of master. This is indicative, the novel suggests, of what is happening across the whole colony in the power vacuum of post-abolition.

Cambridge

After *The Final Passage*, Phillips' novels show clear signs of postmodern narrative style. But this term may need some clarification. Phillips is not, like the postmodern writers Paul Auster, John Barth and Italo Calvino, for example, so concerned with problems of language and representation. He writes neither "historiographic metafiction,"[3] nor a "literature of replenishment."[4] His later novels are confident in their representational claims to assert the tragedy of black experience, and although they weave paths back and forth across history and disrupt narrative time, they do not call into question the processes of history that have conditioned black experience. Phillips, like J.M. Coetzee in his novel *Foe* (1986), uses postmodern form to assert a particular approach to racial issues in the era of multiculturalism. This is not color-blind, blind to history, or pluralist. Mark Poster formulates two positions on multiculturalism in his article "Postmodernity and the Politics of Multiculturalism: The Lyotard-Habermas Debate Over Social Theory." The first is the *consensus* model, which "welcomes all communities to melt down their identities in the crucible of modern democracy"; and the second, the *dissensus* model in which, "the assertion of validity for minority positions reproduces the fullness of identity" (577).

Clearly, Phillips does not attempt to reconcile difference, but to accentuate and extend it. As a West Indian brought to Britain at a very early age, Phillips is a man twice removed from history and place. The long past for Phillips (and for other Caribbean and Afro-American writers) ends abruptly at the moment when his (and their) ancestors are torn from their West African homes. The infamous triangle of Africa, the Americas and Europe, the ruptures of history and their consequences, and the constantly recurring but incomplete past, these form the time-spaces (chronotopes[5]) of all Phillips novels. In *Cambridge*, when the African, Olumide, is sold into slavery and catches a last glimpse of Africa from the boat taking him to the Americas, he realizes that he and his fellow Africans are being snatched from their homes and their history:

> We fellow captives fixed our watery eyes upon the land in a state of mortal grief. Whether affection for one's country is real or imagined, it is not an exaggeration to proclaim that at this moment instinct of nature suffused our being with an overwhelming love for our land and family, whom we did not expect to see again. Our history was truly broken. (Phillips, *Cambridge* 137)

Olumide's history is broken when he is snatched from his home country and, in this moment of parting, Olumide's identity is also taken from him.

From this moment on, his identity is plastic, shaped and re-shaped by others to suit their purposes and desires. They can turn him from virtual Englishman back to African at will.

A major theme in Phillips' novels is this disjunction in the subject's history and the dis-forming of identity that results. The African and West Indian diasporas removed subjects from home, literally, and this geographical dislocation leaves them in an in-between place, floating and rootless. Identity is then formed out of dislocated memories, rather than through continuous attachment to place and history. Being oneself is conditioned by in-between-ness and by the shaping force of others' home culture. Phillips' characters, on the edge of society, are destined to a half-becoming. They are not alienated through existential outsided-ness so much as suffering existential in-between-ness, between two or more cultures. This displacement of identity is a major theme in *Cambridge*, where Phillips presents the African, Olumide, and the Englishwoman, Emily, as two characters "on the edge" in different ways, each shaped and constrained by the demands of patriarchal colonialist society. On the slave ship, Olumide and his fellow slaves are "addressed by one common word, *nigger*, as though we all shared this harsh name" (Phillips, *Cambridge* 137). When he is bought out of slavery and taken to England to the house of a gentleman Liberal, he is given the Christian name, Thomas. This is later changed again to David Henderson after Thomas receives further Christian education and begins to assume Englishness: "Truly I was now an Englishman, albeit a little smudgy of complexion! Africa spoke to me only of a history I had cast aside" (Phillips, *Cambridge* 147). However, despite his education, David Henderson remains a *translated* slave. For him, history is not the ballast that stabilizes his identity but a set of irons he can never cast off. He will never assume full English identity, not because of his lack of education or accomplishments, but because, as a black man in Europe he wears the mark of his race and will be subject to this re-shaping according to the desires of white Europeans.

Taken by force from Africa, Olumide was destined to be other, never to assume the full identity of a sovereign subject, never to become a "true Englishman." In a cruel twist of fate, Olumide alias Thomas Henderson, is sent back to Africa to set up a Christian mission, but is robbed and sold back into slavery. The shock of being taken for an African shows that whatever change he thinks he has wrought in himself, others do not see beyond his blackness. The pain is more keenly felt because Henderson perversely adopts racist attitudes against his own people in his translation into Englishness: "That I, a virtual Englishman, was to be treated as base African cargo, caused me such hurtful pain as I was barely able to endure" (Phillips, *Cambridge* 156). Shipped back to the Caribbean, he is maltreated and taunted by his master whom he eventually kills in a rage. He is then hanged for a murder sensationalized in a newspaper account designed to perpetuate the myth of the "uncivilized Negro." So, once more, Olumide alias Thomas Henderson alias the narrator, Cambridge, is re-shaped by others, having been to "smudgy whiteness" and back again. This trajectory from African to slave to "virtual Englishman" and back to slave is a constant recycling of non-assimilation, and displacement. History for those of the African diaspora is broken, but the history of racism and prejudice is perpetuated.

Later, in *Crossing the River*, history will again reclaim the prejudice, this time as a black GI stationed in England during the Second World War is subjected to racist attacks from his white comrades. A local woman falls in love with him and a child is born. But the woman loses both her lover and the child, taken from her by the authorities. In Phillips' novels, the contact between two cultures never betokens assimilation and reconciliation. Two cultures meet, but a line is drawn under the meeting. The future is curtailed, history is either ruptured, or it loops back on itself, repeating the prejudices and persecutions that difference makes. And in *The Nature of Blood*, discussed below, the black experience of systemic racism and displacement finds a parallel in Jewish histories. This is not a shift in attention, but an extension of Phillips' project to articulate for European and American audiences a sense of how history looks from inside the diaspora. The European Jew is a second marginal perspective, as Phillips sees in Jewish history similar disjunction to that found in the history of the African diaspora.

The introduction of the Jew as the second marginal perspective extends further that of the white female in *Cambridge* (and also in *Crossing the River*) to refract the otherness and prejudice felt by women in patriarchal societies. Phillips' novels are notable for their representation of the female psyche, especially of Englishwomen who are in some sense on the edge, not in control of their destiny, their identity shaped and conditioned by others. Emily in *Cambridge* is a fine example of the second marginal perspective echoing and refracting the plight of the slave Olumide. Like the black slave, who became, for a while, a "virtual Englishman," Emily undergoes shifts in her psyche, as her identity slips from English gentlewoman to virtual Creole. This is a painful process of adaptation and assimilation to the Caribbean, a process that takes her to the brink of madness.

For Emily, the Caribbean impresses itself on her and gradually displaces her attachment to England. Her confinement on the island is also a kind of freedom from her confinement in England, but as for Cambridge, translation leads to a lack of belonging rather than an exchange of belonging. While Cambridge becomes a "virtual Englishman," Emily is creolized, neither at home in the Caribbean nor in England. To return to England would be to place herself again within family, society and home, so she chooses to become a native of no place. In this place-less-ness, her own body becomes home, for a while, to a "little foreigner" (Phillips, *Cambridge* 183), a foetus that is aborted. Recovering from this experience, she can no longer conceive of returning to England. She has changed, and "the corsets and stays" that confined her body in England will no longer fit:

> England. Emily smiled to herself. The doctor delivered the phrase as though this England was a dependable garment that one simply slipped in and out of according to one's whim. Did he not understand that people grow and change? Did he not understand that one day a discovery might be made that this country-garb is no longer of a correct measure? (Phillips, *Cambridge* 177)

When asked in an interview about his considerable skill at realizing female voices, Phillips talked of women's position on the edge of society, central to society, but marginalized by men. This position on the edge, he said, somehow "mirror[s] the rather tenuous and oscillating relationship that all sorts of people, in this case, specifically, black people, have in society, and maybe there is some kind of undercurrent of communicable empathy" (qtd. in Davison 94).

Parenthetically, the popularity of transnational writers in North America and Europe, where they find their main audiences, attests partly to postcolonial guilt and postmodern authority (to reverse the title of an essay by Homi K. Bhabha).[6] Postcolonial guilt recalls, for Western readers, the ugly ghosts of colonialism. But postmodern authority might also imply a guilty pleasure in nostalgia for a past where the world was clearly divided, where differences between nations and races were prescribed. The geopolitical divide is clearly re-established in Mo's *An Insular Possession* (1987), where the island of Hong Kong is presented as more or less an empty space, circumscribed and claimed by the British. Of course, Hong Kong was not an unpopulated island when it was ceded to the British, but that is the way with myths of origin—to erase the past, and start with a blank space. In *An Insular Possession*, criticism of British action in the Opium Wars is muted. The West's involvement in the opium trade, and the belligerence of Britain in protecting the rights of its subjects to free trade, that led directly to the punitive actions against China are described. Yet this is presented in a fairly detached manner through the eyes of two Americans, who are critical of, but in most respects still on the same side as, the British. Mo chooses not to present the other side in this novel, situating the novel in a tradition of English literature with an outsider's view of Chinese history and culture. This perpetuates the idea of a mysterious, closed and untranslatable East. The novel is by no means a meeting ground of cultures, because its feet are firmly planted in the West—the East is at a distance, strange and other.

The Nature of Blood

By contrast, postcolonial guilt can be strongly felt in Phillips' novels, and especially in *The Nature of Blood*, where such guilt is extended to encompass the history of anti-Semitism in Europe. This project extends the idea Phillips expresses in *The European Tribe*, that in Western culture, the Black and the Jew, typified by the Othello and Shylock figures, share a comparable outsider status, and that, as such, there exists a similar "communicable empathy" to that he finds between white women and black people. Both are doomed to being shaped and re-shaped by white, Christian hegemony. For Phillips, the persecution of the Jews and the sufferings of African slaves and their descendants are double and equivalent ghosts in the common memory of European history.

This haunting of history seems to have no beginning and no end, or perhaps many beginnings and no ends, and it is this idea that organizes the disparate fragments of history, memory and imagination in *The Nature of Blood*. The novel jumps between several narrative units. Technically, there are two main stories, both of which are based on historical events. The first is the story of Eva Stern, which takes us through her liberation from a Nazi concentration camp in Poland and her subsequent suicide in London. The climax of the novel is her suicide, and the question of what leads to her suicide is posed and answered by doctors, psychiatrists and historians, whose voices enter the novel as expert witnesses, disturbing the boundaries of fact and fiction. But the answer that matters is probably contained in her own first person narrative, a voice of disjointed dreams and memories, which flashes back to her childhood and adolescence in Germany in the 1930s, in which she witnesses the persecution and forced migration of the Jews. This story resonates with a parallel and overlapping story, told mainly in the third person, of the trial and burning of Jewish moneylenders accused of murdering and sacrificing a Christian boy in Venice in 1480. These two stories significantly and explicitly are about the persecution of Jews in Europe, a practice, it is implied, that has continued across five hundred years or more of history, and that reaches its recent apotheosis in the systematic slaughter of six million or so Jews by the Nazis between 1939 and 1944. The Eva narrative draws in the narrative of Stephan Stern, her uncle. They never meet in the novel, but their memories interconnect. They both remember the crucial moment of Stephan's decision to leave Germany to help establish Israel. The novel begins with

Stephan's conversation with a Romanian boy on the island of Cyprus as he waits to be shipped to his new "home," the modern state of Israel. It ends with his chaste night with an African Jew, Malka, in the 1980s in Israel. In both of these short narrative units, Stephan is haunted by the memory of leaving his family behind to help establish the new Israel. Memory, he says, is now his only companion, although he realizes "that to remember too much is, indeed, a form of madness" (Phillips, *Nature of Blood* 212) Here, memory and identity are again tied in the absence of continuous history and attachment to home. Stephan creates a new homeland, but abandons family and home. His guilt is partly the guilt of surviving; and the paradox of home is that the real home he abandons remains only in his memory, and the new home he is instrumental in creating in Israel has no memory, no attachment, it is only the idea of home.

Eva's narrative is disrupted in two ways. Firstly, it is disorganized, by following the logic of her dysfunctional memory. Much later, the anonymous psychiatrist puts a name to Eva's condition: it is "post-holocaust trauma." Eva is always drawn back into the past, as she attempts, in vain, to re-discover who she is, in, what is for her, the vacuum of the present. A psychiatrist explains the condition, by saying that, "Naturally, their suffering is deeply connected to memory. To move on is to forget. To forget is a crime. How can they both remember and move on?" (Phillips, *Nature of Blood* 157). The voice of the psychiatrist is one of a number of external interjections from unnamed and third-person narrators, who appear outside story time. Like historians, these disinterested and detached voices attempt to make sense of events and experience that evaded all sense and order for those within the historical moment. So the novel moves between the past's present, with its fragments of memory and story; and the present's present with the calm historicizing voice that tries to put the demons of the past to rest.

The second form of disruption to Eva's narrative is brought about by the interlacing, firstly of the narrative of the persecution of the Jews of Portobuffole, near Venice, and secondly by a further narrative which directly links the history of oppression of black people and oppression of Jews—a rewriting of the story of Othello, the Moor. There is a span of nearly five hundred years between the narrative units, and yet the novel as a whole insists on connections and continuity in the master narrative of oppression. The Othello narrative introduces a literary intertext, Shakespeare's *Othello* (first performed in 1604), in which issues of race, and specifically inter-racial marriage, are raised. In Shakespeare's play, the black Moor Othello is driven by jealousy. In Phillips' analysis of the play, this jealousy derives from Othello's insecurity as an outsider in Venetian society, and this analysis clearly informs Phillips' rewriting of the story within this novel (see also the chapter "A Black European Success" in Phillips' *The European Tribe* 45-51). To illustrate, while the deaths of Othello and his wife Desdemona in Shakespeare's play signal an intolerance of inter-racial marriage in white European society, in Phillips' novel the Othello narrative does not reach this conclusion and Othello is left enjoying his conjugal bliss with Desdemona in Cyprus. However, in a similar narrative move to that used in *Crossing the River*, Phillips introduces the trans-historical black narrator, who upbraids Othello for his vanity and foolishness. Othello, like the slave in *Cambridge*, the narrator insists, is playing into the hands of his white masters, by attempting to translate himself into a Venetian. Unlike the slave, however, Othello has chosen to leave home and abandon his wife and son:

> My friend, an African river bears no resemblance to a Venetian canal. Only the strongest spirit can hold both together. Only the most powerful heart can endure the pulse of two such disparate life-forces.... But you run like Jim Crow and leap into their creamy arms. Did you ever think of your wife's soft kiss? Or your son's eyes? Brother, you are weak. A figment of a Venetian imagination. While you still have time, jump from her bed and fly away home. (Phillips, *Nature of Blood* 183)

Othello is set up, not for the tragic denouement of Shakespeare's play, but as a figure for a more general criticism of the white mask:

> And so you shadow her every move, attend to her every whim, like the black Uncle Tom that you are. Fighting the white man's war for him / Wide receiver in the Venetian army / The republic's grinning Satchmo hoisting his sword like a trumpet / You tuck your black skin away beneath their epauletted uniform, appropriate their words (*Rude am I in speech*), their manners, worry your nappy woollen head with anxiety about learning their ways, yet you conveniently forget your own family, and thrust your wife and son to the back of our noble mind. O strong man, O strong arm, O valiant soldier, O weak man. You are lost, a sad black man, first in a long line of so-called achievers who are too weak to yoke their past with their present ... My friend, the Yoruba have a saying: the river that does not know its own source will dry up. (Phillips, *Nature of Blood* 181-182)

This narrator reasserts the essentialism of race, the nature of blood. He implies that black people cannot "cross the river" without compromise.

But the novel as a whole deconstructs racial categories by refracting black experience through Jewish experience and vice versa. The common ground is the experience of broken histories, displacement from home, and being subject to the whims of others' imaginations.

This crossing over is not only implied in the structure of the novel, it occasionally enters the plots of the narrative units. For example, the Othello narrative connects with the Portobuffole narrative when Othello visits the Venetian ghetto and considers the marginalization of the Jews there, and the conditions they suffer: "Surely there was some other land or some other people among whom they might dwell in more tolerable conditions?" (Phillips, *Nature of Blood* 131) In this, and in the interlacing of the Othello narrative with the Eva narrative and the Portobuffole narrative, we are asked to read across history and across the experience of disparate oppressed racial and ethnic groups. The conclusion to the Portobuffole narrative cuts into the Othello narrative as Othello prepares to go to war for the Venetians. The Jews are found guilty of murdering the Christian boy, and are burned at the stake in Venice. The novel then jumps back and forth between the Eva narrative and the Othello narrative several times, with further disruptions from the impersonal narrator and psychiatrist. The key to this highly disrupted section comes at the end of the Portobuffole narrative when the bodies of the innocent Jews are burned: "Later, when the flames had abated, an executioner approached with a long-handled shovel. He put it between the smoking coals and when he pulled it out it was full of white ash. He threw the ash into the air and it dispersed immediately" (Phillips, *Nature of Blood* 156). An end, but an end that prefigures further beginnings. The dust of the burned Jews is scattered to the winds of time and space, to reappear when the Nazis gas and burn the Jews in Eva's concentration camp. The dust, scattered to the wind, is dispersed, but does not disappear; the burning of the Jews is not to be the end of the story.

From this point on, Eva's narrative becomes more and more disjointed. She comes to England to find the sympathetic but feckless British soldier, Gerry, who had asked her to marry him, but who has married someone else in the meantime. She has a breakdown and is admitted to hospital. Gerry brings her a chocolate cake with a knife, and she kills herself with it. In England, Eva's narrative discloses a crisis of identity, a split in her sense of self as she narrates the moments up to her suicide. The Eva who arrives in England is accompanied by her former self, "the other girl, with the swathe of red around her mouth. She is still here. Waiting" (Phillips, *Nature of Blood* 188). Coming to England has not enabled Eva to escape the trauma of the past. The past follows her: "She followed me across the water. In fact she follows me everywhere. I have had to learn to tolerate her. I leave for somewhere, then she arrives moments later" (Phillips, *Nature of Blood* 197). In her final words, Eva describes her attempts to escape this other self, this other Eva from the death camp. She is searching for home, a place where she can escape her memories, but this, she rationalizes, can only be found in death. In the final narrative unit, Stephan, Eva's uncle, who begins the novel describing enthusiastically to a young survivor of the death camps the new homeland being built in Palestine, is drawn to a black Ethiopian woman, Malka, in present-day Israel. In a final contemplation of home, homeland and displacement, Stephan, one of Israel's architects, is forced to realize that he has not found the answer to the question of home, and Malka, being both black and Jewish, is doubly displaced.

Despite the multiple narrative voices in this work, ranging across gender, race and history, there is a stylistic unity that brings together disparate voices, histories and points of view. At the same time, a novel such as *The Nature of Blood* accentuates rifts between cultures, drawing attention to the un-meeting ground between black and white, Jew and non-Jew, the un-meeting ground that has led to persecution throughout European history. On the surface of the novel, voices speak across the disjunctions of time and space producing what Phillips has called "communicable empathy." There is a common ground of sorts, but it is not the common ground that history makes of the past.

Conclusion

Like Rushdie, and unlike Mo, Phillips makes use of postmodern authority to ensure that postcolonial guilt remains an active and positive force for change. Postmodern authority resists hegemony by refusing to reconcile or assimilate difference. The contact between different cultures in Mo's novels is assimilated into history. Difference is either eradicated by removing from the contact zone those subjects that do not fit, or diluted as transculturation and assimilation begin to neutralize the contact zone. In Phillips, it is the subliminal relations to history that determine the extent to which the narrative either concurs with and "puts to rest" history, or inserts silences or "time-gaps," so ensuring that history keeps haunting us and taunting us (see Bhabha, "Postcolonial Authority and Postmodern Guilt").

Notes

[1] The "multi-tongued chorus" is referred to in the over-arching Prologue, and in the Epilogue, which are both narrated by a trans-historical third-person narrator (Phillips, *Crossing the River* 1, 235-237).

[2] The "Middle Passage" is a term for the passage from Africa to the slave colonies. It is also the title of a book (*The Middle Passage* [1962]) by V. S. Naipaul that records his impressions of colonial society in the West Indies and South America. The "Final Passage" might imply conclusion to the African diaspora, but in Phillips' novel the journey to England is only another disjuncture in the histories of black experience.

[3] "Historiographic metafiction" is Linda Huthcheon's catch-all term for postmodernist literature that self-consciously draws attention to the textuality of history and the porous boundaries between history and fiction. See her *A Poetics of Postmodernism: History, Theory, Fiction* (1988).

[4] "The Literature of Replenishment" (1988) is an early manifesto by John Barth on postmodernist fiction.

[5] The term *chronotope* was first used by Bakhtin to refer to the "time-space" of the novel. See "Forms of Time and the Chronotope" in his *The Dialogic Imagination*. For an account of the chronotope as an "optic" for reading the postmodern, see Paul Smethurst, *The Postmodern Chronotope: Reading Space and Time in Contemporary Fiction* (2000).

[6] See Bhabha, "Postcolonial Authority and Postmodern Guilt" (1992). In this essay, Bhabha examines language and temporality especially in Morrison's *Beloved* (1987) and in Rushdie's *Satanic Verses* (1988).

14
Locating Global Links
Arundhati Roy's *The God of Small Things*

Lalitha Ramamurthi

Introduction

This chapter aims at establishing links between the regional and the universal in Arundhati Roy's *The God of Small Things* (1997, identified parenthetically as *GST*), and attempts to locate global links in the narrative through a bicultural approach. I argue that though the narrative is steeped in Indian ethos, the totality of its meaning can be arrived at only through a bicultural approach, as this typical South Indian novel reveals its inner core of universality through its extensive use of techniques that are just as typically postmodern from a Western point of view. It is the recognition of this dual perspective—the native and the foreign—that enriches one's reading of *The God of Small Things*.

The narrative is basically a regional one, rooted in the native soil of Kerala in South India, and acts out the region's cultural, personal and political phases in a timeless continuum lending itself to be situated within a postmodern framework.[1] If explicating the text purely at the regional or national level proves to be somewhat incomplete or not fully satisfactory, to treat it solely as a postmodern creation would be in turn to deprive the text of its unmistakable native flavor. The crux of the matter is that the narrative reach is far beyond the regional and the immediate, as it is universally inclusive in its purport, impact and narrative techniques. Shorn of its external details, this story can take place anywhere—in India or elsewhere. It is the universal story of love and tragedy told in a typical postmodern manner that won Roy the Booker Prize in 1997.

I examine in this chapter the two facets of the novel, the (Eastern) regional story and the (Western) postmodern frame, to illustrate how the recognition of both is necessary for an appraisal of the novel's universality.

The Tragic Tale of Love

The God of Small Things is about the injustice meted out to "small things" — childhood, youth and class/societal gradations. It tells the story of three generations by linking three continents (as represented by three countries: India, the U.K., and the U.S.). The principal character Ammu, the daughter of a rich Syrian Christian Catholic family in Kerala, marries outside her caste. But her husband turns out to be a drunkard, and moreover wants her to yield to the sexual advances of his English employer. Ammu resists; and, on being divorced, returns to her parental home with her six-year-old twins, the boy Estha and the girl Rahel, only to be treated with scorn and disapproval by her own mother, brother and aunt.

The novel opens with (the grown-up) Rahel's return from the United States. It is the recounting of some twenty-four hours in her life at the age of thirty-one, and discloses the days of her childhood when she was just seven years old. Thus the story is narrated at two levels of time, and the novel moves backward and forward, interweaving the present and the past. It recaptures the events leading to the divorced Ammu's illicit affair with the "untouchable" Velutha. As the narrator puts it mimetically, in the caste system, the *paravans*, or the "untouchables," were, "not allowed to walk in public roads, nor allowed to cover their upper bodies, nor allowed to carry umbrellas. They had to put their hands over their mouth when they spoke to divert their polluted breath away from those whom they addressed" (*GST* 74). However, in the text, Velutha is in fact "the god of small things," the master craftsman, the daring darling of the twins—he plays with them, makes toys for them, and does all the menial jobs of the family. It is the act of sex between him and Ammu that shocks the entire social order. He is done to death on flimsy grounds while in police custody. Ammu becomes insane and dies of grief, while Estha turns dumb and immobile after the false witness deposition extracted from him in the police station. Rahel escapes this catastrophe, and returns home after many years from the United States to take her mentally deranged brother into her arms and heal his psychic wounds through the "solace of incest" (B.N. Singh 143).

At first glance, *The God of Small Things* appears to be a novel treating of social issues, as well as an autobiographical narrative projecting a realistic picture of life in the 1960s in the traditional, stratified, caste-ridden, hierarchical Syrian Christian community of the Kottayam district of Kerala. Geographically isolated from the larger context of the national movement for over a century, the community has been trying to find a place for itself; and Roy's mimetic depiction of this community, with all its prejudices and attitudes, is accurately done, as an architect would have designed a building. "Writing *The God of Small Things* was a fictional way of making sense of the world I lived in and the novel was the technical key with which I did it," said the author (qtd. in Aijaz Ahmad, "Reading Arundhati Roy Politically" 106). Ayemenem is believed to be Roy's home in Kottayam. Ammu resembles in some ways the well-known woman activist Mary Roy, the author's mother, who broke the tradition by marrying and then divorcing a Bengali. She made history by fighting for a change in the Christian Succession Act and got a favorable ruling from the Supreme Court that allowed women an equal share. The graphic details of child abuse, and the activities of childhood point towards Roy's own childhood. Pappachi, the head of the family, resembles Roy's grandfather who was an "imperial entomologist" at the Pusa Institute in Delhi, and later became its joint director in independent India.

In the novel, Ammu's father Pappachi is a male chauvinist who imposes his "superiority" by beating his wife Mammachi savagely. Later, when checked by his son Chacko and denied the sadistic pleasure, Pappachi stops talking to his wife and does not let her or anyone else use the Plymouth car he had bought from an Englishman. Chacko was once a Rhodes scholar at Oxford University and married, while a student there, Margaret, the English woman who will later divorce him. Margaret herself faces a series of misfortunes—the failure of her marriage to Chacko, the death of her second husband Joe in an accident, and the death of her daughter and only child Sophie Mol who drowns in the Meenachal River while on visit in Kerala.

The first impression the novel gives vanishes, however, as the narrative emerges as a fluid presentation with many baffling characteristics. It creates different opposing areas of value, but offers no reconciliation among them. By presenting the seamy side of social and personal equations, Roy leaves much unsaid. At the individual level, various characters trace abortive voyages to end where they began—the tragic union of Ammu and Velutha, the unfulfilled love of (Papachi's sister) Kochamma with her fancy for the Christian priest, the paternal love of Chacko for Sophie Mol. At the political level, history is proved to be cyclical and not in accordance with, for instance, the dream of a Marxist. The portrayals of Comrade Pillai and Chacko highlight moreover the unholy alliance between Marxism and the caste system.

There are a number of mild digs at the attitudes and behavior of the members of the community and the society. To illustrate, "Father Mulligan, who was in Kerala for a year on deputation from his seminary in Madras, was studying Hindu scriptures in order to be able to denounce them intelligently" (22). In turn, to make up for its geographical isolation, the community tried to master the English language and sent its children, such as Chacko in the novel, to English colleges in Madras. All these find mimetic resonance in the novel, which caricatures the Western world the characters inhabit: the Imperial Entomologist, the Rhodes scholar, Elvis records, the Plymouth car, playing Handel's *Water Music* on the violin, and old women who have behind them generations of breeding, going back to an ancestor blessed personally by Saint Ignatius of Antioch (who lived in the first century),[2] are all very much part of the "Western" worldview of the community. Roy brings out the irony and pathos of it by twisting the language to suit her storytelling.

The text also exposes the folly of equating revolutionary change with improvement: Velutha, a member of the Communist party, is let down by his own party leader Comrade Pillai; society puts Velutha to torture, and abuses Ammu. Institutions, be they social, religious or political, are incapable of serving the happiness of mankind. What is presented is a problematized reality—a picture of human predicament in turmoil with social anathema, constantly working at cross-purposes with the individuals. While the tapestry of the text reveals no clear ideology, it does throw hints to the observant reader. It unveils certain clearly negative signals related to caste, religion, and false idealism.

Love is a minefield in the narrative. It is through it that all the powers of caste, community, religion and politics are evoked. In the experiences of its major characters, Ammu, Chacko, and Baby Kochamma, the paths of the lovers do not run smooth. It is misdirected, misunderstood and misguided. While Ammu and Chacko are both divorcees, Baby Kochamma fails in her attempts to secure Father Mulligan's love and remains a spinster grudging others' happiness, even conspiring against them. She is instrumental in registering false accusations against Velutha who dies in police custody. Mammachi, who is shocked at her daughter's affair with an untouchable, in contrast condones and even facilitates, in the name of "men's needs," her son Chacko's sexual relationships with low-caste women working in the family's pickle factory. The narrative effectively establishes how something deeply personal as love is bound up with the *love laws* laid down by various institutions. In effect, the novel is not about what happened, but about *how* what happened affected people.

A multiplicity of layers brought into *The God of Small Things* stuns the reader with a surfeit of sights, sounds, names, facts and complicated local information. Roy's art moves through various social, political, religious and purely personal levels. She has succeeded in creating a world compounded of tragedy, farce, brutality, and idealism. There is a magnificent evocation of Ayemenem, with its population of Syrian Christians, Hindus, Communists and the caste gradations of each. However, the Ayemenem house with all its glorious name and values collapses. The decay of the house is reflected in its inhabitants.

The meeting point for the regional and the rest of the world is the gripping love story. It is more or less told already in the first chapter; but then the novel ends in the middle of (the elaborated narrating of) it. In the final pages of the essentially tragic tale that the novel is, there are poignant scenes in which love is redemptive. *The God Of Small Things* ends with Ammu and Velutha making love, and on the word "tomorrow." In the absence of any big plans for the future, the two stick to the immediacy of the future. The commitment they ask of each other is merely:

tomorrow?
tomorrow. (339)

The fact that the novel ends here, at this point, is to say that even though what tomorrow brings may turn out to be terrible, it is wonderful that it has happened at all.

The Narcissistic Narrative

The initial impression of traditional realism is undermined in the text in many other ways, too. The reader has the tantalizing task of moving from the variety, color, and activity of hectic personal lives to the savaging cruelty, pathos and void created therein. Yet, although the text possesses a bustling outer, external reality that appears to dominate the narration, this is only a foil to something internal: the movement in the text seems to be towards a deeper implicit layer that is reflective of a universal situation. Hence, one's initial interpretation of the text remains inadequate if the implicit internal layer is not then culled from the external, outside world that the text portrays at the surface. Nor does the text aim at, or succeed in, creating an ordered universe: the end of the narrative is, in fact, the beginning of yet another unresolved cycle of the disordered worldly events.

An alternative approach would be to analyze the text from the modernist point of view, with a value judgment in favor of strategies that probe the depth of subjective psychology, ambiguity, subtlety or moral dilemma. However, the novel neither internalizes reality nor projects an alternative order of reality. In fact, it differs from the modernist perspective in its abandonment of subjectivity. The fact is that *The God Of Small Things* does not lend itself easily to the modernist mould; for, although the modernist critique recognizes the fragmented nature of the world, it desires to control the discontinuities, at least through artistic closure, which one does not find in the novel.

The typology of the text thus cannot be adequately explicated by treating it either as a realist novel or as a modernist text. The fault line is to be located in its being narcissistic, with features such as multiplicity, time shift, amalgamation, dissemination, fluidity and indeterminacy. This offers scope for reading the text from a postmodern perspective.

I argue that the love story the text unfolds is couched within the postmodernist paradigm, and emerges as a "narcissistic narrative." In Greek mythology, Narcissus fell in love with his own reflection and out of desperation committed suicide. Later turned into a flower, which still bears his name, Narcissus continues to live in two forms—in his own form in the underworld, and as a flower in the other, i.e., the Earth. Narcissistic fiction, likewise, has its form given by the author, supplemented by the reader's creative participation. Such a narrative demands that the reader participate and engage him/herself intellectually in the "co-creation" of fiction.

In *Narcissistic Narrative: The Metafictional Paradox* (1980), Linda Hutcheon identifies as "narcissistic narrative" postmodern texts that exude an intense self-awareness regarding the process of the artistic production while simultaneously playing with the possibilities of meaning and form. A typical narcissistic narrative operates at different levels: in the diegetic mode (i.e., within the storyline), it may incorporate a love story or a private tale with a parallel public or political strand; then, the narrative may also gain strength from the linguistic support of devices such as letters, journals, puns, anagrams; as well as time shifts, or contradictions, etc.

It is the combination of these different modes, that the reader confronts in a narcissistic narrative, that helps to force the text out of "the coherence of domination" (Hutcheon, *Narcissistic Narrative: The Metafictional Paradox* 108). The reader's response and his/her participation in the authorial process together mark both the scope and the limit of the narcissistic narrative.[3]

Postmodernism construes polysemy, the existence of multiple meanings, as a positive principle. In Ayemenem, there are various, seemingly contradictory drives flowing together: on the one hand, there are dreams, illusions, loyalty, whim, and folly; on the other, a vast predetermined socio-cultural force that is ruthless and aggressive. These two differing strands present diverse views of the events taking place, yet they are not truly contradictory in the sense that they both alike discount a rational, orderly sequence of events. Regarding the recounting of events, one identifies, as in all narcissistic narratives, two layers—a highly stratified, caste-ridden, prejudiced social plane; and a parallel personal plane that is being shaped and affected by the former.

The text revels in its polyphony and pluralization of discourses. It is about social gradations. It is a satire on politics. It is a protest novel. Even public administration comes under attack, the police department being one of the targets. The narrative is neither totally social, nor personal; nor is it a moral commentary. It is an amalgamation of all these that the multiple reality radiates. The novelist has not made any effort to integrate the multiple worlds of the discourse into a single ontological plane, or a unified projected world. However, by concentrating on the individuals and then demonstrating how this concentration overlooks the really significant events, Roy demystifies the individualism found in the realist novel and undermines the novel from within. At surface level, the text appears to be regional and culture-bound. Yet, with a postmodern approach, the reader infers that it reflects a complexity that is a multiple reality in a postmodern sense.

The text also exemplifies the postmodern insistence on little narratives. As the very title indicates, Roy's favored characters are small people. Her achievement is never to forget the small things in life—the insects, flowers, wind, water, children, women, the outcaste, and the despised. The most striking is the character of Velutha (white[4]), the low-caste master craftsman whose relationship with the upper-class woman Ammu leads to his disastrous end. Both Ammu and Velutha know that they have no future and that they will be doomed, sooner rather than later. They are victims of the social norms. If in the great mythological stories, evil is punished and destroyed, in this small story it is the innocent who are destroyed. Ammu and Velutha meet their tragic end, but the fact remains that the two had taken up a humble fight against multiple forces of caste, class, power and patriarchy.

Postmodernism postulates that reality is constructed through language. Language contributes in a major way in actualizing Roy's concept of problematized reality. Roy evokes the tropical splendor with a dazzling command of (the English) language and a range of literary strategies that globalize this essentially regional tale. To illustrate, words joined as compounds such as "dinner-plate eyed" (308), "a viable die-able age" (30), "[t]rying not to cry mouth" (300); the joining of two or more words as in "[p]leasedto meetyou" (212), "whatisit?" (6) "[m]o-stunfortunate" (130); sound bite techniques of statements without main verbs, such as "[a] wife with a diamond," "[a] briefcase with important papers" (63), etc. The author's metaphorical exactitude and striking similes add to the charm of the text: "a moonlit river falling from a swimmer's arms like sleeves of silver" (289); "the smell of shit hovering over a village like a hat" (319).

Furthermore, the story is narrated from a child's perspective. The reality projected therein is a child's view of the adult world: the description of the activities in Cochin harbor runs thus:

> Scurrying, hurrying, buying, selling, luggage trundling porter paying children shitting people spitting coming going begging bargaining reservation - checking. (300)

In keeping with the text's overall plan and to provide the text with its specific structure, the conventions of time are set aside. This explains the break in time—another characteristic of narcissistic narratives, labeled *discontinuity* in postmodern terms. The main action takes place in December 1969, and concerns the drowning of the little Anglo-Indian girl (Margaret's daughter from Chacko) Sophie Mol, while on holiday from England. Although the story is told in the first four pages, as mentioned above, Roy employs a circuitous narrative so that events emerge elliptically and out of chronological sequence. The chronological dislocations seem to suggest that since one manifestation is much like the other, it matters little which came first. Roy does this effectively by her technique of going backward and forward in time. She uses cinematic technique—time shifts, endless fast-forwards and reversals, rapid editing—simultaneously to accelerate and delay the coming disaster. The reader is unable at times to understand whether it is the past or the present. An atmosphere of foreboding, lapsing into portentousness, hangs over the narrative. The text deliberately baffles and teases the reader, and compels him/her to explore and organize the fragments. As Hutcheon puts it, the reader of narcissistic narratives "is expected to exercise a kind of balance in the chaos" (*Narcissistic Narrative: The Metafictional Paradox* 157).

This deliberate technique of fracturing time may function to hint that in real life, too, those considering the present are aware of the past and perhaps even of the future. Hence, events do not overtake human beings in neat parcels of time. The narrative's complicated sequence creates this impression. Its suggestion of the flow of life carries with it an insight into the implications of events. These implications may not be more logical or even clearer than in real life. Nonetheless, they do provide an inkling of the contradictory nature of reality presented therein.

As Thomas Doucherty indicates, the reader of a narrative "reads the visible presentation of characters as a mere index of implications" (36). Reading about a character is a process whereby the reader probes and brings to light the depth of the individual essence. Yet, "[i]n existentialist philosophy," Doucherty reminds us, "the notion of an essential reality has been called into question. Appearance versus reality is replaced by appearance versus disappearance" (37). This would signify that character never *is*, but is always about to be endlessly deferred. This elusiveness of character explains the unreadability of a postmodern narrative such as *The God of Small Things* in which the concept of the disappearance of the individual is effectively put into practice. The major characters are presented through the minds of others, and glimpses of them are given from other perspectives, that are in contrast. This leads to yet another typical postmodern situation—*indeterminacy*. This technique seems to stem from an unwillingness to make a clear judgment, which is reflective of the ambiguity of the truth projected. It is also the expression of the creative temperament that refuses to give the normal, expected emphasis, and insists on changing the lens, varying distances; and by the same token keeps distance.

Naturally, any attempt to perceive phenomena as they really are is inevitably colored by the perceptual ability of the individual character filter. Hence, the text necessarily focuses on the subjective process through which each individual may apprehend reality. Roy shifts the interest of her fiction from the human scene to the reflected field. This breaks down the modernist "realism" that assumes a relatively unproblematic contact between the mind and "things" as they really are. Brian McHale considers "[p]ostmodernism as ontological, in the sense that it has abandoned the modernist assumption of the possibility of contact with reality of some kind" (5). This definition appears to assist the reader in comprehending *The God of Small Things* against the epistemological considerations of modernist fiction.

The tale leaves many matters open, suggestive and not spelled out. It meanders through time, weaving a web that entangles one. The reader of *The God of Small Things* is left with more than his/her usual share of freedom to create order and build relationships between parts. The author lets the reader complete the open work, yet implies some kind of inner coherence. The text uses two symbols: the Meenachal River symbolizing the flow of time, and the boat that stands for the "frail vessel of life" (Sarada 57). Much in the tale has to be inferred, comprehended, and deduced, contributing to its complexity. The first part invites and then frustrates the normal objectives of the readers. The average reader's general desire to enter into the book and become one of its characters is carefully baffled. The reader attempts to identify him/herself with one figure or the other and use that figure's viewpoint as a post of observation, but the opportunity is withdrawn as soon as it is offered. The reader tries to live through imagined experience, and through the senses of the characters. But every promised lead is broken off after a few pages. The reader is never allowed to settle down. By shifts of time, scene, emphasis, focus and point of observation, the author mischievously hinders the reader's progress. What the narrative does achieve is to subject the reader to a new, strange and largely frustrating experience truly characteristic of a narcissistic narrative in which the writer constructs her vision of reality accessible only to the "ideal reader."

Conclusion

The God of Small Things is a tale of love recounted in a refreshingly new way. This simple tale that takes place in a specific locale in India derives its global dimensions in its bold, postmodern conception, execution and interpretation of reality. A bicultural approach that allows one to appraise both aspects needs to be adopted to arrive at the totality of the text. Perhaps a narcissistic reading holds the key to one dimension of the text. To that end, the reader must collaborate not only in the reading of the text, but also in the writing of the region's history. The recognition of this problematized nature of the text is to acknowledge the presence of postmodern trends.

As one closes the book, conflicting visions leave no vision whole. The novel ends curiously with *nalee* ("tomorrow")—with reference to the lovers' next appointment. Having told a tragic tale, Roy contrives to end expectantly by re-playing the ecstasy of the ill-starred lovers. She lets the reader into her fictional world, not conventionally or habitually but differently, as if for the first time, projecting a multiple, ambiguous and perhaps "truer" vision of reality.

Notes

[1] As Edmund J. Smyth puts it, "[t]he evaluative criteria for deciding upon the admission of a work into the postmodernist canon can be applied to almost any literary work from any given period" (11).

[2] In India, heredity and the past history of a family count significantly. The old women belong to a family which has maintained good status for generations, with an ancestor in the past fortunate enough to have been blessed by St. Ignatius himself.

[3] Narcissistic texts are covert, and unveil only hints to the reader concerning their explication. The reader is left to make sense of the built-in artifices—ambiguities, paradoxes, and even contradictions. S/he has to exercise a kind of balance in the chaos. But the reader's attempt to systematize or bring order to the text by conventional means is frustrated. There is amalgamation of characters wherein one character appears to be reflected in many others. There are also unconventional notions of time. The narrative clock and calendar work against all plot logic. The narrative has an open, nebulous form, and is incomplete unless the reader comprehends, reacts, participates and co-creates the text.

[4] *Velutha* means *white* in Malayalam, Roy's mother tongue and the language spoken in Kerala where the novel is set.

Works Cited

Adıvar, Halide Edib. *The Clown and his Daughter*. London: Allen and Unwin, 1935.
_____. *Sinekli Bakkal* (The Flea-ridden Grocer). İstanbul: Ahmet Halit Kitabevi, 1942.
Ahmad, Aijaz. "Reading Arundhati Roy Politically." *Frontline*. 8 August 1997. 103-108.
Ahmad, Akbar S. *Postmodernism and Islam*. London:Routledge, 1992.
Ahmad, Nadia. "*Cracking India*: Cultural and Religious Representation in Indo-Anglian Literature (1947 to Present)." *Queen: A Journal of Rhetoric and Power*. Special issue on "Power and Recolonization." vol.2.1. Accessed on January 2005. (http://www.as-rhetorica.net/Queen/Volume21/Articles/Ahmad.html).
Aigner-Varoz, Erika. "Metaphors of a Mestiza Consciousness: Anzaldúa's *Borderlands/La Frontera*." *MELUS* 25. 2 (Summer 2000): 47-62.
Aiken, Susan Hardy. *Isak Dinesen and the Engendering of Narrative*. Chicago: University of Chicago Press, 1990.
Aixelá, Javier Franco. "Culture-specific Items in Translation." *Translation, Power, Subversion*. Eds. Román Álvarez and M. Carmen Africa Vidal. Clevedon, Philadelphia, and Adelaide: Multilingual Matters Ltd., 1996. 52-78.
Alangu, Tahir. *Keloğlan Masalları* (Tales of Keloğlan). İstanbul: Keloğlan Yayınevi, 1967.
Al-Attas, Syed Muhammad al-Naguib. *Islam and Secularism*. Kuala Lumpur: Muslim Youth Movement of Malaysia, 1978.
Alba, Richard D. *Ethnic Identity: The Transformation of White America*. New Haven: Yale University Press, 1990.
Allen, Paula Gunn. "'Border' Studies: The Intersection of Gender and Color." *Introduction to Scholarship in Modern Languages and Literatures*. Ed. Joseph Gibaldi. New York: Modern Language Association of America, 1992. 303-319.
The American Heritage Dictionary of the English Language. Fourth edition. Boston: Houghton Mifflin Company, 2000.
Anderson, Benedict. *Imagined Communities: Reflections on the Origin and Spread of*

Nationalism. 1983. Rev. ed. London and New York: Verso, 1991.

Anquetil, Gilles. "Quand Jacques le Goff interviewe Umberto Eco." *Le Nouvel Observateur.* 8 Février 1990. 73-74.

Antin, Mary. *The Promised Land.* Boston and New York: Houghton Mifflin Co., 1912.

Anzaldúa, Gloria. *Borderlands/La Frontera: The New Mestiza.* 1987. San Francisco: Aunt Lute, 1999.

Apollon, Willy. "Psychoanalytic Treatment of Psychosis." *Lacan and the Subject of Language.* Eds. Ellie Ragland-Sullivan and Mark Bracher. New York: Routledge, 1991. 116-140.

Appiah, Kwame Anthony. "Thick Translation." *Callaloo* 16:4 (1993): 808-819.

―――. "Race, Culture, Identity: Misunderstood Connections." *Color Conscious: The Political Morality of Race.* Eds. Anthony Appiah and Amy Gutman. Princeton: Princeton University Press, 1996. 30-105.

The Arabian Nights. Trans. Husain Haddawy, based on the text of the fourteenth-century Syrian manuscript. Ed. Muhsin Mahdi. New York: Norton, 1990.

Arguedas, José María. *Agua* (Water). *Relatos Completos* (Complete Stories). 1935. Lima: Horizonte, 1987.

―――. *Yawar Fiesta* (*Yawar* [Blood] Feast). Lima: CIP, 1941. *Yawar Fiesta - Fiesta de Sangre* (Blood). Extended 2. ed. Lima: Editorial Horizonte, 1980.

―――. "La Novela y el Problema de la Expresión Literaria en el Perú (The Novel and the Problem of Literary Expression in Peru)." 1950. *Yawar Fiesta - Fiesta de Sangre.* Lima: Horizonte, 1980. 7-17.

―――. *Diamantes y Pedernales* (Diamonds and Flint). 1954. México: Patria and Alianza, 1994.

―――. *Los Ríos Profundos.* Madrid: Alianza, 1958. Madrid: Ediciones de Cultura Hispánica, 1992. *Deep Rivers.* Trans. Frances Horning Barraclough, with an introduction by John V. Murra and afterword by Mario Vargas Llosa. Austin and London: University of Texas Press, 1978.

―――. *Todas las Sangres* (All Bloods). 1964. Madrid: Alianza, 1988.

―――. *El Zorro de Arriba y el Zorro de Abajo* (The Fox from Above and the Fox from Below). Ed. Eve-Marie Fell. Colección Archivos, n. 14. Madrid: Consejo Superior de Investigaciones Científicas, 1971. Ed. Eve-Marie Fell. ALLCA XXe, Université Paris X. Nanterre: Centre de Recherches Latino-américaines, 1990.

Aristotle. *The Poetics of Aristotle.* Trans. with a commentary by Stephen Halliwell. London: Duckworth, 1987.

Arrizón, Alicia. *Latina Performance. Traversing the Stage.* Bloomington: Indiana University Press, 1999.

Arteaga, Alfred. *Chicano Poetics. Heterotexts and Hybridities.* Cambridge, U.K. and New York: Cambridge University Press, 1997.

Ashcroft, Bill, Gareth Griffiths and Helen Tiffin. *The Empire Writes Back: Theory and Practice in Post-Colonial Literatures.* London and New York: Routledge, 1989. 1994.

―――. *Key Concepts in Post-Colonial Studies.* London and New York: Routledge, 1998.

Azim, Firdous. *The Colonial Rise of the Novel.* London and New York: Routledge, 1993.

Bagchee, Shyamal. "Poetry and Nationalism at the Margins: Hopkins and Tagore." *Studies.* Summer 1995 (Vol. 84, No. 334). 141-151.
Baker, Jr., Houston A., ed. *Three American Literatures: Essays in Chicano, Native American, and Asian-American Literatures for Teachers of American Literature.* With an Introduction by Walter J. Ong. New York: Modern Language Association of America, 1982.
Bakhtin, Mikhail M. *The Dialogic Imagination. Four Essays by M.M. Bakhtin.* Trans. Caryl Emerson and Michael Holquist. Ed. M. Holquist. Austin: University of Texas Press, 1981.
Bal, Mieke. "Tricky Thematics." *Semeia: An Experimental Journal for Biblical Criticism* 42 (1988): 133-155.
Balibar, Etienne. "Is there a Neo-Racism?" *Race, Nation, Class: Ambiguous Identities.* Eds. Etienne Balibar and Immanuel Wallerstein. London: Verso, 1991. 17-28.
Balibar, Etienne and Immanuel Wallerstein. *Race, Nation, Class: Ambiguous Identities.* London: Verso, 1991.
Bandia, Paul. "Translation as Culture Transfer: Evidence from African Creative Writing." *Traduction, Terminologie, Redaction* 6:2 (1993): 55-78.
Barnstone, Willis. *The Poetics of Translation: History, Theory, Practice.* New Haven and London: Yale University Press, 1993.
Barth, John. *Chimera.* New York: Random House, 1972.
_____. *The Last Voyage of Somebody The Sailor.* Boston: Little, Brown, 1991.
_____. "The Literature of Replenishment." *The Atlantic.* 245. 1 (1988). 65-71.
Bassnett, Susan. *Comparative Literature: A Critical Introduction.* Oxford, UK and Cambridge, MA: Blackwell, 1993.
_____. "The Meek or the Mighty: Reappraising the Role of the Translator." *Translation, Power, Subversion.* Eds. Román Álvarez and M. Carmen Africa Vidal. Clevedon, Philadelphia, and Adelaide: Multilingual Matters Ltd., 1996. 10-24.
Bassnett, Susan and Harish Trivedi. "Introduction: Of Colonies, Cannibals and Vernaculars." *Post-colonial Translation Theory and Practice.* Eds. Susan Bassnett and Harish Trivedi. London and New York: Routledge, 1999. 1-8.
_____. eds. *Post-colonial Translation Theory and Practice.* London and New York: Routledge, 1999.
Baum, L. Frank. *The Wonderful Wizard of Oz.* Chicago and New York: G.M. Hill Co., 1900.
Beaumont, Daniel. "Introduction." *Slave of Desire: Sex, Love, and Death in the 1001 Nights.* Madison (NJ): Fairleigh Dickinson University Press, 2002. Accessed 12 April 2004. http://www.arabiannights.org/index2.html.
Beauregard, Guy. "'Race,' Writing and Deference? Asian Canadian and Asian American Literary Studies in Comparative Perspective." John A. Sproul Lecture in Canadian Studies, University of California, Berkeley, 9 November 2000.
Beidelman, T.O. "The Moral Imagination of the Kaguru: Some Thoughts on Tricksters, Translation and Comparative Analysis." *Mythical Trickster Figures: Contours, Contexts, and Criticisms,* eds. William J Hynes and William G. Doty. Tuscaloosa and London: University of Alabama Press, 1993. 174-192.

Benjamin, Walter. "The Storyteller." *Illuminations*. Ed., with an introduction by Hannah Arendt. Trans. Harry Zohn. New York: Schocken Books, 1968. 83-109.
Beauregard, Guy. "'Race,' Writing and Deference? Asian Canadian and Asian American Literary Studies in Comparative Perspective." Unpublished lecture delivered as the John A. Sproul Lecture in Canadian Studies at the University of California, Berkeley, 9 November 2000.
Bhabha, Homi K. "Postcolonial Authority and Postmodern Guilt." *Cultural Studies*. Eds. Lawrence Grossberg *et al*. New York: Routledge, 1992. 56-68.
———. *The Location of Culture*. London and New York: Routledge, 1994. 1995. *The Bhagavad-Gita: Krishna's Counsel in Time of War*. Trans. Barbara Stoler Miller. New York: Bantam Books, 1986.
Blackburn, Stuart H. *et. al*., eds. *Oral Epics in India*. Berkeley, Los Angeles and London: University of California Press, 1989.
Bloom, Harold. *The Anxiety of Influence: A Theory of Poetry*. New York: Oxford University Press, 1973.
Bohannan, Paul. *How Culture Works*. New York: The Free Press and Simon and Schuster, 1995.
Borges, Jorge Luis. "Pierre Menard, Author of the *Quixote*." *Labyrinths: Selected Stories and Other Writings*. Edited by Donald A. Yates and James E. Irby. New York: New Directions Publishing Co., 1964. 36-44.
Bost, Suzanne. "Transgressing Borders: Puerto Rican and Latina *Mestizaje*." *MELUS* 25.2 (Summer 2000): 187-211.
Bradbury, Malcolm. *Dangerous Pilgrimages: Transatlantic Mythologies and the Novel*. London: Penguin Books, 1995.
Braidotti, Rosi. *Nomadic Subjects: Embodiment and Sexual Difference in Contemporary Feminist Theory*. New York: Columbia University Press, 1994.
Brennan, Tim. "Cosmopolitans and Celebrities." *Race and Class*. 31. 1 (1989). 1-19.
Broumas, Olga. *Beginning with O*. New Haven: Yale University Press, 1977.
Bunyan, John. *Pilgrim's Progress*. 1678. Ed. with an introduction and notes by N.H. Keeble. Oxford and New York: Oxford University Press, 1998.
Burstein, Janet Handler. "Two Locked Caskets: Selfhood and 'Otherness' in the Work of Isak Dinesen" *Texas Studies in Literature and Language*, 20 (1978): 615-632.
Butalia, Urvashi. *The Other Side of Silence: Voices from the Partition of India*. New Delhi: Viking, 1998.
Butler, Judith P., *Bodies that Matter*. London: Routledge, 1993.
Cahan, Abraham. *The Rise of David Levinsky*. 1917. New York: Harper Torchbooks, 1960.
Calderón, Héctor and José D. Saldívar, eds. *Criticism in the Borderlands. Studies in Chicano Literature, Culture and Ideology*. Durham and London: Duke University Press, 1994.
Carroll, Lewis. *Alice's Adventures in Wonderland and Through the Looking Glass*. 1861. Ed. with an introduction by Martin Gardner. New York and London: W.W.W. Norton and Company, 2000.
Chan, Jeffery Paul, *et al*., eds. *The Big Aiiieeeee! An Anthology of Chinese American and Japanese American Literature*. New York: Meridian, 1991.

Chandra, Vikram. "Dharma." *The Paris Review*. 130 (1994): 258-282.
_____. "Shakti." *The New Yorker*. December 24, 1994/January 2. (1995). 108-129.
_____. *Red Earth and Pouring Rain*. London: Faber and Faber, 1995.
_____. *Love and Longing in Bombay*. London: Faber and Faber, 1997.
_____. "Eternal Don." *The New Yorker*. June 23 and 30, 1997. 130-141.
_____. Personal communication with Dora Sales Salvador. 21 May 1997.
_____. Personal communication with Dora Sales Salvador. 4 October 1997.
_____. Personal communication with Dora Sales Salvador. 17 September 1999.
_____. Personal communication with Dora Sales Salvador. 11 November 1999.
_____. "The Cult of Authenticity. India's Cultural Commissars Worship 'Indianness' Instead of Art." *Miscelánea: A Journal of English and American Studies*. Vol. 22. University of Zaragoza. 2000. 175-200.
_____. "Finding a Form." Unpublished lecture delivered at diverse Spanish universities (Zaragoza, Lleida, Autónoma of Barcelona and Castellón) during the author's visit to Spain, promoted by The British Council in Spain, 18-26 November 2000.
Chatterjee, Partha. "The Nationalist Resolution of the Women's Question." *Recasting Women: Essays in Colonial History*. Eds. Kumkum Sangari and Sudesh Vaid. New Delhi: Kali for Women, 1989. 233-253.
Chaudhuri, Amit. "Lure of the Hybrid." *The Times Literary Supplement*. September 3, 1999. 5-6.
Cheung, King-Kok, ed. *An Interethnic Companion to Asian American Literature*. Cambridge, UK: Cambridge University Press, 1997.
Chin, Frank. "Preface." *Aiiieeeee! An Anthology of Asian American Writers*. Eds. Frank Chin, *et al*. Washington, D.C.: Howard University Press, 1974. xxi-lxiii.
_____. "Afterword." *No-No Boy*. John Okada. Seattle: University of Washington Press, 1976. 253-260.
_____. "Come All Ye Asian American Writers of the Real and the Fake." *The Big Aiiieeeee!: An Anthology of Chinese American and Japanese American Literature*. Eds. Jeffery Paul Chan *et al*. New York: Meridian, 1991. 1-92.
Chin, Frank *et al*., eds. *Aiiieeeee! An Anthology of Asian American Writers*. Washington, D.C.: Howard University Press, 1974.
Chirikure, Chirikure. "The Shona Novel - Originality and Depth." *An Editor's Manual*. Compiled by the Literature Bureau. Gweru, Zimbabwe: Mambo Press, 1992. n. p.
Cisneros, Sandra. *The House on Mango Street*. 1984. New York: Vintage, 1991.
Clifton, James, ed. *Being and Becoming Indian: Biographical Studies of North American Frontiers*. Chicago: The Dorsey Press, 1989.
Clifford, James. "The Transit Lounge of Culture." Times Literary Supplement. 3 May 1991. 7-8.
_____. "Traveling Cultures." *Cultural Studies*. Eds. Lawrence Grossberg, Cary Nelson and Paula Treichler. New York and London: Routledge. 1992. 96-116.
_____. *Routes Travel and Translation in the Late Twentieth Century*. Cambridge, MA: Harvard University Press, 1997.
Coetzee, J.M. *Foe*. London: Secker and Warburg, 1986.
The Columbia Encyclopedia. Sixth edition. New York: Columbia University Press, 2004.

Columbus, Claudette Kemper. *Mythological Consciousness and the Future: José María Arguedas*. Berne, Frankfurt and New York: Peter Lang, 1986.
Crocker, John. "The Book of the Thousand and One Nights." Accessed 14 April 2004.http://www.crock11.freeserve.co.uk/arabian.htm.
Curti, Lidia. "What is Real and What is Not: Female Fabulations in Cultural Analysis." *Cultural Studies*. Eds. Lawrence Grossberg, Cary Nelson and Paula Treichler. New York and London: Routledge. 1992. 134-153.
Cypess, Sandra Messinger. *La Malinche in Mexican Literature: From History to Myth*. Austin, TX: Universty of Texas Press, 1991.
Dante Alighieri, *Divina Commedia. The Divine Comedy: the Inferno, the Purgatorio, and the Paradiso*. Translated by John Ciardi. New York: New American Library, 2003.
Das, Bijay Kumar. "The Art of Story-Telling: A Study of Vikram Chandra's *Love and Longing in Bombay*." *50 Years of Indian Writing. A Commemorative Volume Highlighting the Achievement of Post-Independence Indian Writing in English and Literature in Translation*. Ed. R.W. Dhawan. New Delhi: Sangam Books and Prestige, 1999. 51-60.
Davidson, Temma Catherine. *The Priest Fainted*. New York: Henry Holt and Co., 1998.
Davison, Carol Margaret. "Crisscrossing the River: An Interview with Caryl Phillips." *Ariel*. 25. 4 (1994). 91-99.
Defoe, Daniel. *The Fortunes and Misfortunes of the Famous Moll Flanders*. 1772. Ed. with an introduction by Juliet Mitchell. Harmondsworth: Penguin, 1978.
Derrida, Jacques. "Structure, Sign and Play in the Discourse of the Human Sciences." *The Structuralist Controversy: The Language of Criticisms and the Sciences of Man*. Eds. Richard Macksey and Eugene Donato. Baltimore, MD: The John Hopkins University Press, 1970. 247-272.
_____. *Of Grammatology*. Trans. Gayatri Chakravorty Spivak. Baltimore and London: Johns Hopkins University Press, 1997.
Desai, Anita. "Introduction." *Sunlight on a Broken Column* by Attia Hosain. With a new introduction by Anita Desai. New York: Penguin Books-Virago Press, 1989. Delhi: Penguin Books, 1992.
Devy, G.N. *Of Many Heroes: An Indian Essay in Literary Historiography*. New Delhi: Sangam Books and Prestige, 1998.
Dhawan, R.W., ed. *50 Years of Indian Writing. A Commemorative Volume Highlighting the Achievement of Post-Independence Indian Writing in English and Literature in Translation*. New Delhi: Sangam Books and Prestige, 1999.
Dimock, Edward C. et al. *The Literatures of India. An Introduction*. Chicago and London: The University of Chicago Press, 1974.
Dinesen, Isak. *Seven Gothic Tales*. English ed. London: Putnam, 1934.
_____. "The Deluge at Norderney." *Seven Gothic Tales*. English ed. London: Putnam, 1934. 1-79.
_____. *Den Afrikanse Farm*. København: Gyldendal, 1937. *Out of Africa*. London: Putnam, 1937.
_____. *Babettes Gaestebud*. København: Forlaget Fremad, 1952. *Babette's Feast and Other Anecdotes of Destiny*. New York: Vintage Books, 1988. –48.
_____. *Skygger Paa Graesset*. København: Gyldendal, 1960. *Shadows on the Grass*.

London: M. Joseph, 1960.
____. *Letters from Africa 1914-1931.* Trans. Anne Born. Ed. Frans Lasson. ChicagoUniversity of Chicago Press, 1981.
____. *Out of Africa* and *Shadows on the Grass.* New York: Vintage Books, 1989.
Dingwaney, Anuradha. "Introduction: Translating 'Third World' Cultures." *Between Languages and Cultures: Translation and Cross-Cultural Texts.* Eds. Anuradha Dingwaney and Carol Maeir. Pittsburgh and London: University of Pittsburgh Press, 1995. 3-15.
Dingwaney, Anuradha and Carol Maeir, eds. *Between Languages and Cultures: Translation and Cross-Cultural Texts.* Pittsburgh and London: University of Pittsburgh Press, 1995.
____. "Translation as a Method for Cross-Cultural Teaching." *Between Languages and Cultures: Translation and Cross-Cultural Texts.* Eds. Anuradha Dingwaney and Carol Maeir. Pittsburgh and London: University of Pittsburgh Press, 1995. 303-319.
Divakaruni, Chitra Banerjee. *The Mistress of Spices.* London: Black Swan, 1997.
Docherty, Thomas. *Alterities: Criticism, History, Representation.* Oxford, U.K. and New York: Clarendon Press, 1996.
Doody, Margaret Anne. *The True Story of the Novel.* New Brunswick, New Jersey: Rutgers University Press, 1996.
Doueihi, Anne. "Trickster: On Inhabiting the Space Between Discourse and Story." *Soundings: An Interdisciplinary Journal* 67:3 (1984): 283-311.
Durrell, Lawrence. *Bitter Lemons.* New York: Dutton, 1957.
____. *The Greek Islands.* New York: Viking Press, 1978.
Dwyer, Rachel. *All You Want is Money, All You Need is Love. Sex and Romance in Modern India.* London and New York: Cassell, 2000.
Dyson, Ketaki Kushari. *In Your Blossoming Flower Garden: Rabindranath Tagore and Victoria Ocampo.* New Delhi: Sahitya Akademi, 1988.
Eagleton, Terry. *Literary Theory: An Introduction.* 1983. Minneapolis: University of Minnesota Press, 1996.
____. *After Theory.* London and New York: Allen Lane, 2003.
"Editorial." *Te Ao Hou.* Wellington: Maori Affairs Department, 1952. 1
Egerer, Claudia. *Fictions of (In)Betweenness.* Göteborg, Sweden: Acta Universitatis Gothoburgensis. 1997.
Ekstrom, Margaret V. "Interpreting Ethnicity: Differing Views of Biculturalism in Arguedas, Carpentier, Castellanos, and Valle-Inclán." *Translating Latin America: Culture as Text.* Eds. William Luis and Julio Rodríguez-Luis. Translating Perspectives VI. Binghamton: Center for Research in Translation, State University of New York, 1991. 173-178.
Elliott, Emory et al., eds. *Columbia Literary History of the United States.* New York: Columbia University Press, 1988.
____. eds. *The Columbia History of the American Novel.* New York: Columbia University Press, 1991.
Escobar, Alberto. *Arguedas o la Utopía de la Lengua* (Arguedas, or the Utopia of Language). Serie Lengua y Sociedad n. 6. Lima: Instituto de Estudios Peruanos, 1984.
Evans, Dylan. *An Introductory Dictionary of Lacanian Psychoanalysis.* New York:

Routledge, 1996.
Even-Zohar, Itamar. *Polysystem Studies. Poetics Today* 11(1). Special issue. 1990.
Fabb, Nigel. *Linguistics and Literature*. Malden, MA: Blackwell, 1997.
Fanon, Frantz. *Peau Noire, Masques Blancs*. 1952. *Black Skin, White Masks*. Trans. Charles Lam Markmann. New York: Grove Press, 1967. With a foreword by Homi K. Bhabha. London: Pluto, 1986.
Feldstein, Richard. *Political Correctness*. Minneapolis: University of Minnesota Press, 1997.
Feliciano, Wilma. "'I Am a Hyphenated American': Interview with Dolores Prida". *Latin American Theatre Review* 29. 1 (Fall 1995): 113-118.
Fink, Bruce. *A Clinical Introduction to Lacanian Psychoanalysis*. Cambridge, MA: Harvard University Press, 1997.
———. *The Lacanian Subject*. Princeton, NJ: Princeton University Press, 1995.
Forster, E.M. *A Passage to India*. London: Harvest/Harcourt Brace Jovanovich, 1924.
Fortune, G[eorge]. *Ideophones in Shona: An Inaugural Lecture Given in the University College of Rhodesian and Nyasaland on 28 April 1961*. London: Oxford University Press, 1962.
Foucault, Michel. *La Volonté de Savoir*. (*Histoire de la Sexualité*. Vol. I). Paris: Éditions Gallimard, 1976. *The History of Sexuality*. Trans. Robert Hurley. New York: Pantheon Books, 1978. *The History of Sexuality: An Introduction*. Vol. I. Trans. Robert Hurley. New York: Vintage, 1990.
Fox-Genovese, Elizabeth. "My Statue, My Self: Autobiographical Writings of Afro-American Women." *The Private Self*. Ed. Shari Benstock. Chapel Hill: University of North Carolina Press, 1988. 63-89.
Fresno Calleja, Paloma. *Patricia Grace: Diálogo Intercultural e Identidad Maorí*. Oviedo: KRK, 2000.
Frye, Marilyn. "The Necessity of Differences: Constructing a Positive Category of Women." *Signs* 21.4 (1996): 991-1010.
Fuentes, Carlos. "Elogio del Mestizaje." *El Urogallo* 90 (Nov. 1993): 8-13.
Gans, Herbert. "Symbolic Ethnicity: The Future of Ethnic Groups and Cultures in America." *On the Making of Americans: Essays in Honor of David Riesman*. Eds. Herbert Gans et al. Philadelphia: University of Pennsylvania Press, 1979. 193-220.
Gans, Herbert et al., eds. *On the Making of Americans: Essays in Honor of David Riesman*. Philadelphia: University of Pennsylvania Press, 1979.
Gates, Henry Louis Jr., *The Signifying Monkey: A Theory of African-American Literary Criticism*. New York and Oxford: Oxford University Press, 1988.
Gatura, Kamante, and Peter Beard. *Longing for Darkness: Kamante's Tales from Out of Africa*. San Francisco: Chronicle Books, 1990.
Geok-lin, Shirley and Amy Ling, eds., *Reading the Literatures of Asian America*. Philadelphia: Temple University Press, 1992.
Giménez Micó, José Antonio. "José María Arguedas y la Modernidad (José María Arguedas and Modernity)." *Revista Canadiense de Estudios Hispánicos/ Canadian Review of Hispanic Studies*. Vol. XX, 1996. 241-267.
"Globalizing Literary Studies." *PMLA* January 2001 (v. 116, n. 1).
Goldman, Anne. "'I Yam What I Yam': Cooking, Culture, and Colonialism."

De/Colonizing the Subject. The Politics of Gender in Women's Autobiographies. Eds. Sidonie Smith and Julia Watson. Minneapolis: University of Minnesota Press, 1992. 169-195.
Grace, Patricia. *Waiariki*. Auckland: Longman Paul, 1975.
_____. *Mutuwhenua: The Moon Sleeps*. Auckland: Longman Paul, 1978.
_____. *Potiki*. Auckland: Penguin, 1986.
_____. *Cousins*. Auckland: Penguin, 1992.
_____. *Baby No-Eyes*. Auckland: Penguin, 1998.
Grace, Patricia and Witi Ihimaera. "The Maori in Literature." *Tihe Mauri Ora. Aspects of Maoritanga*. Ed. Michael King. Auckland: Methuen, 1978. 80-85.
Grosjean, François. *Life with Two Languages: An Introduction to Bilingualism*. Cambridge, MA and London: Harvard University Press, 1982.
Gün, Güneli. *Book of Trances: A Novel of Magic Recitals*. London: Julian Friedman, 1979.
_____. *On the Road to Baghdad: A Picaresque Novel of Magical Adventures, Begged, Borrowed, and Stolen from the Thousand and One Nights*. 1991. London and Basingstoke: Picador, 1994. *Bağdat Yollarında: Sihirli Serüvenlerin Romanı*. Trans. Yurdanur Salman. İstanbul: Simavi Yayınları, 1993.
Hall, Stuart. "Cultural Identity and Diaspora." *Colonial Discourse and Post-Colonial Theory*. Eds. Patrick Williams and Laura Christman. New York: Columbia University Press, 1994. 392-403.
Hammond, Dorothy and Alta Jablow. *The Africa That Never Was: Four Centuries of British Writing about Africa*. New York: Twayne, 1970.
Harlow, Barbara. *Resistance Literature*. New York and London: Methuen, 1987.
Hartsock, Nancy. "Rethinking Modernism: Minority vs. Majority Theories." *Cultural Critique* 7. 187-206.
Hasan, Mushirul. "Partition: The Human Cost" *History Today*. Vol. 47. n. 9. September 1997.
Hasty, Christopher Francis. *Meter as Rhythm*. New York and Oxford: Oxford University Press, 1997.
Hegel, G.W.F. *The Philosophy of History*. Trans. John Sibree. New York: Dover Publications, 1956.
Heim, Otto. *Writing Along Broken Lines: Violence and Ethnicity in Contemporary Maori Fiction*. Auckland: Auckland University Press, 1998.
Henderson, Mae G, ed. "Introduction". *Borders, Boundaries, and Frames. Cultural Criticism and Cultural Studies*. New York and London: Routledge, 1995. 1-30.
Herder, Johann Gottfried von. *Philosophical Writings*. Translated and edited by Michael N. Forster. Cambridge, U.K. and New York: Cambridge University Press, 2002.
Hicks, D. Emily. *Border Writing: The Multidimensional Text*. Minneapolis: University of Minnesota Press, 1991.
Hobsbawm, Eric and Terence Ranger, eds. *The Invention of Tradition*. Cambridge, U.K.: Cambridge University Press, 1983.
Hollinger, Davidson A. *Postethnic America: Beyond Multiculturalism*. New York: Basic Books, 1995.
Homer. *The Odyssey*. Trans. Edward McCrorie; with an introduction and notes by

Richard P. Martin. Baltimore: Johns Hopkins University Press, 2004.
hooks, bell. "Postmodern Blackness." *Yearning: Race, Gender and Cultural Politics.* Boston: South End Press, 1991. 23-31.
———. "'this is the oppressor's language / yet I need it to talk to you': Language, a place of struggle." *Between Languages and Cultures: Translation and Cross-Cultural Texts.* Eds. Anuradha Dingwaney and Carol Maeir. Pittsburgh and London: University of Pittsburgh Press, 1995. 295-301.
Horno-Delgado, Asunción et al., eds. *Breaking Boundaries. Latina Writing and Critical Essays.* Amherst, MA: University of Massachussets Press, 1989.
Hosain, Attia. *Sunlight on a Broken Column.* 1961. With a new introduction by Anita Desai. New York: Penguin Books-Virago Press, 1989. Delhi: Penguin Books, 1992.
House, Juliane. *Translation Quality Assessment: A Model Revisited.* Tübingen: G. Narr, 1997.
Hulme, Keri. *the bone people.* Auckland: Spiral, 1983.
Humm, Maggie. *Border Traffic: Strategies of Contemporary Women Writers.* Manchester and New York: Manchester University Press, 1991.
Hunn, Jack Kent. *Report on the Department of Maori Affairs with Statistical Supplement.* Wellington: Owen, 1961.
Huntington, Samuel P. *The Clash of Civilizations and the Remaking of World Order.* New York: Simon and Schuster, 1996.
Hutcheon, Linda. *Narcissistic Narrative: The Metafictional Paradox.* Waterloo, Ont.: Wilfrid Laurier University Press, 1980.
———. *A Poetics of Postmodernism: History, Theory, Fiction.* London: Routledge, 1988.
Hynes, William J. "Mapping the Characteristics of Mythic Tricksters: A Heuristic Guide." *Mythical Trickster Figures: Contours, Contexts, and Criticisms.* Eds. William J. Hynes and William G. Doty. Tuscaloosa and London: University of Alabama Press, 1993. 33-45.
Hynes, William J. and William G. Doty. "Historical Overview of Theoretical Issues: The Problem of the Trickster." *Mythical Trickster Figures: Contours, Contexts, and Criticisms.* Eds. William J. Hynes and William G. Doty. Tuscaloosa and London: University of Alabama Press, 1993. 13-32.
———. "Introducing the Fascinating and Perplexing Trickster Figure." *Mythical Trickster Figures: Contours, Contexts, and Criticisms.* Eds. William J. Hynes and William G. Doty. Tuscaloosa and London: University of Alabama Press, 1993. 1-12.
———. eds. *Mythical Trickster Figures: Contours, Contexts, and Criticisms.* Tuscaloosa and London: University of Alabama Press, 1993.
Ibn al-Naqīb al-Misri, Ahmad ibn Lu'lu'. *'Umdat Al-sālik Wa-'uddat Al-nāsik. Reliance of the Traveller: The Classic Manual of Islamic Sacred Law.* In Arabic with facing English text. Ed. and trans. Nuh Ha Mim Keller. Rev. ed. Beltsville, MD: Amana Publications, 1999.
Ihimaera, Witi. *Pounamu Pounamu.* Auckland: Heinemann, 1972.
———. "Maori Life and Literature: a Sensory Perception". *The Turnbull Library Record.* Vol. XV, 1. 1982. 45-55.
———. *The Matriarch.* Auckland: Reed, 1986.

Ihimaera, Witi et al. *Te Ao Marama.* 5 vol. Auckland: Reed Books, 1992.
Inada, Lawson Fusao. "Introduction." *No-No Boy.* John Okada. Seattle: University of Washington Press, 1976. iii-vi.
_____. "Of Place and Displacement: The Range of Japanese-American Literature." *Three American Literatures: Essays in Chicano, Native American, and Asian-American Literatures for Teachers of American Literature.* Ed. Houston A. Baker, Jr. New York: Modern Language Association, 1982. 254-265.
Inden, Ronald. *Imagining India.* Oxford: Blackwell, 1990.
Irigaray, Luce. *The Speculum of the Other Woman.* Trans. Gillian C. Gill. Ithaca: Cornell University Press, 1985.
_____. *This Sex Which is Not One.* Trans. Catherine Porter with Carolyn Burke. Ithaca: Cornell University Press, 1985.
Irving, Washington. "Rip van Winkle." *The Sketchbook of Geoffrey Crayon, Gent.* 1819. *Rip van Winkle.* Ed. Robert Dewsnap. Copenhagen: Aschehoug, 1995.
Iyer, Pico. *The Global Soul: Jet Lag, Shopping Malls and the Search for Home.* London: Bloomsbury, 2000.
Jameson, Fredric. "Third World Literature in the Era of Multinational Capitalism." *Social Text,* 15 (Fall): 65-88.
_____. *Postmodernism or The Cultural Logic of Late Capitalism.* Durham: Duke University Press, 1991.
JanMohammed, Abdul R. *Manichean Aesthetics: The Politics of Literature in Colonial Africa.* Amherst: University of Massachusetts Press, 1983.
_____. "Worldliness-Without-World, Homelessness-As-Home: Toward Definition of the Specular Border Intellectual." *Edward Said. A Critical Reader.* Ed. Michael Sprinker. Oxford, UK and Cambridge, MA: Blackwell, 1992. 96-120.
The Joy Luck Club, directed by Oliver Stone, 1994.
Kachru, Braj B. *The Indianization of English. The English Language in India.* Delhi. Oxford University Press, 1983.
_____. *The Alchemy of English. The Spread, Functions, and Models of Non-Native Englishes.* Urbana and Chicago: University of Illinois Press, 1986. 1990.
Kalogeras, Yiorgos D. "Greek American Literature: Who Needs It? Some Canonical Issues Concerning the Fate of An Ethnic Literature." *New Directions in Greek American Studies.* Eds. Dan Georgakas and Charles C. Moskos. New York: Pella Publishing Company, Inc., 1991. 129-141.
_____. "Greek-American Literature." *New Immigrant Literatures in the United States: A Sourcebook to Our Multicultural Literary Heritage.* Ed. Alpana Sharma Knippling. Westport, CT.: Greenwood Press, 1996. 253-264.
_____. "The 'Other Space' of Greek America." *American Literary History* 10:4 (1998): 702-723.
Kaplan, Caren. "Deterriorializations: The Rewriting of Home and Exile in Western Feminist Discourse." *Cultural Critique* 6 (Spring 1987).
Kapur, Manju. *Difficult Daughters.* London: Faber and Faber, 1998.
Karasu, Bilgé. *Night.* Trans. Güneli Gün, with the author. Baton Rouge: Louisiana State University Press, 1994.
Kaviraj, Sudipta. "Modernity and Politics in India." *Daedalus* (Winter 2000): 137-161.
Kawash, Samira. *Dislocating the Color Line. Identity, Hybridity, and Singularity in*

African-American Narrative. Stanford, CA: Stanford University Press, 1997.
Kedgley, Sue. *Our Own Country: Leading New Zealand Women Writers Talk About Their Writing and Their Lives*. Auckland: Penguin, 1989.
Kerouac, Jack. *On the Road*. Text and Criticism. Ed. Scott Donaldson. New York: Viking Press, 1979.
Kherdian, David. *Monkey: The Journey to the West*. A retelling of the Chinese folk novel by Wu Ch'eng-en. Boston and London: Shambhala, 1992.
Khilnani, Sunil. *The Idea of India*. London: Penguin, 1997.
Kim, Elaine H. *Asian American Literature: An Introduction to the Writings and Their Social Context*. Philadelphia: Temple University Press, 1982.
Kingston, Maxine Hong. *The Woman Warrior: Memoirs of a Girlhood Among Ghosts*. New York: Knopf, 1976. New York: Vintage Books, 1989.
_____. *Tripmaster Monkey. His Fake Book*. 1989. New York: Vintage Books, 1990.
Klages, Mary. "Jacques Lacan." Accessed June 14, 2004. http://www.colorado.edu/English/ENGL2012Klages/lacan.html.
Kristeva, Julia. *La Révolution du Langage Poétique: L'Avant-garde à la Fin du XIXème Siècle, Lautréamont et Mallarmé*. Paris: Éditions du Seuil, 1974. *Revolution in Poetic Language*. Trans. Margaret Waller, with an introduction by Léon S. Roudiez. New York: Columbia University Press, 1984.
Konuk, Kader. "Sufism and Postmodernism in Güneli Gün's *On the Road to Baghdad*." *"Wandering Selves: Essays on Migration and Multiculturalism*. Eds. Christian Berkemeier and Michael Porsche. Essen: Verlag Die Blaue Eule, 2001. 89-102.
Kroeber, Karl. *Retelling/Rereading: The Fate of Storytelling in Modern Times*. New Brunswick: Rutgers University Press, 1992.
Kruger, Alet and Kim Wallmach. "Research Methodology for the Description of a Source Text and Its Translation(s) - A South African Perspective." *South African Journal of African Languages* 17:4 (November 1997): 119-127.
Krupat, Arnold. *Ethnocriticism: Ethnography, History, Literature*. Berkeley, CA: University of California Press, 1992.
Kureishi, Hanif. *The Buddha of Suburbia*. London: Faber and Faber, 1990.
Lacan, Jacques. *Écrits: A Selection*. Trans. Alan Sheridan. New York: Norton, 1977.
_____. *Le Séminaire de Jacques Lacan*. Texte établi par Jacques-Alain Miller. Paris: Seuil, 1973.
_____. *The Psychoses*. The Seminar Book III 1955-1956. Trans. with notes by Russell Grigg. Ed. Jacques-Alain Miller. London: Routledge, 1993.
Lamming, George. *In the Castle of My Skin*. 1953. Harlow: Longman Caribbean Writers, 1986.
Landy, Marcia. "Anecdote as Destiny: Isak Dinesen and the Storyteller." *The Massachusetts Review*. 19 (1978): 389-406.
Landreau, John C. "Translation, Autobiography, and Quechua Knowledge." *José María Arguedas: Reconsiderations for Latin American Cultural Studies*. Eds. Ciro A. Sandoval and Sandra M. Boschetto-Sandoval. Athens: Ohio University Center for International Studies, 1998. 88-112.
Langbaum, Robert. *Out of Africa in The Gayety of Vision: A Study of Isak Dinesen's Art*. New York: Random House, 1965.
Lanyon, Anna. *Malinche's Conquest*. New South Wales, Australia: Allen and Unwin, 1999.

Larsen, Nella. *Passing*. 1929. Ed. Deborah E. McDowell. New Brunswick, NJ: Rutgers University Press, 1986.
Lauter, Paul et al., eds. *The Heath Anthology of American Literature*. 2 vols. Lexington, MA: D.C. Heath and Company, 1990.
Ledent, Benedicte. "Overlapping Territories, Intertwined Histories: Cross-Culturality in Caryl Phillips' *Crossing the River*." *Journal of Commonwealth Literature*. 30. 2 (1995).
Lee, Judith. "The Mask of Form in *Out of Africa*." *Isak Dinesen: Critical Views*. Ed. Olga Anastasia Pelensky. Athens: Ohio University Press, 1993. 267-282.
Levins Morales, Aurora and Rosario Morales. *Getting Home Alive*. Ithaca, NY: Firebrand, 1986.
Lienhard, Martin. *Cultura Popular Andina y Forma Novelesca: Zorros y Danzantes en la Última Novela de Arguedas* (Andean Popular Culture and the Novel Form: Foxes and Minstrels in Arguedas's Last Novel). 1981. Lima: Horizonte and Tarea, 1990.
Ling, Jingi. "Race, Power, and Cultural Politics in John Okada's *No-No Boy*." *American Literature* 67.2 (1995): 359-381.
Long, D. S. and Witi Ihimaera, eds. *Into the World of Light*: An Anthology of Maori Writing. Auckland: Heinemann, 1982.
Lugo, Alejandro. "Reflections on Border Theory, Culture, and the Nation." *Border Theory: The Limits of Cultural Politics*. Eds. Scott Michaelsen and David E. Johnson. Minneapolis and London: University of Minnesota Press, 1997. 43-67.
Lugones, Maria. "Purity, Impurity, and Separation." *Signs* 19.2 (Winter 1994): 458-479.
Lukács, Georg. *The Historical Novel*. Trans. Hannah and Stanley Mitchell. 1962. Harmondsworth: Pelican Books, 1982.
Ma, Sheng-mei. *Immigrant Subjectivities in Asian American and Asian Diaspora Literature*. New York: State University of New York Press, 1998.
The Mahabharata. Ed. Chakravarti Rajagopalchari. Bombay: Bharatiya Vidya Bhavan, 2001.
Maier, Carol. "Toward a Theoretical Practice for Cross-Cultural Translation." *Between Languages and Cultures: Translation and Cross-Cultural Texts*. Eds. Anuradha Dingwaney and Carol Maeir. Pittsburgh and London: University of Pittsburgh Press, 1995. 21-38.
Maira, Sunaina. "Henna and Hip Hop: The Politics of Cultural Production and the Work of Cultural Studies." *Journal of Asian American Studies* (October 2000): 329-369.
Man, Paul de. "Autobiography as De-Facement." *The Rhetoric of Romanticism*. New York: Columbia University Press, 1984. 67-81.
Mandeville, John, Sir. *The Travels of Sir John Mandeville*. 1356. Trans. from Anglo-Norman with an introduction by Charles W.R.D. Moseley. Harmondsworth and New York: Penguin Books, 1983.
Marechera, Dambudzo. *House of Hunger. A Novella and Short Stories*. New York: Pantheon Books, 1978.
Mazrui, Alamin M. "Shakespeare in Africa: Between English and Swahili Literature." *Research in African Literatures* 27:1 (Spring 1996): 1-10.

McDonald, Dorothy Ritsuko. "After Imprisonment: Ichiro's Search for Redemption in *No-No Boy*." *MELUS* 6.3 (1979): 19-26.
McHale, Brian, "Introduction." *Postmodernist Fiction*.Ed. Brian McHale. New York: Methuen, 1987.
____, ed. *Postmodernist Fiction*. New York: Methuen, 1987.
McRae, Jane. "Interview with Patricia Grace." *In the Same Room: Conversations with New Zealand Writers*. Eds. Elizabeth Alley and Mark Williams. Auckland: Auckland University Press, 1992. 285-296.
____. "Patricia Grace and Complete Communication." *Australian and New Zealand Studies in Canada*. Vol. 10 (1993). 66-86.
Metcalf, Barbara D. *Islamic Contestations: Muslims in India and Pakistan*. Delhi: Oxford University Press, 2004.
Michaelsen, Scott and David E. Johnson, eds. *Border Theory: The Limits of Cultural Politics*. Minneapolis and London: University of Minnesota Press, 1997.
Migel, Parmenia. *Titania: The Biography of Isak Dinesen*. New York: Random House, 1967.
Les Mille et Une Nuits Contes Arabes. Trad. Antoine Galland, avec une introduction par (with an introduction by) Jean Paul Sermain et (and) Aboubakr Chraïbi. 3 vols. Paris: GF, 2004.
Miller, Henry. *The Colossus of Maroussi*. 1941. New York, New Directions, 1958.
Miller, Jacques-Alain. "An Introduction to Lacan's Clinical Perspectives." *Reading Seminars I and II*. Eds. Richard Feldstein, Bruce Fink and Maire Jaanus. New York: State University of New York Press, 1996. 241-247.
Miner, Earl. *Comparative Poetics. An Intercultural Essay on Theories of Literature*, Princeton, NJ: Princeton University Press, 1990.
Mirriam-Goldberg, Caryn. *Sandra Cisneros. Latina Writer and Activist*. Berkeley Heights, NJ: Enslow, 1998.
Mitra, Indrani. "'I Will Make Bimala One with My Country': Gender and Nationalism in Tagore's *The Home and the World*." *Modern Fiction Studies*. Vol. 41. n. 2 (Summer 1995). 243-264.
Mo, Timothy. *Sour Sweet*. London: Deutsch, 1982.
____. *An Insular Possession*. London: Picador, 1987.
Mohan, Chandra, ed. *Aspects of Comparative Literature. Current Approaches*, New Delhi: India Publishers and Distributors, 1989.
Monsma, Bradley John. "'Active Readers . . . Obverse Tricksters': Trickster Texts and Cross-Cultural Reading." *Modern Language Studies* 26:4 (1996): 83-98.
Morrison, Toni. *Beloved*. New York: Knopf, 1987.
Mukherjee, Bharati. "The Road from Ballygunge." *Half and Half: Writers on Growing up Biracial and Bicultural*. Ed. Claudine Chiawei O'Hearn. New York: Pantheon Books, 1998. 71-79.
Mukherjee, Sujit. *Translation as Discovery*. Delhi: Allied Publishers, 1981.
Mungoshi, Charles. *Makunun'unu Maodzamwoyo* (Deep Considerations of a Rotting Heart). 1969. Salisbury: College Press, 1970.
____. *Coming of the Dry Season*. Nairobi: Oxford University Press, 1972.
____. *Ndiko Kupindana Kwamazuva* (How Days Pass). Gwelo, Rhodesia: Mambo Press, 1975.
____. *Waiting for the Rain*. 1975. Harare: Zimbabwe Publishing House, 1991.

———. *Inongova Njakenjake* (It Pulls Each in His Own Direction). Salisbury: Longman, 1980.
———. *Kunyarara Hakusi Kutaura?* (Is to be Silent not to Speak?) Harare: Zimbabwe Publishing House, 1983.
Naipaul, V.S. *The Middle Passage: Impressions of Five Societies, British, French, Dutch, in the West Indies and South America.* London: A. Deutsch, 1962.
———. *The Mimic Men.* New York: Macmillan, 1967.
———. *The Enigma of Arrival.* New York: Knopf, 1987.
Nayak, H. M., ed. *Epic in Indian Literature.* Mysore: University of Mysore Institute of Kannada Studies, 1985.
The New College Latin and English Dictionary. Ed. John C. Traupman. New York: Amsco School Publications, 1966.
New Redhouse Turkish-English Dictionary, 12. ed. İstanbul: Redhouse Yayınevi, 1991.
Ngugi wa Thiong'o, James. *Weep Not Child.* 1964. With introduction and notes by Ime Ikiddeh. London and Ibadan: Heinemann, 1967.
———. *The River Between.* Oxford, England: Heinemann, 1965.
———. *A Grain of Wheat.* London: Heinemann, 1967. Harare: Zimbabwe Publishing House, 1984. Oxford: Heinemann, 1986. *Tsanga Yembeu.* Trans. Charles Mungoshi. Harare: Zimbabwe Publishing House, 1987.
———. *Petals of Blood.* London: Heinemann, 1977.
———. *Caitaani Mutharabaini.* Nairobi: Heinemann Educational Books, 1980. *Devil on the Cross.* Translated from Gikuyu into English by the author. London: Heinemann, 1982. *Shetani Msalabani.* Trans. from Gikuyu into Kiswahili by Clement M. Kabugi. Nairobi: Heinemann, 1982.
———. "The Language of African Theatre." Unpublished presentation given at at the University of Zimbabwe in 1984.
———. "The Language of African Fiction." Unpublished presentation given at at the University of Zimbabwe in 1984.
———. *Decolonising the Mind: The Politics of Language in African Literature.* 1981. Harare: Zimbabwe Publishing House, 1987. 1994.
———. *Moving the Centre: The Struggle for Cultural Freedoms.* London: James Currey/Heinemann, 1993.
———. "A conversation with Ngugi wa Thiong'o." Interview with D. Venkat Rao. *Research in African Literatures* 30:1 (Spring 1999): 162-168.
Ngugi [wa Thiong'o], James and Ngugi wa Mirii. *I Will Marry When I Want* (translation by the authors of *Ngaahika Ndeenda* from Gikuyu). London: Exter, N.M.: Heinemann, 1982.
Nomura, Gail M., et. al., eds. Frontiers of Asian American Studies: Writing, Research, and Commentary. Pullman, WA: Washington State University Press, 1989.
Noss, Philip A. "The Ideophone: A Dilemma for Translation and Translation Theory." *New Dimensions in African Linguistics and Languages.* Ed. Paul F.A. Kotey. Trenton, NJ: Africa World Press, 1999. 261. 272.
O'Hearn, Claudine Chiawei. "Introduction." *Half and Half: Writers on Growing up Biracial and Bicultural.* Ed. Claudine Chiawei O'Hearn. New York: Pantheon Books, 1998. vii-xiv.

_____. ed. *Half and Half: Writers on Growing up Biracial and Bicultural*. New York: Pantheon Books, 1998.
Okada, John. *No-No Boy*. 1957. Seattle: University of Washington Press, 1976.
Ortiz, Fernando. *Contrapunteo Cubano del Tabaco y el Azúcar* (Advertencia de Sus Contrastes Agrarios, Económicos, Históricos y Sociales, Su Etnografía y Su Transculturación). Prólogo de Herminio Portell Vilá, introducción por Bronislaw Malinowski. La Habana: J. Montero, 1940. La Habana: Direccion de Publicaciones Universidad Central de las Villas, 1963. Barcelona: Ariel, 1963. 1973. *Cuban Counterpoint: Tobacco and Sugar*. Prologue by Herminio Portell Vilá, introduction by Bronislaw Malinowski. Trans. Harriet de Onis. New York: A.A. Knopf, 1947. With a new introduction by Fernando Coronil. Durham: Duke University Press, 1995.
Ortiz Cofer, Judith. *Silent Dancing: A Partial Remembrance of a Puerto Rican Childhood*. Houston, TX: Arte Publico Press, 1990.
Oster, Judith. "See(k)ing the Self: Mirrors and Mirroring in Bicultural Texts." *MELUS* 23.4 (Winter 1998): 59-83.
Overland, Orm. "West and Back Again." *On the Road*. Text and Criticism. Ed. Scott Donaldson. New York: Viking Press, 1979. 451-464.
Out of Africa, directed by Sydney Pollack, 1985.
Owusu, Kofi. "Point of View and Narrative Strategy in Nguge's [sic] *A Grain of Wheat*." *Notes on Contemporary Literature* 17:1 (1987): 2-3.
Paksoy, Hasan Bülent. *The Bald Boy Keloglan and the Most Beautiful Girl in the World*. Lubbock, TX: Archive of Turkish Oral Narrative, 2001. Full-text available at http://www.ku.edu/carrie/texts/carrie_books/paksoy-8/
Palumbo-Liu, David. "Discourse and Dislocation: Rhetorical Strategies of Asian-American Exclusion and Confinement." *Literature Interpretation Theory* 2 (1990): 1-7.
Pamuk, Orhan. *The Black Book*. Trans. Güneli Gün. New York: Farrar, Straus, and Giroux, 1994.
_____. *The New Life*. Trans. Güneli Gün. New York: Farrar, Straus, and Giroux, 1997.
Pandit, Lalita. "Caste, Race, and Nation: History and Dialectic in Rabindranath Tagore's *Gora*." *Literary India: Comparative Studies in Aesthetics, Colonialism and Culture*. Eds. Patrick Colm Hogan and Lalita Pandit. Albany: State University of New York Press, 1995. 207-233.
Papandreou, Nicholas. *Father Dancing: An Invented Memoir*. London: Viking, 1996.
_____. *A Crowded Heart*. New York: Picador, 1998.
Paz, Octavio. "Literature and Literalness." *Convergences: Essays on Art and Literature*. Trans. Helen Lane. San Diego, New York and London: Harcourt Brace Jovanovich, 1987. 184-200.
_____. "Los Hijos de la Malinche" (The Sons of La Malinche). *El Laberinto de la Soledad*. 1950. Mexico City: Fondo de Cultura Económica, 1959. Madrid: Cátedra, 1993. 202-227.
Pelensky, Olga Anastasia. *Isak Dinesen: The Life and Imagination of a Seducer*. Athens: Ohio University Press. 1991.
Pelton, Robert D. *The Trickster in West Africa: A Study of Mythic Irony and Sacred Delight*. Berkeley, Los Angeles and London: University of California Press, 1980.

Peres Vieira, Else Ribeiro. "Liberating Calibans: Readings of Anthropofagia and Haroldo de Campos' Poetics of Transcreation." *Post-colonial Translation Theory and Practice*. Eds. Susan Bassnett and Harish Trivedi. London and New York: Routledge, 1999. 95-113.

Pérez Firmat, Gustavo. "Transcending Exile: Cuban-American Literature Today." Occasional Paper Series Dialogues. Ed. Richard Tardanico. Miami: Florida International University Press, 1987. 3-23.

_____. *The Cuban Condition. Translation and Identity in Modern Cuban Literature*. Cambridge: Cambridge University Press, 1989.

Phillips, Caryl. *The Final Passage*. 1985. London: Picador, 1995.

_____. *The European Tribe*. 1987. London: Picador, 1992.

_____. *Cambridge*. 1991. London: Picador, 1992.

_____. *Crossing the River*. 1993. London: Picador, 1994,

_____. *The Nature of Blood*. London: Faber and Faber, 1997.

_____. *Extravagant Strangers: A Literature of Belonging*. London: Faber and Faber, 1997.

_____. *The Atlantic Sound*. London: Faber and Faber, 2000.

Planet of the Apes, directed by Franklin J. Schaffner, 1968.

Poster, Mark. "Postmodernity and the Politics of Multiculturalism: The Lyotard-Habermas Debate Over Social Theory." *Modern Fiction Studies*. 38. 3 (1992). 567-596.

Pratt, Mary Louise. *Imperial Eyes: Travel Writing and Transculturation*. London and New York: Routledge, 1992.

Prida, Dolores. "Coser y Cantar." *Beautiful Señoritas and Other Plays*. Houston: Arte Público, 1990. 49-67.

Pultar, Gönül. *Technique and Tradition in Beckett's Trilogy of Novels*. Lanham, MD: University Press of America, 1996.

The Quran. Trans. M.A.S. Abdel Haleem. Oxford and New York: Oxford University Press, 2004.

Raban, Jonathan. "The Sloop of Araby. *New York Times Books*. Late Edition. February 3, 1991, Sunday. Accessed 10 April 2004. http://www.nytimes.com/books/98/06/21/specials/barth-voyage.html.

Radhakrishnan, Rajagopalan. *Diasporic Mediations: Between Home and Location*. Minneapolis: University of Minnesota Press, 1996.

Rama, Ángel. *Transculturación Narrativa en América Latina* (Narrative ransculturation in Latin America). México, D.F.: Siglo Veintiuno Editores, 1982.

Ramadan, Hanan. "Arabian Nights: Its Origin and Legacy." Accessed 14 April 2004. htttp://www.middleeastuk.com/culture/mosaic/arabian.htm.

The Ramayana of Valmiki. Trans. from Sanskrit and edited by Arshia Sattar. New Delhi: Penguin Books, 1996. 2000.

Ranger, Terence. "The Invention of Tradition in Colonial Africa." *The Invention of Tradition*. Eds. Eric Hobsbawm and Terence Ranger. Cambridge, U.K.: Cambridge University Press, 1983. 211-262.

Rao, Raja. *Kanthapura*. 1938. New Delhi: Oxford University Press, 1989.

Reuman, Ann E. "Coming into Play: An Interview with Gloria Anzaldúa." *MELUS* 25. 2 (Summer 2000): 3-45.

Rigal-Cellard, Bernadette. "*No-No Boy* de John Okada (1957): Les Japonais Nisei après la Deuxiéme Guerre Mondiale et les Affres de l'Américanisation (John Okada's *No-No Boy* (1957): The Nisei Japanese after the Second World War and the Throes of Americanization)." *Séminaires.* Talence: Centre de Recherches sur l'Amérique Anglophone, 1986. 89-104.

Riley, Joan. *The Unbelonging.* London: Women's Press, 1985.

Roberson, Susan L., ed. *Women, America, and Movement. Narratives of Relocation.* Columbia: University of Missouri Press, 1998.

Robinson, Basil William. *The Persian Book of Kings: An Epitome of the Shahnama of Firdawsi.* Adaptation of *The Shāhnāma* of Abu al-Qasim Hasan Firdawsī, tr. into English by A.G. Warner and E. Warner. London and New York: RoutledgeCurzon, 2002.

Robinson, Francis. "The Muslims and Partition." *History Today.* V. 47. n. 9. September 1997.

Rodríguez Aranda, Pilar E. "On the Solitary Fate of Being Mexican, Female, Wicked and Thirty-three: An Interview with Writer Sandra Cisneros." *The Americas Review* 18.1: 64-80.

Rodríguez, Richard. *Days of Obligation: An Argument with my Mexican Father.* 1992. New York: Penguin, 1993.

Rojas, Lourdes. "Latinas at the Crossroads: An Affirmation of Life in Rosario Morales and Aurora Levins Morales' *Getting Home Alive.*" *Breaking Boundaries. Latina Writing and Critical Essays.* Eds. Asunción Horno-Delgado et al. Amherst, MA: University of Massachusetts Press, 1989. 166-177.

Rowe, William. *Mito e Ideología en la Obra de José María Arguedas* (Myth and Ideology in the Work of José María Arguedas). Lima: Instituto Nacional de Cultura. V. Cuadernos del INC, n. 3, 1979.

Roy, Arundhati. *The God of Small Things.* New Delhi: India Ink, 1997.

Rushdie, Salman. *Midnight's Children.* 1980. London: Picador, 1981. New York: Knopf, 1981.

_____. *The Satanic Verses.* London: Viking, 1988.

_____. *Haroun and the Sea of Stories.* London: Granta Books, 1990. New York: Penguin Books, 1990.

_____. "Imaginary Homelands." *Imaginary Homelands. Essays and Criticism 1981-1991.* London: Granta Books, 1991. New York: Penguin Books, 1991. 9-21.

_____. "Damme, This is the Oriental Scene for You!" *The New Yorker.* June 23 and 30, 1997. 50-61.

_____. *The Ground Beneath her Feet.* London: Vintage, 1999.

Said, Edward. *Orientalism: Western Conceptions of the Orient.* Harmondsworth, U.K. and New York: Penguin, 1978.

_____. "Identity, Authority and Freedom: The Potentate and the Traveler." *Pretexts* 3: 1-2 (1991): 67-81.

Saldívar, José David. "Introduction. Tracking Borders." *Border Matters. Remapping American Cultural Studies.* Berkeley, Los Angeles, London: U of California P, 1997. 1-14.

Saldivar-Hull, Sonia. "Feminism on the Border: From Gender Politics to Geopolitics." *Criticism in the Borderlands: Studies in Chicano Literature, Culture, and Ideology.* Eds. Héctor Calderón and José David Saldívar.

Durham and London: Duke University Press, 1994. 203-220.
———. *Feminism on the Border. Chicana Politics and Literature*. Berkeley, Los Angeles and London: University of California Press, 2000.
Sales Salvador, Dora. "*Love and Longing in Bombay*, by Vikram Chandra: Forever Listening." *Miscelánea. A Journal of English and American Studies*. Vol. 18. University of Zaragoza (Spain), 1997. 357-362.
———. *Identidad Étnica Ttraducción Cultural y Oralidad en Las Narrativas de José María Arguedas y Vikram Chandra* (Ethnic Identity, Cultural Translation and Orality in the Narratives of José María Arguedas and Vikram Chandra). Unpublished M.A. Thesis. Castellón: Universidad Jaume I de Castellón (Spain), 1998.
———. "El Intertexto Musical Quechua en el Discurso Narrativo de José María Arguedas: *Los Ríos Profundos, Haylli Taki* (The Quechua Musical Intertext in the Narrative Discourse of José María Arguedas: *Deep Rivers, Haylli Taki*)." *Intertextualitat y Recepció* (Intertextuality and Reception). Eds. Lluís Meseguer and María Luisa Villanueva. Collecció Summa Filologia 11. Castellón: Universitat de Castelló, 1998. 423-438.
———. "Vikram Chandra's Constant Journey: Swallowing the World." *JES. Journal of English Studies. Special Issue: New Voices in Literature*. Volume 2. 2000. Logroño, Universidad de La Rioja. 93-111.
———. "Vikram Chandra's Transcultural Narrative: *Red Earth and Pouring Rain*, Much More than a Novel." *Beyond Borders: Re-defining Generic and Ontological Boundaries*. Eds. Ramón Pló-Alastrué and Maria Jesús Martínez-Alfaro. Heidelberg: Universitätsverlag C. Winter, 2002. 175-184.
———. "Vikram Chandra's *Love and Longing in Bombay*: The Order of Emotion." *Ac(unofficial)knowledging Cultural Studies in Spain*. Eds. David Walton and Dagmar Scheu. Bern: Peter Lang, 2002. 91-107.
Sandoval, Ciro A. and Sandra M. Boschetto-Sandoval, eds. *José María Arguedas: Reconsiderations for Latin American Cultural Studies*. Latin American Series number 29. Athens: Ohio University Center for International Studies, 1998.
Sarada T. "Visions of Childhood in Arundhati Roy's *The God of Small Things*." *Critical Practice* Vol.VI, No.2. June 1998. 53-58.
Sarkar, Sumit. *Modern India 1885-1947*. Delhi: Macmillan, 1983.
Sarti, Antonella. *Spiritcarvers. Interviews with Eighteen Writers from New Zealand*. Amsterdam: Rodopi, 1998.
Sarup, Madan. *Jacques Lacan*. Toronto: University of Toronto Press, 1992.
Sato, Gayle K. Fujita. "Momotaro's Exile: John Okada's *No-No Boy*." *Reading the Literature of Asian America*. Eds. Shirley Geok-lin and Amy Ling. Philadelphia: Temple University Press, 1992.
Satz, Martha. "Returning to One's House: Interview with Sandra Cisneros." *Southwest Review* 82.2 (March 1, 1997): 166-185.
Sawhney, Sabina. "Mother India through the Ages: The Dilemma of Conflicting Subjectivities." *Narratives of Nostalgia, Gender, and Nationalism*. Eds. Jean Pickering and Suzanne Kehde. New York: New York University Press, 1997. 88-106.
Sayers, Dorothy L. "Introduction." *The Comedy of Dante Alighieri, the Florentine*.

Hell. Vol. 1. London: Penguin Books, 1949. 25-52.
Schiller, Friedrich von. *On The Aesthetic Education Of Man: In A Series Of Letters*. Trans. and edited by Elizabeth Wilkinson and Leonard Ashley Willoughby. Oxford: Oxford University Press, 1967.
Schwimmer, Erik. "The Aspirations of the Contemporary Maori." *The Maori People in the Nineteen-Sixties. A Symposium*. Ed. Erik Schwimmer. 1968. Auckland: Blackwood and Janet Paul, 1969. 9-64.
_____. ed. *The Maori People in the Nineteen-Sixties. A Symposium*. 1968. Auckland: Blackwood and Janet Paul, 1969.
Seyhan, Azade. *Writing Outside the Nation*. Princeton: Princeton University Press, 2001.
Shakespeare, William. *Othello*. Ed. Norman Sanders. Cambridge, U.K.: Cambridge University Press, 2003.
Sharp, Andrew. "Why Be Bicultural?" *Justice and Identity: Antipodean Practices*. Eds. Margaret Wison and Anna Yeatman. Wellington: Bridget Williams Books, 1995. 116-133.
Shea, Lisa. "Ancient Wisdom." *New York Times Book Review*. 14 June 1998, late ed. F1+.
Sidwa, Bapsi. *Cracking India*. Minneapolis: Milkweed Publication, 1991.
Silkü, Rezzan Kocaöner. "*Bağdat Yollarında* Romanında Kimlik Arayışı ya da Türk Kültüründe Diasporik Açılımlar (Search for Identity in the Novel *On the Road to Baghdad* or Diasporic Gateways in Turkish Culture)." *Kültür ve Modernite* (Culture and Modernity). Eds. Gönül Pultar, Emine O. İncirlioğlu and Bahattin Akşit. İstanbul: Türkiye Kültür Araştırmaları Grubu ve (and) Tetragon Yayınları, 2003. 315-330.
Singh, B.N. "Combating Caste and Sexuality in God's Own Country: A Feminist Reading of Arundhati Roy's *The God of Small Things*." *Contemporary Indian Women Writers in English: A Feminist Perspective*. Ed. Surya Nath Pandey. New Delhi: Atlantic Publishers and Distributors, 1999. 142-161.
Singh, Khuswant. *Train to Pakistan*. London: Chatto and Windus, 1956.
"Sir Gawain and the Green Knight." *The Norton Anthology of English Literature*. Sixth ed. Vol. 1. New York and London: W.W.W. Norton and Company, 1993. 200-254.
Smethurst, Paul. *The Postmodern Chronotope: Reading Space and Time in Contemporary Fiction*. Amsterdam and Atlanta, GA: Rodopi Editions, 2000.
_____. "Postmodern Blackness and Unbelonging in the Works of Caryl Phillips." *Journal of Commonwealth Literature*. Vol. 37, no. 2, 2002. 5-19.
Smith, Sidonie. *A Poetics of Women's Autobiography: Marginality and the Fictions of Self-Representation*. Bloomington: Indiana University Press, 1987.
Smyth, Edmund J. *Postmodernism and Contemporary Fiction*. London: Batsford, 1991.
Sollors, Werner. *Neither Black Nor White Yet Both: Thematic Explorations of Interracial Literature*. 1997. Cambridge, MA: Harvard University Press, 1999.
Soyinka, Wole. *The Lion and the Jewel*. London: Oxford University Press, 1963.
_____. *Myth, Literature, and the African World*. Cambridge, U.K. and New York: Cambridge University Press, 1976.
Spivak, Gayatri Chakravorty. "The Politics of Translation." *Outside in the Teaching*

Machine. Routledge: New York and London, 1993. 179-200.

———. *Death of a Discipline*. New York: Columbia University Press, 2003.

Spoonley, Paul. *Racism and Ethnicity*. Auckland: Oxford University Press, 1989.

Stambaugh, Sara. *The Witch and the Goddess in the Stories of Isak Dinesen: A Feminist Reading*. Ann Arbor: UMI Research Press, 1988.

Stewart, Susan. *Nonsense: Aspects of Intertextuality in Folklore and Literature*. Baltimore: The Johns Hopkins University Press, 1989.

Sumida, Stephen H. "Japanese American Moral Dilemmas in John Okada's *No-No Boy* and Milton Murayama's *All I Asking for Is My Body*." *Frontiers of Asian American Studies*. Eds. Gail M. Nomura *et al*. Seattle: Washington State University Press, 1989. 224-226.

Syal, Meera. *Anita and Me*. London: Flamingo, 1996.

Tagore, Rabindranath. *Nashtanid* (The Broken Nest). 1903. [In] *Rabindra Rachanabali*. 15 vols. Calcutta: Visvabharati, 1961. Vol. 7. 433-474.

———. *Gora*. 1910. [In] *Rabindra Rachanabali*. 15 vols. Calcutta: Visvabharati, 1961. Vol. 9. 1-350.

———. *Ghare Baire* (The Home and the World). 1916. [In] *Rabindra Rachanabali*. 15 vols. Calcutta: Visvabharati, 1961. Vol. 9. 405-550.

———. *Nationalism*. New York: Macmillan, 1917.

———. *Reminiscences*. London: Macmillan, 1920.

———. *Char Adhyay* (Four Chapters). 1934. [In] *Rabindra Rachanabali*. 15 vols. Calcutta: Visvabharati, 1961. Vol. 9. 875-923.

———. *Crisis in Civilization*. Calcutta: Visvabharati, 1941.

———. *Europe Probashir Patra* (Letters of a European Sojourn). [In] *Rabindra Rachanabali*. 15 vols. Calcutta: Visvabharati, 1961. Vol. 10. 229-341.

———. *Europe Jatrir Diary* (European Diary). [In] *Rabindra Rachanabali*. 15 vols. Calcutta: Visvabharati, 1961. Vol. 10. 343-476.

Tan, Amy. *The Joy luck Club*. New York: Putnam, 1989.

Taylor, Charles. "Examining the Politics of Recognition." *Multiculturalism and the Politics of Recognition*. Ed. Amy Gutmann. Princeton, NJ: Princeton University Press, 1994. 25-74.

Thompson, Katrina. "A Trickster Translation: How *A Grain of Wheat* Becomes *Tsanga Yembeu*." Unpublished M.A. Thesis. University of Wisconsin-Madison. 1999.

Thurman, Judith. *Isak Dinesen: The Life of A Storyteller*. New York: Picador, 1982.

Toury, Gideon. *Descriptive Translation Studies and Beyond*. Amsterdam and Philadelphia: John Benjamins, 1995.

Tsang, Lori. "Postcards from 'Home.'" *Half and Half: Writers on Growing up Biracial and Bicultural* Ed. Claudine Chiawei O'Hearn. New York: Pantheon Books, 1998. 197-215.

Tuwhare, Hone. *No Ordinary Sun*. Auckland: Blackwood and Janet Paul, 1964.

The Upanishads. Translated from the Sanskrit with an introduction by Juan Mascaro. Harmondsworth, U.K.: Penguin Books, 1965.

Vargas Llosa, Mario. *La Utopía Arcaica. José María Arguedas y las Ficciones del Indigenismo* (The Archaic Utopia. José María Arguedas and the Fictions of Indigenism). México City: Fondo de Cultura Económica, Colección Tierra Firme, 1996.

Vasil Raj. *Biculturalism: Reconciling Aotearoa with New Zealand*. Wellington: Institute of Policy Studies, 2000.
Veit-Wild, Flora. *Teachers, Preachers, Non-Believers: A Social History of Zimbabwean Literature*. Harare: Baobab Books, 1993.
Vizenor, Gerald. *Manifest Manners: Postindian Warriors of Survivance*. Hanover, NH: University Press of New England, 1994.
―――. *Fugitive Poses: Native American Indian Scenes of Absence and Presence*. Lincoln: University of Nebraska Press, 1998.
Voltaire. *Candide ou L'optimisme*. 1759. Ed. André Magnon. Paris: Bordas, 1981.
Wah, Fred. "Half-Bred Poetics." *absinthe* 9.2 (1996): 60-65.
Walsh, Michael. "Reading the Real in the Seminar on the Psychoses." *Interpreting Lacan*. Eds. Joseph H. Smith and William Kerrigan. New Haven: Yale University Press, 1983.
Wang, Qun. "'Double Consciousness,' Sociological Imagination, and the Asian American Experience." *Race, Gender and Class* 4.3: 88-94.
Waters, Mary C. *Ethnic Options: Choosing Identities*. Berkeley: University of California Press, 1990.
Watt, Ian. *The Rise of the Novel: Studies in Defoe, Richardson and Fielding*. 1957. London: Pelican Books, 1972.
Webster's Encyclopedic Unabridged Dictionary of the English Language. New York: Grammercy Books, 1996.
Wong, Sau-ling. "Autobiography as Guided Chinatown Tour? Maxine Hong Kingston's *The Woman Warrior* and the Chinese-American Autobiographical Controversy." *Multicultural Autobiography: American Lives*. Ed. James Payne. Knoxville: University of Tennessee Press, 1992. 248-279.
Yarbro-Bejarano, Yvonne. "Gloria Anzaldúa's *Borderlands/La Frontera*: Cultural Studies, 'Difference,' and the Non-Unitary Subject." *Cultural Critique* (Fall 1994): 5-28.
Yeh, William. "To Belong or Not to Belong: The Liminality of John Okada's No-No Boy." *Amerasia Journal* 19.1(1993): 121-133.
Yeğenoğlu, Meyda. *Colonial Fantasies: Toward a Feminist Reading of Orientalism*. New York and Cambridge, UK: Cambridge University Press, 1998.
Yogi, Stan. "'You Had to Be One or the Other': Opposition and Reconciliation in John Okada's No-No Boy." *MELUS* 21.2 (1996): 63-77.
―――. "The Collapse of Difference: Dysfunctional and Inverted Celebrations in John Okada's No-No Boy." *Revue Française d'Études Americaines* 53 (1992): 233-244.
Young, Robert J. C. *Colonial Desire: Hybridity in Theory, Culture and Race*. London and New York: Routledge, 1995.
Youngs, Tim. *Travelers in Africa*. New York: St. Martin's Press, 1994.
Zizek, Slavoj. *The Sublime Object of Ideology*. London and New York: Verso, 1989.
―――. *Enjoy Your Symptom: Jacques Lacan in Hollywood and Out*. New York: Routledge, 1992.
―――. "The Undergrowth of Enjoyment." *The Zizek Reader*. Eds. Elizabeth Wright and Edmond Wright. Malden, MA: Blackwell, 1999. 11-36.
Zyla, Wolodymyr T. and Wendell M. Aycock, eds. *Ethnic Literatures Since 1776: The Many Voices of America*. Ninth Comparative Literature Symposium,

Texas Tech University, 1976. Lubbock: Interdepartmental Committee on Comparative Literature, Texas Tech University, 1978. 2 vols.

Notes on Contributors

Esther Alvarez Lopez is Associate Professor at the University of Oviedo (Spain), where she teaches American Literature and American Drama. She has been President of the Women and Literature Association (University of Oviedo) since 1999. Her research interests are focused on gender and ethnicity. She has published numerous essays on African-American and Latina women writers of the United States, and is co-editor of *Tramas Postmodernas: Voces Literarias para una Década (1990-2000)* (2002), a volume of essays on contemporary literature.

Mita Banerjee is the Chair of the Department of American Studies at the University of Siegen, Germany. Her publications include *The Chutneyfication of History: Salman Rushdie, Michael Ondaatje, Bharati Mukherjee and the Postcolonial Debate* (2002), and *Race-ing the Century* (forthcoming) which looks at the ways in which the concepts of "race" and "ethnicity" are articulated in twentieth-century American literature, film, music, and art. She is currently working on a postcolonial study of the American Renaissance.

Sriparna Basu obtained her Ph.D. in Comparative Literature from the University of Illinois, Urbana-Champaign, in 1999. She is an independent scholar working in the area of critical theory and South Asian women's cultural history.

William Boelhower teaches American Literature and Trans-Atlantic Studies at the University of Padua, Italy. He is Vice-President of MESEA (Multiethnic Studies: Europe and the Americas) and an editor of the new Routledge journal *Atlantic Studies*. He has translated Antonio Gramsci and

Lucien Goldmann, and his essays have appeared in major journals of the field. His books include *Immigrant Autobiography in the United States* (1982), *Through a Glass Darkly, Ethnic Semiosis in American Literature* (1987, 1992), and *Autobiographical Transactions in Modernist America* (1992). He has edited the volume *The Future of American Modernism* (1990), and coedited *Adjusting Sites, New Essays in Italian American Studies* (1999), *Multiculturalism and the American Self* (2000), *Public Space, Private Lives: Race, Class, Gender, and Citizenship in New York 1890 - 1929* (2004), and *Working Sites: Text, Territory and Cultural Capital* (2004).

Fu-jen Chen is Assistant Professor in the Department of Foreign Languages and Literatures at National Sun Yat-sen University, Taiwan, where he teaches American and Asian-American literatures. His interest in Asian-American writing is complemented by an interest in psychoanalytical theory and children's literature. His work as articles in journals has appeared or is forthcoming in *Canadian Children's Literature, Women's Studies: An Interdisciplinary Journal*, and *Canadian Children's Literature*; and as chapters of books in *Trompe(-)l'oeil, Imitation et Falsification* (eds. Philippe Romanski and Aissatou Sy-Wonyu, 2002); and *Yellow Peril, Model Minority, Karate Kid* (ed. Dolores de Manuel, forthcoming). He has also contributed numerous entries in bio-bibliographical sourcebooks.

Paloma Fresno Calleja holds a Ph.D. in English Literature from the University of Oviedo, and is currently a lecturer at the University of the Balearic Islands. Her research so far has focused on postcolonial writing from New Zealand, Australia and the South Pacific.

Kuldip Kuwahara is an Associate Professor of English at North Carolina Central University. She is the author of *Jane Austen at Play: Self-Consciousness, Beginnings, Endings* 1993) and is presently working on her forthcoming "Magical Realism in Asian-American Women's Literature." A British Council scholar at the University of Edinburgh and NEH fellow at the University of California Santa Barbara, Kuwahara teaches graduate and undergraduate courses in Images of Women in World Literature, Contemporary Multi-Ethnic Literature, Postcolonial and Diasporic Studies. Her work in Enlightenment and Empire includes a re-examination of nineteenth and twentieth-century literary texts from a postcolonial perspective.

Gönül Pultar is the founding president of the Cultural Studies Association of Turkey. She has taught at Bilkent, Boğaziçi and Middle East Technical universities, and was a research fellow at Harvard University. She combines interests in the twentieth-century novel, American ethnic fiction and comparative cultural studies. Her published works include *Technique and Tradition in Beckett's Trilogy of Novels* (1996); various edited books; encyclopedia entries, journal articles and chapters in books; and two novels. The founding editor of *Journal of American Studies of Turkey*, Pultar is currently an Editorial Advisory Board member of *Journal of Popular Culture*, and will be guest-editing the 2006 special issue on American literature in languages other than English of *Comparative American Studies*. Pultar was chair of the Group for Cultural Studies in Turkey, vice-president of the American Studies Association of Turkey, and held or is holding at present various posts in MLA, ASA, MESEA, and MELUS-India.

V. Lalitha Ramamurthi is a Reader in the Department of English at All Saints' College, University of Kerala (1983-). He is a graduate of the University of Madras where he also received his Ph.D. in English Literature (1985). He is the author of *A Textbook of English Language* (1997), as well as of numerous articles in journals and chapters in books, and the editor of *Joseph Conrad: An Anthology of Recent Criticism* (1998). He was the recipient of the "Most Favoured College Teacher Award" given by the Kerala State Women's Development Corporation in March 1996; of the "Prof. Sivaprasad Award for the Most Outstanding College Teacher in the State" given in June 1996; and of the "Rev. Fr. Mathias Award for the Most Innovative Teacher" given in June 2000.

Dora Sales Salvador is Lecturer in the Department of Translation and Communication at the University Jaume I of Castellón (Spain), where she has taught literary theory, comparative literature and, currently, documentation. Her research interests and publications deal with Latin American fiction; Indian literatures in English; Western and non-Western literary theory; comparative literature; translation studies; cultural studies; and, intercultural communication and mediation. She holds a PhD in Translation Studies. She has translated Indian fiction from English to Spanish and is the author of *Puentes sobre el mundo: Cultura, Traducción y Forma literaria en las narrativas de transculturación de José María Arguedas y Vikram Chandra* (2004).

Paul Smethurst is Associate Professor at the University of Hong Kong where he teaches postmodernism, contemporary fiction and travel writing. He is the author of *The Postmodern Chronotope: Reading Space and Time in Contemporary Fiction* (2000), as well as a number of articles on postmodernism and travel writing. He is currently working on his next monograph, "The Poetics of Travel."

Katrina Daly Thompson earned her MA (1999) and Ph.D. (2004) in African Languages and Literatures at the University of Wisconsin-Madison, where she currently teaches Swahili language and culture. She is currently working on a manuscript entitled "Viewing the Foreign and the Local in Zimbabwe: Film, Television and Shona Viewers."

Rachel Trousdale is an Assistant Professor of English at Agnes Scott College (2002-). She received her M.A. (1997), M.Phil. (1998), and Ph.D. (2002) with a dissertation entitled: "Imaginary Worlds and Cultural Hybridity in Isak Dinesen, Vladimir Nabokov, and Salman Rushdie" from Yale University. She was a teaching fellow (1998-1999), and a part-time acting instructor (2000-2002) at Yale University, and has published numerous articles in journals and entries in encyclopedias.

Theodora Tsimpouki is Professor at the Faculty of English Studies, University of Athens, where she teaches American Literature and Culture. She studied at the University of Athens, the Sorbonne and at New York University from where she obtained her Ph.D. Her books are on modernist American writers (Faulkner and Fitzgerald) and contemporary ethnic American writers (Chicano, Native American and Afro-American literature). Her articles and reviews on contemporary English and American writing, identity politics and feminist theory have appeared in periodicals and conference proceedings. Her most recent publication is a literary history of American Literature (co-authored with Paul Levine) in 2002. She was the president of the Hellenic Association for American Studies. She is co-editor of *Culture Agonistes: Debating Culture, Re-reading Texts* (2002) and *Greek Literature in an International Perspective* (2002).

Index

acculturation 7, 90, 99, 130
adab 209, 216
Adıvar, Halide Edib 60, 299
After Theory 2, 305
Ahmad, Aijaz 291, 299
Ahmad, Akbar S. 208, 299
Anderson, Benedict 27, 299
Antin, Mary 49, 300
Anzaldúa, Gloria 89, 91, 92, 93, 94, 102, 299, 300, 315, 320
Appiah, Kwame Anthony 66, 143, 144, 146, 163, 300
The Arabian Nights 53-54, 193-194, 300, 315
    as *Les Mille et Une Nuits* 55, 62, 312
    see also *The Thousand and One Nights*
Arguedas, José María 8, 11, 109, 110, 111, 112, 113, 114, 115, 116, 117, 119, 121, 123, 124, 125, 127, 128, 129, 131, 134, 135, 137, 138, 300, 304, 305, 306, 310, 311, 316, 317, 319, 324
Aristotle, 120, 300
Ashcroft, Bill, Gareth Griffits and Helen Tiffin 50, 300
assimilation 7, 28, 29, 34, 97, 184, 224, 227, 274, 281, 287
assimilationism 68, 250
assimilationist 96

Baby No-eyes 41-43, 307
Bakhtin, Mikhail 32, 214, 274, 288, 301
Balibar, Etienne 68, 69, 81, 301
Barth, John 55, 56, 57, 62, 136, 279, 288, 301, 315
Bassnett, Susan 137, 144, 145, 158, 301, 315
belonging 10, 21, 25, 28, 31, 41, 69, 97, 100,102, 128, 173, 174, 233, 273, 274, 276, 281
Benjamin, Walter 189, 302
Bhabha, Homi K. 3, 7, 22, 25, 50, 69, 91, 92, 105, 131, 132, 169, 282, 287, 288, 302, 306
Bhagavad Gita (The) 239, 302
bicultural 2, 3, 5, 7, 9, 11, 12, 26, 27, 28, 29, 30, 31, 32, 33, 35, 36, 37 39, 40, 43, 44, 49, 50, 60, 61, 84, 91, 96, 97, 99, 109, 111, 112, 113, 116, 119, 121, 122, 124, 127, 129, 130, 132, 133, 137, 143, 146, 164, 220, 229, 230, 231, 239, 244, 251, 273, 274, 289, 298, 312, 313, 314, 318, 319, 320
bicultural heritage 26
bicultural identity 16, 21, 22, 24, 25, 89, 105, 233
biculturalism 3, 27, 28, 29, 30, 31, 34, 36, 37, 41, 43, 44, 50, 51, 60, 99, 112, 113, 114,124, 129, 193, 305, 320
    see also traveling biculturalism 51, 60
biculturality 10, 11, 65
bilingual 38, 93, 95, 96, 97, 99, 113, 114, 159
bilingualism 113, 114, 307
Bloom, Harold 158, 302
borderlands 89, 91, 92, 103, 105, 129, 302, 316
Borderlands/La Frontera 89, 90, 92, 299, 300, 320
Borges, Jorge Luis 131, 157, 302
Bradbury, Malcolm 47, 302
Braidotti, Rosi 107, 302
Brennan, Tim 7, 274, 275, 302
Bunyan John 58, 302

Index   327

Butler, Judith 7, 16, 26, 302

Cahan, Abraham 49, 302
Cambridge 275, 277, 278, 279-282, 285, 315
cannibalism 145
Chandra, Vikram 7, 11, 109-115, 120-121, 123-129, 134-137, 303-304, 317, 324
Char Adhyay 9, 221, 225, 236-238, 240, 242, 244-245, 319
Chatterjee, Partha 246, 303
"Child of the Americas" 90, 104
Chin, Frank 249-250, 271, 303
chora 263
chronotope 279, 288, 318, 324
Cisneros, Sandra 90, 99, 101, 303, 312, 316, 317
Clifford, James 10, 50-51, 60, 303
Coetzee, J.M. 279, 303
colonial 1, 3, 16, 23, 25, 28-29, 36, 39, 41, 73, 115, 122, 128-129, 141-142, 144-146, 149, 159, 161-164, 169-171, 192, 208, 211-212, 215, 220, 223-225, 227-228, 232, 237, 245-246, 274, 278, 288, 300, 303, 307, 309, 320
colonialism 3, 50, 73, 107, 144, 163, 208-209, 210-211, 213, 225, 282, 306, 314
colonialist 73, 126, 280
colonist 170, 189
colonized 20, 25, 39, 133, 142, 144-146, 153, 159, 163-164, 169, 208, 215, 220
colonizer 39, 50, 121, 123, 133, 144, 162, 169, 209, 215, 220
colonization 28, 50, 130, 133, 209, 214
colony/ies 10, 28, 144-145, 208, 273, 278, 288, 301
contact zone 50, 89, 107, 129, 169, 287
Coser y Cantar 90, 95-96, 99, 07, 315
Cousins 40-41, 43-44, 307
cross-culturality 105, 311
culture 2-5, 8, 10-11, 16-26, 27-36, 39, 41, 44, 47-52, 54, 56, 60-62, 65-66, 69-72, 74-85, 89-94, 96-97, 100-103, 105-107, 109-115, 117-122, 124-135, 137, 139, 142-148, 150, 155, 158-162, 164-165, 169-171, 176, 181-184, 186-188, 192-193, 199-200, 202, 204, 206-209, 212, 215, 219-220, 222, 224, 228, 236, 238, 242, 245, 251, 255, 265, 267-268, 270-271, 274, 276, 280-281, 283, 287, 295
cultural criticism 107, 132, 253
cultural heritage 1, 9, 18, 26, 30
cultural hybrid 23, 91-92, 103, 106, 132, 325
cultural incompatibility 69
cultural interaction 30-31, 83
cultural mirroring 251, 253-255
cultural nationalism 9, 220, 221, 225, 227, 228, 229, 236,
cultural tradition 21, 23, 24, 132
cultural translation 8, 11, 113, 125, 143

Dante Alighieri 243, 247, 304, 317
Davidson, Catherine Temma 17-18, 21, 25, 304
Death of a Discipline 2, 319
Decolonising the Mind 50, 141-142, 148, 164-165, 313
deconstruction 15-16, 50, 60, 66, 68-70
deculturation 90
Defoe, Daniel 60, 304, 320
Deep Rivers 112, 125, 135, 138-139, 300, 317
Derrida, Jacques 2, 15, 56, 159, 264, 268, 304
Desai, Anita 203, 304, 308
diaspora 10, 22, 49, 104, 107, 155, 271, 273, 278, 280-281, 288, 307, 311
diasporic 1, 10, 251, 315, 318, 323
Difficult Daughters 200, 203-204, 209, 212-213, 309
Dinesen, Isak 8, 10, 169-190, 302, 304, 305, 310, 311, 312, 314, 319, 325
Divakaruni, Chitra Banerjee 8, 65, 74-80, 82-84, 85, 305
La Divina Commedia 243, 304
Durrell, Lawrence 22, 305

Eagleton, Terry 2, 158, 305
ego ideal 252-253, 255, 258, 272
essentialism 12, 68, 71, 74-75, 105, 275-

Index

277, 285
ethnic 2, 5, 7, 9, 15-18, 20-21, 25-26, 48-49, 60, 61, 66-69, 77, 81, 96-97, 112, 125, 135, 137, 193, 197, 250-251, 255, 264, 271, 286, 299, 306, 309, 311, 320, 323, 324, 325
ethnic heritage 17-18
ethnicity 16, 26, 28, 36, 44, 67-71, 79-81, 91, 111-112, 197, 253, 255, 275-277, 305, 307, 306, 319, 322

Fanon, Frantz 7, 50, 113, 254-255, 306
Father Dancing 18, 25, 314
Faulkner, William 274, 325
The Final Passage 273, 275, 277-279, 315
Fink, Bruce 253, 255, 260, 262, 306, 312
Forster, E.M. 222, 224-225, 306
Foucault, Michel 238-239, 306
Fox-Genovese Elizabeth 16, 306
Fuentes, Carlos 90, 306

Gates Henry-Louis Jr. 154-156, 158-159, 306
gender 7, 10, 16, 24-25, 38, 53, 90-91, 94, 101, 105-106, 155, 204, 209, 213, 227, 241, 253, 275, 277-278, 287, 305, 307, 308, 312, 316, 317, 320, 322, 323
Ghare Baire 221, 225, 228-229, 235-239, 241, 244-246, 319
The God of Small Things 9, 289-293, 297-298, 316, 317, 318
Gora 9, 219, 221, 225, 231, 236-239, 242, 244-245, 314, 319
Grace, Patricia 7, 9, 27-29, 31-44, 306, 307, 312
A Grain of Wheat 10, 142, 146-152, 154, 156, 158-162, 164-165, 313, 314, 319
Gün, Güneli 7, 11, 47-49, 53-55, 57-60, 61-63, 307, 309, 310, 314

Hall, Stuart 102, 307
Haroun and the Sea of Stories 11, 62, 191-193, 197, 316
Hegel, G.W.F. 245, 307
heteroglossia 274
Hindu 73, 120, 128, 200-201, 204, 206, 211-212, 213, 214, 216, 217, 226, 229, 231-232, 246, 291-292,
Hinduism 73, 139, 217, 230
The House on Mango Street 90, 99, 102, 303
hooks, bell 163, 277, 308
Hosain, Attia 8, 200, 203, 205-207, 213, 215, 304, 308
Huntington, Samuel P. 68, 308
Hutcheon, Linda 294, 296, 308
hybrid 3, 9, 10, 23,
hybridity 8, 9, 10, 16, 21,

ideal ego 252-253, 255, 267, 272
identity/identities 9, 11, 16-18, 21-26, 28, 32-34, 39-41, 50, 59, 66-68, 72, 83, 89-91, 93-96, 99, 102-105, 107, 111-113, 120, 125, 127-128, 130, 132, 137, 144, 147, 171, 174, 188, 193, 195, 199-200, 207, 212, 216, 219-221, 228, 231-233, 237, 241-242, 245, 249-251, 255, 257, 265, 267, 273-274, 276-277, 279-281, 284, 286, 299, 300, 301, 307, 309, 315, 316, 317, 318, 320, 325
ideophone 143, 152-153, 157, 160, 163, 165, 306, 313
Ihimaera, Witi 27, 33, 36, 38, 44, 307, 308, 309, 311
Imaginary Phallus 257-258
immigrant 7, 10, 17, 49, 60, 96, 250-251, 256, 271, 273-274, 309, 311, 323
integration 29, 30, 97, 112, 266
intercultural 30, 32-34, 41, 45, 51, 67, 69, 82, 109-110, 116, 130-131, 133, 136-137, 306, 312
intercultural communication 31, 32, 36, 37, 141, 324
intercultural negotiation 67, 83
interculturality 8, 10, 67, 69, 70, 80, 82, 83, 84,
Irigaray, Luce 23, 309
Islam 26, 73, 204, 206-209, 216, 299
Islamic 52, 204, 207, 209, 215-216, 308, 312
  see also Muslim(s)
Iyer, Pico 129, 309

Jameson, Fredric 50, 214, 309

JanMohammed, Abdul R. 89, 169, 309

Kalogeras, Yiorgos D. 17, 18, 61, 309
Kapur, Manju 8, 200, 204, 210-213, 309
Kerouac, Jack 58, 310
Kim, Elainde H. 250, 271, 310
Kingston, Maxine Hong 7, 11, 48, 67, 77-78, 82, 137, 191-193, 195, 197, 310, 320
Kristeva, Julia 107, 263, 310
Krupat, Arnold 92, 310
Kureishi, Hanif 137, 310

Lacan, Jacques 108, 251-254, 256, 258, 261, 264-270, 271, 272, 300, 310, 312, 317, 320
Legba 11, 155-160
Levins Morales, Aurora and Rosario Morales 90, 104-105, 311, 316
literary tradition 4, 115, 143, 158, 165, 251
The Location of Culture 3, 22, 25, 50, 69, 91, 105, 132, 169, 302
Lukács, Georg 52, 311

Macaulay, Thomas Babington 208
Madonna 80-82
magical realism 49, 60-61, 197, 323
magical realist 48
The Mahabharata 124, 139, 193, 311
Man, Paul de 171, 317
Mandeville, Sir John 58, 311
Melville, Herman 274
mestizaje 11, 90-93, 104, 106-107, 302, 306
mestiza 89, 92, 93-94, 103-104, 299, 300,
mestizo 91, 93, 107, 112, 128, 134
Midnight's Children 3, 62, 65, 70-75, 84, 126, 316
The Mistress of Spices 65, 74-78, 80, 82, 84, 305
mirror stage 251-255, 266-267, 269-270, 272
mixed heritage 31, 36
Mo, Timothy 273-274, 282, 287, 312
modern 18-19, 38, 73, 76, 111-112, 124-125, 128, 130, 151, 199, 202-207,
211-213, 230, 232, 239-240, 246, 276, 278-279, 284, 305, 310, 312, 315, 317
modernism 203-204, 208-209, 307, 323
modernist 204, 293-294, 297, 323, 325
modernity 10, 22, 73, 110, 124, 125, 128, 199, 200, 202, 203, 204, 206-213, 215, 229, 233, 234, 306, 309, 318
Mohammedan *see* Muslim
Morrison, Tony 274, 288, 312
Moslem *see* Muslim
multicultural 2, 29, 47-48, 59-60, 65, 70-71, 73, 110, 127, 133, 137, 139, 142-143, 146, 153, 162, 164, 220, 264, 309, 320,
multiculturalism 2, 29, 32, 65, 84, 111, 157, 192, 279, 307, 310, 315, 319, 323
multiculturalist 49, 74
Mungoshi Charles 142, 146-153, 154-162, 163, 164, 165, 312, 313
Muslim(s) 73, 200-201, 204, 206-209, 211-213, 215-217, 229, 299, 312, 316
as Moslem(s) 53
as Mohammedan(s) 223
Mutuwhenua 35-37, 307

Naipaul, V.S. 47, 50, 273-274, 288, 313
narcissistic narrative 293-294, 296, 298, 308
nationalism 9, 15, 73, 128, 200, 204, 210-212, 219-221, 221-223, 228-231, 236, 238, 240-241, 245, 250, 257, 300, 301, 312, 317, 319
see also cultural nationalism
The Nature of Blood 275, 277, 281, 283-287, 315
neo-culturalism 69
neoculturation 90, 131
Ngugi wa Thiong'o 7, 10, 129, 141-142, 146-153, 156-157, 159-162, 163-165, 313
No-No Boy 10, 249-251, 255-256, 271, 303, 309, 311, 312, 314, 316, 317, 319, 320

Okada, John 8, 10, 249-250, 255, 271, 303, 309, 311, 314, 316, 317, 319, 320
On the Road to Baghdad 5, 11, 47-53, 55,

57-60, 62, 307, 310, 318
oral tradition 53, 111, 125, 128, 154, 158
Orientalism **3, 16, 20, 189, 316**
Orientalism 24, 66-68, 71-72, 80, 84, 189, 320
Ortiz, Fernando 90,130-131, 137, 314
Ortiz Cofer, Judith 91, 106, 314
Othello 284, 318
Out of Africa 10, 169-171, 173-174, 176, 180-181, 186-190, 304-306, 310-311
Øverland, Orm 58, 314

Pamuk, Orhan 61, 314
Papandreou, Nicholas (Nikos) 7, 17-18, 314
Paz, Octavio 107, 156, 159, 314
Pérez Firmat, Gustavo 130, 315
phallus/Phallus 94, 257-258, 261-262, 268-271,
  see also Imaginary Phallus
Phillips, Caryl 4, 8, 10, 273-288, 304, 311, 315, 318
Polysystem theory 128, 132-133 306
postcolonial 1, 4, 7, 9, 16, 21, 29, 36, 48, 65-66, 68-71, 115, 121, 125-126, 130, 142,
  145, 154, 158, 163, 192, 200, 206, 213, 251, 274-275, 282-283, 287-288, 302, 322, 323
postmodern 5, 9, 11, 21, 61, 76, 105, 120, 154, 192, 220, 275-279, 282, 287, 288, 289, 294-298, 302, 308, 318, 324
postmodernism 2, 8, 10, 74, 214, 273, 276-277, 294-295, 300, 308-309, 318, 324
postmodernist 48-49, 55, 58, 65, 75, 273, 288, 294, 298, 312
postmodernity 274, 276, 279, 315
post-structuralism 21
Potiki 36-37, 39-43, 307
Pratt, Marie Louise 7, 39, 89, 107, 129-130, 139, 169, 315,
Prida, Dolores 90, 95-96, 98-99, 108, 306, 315
The Priest Fainted 18, 21, 25, 26, 304

Ramayana (The) 124, 139, 193, 315

Red Earth and Pouring Rain 112, 120, 122-124, 126, 129, 136-137, 303, 317
Los Rios Profundos 112, 116-118, 124-125, 129, 135, 300, 317
Roy, Arundhati 7, 9, 289, 290,291, 292, 295, 296, 297, 298, 299, 316, 317, 318
Rushdie, Salman 3, 4, 7, 11, 48, 62, 65, 70, 74-75, 82-84, 109, 115, 121, 123, 126, 170, 191-194, 197, 273-274, 288, 316, 322, 325

Said, Edward 2-3, 7, 10, 20, 56, 93, 189, 309, 316
Saldívar José David 89, 302, 316,
Saldívar-Hull, Sonia 92, 106, 316
self-Orientalizing 62, 74-78
Shakespeare, William 145, 284-285, 311, 318
Sollors, Werner 49, 53, 62, 318
Soyinka, Wole 192, 318
Spivak, Gayatri Chakravorty 2, 7, 144-145, 613, 304, 318
subaltern/ity 2, 3, 50, 94
Sunlight on a Broken Column 200, 203-205, 208-209, 213, 215, 304, 308

Tagore, Rabindranath 5, 8-9, 73, 219-227, 229, 234, 236, 239, 242, 244-246, 301, 305, 312, 314, 319
Tan, Amy 48, 319
Taylor, Charles 32, 319
The Thousand and One Nights 3, 48, 51, 53-57, 60-62, 304, 307,
  see also The Arabian Nights
Toury, Gideon 143, 149, 151-152, 158-159, 164, 319
tradition 1, 3-4, 9, 11, 25, 31, 35, 42, 54, 58, 60, 61, 62, 68, 72-73, 81, 92, 100, 110-112, 124-128, 154, 156, 158, 164, 199-200, 202-204, 206-208, 210, 212, 215, 230, 235-236, 246, 274, 282, 291, 307, 315, 324
  see also cultural tradition
  see also literary tradition
  see also oral tradition
traditional/ly 1, 22-24, 27-28, 30, 35, 38-40, 45, 51, 53, 62, 84, 90, 94, 96,

98, 100-102, 110-112, 119, 120, 124, 127, 135, 139, 151, 175, 191, 203, 205-207, 210, 213, 230-232, 234, 242, 246, 290, 293
transculturation 2, 8, 10, 39, 90, 96, 98-99, 107, 110-112, 130-133, 137, 139, 287, 315
thick translation 143, 300
translation 10, 11, 18, 44, 55, 62, 95, 111, 113, 115-116, 122, 130, 132, 135, 138, 141-165, 238, 245, 247, 254, 264, 272, 280-281, 299, 301, 303, 304, 305, 310, 312, 313, 315, 317, 318, 319, 324
see also cultural translation
transnational 8-9, 47, 84, 124, 219, 274, 277-278, 282
transnationalism 1, 8, 10
traveling biculturalism 51, 60
trickster 11, 39, 76, 80, 142, 146, 153-159, 161-162, 188, 193, 301, 305, 308, 312, 314, 319
trickster translator 142, 143, 146, 153-157, 159, 161-162
Tripmaster Monkey 11, 67, 191-193, 195, 197, 310

Tsanga Yembeu 10, 142, 146, 148, 151-155, 159-162, 164, 313, 319

unbelonging 273-274, 276, 316, 318
universal humanism 9, 219, 225, 236-237, 242, 244-245
The Upanishads 230, 246, 319

Vargas Llosa, Mario 124-125, 127, 274, 300, 319
Vizenor, Gerald 76, 80-81, 84
Voltaire 59, 320

Waiariki 27, 34-36, 307
Watt, Ian 127, 320
The Woman Warrior 48, 60, 77-78, 137, 310, 320
Wong, Sau-ling 77-78, 320

Yeğenoğlu, Meyda 16, 23, 320
Young, Robert J.C. 50, 91, 169, 320

Zizek, Slavoj 258-260, 262-263, 272, 320

www.ingramcontent.com/pod-product-compliance
Lightning Source LLC
Chambersburg PA
CBHW031308150426
43191CB00005B/125